Defining the Field of Comparative Constitutional Law

Defining the Field of Comparative Constitutional Law

Edited by
Vicki C. Jackson and Mark Tushnet

FOREWORD BY WILLIAM H. REHNQUIST
Chief Justice of the United States

PRAEGER

Westport, Connecticut
London

Library of Congress Cataloging-in-Publication Data

Defining the field of comparative constitutional law / edited by Vicki C. Jackson and Mark Tushnet ; foreword by William H. Rehnquist.
p. cm.
Includes bibliographical references and index.
ISBN 0–275–97069–8 (alk. paper)
1. Constitutional law. I. Jackson, Vicki C. II. Tushnet, Mark V., 1945–
K3165.D44 2002
342—dc21 2002019629

British Library Cataloguing in Publication Data is available.

Library of Congress Catalog Card Number: 2002019629
ISBN: 0–275–97069–8

First published in 2002

Praeger Publishers, 88 Post Road West, Westport, CT 06881
An imprint of Greenwood Publishing Group, Inc.
www.praeger.com

Printed in the United States of America

The paper used in this book complies with the Permanent Paper Standard issued by the National Information Standards Organization (Z39.48–1984).

P

Copyright Acknowledgments

Grateful acknowledgement is given for permission to reprint the following: Roberto MacLean, "Judicial Discretion in the Civil Law," 43 *Louisiana Law Review* 45 (1982); Roberto MacLean, "The Culture of Service in the Administration of Justice," 6 *Transnational Law & Contemporary Problems* 139 (spring 1996); Ratna Kapur and Brenda Cossman, *Secularism's Last Sigh? Hindutva and the (Mis)Rule of Law* (New York: Oxford University Press, 1999); "Law Like Love," copyright 1940 and renewed 1968 by W.H. Auden, from *W.H. Auden: The Collected Poems by W.H. Auden*. Used by permission of Random House, Inc., and Faber and Faber Ltd.

In order to keep this title in print and available to the academic community, this edition was produced using digital reprint technology in a relatively short print run. This would not have been attainable using traditional methods. Although the cover has been changed from its original appearance, the text remains the same and all materials and methods used still conform to the highest book-making standards.

Contents

Foreword

Chief Justice William H. Rehnquist

This collection should stimulate a great deal of thought and discussion about the emerging field of comparative constitutional law, and it is certainly a distinguished group of scholars, jurists, and government officials who have contributed from throughout the world.[1]

Those who believe in constitutional government basically put their trust in the idea that political power should be constrained by law. This idea is well expressed in the Latin expression used by the early English legal writer Henri de Bracton, *non sub homine sed sub deo ad legis*: "Not under man, but under God and law."

Two centuries ago, when the United States had just begun to operate under its constitution, the idea of a written constitution such as we had was a novel one. Almost at the beginning of that era, our Supreme Court decided that this written constitution gave the Court the authority to declare legislative actions invalid or unconstitutional. This was a dramatic departure, a really novel proposal, unknown anywhere else in the world.

For the next century and a half, the United States, almost alone among nations, operated under this system. But within the past half century, especially after the Second World War, numerous other nations have adopted written constitutions or basic laws that entrusted their courts with the power of judicial review. Germany, Italy, France, Hungary, Spain, Japan, India, South Africa, Canada, among other countries, have all given some or all of their courts the power of judicial review.

The provisions of the constitutions vary, the structure of the court systems may differ, but the underlying ideas are the same, even in countries that do not have a written constitution and therefore have no judicial review in the American sense of that phrase—the United Kingdom, for example—or those countries that have a written constitution which in theory grants judicial review but in which that power is unexercised, such as Sweden.

When I was visiting Sweden five or six years ago, I was talking to the attorney general and several people on her staff. One of the questions I asked was, "Does the Supreme Court of Sweden have the authority to declare an act of Parliament unconstitutional?" After conferring with two or three of her staff members, with Parliament, she said, "Yes, it does." I asked "Well, has it ever exercised that power?" And she said, "No."

In these countries, there is considerable discussion about the desirability of granting the authority to the Court. The European Court of Justice of the European Union, which sits in Luxembourg City, now has the power of judicial review for those countries adhering to the Treaty of Rome. It may not be in the same form as ours, but nonetheless they certainly have the power. The European Court of Human Rights, sitting in Strasbourg, also provides a form of international judicial review.

Thus, more and more courts around the world are exercising this power. The efficacy of judicial review of courts can hinge to a large degree on an independent judiciary; that is, a judiciary free of the political pressures of and from the other branches of government. Our American history has shown that establishing and maintaining an independent judiciary presents continuing challenges, and we see those challenges in other countries that have created a constitutional form of government.

Recently we witnessed the resignation of the president of the Supreme Court of Venezuela, Cecilia Sosa, who had served on the Court since 1989. President Sosa resigned from office because she felt that the new constituent assembly, created to write a new constitution for the country, was threatening the independence of both the legislative and judicial branches of government.

As to the comparative aspects of constitutional law, for nearly a century and a half, courts of the United States exercising the power of judicial review had no precedents to turn to except their own, because our Court alone exercised this sort of authority. When many new constitutional courts were created after the Second World War, these courts naturally looked to the decisions of the Supreme Court of the United States, among other sources, for developing their own law.

But now that constitutional law is solidly grounded in so many countries, I am simply repeating now what I've said previously: it's time the U.S. courts began looking to the decisions of other constitutional courts to aid in their own deliberative process. U.S. courts and legal scholarship in our country generally have been somewhat laggard in relying on comparative law decisions of other countries.

We had a judicial exchange program between Canada and the United States about ten years ago, and one of the things the justices of Canada's Supreme

Court asked was, "We cite your Constitution; why don't you cite ours?" What I answered that time was that the Charter of Rights and Freedom was only seven years old. Of course, now their Charter of Rights and Freedom, adopted in 1982, is about seventeen years old, so it's less defensible to say that we're not familiar with it.

As I predicted in the past, with so many thriving constitutional courts in the world today, we'll see a change in this approach in the U.S. courts, and certainly this volume is another step in that direction.

NOTE

1. This foreword is based on an edited transcript of introductory comments delivered at the conference "Comparative Constitutional Law: Defining the Field," held at Georgetown University Law Center on September 17, 1999, in conjunction with the 1999 meeting of the American Association of Comparative Law.

Introduction

Vicki C. Jackson and Mark Tushnet

In September 1999, Georgetown University Law Center hosted a conference on Comparative Constitutional Law: Defining the Field. Held in conjunction with the 1999 meeting of the American Association of Comparative Law, the conference attracted scholars from across the United States and from many other nations. Scholars from every major continent were present and spoke, bringing perspectives from the constitutional experiences of Canada, Egypt, France, Germany, India, Japan, Peru, South Africa, Switzerland, the United Kingdom, and the United States to the forum. The conference began with brief introductory comments by William H. Rehnquist, Chief Justice of the United States.

At least since the end of World War II, constitutionalism has spread in tandem with the growth of international law commitments to human rights law and the development of transnational legal regimes for trade and commerce. Law itself has exploded in development and in availability; more nations exist and more nations have adopted written constitutions; and constitutional law has been influenced and developed not only within domestic national courts, but also through transnational tribunals, such as the European Court of Human Rights, engaged in quasi-constitutional adjudication. All of these factors help account for the renewal of interest among scholars and jurists in the constitutional developments of other nations and tribunals. But this kind of interest is not new; it goes back at least to the time of Aristotle. In the United States, James Madison, in Federalist No. 63, announced that

> An attention to the judgment of other nations is important to every government . . . [because] in doubtful cases, particularly where the national councils may be warped by

some strong passion, or momentary interest, the presumed or known opinion of the impartial world may be the best guide that can be followed . . . [H]ow many errors and follies would [the United States] have avoided, if the justice and propriety of her measures had in every instance been previously tried by the light in which they would probably appear to the unbiased part of mankind? (G. Wills, ed., The Federalist Papers 318, 1982)

Madison can be read as suggesting that we might refrain from making unwise or unjust decisions if we recognize that our public decisions—of constitutional design, interpretation, and implementation—will be subject to scrutiny in other nations.[1] Others might suggest that we value the opinions of other nations not because they are "unbiased" but rather, or at least as much, because they have been engaged in struggling with similar problems.[2]

Madison's comment, then, suggests that comparative constitutional study and the dissemination of knowledge about comparative constitutional practices can serve at least two overarching functions—enhancing accountability of constitutional decision-making and learning from comparable experience. Neither can happen, however, without having as a predicate a community of scholars with the ability to learn about other systems, to analyze those systems and constitutional practices, and to communicate with one another about foreign and domestic experiences. Exchanges such as those that took place at the conference in 1999, and as are embodied in this book, are thus part of a project of transnational constitutional discourse, providing the infrastructure both for comparative constitutional experience as a form of external accountability constraining otherwise bad choices and as a positive source of learning about different approaches or solutions to similar challenges.

In asking our authors to think about how one should define the field of comparative constitutional law, we hoped to illuminate a number of questions. An important one is this: What, if anything, distinguishes the study of comparative *constitutional* law from the study of comparative law in general? Obviously, the subject matter of the field is narrower. Equally obvious, some of the benefits of comparative study accrue to studying constitutional law comparatively. So, for example, one interested in domestic constitutional law might gain some critical perspective on particular issues by seeing them from a distance. The fact that judges serving on constitutional courts usually have limited terms may help U.S. scholars and students understand that judicial independence can be secured by means other than life tenure. It may also help such scholars and students reflect on what might be distinctive in the U.S. legal-constitutional culture that makes life tenure appropriate in the United States even though other democracies have chosen other ways to staff their constitutional courts. Here comparativism brings to the fore the need to see particular legal institutions and doctrines in the political, legal, economic, and social contexts in which they are found. Thus, as Professor Kazuyuki Takahashi asserts, two important purposes of comparative constitutional study include finding functional solutions to similar problems and pursuing what he terms a "general curiosity": becoming aware of new perspectives and issues and providing a kind of intellectual distance from one's immediate interests that can help to avoid risks of distorted perception and judgment in favor of those interests.

Comparativists who focus on private law sometimes examine the ways in which diverse legal systems address problems that are functionally similar: the principles and institutions used to resolve problems caused by automobile accidents or contractual disputes between businesses. Functional inquiries can be undertaken with constitutional law as their subject matter. For example, one might examine the ways in which democracies secure civilian control of the military and attempt to identify which institutional arrangements secure civilian control more effectively. But, as critical comparativists have suggested, the task of identifying functional equivalents across legal cultures is fraught with peril. A self-reflective comparativist, after engaging in a functional inquiry, might then ask *whether* the areas examined are indeed functionally equivalent, or *why* a person coming from the comparativist's particular legal culture would identify these institutions or principles as functionally equivalent, as is suggested by Professor Takahashi in questioning the functional categories to compare in thinking about government control of school texts.

Neither learning by gaining critical distance nor functional analysis is particularly distinctive to the study of comparative constitutional law. Nor are many other characteristics often attributed to comparative legal study, such as the sheer interest of learning about other legal systems or the general cultural enhancement that comes from expanding one's base of knowledge. But, we think we can identify at least some distinctive issues that arise in studying comparative constitutional law.

The present generation's interest in comparative constitutional law has been fueled, we think, by the confluence of the great wave of constitutional reform that flowed around the world—from Central and Eastern Europe to South Africa and Latin America—in the 1980s and 1990s, with the development of a strong community associated with international human rights. The connection between domestic constitutional law and international human rights is complex but of increasing importance. Professor Lorraine E. Weinrib notes, critically, Justice Scalia's rejection of the relevance of comparative practice in resolving whether imposition of the death penalty on juveniles violates the Eighth Amendment. Justice Scalia gives primacy instead to the decisions of the state legislatures of the people of the United States and, in Professor Weinrib's view, to a distorted reading of the values expressed in those decisions. She contrasts Justice Antonin Scalia's positivist, exceptionalist view of U.S. constitutional law with what she calls the new "postwar conception" of constitutions as most fundamentally committed to human dignity as a value to be elaborated—as Kant foresaw—by a " 'universal community' made up of the 'peoples of the earth.' " Professor Donald Kommers, too, noting how "constitutional ideas have been floating unimpeded across national boundaries," questions whether the United States should insulate itself from what he terms a "transcultural normative value system."

For the present, we wish to focus attention on some institutional dimensions of the interaction between international human rights law and domestic constitutional law that might be illuminated by comparative study. First, we might note that some aspects of international human rights law have developed initially by flowing *up* from domestic legal systems into the international arena and then *down* to domestic legal systems, sometimes even those systems that were sources for the international human rights norms in the first place.

Consider, for example, Canada's experience with the question of whether Canadian officials may accede to extradition requests that would result in the exposure of the defendant to the death penalty in the United States. Initially the Canadian Supreme Court held that vesting discretion in government officers to extradite or not, as they chose, did not violate Canadian law.[3] A decade later, however, the Court reconsidered and held that extradition without assurances that the defendant would not be subject to the death penalty was generally impermissible.[4] In the intervening years the international norm against capital punishment strengthened materially. Notably, though, the Canadian Supreme Court offered a *domestically* oriented explanation for the new rule. Canadian constitutional law has come to make central to the nation's self-understanding the idea that Canada is a multicultural society. The Canadian Supreme Court explained its most recent extradition decision by referring to the way in which leadership in international human rights was part of that self-understanding. The Court gave this heading to one of the sections of its opinion: "The Abolition of the Death Penalty Has Emerged as a Major Canadian Initiative at the International Level and Reflects a Concern Increasingly Shared by Most of the World's Democracies." While reviewing the position of the death penalty in international human rights law generally, this section of the opinion repeatedly stressed the positions the Canadian government had taken in international discussions. The Court concluded that "a rule requiring that assurances be obtained prior to extradition in death penalty cases not only accords with Canada's principled advocacy on the international level, but is also consistent with the practice of other countries with whom Canada generally invites comparison, apart from the retentionist jurisdictions in the United States."

The U.S. experience with international human rights treaties provides a valuable contrast. Typically, U.S. accession to international human rights agreements includes statements, sometimes formal and sometimes informal, that the agreements require nothing more of the United States than that it comply with norms already embedded in the U.S. Constitution. Such statements might imply that the United States would have to reconsider the concrete applications of U.S. constitutional norms in light of international understandings about what the parallel international human rights norms require. But they need not have that implication. They might simply express the view that the United States already complies with international human rights norms, so that joining agreements embodying those norms is costless to the United States.

The U.S. position on treaty accession suggests that the upward-and-downward flow we have described might operate differently in different domestic constitutional systems. Specifically, it suggests that the United States as a hegemonic power might stand in a different relation, domestically, to international human rights norms than do many other nations. That is, the United States may insist that other nations adhere to international human rights norms while resisting criticisms from other nations that U.S. practices depart from those norms. The insistence by Western European nations that Central and Eastern European nations accept the (nominally) optional Protocol No. 6 to the Convention for the Protection of Human Rights and Fundamental Freedoms Concerning the Abolition of the Death Penalty, which outlaws the death penalty, as a condition of full membership in the community of European nations, is another example of the same phenomenon. The Protocol is formally optional for Western European nations, but functionally compulsory for Eastern and Central European ones. Notably, Hungary complied with this requirement not by amending its domestic constitution nor by abolishing the death penalty by parliamentary action, but by a decision of the Hungarian Constitutional Court.[5]

There may be parallel instances of transnational institutional influences on the development of domestic nonconstitutional law, perhaps through the influence of transnational corporations. Identifying the processes through the study of comparative constitutional law might provide a useful basis for comparing institutional developments in the private and public law fields. A focus on the processes of influence might also be useful in understanding changes in receptivity that may be emerging, for example, among U.S. jurists on the relevance of the decisions of foreign tribunals on constitutional questions, as is suggested by Chief Justice William H. Rehnquist's foreword's call for courts in the United States to become more familiar with the constitutional experiences of other nations.

The study of comparative constitutional law might be distinctive in another way. The distinction between civil law and common law systems, frequently supplemented by distinguishing between those systems and still others, has been one of the central organizing principles of the field of comparative law. The same cannot be said, at least initially, about constitutional law. There is, in a sense, an absent term in comparative constitutional law: If civil law is an organizing "counterpart" to "common law," what is the organizing counterpart to "constitutional law"? The accepted meaning in comparative study of constitutions and constitutional law is part of the difficulty: if constitutional law is understood as what is produced by courts empowered to interpret and apply the constitution to constrain political actors, then perhaps constitutional law can be counterposed to legislative supremacy systems. Professor Geoffrey Marshall's chapter strongly links judicial enforceability with full realization of constitutional rights. But even before the Human Rights Act of 1998, British constitutionalists insisted that Britain had a constitution, not entirely written, scattered in different documents and conventions, and not subject to being enforced by courts as against the will of Parliament—but a constitution nonetheless. If constitutional law is understood to embrace legal norms not fully enforceable by courts but complied with by the legal system and political branches more generally, then the UK would be not a counterexample, but an example. If the definition broadens in this way, however, then the question is whether there is an organizing counterpart to "constitutional law."

Moreover, civil law systems and common law systems are arguably equally defensible in overall normative terms. By this we mean that neither the common law nor the civil law is likely to come out clearly ahead of the other as long as one specifies a sufficiently rich set of normative criteria: Civil law might come out ahead on some criteria, common law on others, but overall the normative judgments on the systems may well be that both are reasonably acceptable ways of accomplishing the purposes of law. We can counterpose common law to civil law without raising overall normative questions, but it is much harder to counterpose constitutional law to—what? anticonstitutional law? anarchy? totalitarianism?—without raising such questions.

Answering those questions invites analysis of the normative goals of constitutions and, in efforts to create counterpart categories, a tendency to identify transnational norms that permit the categorization of systems as having, or not having, constitutional law. To the extent that comparative constitutional inquiry converges on efforts to identify transnational normative goals for a constitution, it overlaps considerably with normative political theory and invites a search for general truths with which some scholars today might be uncomfortable. Although part of the discomfort may be a generational mistrust of the assertion that there are universal rules for anything, discomfort about the search for universal constitutional norms also relates to the underdeveloped character of the categories for understanding constitutions. There is a kind of implicit normativity associated with the claim that there is a "constitution" that does not arise with the claim that one has either a common law or civil law system. To dispute that there is "really" a constitution claimed to exist requires a normative theory of the range of things constitutions do, or the form they take, or the procedure by which they are recognized.

Analysis of the different normative goals of laws regarded as "constitutional" is a rich field for exploration, provided that the scholar strives to retain the stance of "distancing." This may be difficult, especially if the scholar embraces the proposition that domestic constitutional law should reflect or be interpreted to conform to the best normative political theory available.[6] To the extent that one is suffused with normative regard for the aspirations of one's own system, there may be a temptation to see other constitutional systems as imperfect realizations of what that scholar's domestic system is already committed to. Yet a failure to attend explicitly to the normative questions about the definitions of constitutional law may risk this temptation through unexamined beliefs to a far greater extent than efforts to identify and critically analyze the range of goals or characteristics that are associated with the category of *constitution*.

Indeed, noticing the absent term in comparative constitutional law might itself deepen our understanding of comparative constitutional law. It helps raise important questions. We can ask whether constitutions have any necessary normative components, without prejudicing the answer by equating constitutions with some normative definition of constitutionalism. We can ask whether it is helpful to think of constitutions as the means of organizing governments and nothing more, and, if it sometimes is, whether there are conditions under which a minimalist understanding of constitutions is more or less helpful.

The chapters in this collection attempt to define the field of constitutional law, sometimes expressly but more often by illustrating the way in which each author thinks about comparative constitutional law.

When we originally envisioned the 1999 conference, we had thought that geographic proximity might be reflected in distinctive constitutional questions or concerns. But we found instead that the larger constitutional questions transcended geographic and cultural differences, though how nations responded to those questions or concerns might differ substantially, based on different histories, traditions, and experiences. Let us identify three common themes reflecting common questions in the chapters that follow.

First, several scholars focused on the relationships of constitutionalism and constitutional law to popular understandings and political contexts, what Professor Takahashi calls "daily narratives" and their relationship to constitutional understandings and transformations. Professor Ratna Kapur in her chapter explains the differing concepts of tolerance and equal respect competing for the "popular imagination" in India. Minister Dullah Omar's chapter delves into the history of the unjust uses of law in the colonial and apartheid era, while exploring the need to develop institutions of civil society in order to promote constitutionalism under the new South African Constitution. Ambassador Roberto G. MacLean's discussion of the prerequisites for successful court systems and Justice Adel Omar Sherif's chapter on the importance of the "political atmosphere" for the successful functioning of judicial review—both of these may be taken to imply a broader or different role for constitutional law teachers and scholars, one that requires greater knowledge of and engagement with the broader context in which law and legal decisions occur.

For example, Professor Kapur argues for regrounding the value of tolerance for different religions in legal sources and precedents, rather than in religious traditions, in order to help resecularize popular and constitutional understandings of treatment of religious groups. Such an argument implies that constitutional scholars must be or become concerned with a broader base of knowledge than the cases and formal legal principles of their systems as such. Professor Winfried Brugger argues that the common good is the measure by which to evaluate a legal regime, according to three "pillars"—legal certainty, legitimacy, and practicality. The idea of practicality for Brugger entails acting on valid empirical assumptions with enough means-ends efficiency, and consideration to the structure of the relevant sphere of life—none of which can be determined solely through formalist analysis of laws themselves. And Ambassador MacLean envisions a role for judges in bridging the gap between law and society in peaceful ways by giving real meaning to law. For judges to be willing and able to do so, however, requires specific social and political conditions, including physical security for the courts; the willingness of judges to understand themselves as, in part, providing a service; and some minimum level of acceptance of the courts and the government by the community. For Commissioner Counselor Sherif, judicial review in Egypt emerged out of the struggles toward political liberalization and depends on a liberal political environment to flourish.

If it is correct that both constitutional law and constitutional systems depend importantly on popular understandings and the political-social environment, then the work of constitutional law and comparative constitutional law cannot carry forward in intellectual isolation from the work of other disciplines of political science, sociology, cultural anthropology, the cognitive sciences, or economics. There is an old debate, of a disciplinary character, in the United States: Is law an autonomous intellectual discipline or even an independent "science," or, rather, is law to be seen as an interconnected part of a broader interdisciplinary understanding of people, their societies, and their needs for governance? One famous story concerns the founding of the University of Chicago Law School: A Harvard-educated prospective dean would not take the deanship unless Ernst Freund's proposed curriculum—which would have included comparative political science—was rejected. Comparative constitutional study may well revive interest in the direction of broader understandings of relevant knowledge, for, as comparative scholars, many of us find we cannot understand even the formal meanings of the texts we study without understanding the broader legal system and cultural and political value structure in which they are embedded.

A second set of concerns revolves around dilemmas of equality, and here we note two different dilemmas familiar to many constitutional systems. First, there are tensions between different versions of equality—formal and substantive versions of equality, for example. Second, there are tensions in rule-of-law based constitutional systems between the value of equality, on the one hand, and the value of tolerance for difference, on the other. These are among the most ubiquitous and difficult of problems for most constitutional systems, whether in Canada, in the United States, in South Africa, in Egypt, in the UK, or in India.

The dilemma of equality of form or substance is played out in the United States in debates over race and affirmative action and of accommodation of minority religious practices. Professor Jean-Pierre Théron posits a tension between the idea of rights as universal and the second-generation claims to social and economic rights, which, one might say, are distributed according to notions of substantive, rather than formal equality. As Professor Théron emphasizes, for "second generation" constitutional rights, the state is no longer the enemy of freedom. And Minister Omar's chapter suggests that effectively providing for human rights, including social and economic improvements, may be essential for the legitimacy of emerging constitutional orders. Such efforts to link constitutional approaches to equality with efforts to define legitimacy will bring us again into realms of political science and other social sciences.

As the chapters suggest, the two dilemmas of equality can intersect and overlap with each other. Claims to gender equality, for example, are often in conflict with claims of cultural or religious autonomy—that is, with rights to difference and tolerance. Yet this same set of conflicts can be recharacterized as conflicts between different kinds of equality claims: gender equality claims in conflict with "equality" rights of different cultural or religious groups to be treated with equal respect. In the context of India's constitutional approaches to religious freedom and equal respect for religions, Professor Kapur's chapter explores whether constitutional law can link values of respect for group differences with requirements for internal group democracy or accountability. And yet a striking question is raised in Judge Dennis M. Davis' chapter, in the context of South Africa's new constitutional system: Do constitutional efforts to insist on equality as a higher norm than recognition of cultural difference, by requiring that groups seeking some form of cultural autonomy respect the equality of their own members, impair the overall legitimacy of the constitutional system?

Finally, explicit or implicit in virtually all of these chapters is the theme that globalization as a phenomenon requires comparative constitutional study. Why? A number of answers are suggested. First, to understand the forms, the very vocabulary, through which constitutional discourse is had, Professor Thomas Fleiner's thoughtful chapter explores differences between civil law and common law orientations to the state. These differences, he suggests, cause the "rule of law" to have different meanings in Europe and in the United States—in Europe, government is limited by normative decisions of sovereignity in the constitution, whereas, he asserts, in the United States, the rule of law itself is preconstitutional. Yet, as Professors Weinrib's and Kommers's chapters suggest, there is some degree of convergence among constitutional courts around the world on the construction of an increasingly internationalized or cosmopolitan law of human rights in which the constitutional decisions of major court systems are regarded as a shared legal product.

Globalization and its pressures must be understood as well, Ambassador MacLean's chapter suggests, to help identify and support the instrumental and functional needs of creating stable judicial systems. Commissioner Counselor Sherif's chapter emphasizes the need for comparative constitutionalists to understand the multiple global influences in Egypt where, he explains, the legal system as a whole has been most influenced by civil law tradition, yet the Constitutional Court has been most influenced by the U.S. judiciary, while Islamic legal traditions also play an influential role. And the increased globalization of constitutional law is significant as a tool and a backdrop for evaluating the quality and import of change in the legal orders of particular regimes, as both Professor Marshall suggests for the UK and Professor Brugger for the European Community.

Indeed, Professor Weinrib has suggested that there is an ongoing process of institutionalizing comparative constitutional study as a basic and foundational part of law, and thus, of legal training. Professors Weinrib and Takahashi offer complementary frameworks for conceiving of the questions of comparative constitutional law—and many of the other chapters illustrate one or more of their suggested approaches. According to Professor Weinrib, a post–World War II constitutional order has emerged that is transnational in character and most fundamentally defined by its commitment to human dignity as the core constitutional value. Professor Takahashi, on the other hand, emphasizes both structural and individual rights components as core elements of the comparative study of constitutional law and systems. He identifies four basic principles of modern constitutionalism—guarantees of rights, separation of powers, popular sovereignty, and rule of law.

Professor David Schneiderman's chapter contains an important caution: that preoccupation with constitutionalism risks obscuring the transfers of power to private businesses that the globalization of the economy entails, and that a focus on individual rights may cause comparative constitutionalists to fail to come to grips with the significance of limiting their concerns to constraints on governments rather than exploring government's role in constraining the economic power of markets. His chapter is an elegant reminder of the importance of sustaining a critical distance to the very categories of legal phenomenon we as scholars analyze, to question what is implicit in the choice of what we write about and what we treat as within and without the domain of comparative constitutional law. As we have tried to suggest in this introduction, and as is illustrated by the chapters that follow, the domain of comparative constitutional law is yet working to define itself and should be seen as having at best highly porous boundaries from (and perhaps more accurately overlapping concerns with) both domestic constitutional law and international law, as well as with the fields of comparative government, history, economics, sociology, and cultural studies.

In an organization that is necessarily somewhat arbitrary, Part I of this book is organized around chapters whose central questions go to what Professor Weinrib calls "constitutional conceptions" and directly address how the inquiries of this field might be framed. In addition to Professor Weinrib's chapter focusing on the elaboration of human dignity as a transnational constitutional conception, this part includes Professor Takahashi's argument as to the purposes of comparative constitutional law and the core features of constitutions, Professor Kommers' chapter on how U.S. and German approaches to human dignity and human rights illuminate comparative constitutional understanding, Commissioner Counselor Sherif's elaboration of the need to understand the complex of factors influencing the emergence of constitutional law and the Constitutional Court in Egypt, and Professor Fleiner's elucidation of conceptual differences between civil and common law backgrounds that infiltrate understandings of constitutionalism and the rule of law. Part II includes four chapters that focus on the relations between constitutions, courts, and governmental legitimacy: Professor Brugger's analysis of the normative categories by which to evaluate the emerging constitution in the European Union (EU), Professor Marshall's critique of British reluctance to fully embrace judicial enforcement of human rights, Ambassador MacLean's argument that courts must see themselves and be seen as serving the people in order to have the legitimacy to perform their roles, and Minister Omar's emphasis on the melding of high aspiration with very difficult and conflictual politics in the creation of the new South African Constitution. And Part III, which we have titled "Constitutions, Rights, and Reframing," includes chapters that focus on rights—on different conceptions of equality, as discussed by Professor Kapur and Judge Davis; on different conceptions of negative and positive rights, as discussed by Professor Théron; and on the question of rights against whom and to, or for, what, implicitly raised by Professor Schneiderman's chapter on the risks of private power. His challenge to the effects of how constitutional questions are framed seemed a suitable closing chapter, forcing reflection again on the constitutional conceptions advanced throughout the preceding chapters.

NOTES

1. The power of awareness of external judgments might be reflected in what Amnesty International and Father Robert F. Drinan have called the "mobilization of shame"—the use of the judgments of an international community to restrain human rights violations. See Robert F. Drinan, S.J., *The Mobilization of Shame: A World View of Human Rights* (New Haven: Yale University Press, 2001).

2. See, e.g., Bill Lann Lee, Henry and Lucy Moses Foundation Lecture, Columbia University Law School (April 10, 2001).

3. *Kindler v. Canada* (Minister of Justice), [1991] 2 S.C.R. 779; Reference re Ng Extradition (Can.), [1991] 2 SCR 858.

4. *United States v. Burns*, [2001] Can. Sup. Ct. LEXIS 9, [2001] SCC 7.

5. Decision No. 23/1990 (X.31) AB, (Capital Punishment Case, Const. Court of the Republic of Hungary, October 31, 1990), translated and reproduced in 1 *East Eur. Case Rep. Const. Law* 177 (1994).

6. See, e.g., Ronald Dworkin, *A Matter of Principle* (Cambridge, Mass.: Harvard University Press, 1985).

Abbreviations

ABA	American Bar Association
ADR	Alternative Dispute Resolution
AI	Amnesty International
ANC	African National Congress
BIT	bilateral investment treaty
BJP	Bhartiya Janata Party
CBOs	community-based organizations
EC	European Community
ECJ	European Court of Justice
ECT	European Community Treaty
EP	European Parliament
EU	European Union
FCC	Federal Constitutional Court (German)
FDI	foreign direct investment
GATT	General Agreement on Tariffs and Trade
GHQ	General Headquarters
ICC	International Criminal Court
ICSID	International Centre for Settlement of Investment Disputes
ILD	Institute for Liberty and Democracy
NAFTA	North American Free Trade Agreement

NGOs	nongovernmental organizations
PCIA	Personal Communications Industry Association
SDF	Self-Defence Force
TEU	Treaty on European Union
UNCITRAL	United Nations Commission on International Trade Law
UNIDROIT	International Institute for the Unification of Private Law
UNO	United Nations Organization
USAID	United States Agency for International Development
WTO	World Trade Organization

Part I

Constitutional Conceptions

1

Constitutional Conceptions and Constitutional Comparativism

Lorraine E. Weinrib

> Since the (narrower or wider) community of the nations of the earth has now gone so far that a violation of right on *one* place of the earth is felt in *all*, the idea of a cosmopolitan right is no fantastic and exaggerated way of representing right; it is, instead, a supplement to the unwritten code of the right of a state and the right of nations necessary for the sake of any public rights of human beings and so for perpetual peace; only under this condition can we flatter ourselves that we are constantly approaching perpetual peace.[1]

I. INTRODUCTION

The proliferation of rights-protecting instruments has become a familiar feature of legal development over the last half century. At both the national and supranational levels, these instruments enshrine aspects of human dignity to give legal expression to shared revulsion at totalitarianism and the horrors of Nazi barbarity. Rights have thus become a staple both of new international forms of cooperation and of the emergence, maturation, or transformation of particular democracies.

These developments have awakened considerable interest in comparative law.[2] Well-established in academic law and in the preparatory work that typically precedes the creation of new instruments, comparative analysis now plays a more extensive and more controversial role. It has come to occupy an accepted place within judicial review under both new and established systems of rights protection, appearing expressly in the judgments of courts and providing material for the academic assessment of those judgments. Where this "new comparativism" has taken hold, comparative analysis is regarded as internal to the activity of constitutional adjudication or as supplying commentators with insights appropriate to the internal workings of specific constitutional regimes. The new comparative engagement is wide-ranging. It includes consideration of the general features of a constitutional system (e.g., fundamental values and their hierarchy, institutional roles, and modes of reasoning), as well as analysis of particular elements, such as text and doctrine.

The constitutional jurisprudence of the United States has remained remarkably untouched by the new constitutional comparativism. Because the United States has the world's oldest and most influential system for the judicial review of constitutional rights, one might expect its constitutional jurisprudence to be exemplary in this respect, as it has been in others. The Supreme Court of the United States does not, however, engage in this type of comparative analysis. In fact, the propriety of comparative engagement has become a matter of comment on the Court.

The almost complete absence of any comparative analysis in the American jurisprudence calls for some explanation. Why is it that a phenomenon so easily accepted among other constitutional democracies plays virtually no role in the American constitutional discourse? What does acceptance or rejection of comparative analysis reveal about contemporary notions of constitutionalism?

My contention is that the role assigned to comparativism does not stand apart from other elements of constitutional analysis. It is an integral component of one's overall conception of a constitution. By a conception of a constitution I mean the collection of interrelated ideas that one brings to the understanding of a particular system of constitutional law. Such a conception has substantive aspects that go to the nature of the guaranteed rights, the hierarchy among those rights, and the values implicit in them. Its institutional aspects relate to the different roles of legislatures, the executive, and courts and thus implicate basic constitutional structural features, such as the rule of law, the separation of powers, and the independence of the judiciary. Moreover, it has interpretative aspects that go to the mode of adjudicative reasoning, the exhaustiveness (or otherwise) of the constitutional text, the coherence of constitutional doctrine, and the relationship of constitutional development to nonlegal bodies of knowledge and to social change. A conception of the constitution brings these aspects together at the appropriate level of generality, so that they are understood as mutually dependent and informing.

The new comparativism has arisen within systems of rights protection that share a similar conception of constitutional values. This value structure dictates certain institutional arrangements as well as a particular interpretative methodology. The conception is sufficiently general to allow different constitutions to develop in accordance with their own histories, constitutional arrangements, and challenges. It welcomes—indeed, it requires—significant cross-fertilization. Judges and scholars within this conceptual paradigm deepen their understanding of their own constitutions when they come to appreciate the range of similarities and differences that arise under the cognate constitutions within this paradigm. In particular, they benefit by seeing their own systems through the eyes of foreign judges, academics, and commentators. In the absence of shared, general ideas informing the conception of the constitution, however, such comparative engagement is incoherent. Thus, if one understands a constitution as the embodiment in higher law of a unique nation's experience, a fixed moral code, and/or a concrete political practice, then the new comparativism will challenge one's most basic constitutional presuppositions.

The close connection between conceptions of constitutionalism and the acceptance of the new comparativism is well illustrated by Justice Scalia's now-ascendant views on the constitutionality of executing felons who were young adolescents at the time of their crimes. In *Thompson v. Oklahoma*[3] in dissent, and a year later in *Stanford v. Kentucky*[4] for the plurality, he sets out a complex frame of argument supporting the constitutional permissibility of juvenile execution. In this context, he also goes out of his way to express his emphatic objection to even the most formulaic reference to legal rules in other Western democracies. There are other indicators that exclusion of any and all external influences is essential to the internal structure of his particular conception of the U.S. Constitution.[5] Therefore, this attitude, even if it is extreme, is worth examining. After presenting an account of the conception of the constitution implicit in these opinions, I will contrast it with the conception that has generated and supports the pervasive comparativist engagement now integrated in the constitutional analysis of most other constitutional democracies. In conclusion, I will examine some of the challenges that the new comparativism poses within new and established constitutional systems.

II. CAPITAL PUNISHMENT OF MINORS

The recent American death penalty case law presents an excellent case study for comparative engagement because it presents such a dramatic divergence from the general abolitionist trend in other democracies, especially in respect to juvenile offenders.[6] This trend stands as the product of judicial rulings under constitutional or international rights-protecting instruments that may well have taken the Eighth Amendment as their model or, by law, reform under the influence of such instruments. If this trend, or its principled foundation, were relevant to the deliberations of the Supreme Court of the United States, then it would have some salience for cases arising under the Eighth Amendment. At the very least, the Court would feel called upon to account for the divergence.

Such divergence is permissible under the postwar constitutional paradigm that has spawned the new comparativism. This paradigm generates a considerable degree of homogeneity on similar questions, but does not slavishly impose the same response to every rights claim in all legal systems. The shared constitutional conception that informs judicial methodology precipitates a systematic mode of reasoning that includes reflection on the resolution of similar claims under other rights-protecting systems. Marked departures from general trends in analysis or result in a particular national context rest on reasoning rooted both in the general constitutional conception as well as the particularities of national context compatible with that conception.

The constitutional analysis employed by Justice Scalia in the cases under review, however, expresses a conception of the constitution that is totally inconsistent with the one that fosters and thrives on the new comparativism. Consequently, he repudiates even a relatively limited comparative engagement. Thus, he takes objection to an omnibus listing of the legal position on the execution of juvenile felons in other democracies and under various rights-protecting systems. How much more adamantly he would have to object to the more rigorous, analytic comparative engagement that is the hallmark of the new comparativism.

While Justice Scalia insists upon a fully American constitutional methodology, his distaste for comparative reflection is not an established feature of American constitutional jurisprudence.[7] The text of the Eighth Amendment, originally applicable to the federal government and later extended to the states, prohibits the imposition of "cruel and unusual punishments." The doctrinal tradition spawned by this provision has not remained fixed to the Framers' particular opinions of acceptable punishments in their day. Nor did it seem, until recently, to be constrained by national borders.

Judges have thus read the Eighth Amendment to stipulate that modes of punishment must conform to "evolving standards of decency that mark the progress of a maturing society," interpreted "in a flexible and dynamic manner."[8] As late as 1988 in *Thompson v. Oklahoma*,[9] citing a line of prior decisions, the Supreme Court by plurality affirmed the judiciary's duty to apply this standard progressively,[10] so as to acknowledge "new threats to an established constitutional value."[11] Accordingly, as time passed, and new "conditions and purposes emerged," the vitality of a constitutional principle would come to depend on its extension beyond the specific mischief that prompted its adoption.[12] In this spirit, the "evolving standard of decency" that marks "the progress of a maturing society," took note of the principled rejection of particular kinds of punishment in other democracies. Accordingly, a majority found unconstitutional the execution of offenders who were below the age of 16 when they committed their crimes, at least when legislatures had not explicitly authorized such executions.

The judicial search for contemporary standards extended in *Thompson*, as in earlier decisions, beyond national borders to canvass practices in other countries, chosen because they shared the Anglo-American heritage, as well as in Western Europe, and even the Soviet Union.[13] The plurality opinion also referred to three supranational, rights-protecting instruments, noting that the first two had been signed, and the third both signed and ratified, by the United States.[14] These were the International Covenant on Civil and Political Rights,[15] the American Convention on Human Rights,[16] and the Geneva Convention Relative to the Protection of Civilian Persons in Time of War.[17]

It would be an exaggeration to claim that these comparative references did more than add some extra weight to the Court's ruling that the execution of someone under 16 years of age at the time of the offense was unacceptable constitutionally. After setting out the long list of comparators taken from Amnesty International's brief, Justice Stevens' plurality opinion offered no analysis. He simply observed that this ruling was "consistent" with the "views" of other nations.[18] This material seemed to rank in importance at the same level as the similar views of expert, domestic professional organizations.[19] One might say that it was supportive, rather than persuasive or authoritative.[20] Such use of comparative material is not as rigorous, analytic, or broad-based as the "new comparativism."

Just one year later, in *Stanford v. Kentucky*, when the Court ruled that there was no constitutional impediment to executing persons who were slightly older, that is, age 16 or 17 at the time of the offense, it relegated comparative material to an even more marginal role. Justice Scalia, now speaking for the plurality, stipulated that only "American conceptions of decency . . . are dispositive."[21] The "standards of decency" that mark the "progress of a maturing society" might evolve, but not to reflect legal developments beyond the borders of the United States, even when these developments were formulated in terms similar to the Eighth Amendment and may well have taken inspiration from it. His methodology focussed not merely on American material, but exclusively on domestic statute law and jury practice: "A revised national consensus so broad, so clear, and so enduring as to justify a permanent prohibition upon all units of democratic government must appear in the operative acts (laws and the application of laws) that the people have approved."[22]

Two aspects of Justice Scalia's conception of the constitution come together in his treatment of capital punishment for minors. The first is that, because the United States is a democracy, the expression of the people's will through legislation is entitled to extreme deference. The second is that constitutional standards should not reflect the merely subjective views of the judiciary. These two aspects are related, in that deference to legislation both reflects the legitimacy of democracy's most authentic voice and avoids the subjectivity of court judgments. Accordingly, if the invalidation of capital punishment for minors requires reference to the evolving standards of decency in American society, "the most reliable objective signs consist of the legislation that society has enacted. It will rarely if ever be the case that Members of this Court will have a better sense of the evolution in views of the American people than do their elected representatives."[23]

The strong presumption of constitutionality embodied in this test does not preclude reference to the sentencing practices of other democracies altogether. The primary concern for Eighth Amendment purposes, however, is the punishment that the people of the United States stipulate and permit. Even a practice accepted as uniform among the American people might, however, require further confirmation of its pervasive acceptance elsewhere to warrant judicial acknowledgment that it is "implicit in the concept of ordered liberty" and, thus, not merely an ephemeral trend in social mores.[24] Accordingly, "where there is not first a settled consensus among our own people, the views of other nations, however enlightened the Justices of this Court may think them to be, cannot be imposed upon Americans through their Constitution."[25]

Justice Scalia rejected the critique leveled by the dissent that he had transformed the Eighth Amendment's protection against cruel and unusual punishment into a shield protecting political majorities.[26] More stringent review, released from the "historical moorings" of the issue or the social values of the American people as reflected in the laws produced by their democratic process, he insisted, would invite elite and nonelected judges to impose their personal preferences by judicial fiat.[27] As the "servants," "creatures and agents" of the American people, judges must not impose norms that the people's political institutions have not democratically espoused.[28]

This constitutional conception relegates courts to mechanical tasks, such as determining the social consensus on the execution of juvenile felons by conducting an audit of the domestic statute books. It cannot, however, eliminate the interpretative function altogether. What social consensus is the judiciary to discern embodied in statutes that proscribe capital punishment without making any reference to juveniles? Of what relevance is the widespread propensity to set the responsibilities of juveniles to accord with the maturation process? What social meaning can judges derive from jurisdictions that make no express reference to juvenile execution, but seem to allow it through the combined operation of statutes enacted at different times? Justice Scalia's conception of the constitution demands an "objective" domestic methodology, to preclude judicial imposition of personal preferences or foreign influence that would undermine fidelity to popular sovereignty, federal arrangements, and legislative supremacy. The application of that methodology to each of these questions demonstrates that the rejection of comparativism arises as part of a constitutional conception that offers only an illusory flight from substantive values and judicial authority.

Consider first the relevance of state laws that do not impose the death penalty. Justice Scalia considers these statutes unhelpful in discerning the social consensus on juvenile execution. To register its constituents' aversion to juvenile capital punishment, a state legislature opposed to capital punishment must, one infers, expressly ban both adult and juvenile executions. In consequence, the petitioners bear the burden of establishing a national consensus against the death penalty for juvenile felons without being able to call in aid the legislation in fourteen states, plus the District of Columbia, that have abolished capital punishment altogether.

To illuminate his insistence on specific statutory embodiment of a consensus directed against the execution of juvenile felons, rather than against capital punishment generally, Justice Scalia offers a striking analogy. A general proscription against capital punishment, he observes, fails to express any social consensus on juvenile execution, just as a general ban on wagering would reveal no specific consensus as to the inhumanity of cockfights.[29] The analogy is inapposite. Although cockfights are staged for wagering purposes, the cruelty of cockfights is a moral issue independent of the undesirability of wagering. Because one can be opposed to wagering generally for reasons that have nothing to do with the cruelty of cockfights, a consensus against the former does not necessarily reflect a consensus against the latter. The situation is different with respect to capital punishment. Here, the general and specific bans express the same moral values. The stronger opposition to execution of juveniles rests on additional grounds related to the same moral values.

Justice Scalia offers nothing more than this faulty analogy to support his belief that it is beyond a judge's institutional capacity to infer a social attitude opposed to juvenile capital punishment from state law that does not authorize capital punishment. One must therefore delve deeper into his methodology to make sense of this part of his opinion. The social consensus that he seeks is very particular. It is not that a particular state has by statute authorized execution of juvenile felons or not. The state must have expressly and specifically legislated to exempt this age cohort from a regime of execution. This, it appears, would be the only "reliable objective sign" of public aversion to juvenile execution as a matter of evolving standards of decency related to capital punishment.

Framing the issue in this peculiar way removes from the canvass of social consensus a number of arguably important elements. It excludes, for example, the result of standard statutory interpretation. No judge would read a general ban as authorization for the execution of juvenile offenders. Moreover, it excludes precisely the political units whose constituents may hold the strongest views against juvenile execution, that is, because abhorrence of all capital punishment is part of a more comprehensive view.

Similarly, this framing excludes reference to any comparative example or reasoning on the relationship between juvenile capital punishment and capital punishment generally. A judge would be hard-pressed to find an example—domestic or foreign, past or present—of a legal regime (excluding cultures that perform child sacrifice) that imposes juvenile, but not adult, capital punishment. Comparative research would, therefore, further undermine the proposition that a general rejection of the death penalty does not express social consensus precluding execution of juveniles. It would also provide extensive evidence of the rejection by democratic nations of the death penalty as an expression of commitment to the rule of law, due process, and equality.

Having failed to offer reasoning or example to support the dubious claim that a consensus against capital punishment is not, *a fortiori*, a consensus against juvenile executions, Justice Scalia also fails to account for his view that the only social consensus that counts for determining the constitutionality of the execution of juvenile felons under the Eighth Amendment is that of states that impose the death penalty, whether on minors or not. The methodology restricting judges to "the most reliable objective signs" of American society's evolving standard of decency, erected to prevent judicial usurpation of the legislative prerogative, seems to filter out standard statutory interpretation as well as common sense. In application, it denies judges the very material that might signal a changing social consensus at home, including insight derived from examination of similar tendencies in democracies elsewhere. The second and third interpretative challenges provide greater insight into this curious methodology.

The second interpretative question relates to the social significance of public policy that generally treats adolescents differently from the rest of the population. Statutes abound that establish a delayed and graduated transition to adult freedoms and responsibilities. These statutes regulate the lives of young persons in a wide range of personal, social, and public activities. For example, Western democracies systematically prevent adolescents from voting, sitting on juries, marrying without parental consent, giving consent to medical treatment, driving, leaving school, participating in organized gambling, using pool halls or pawn shops, consenting to sexual relations, or buying pornography, cigarettes, or alcohol. These rules are generally understood to reflect a societal consensus that adolescents are incapable of making responsible decisions, even about their own best interests, when evaluating the long-term consequences of present indulgences and impulsive behavior. How much less do we expect them to appreciate fully the consequences to others of their actions, or to the working of the legal system in response to these actions? One might reasonably suppose that the legislative restrictions that insulate adolescents from both the immediate and long-term repercussions of their actions would constitute an important element of any reading of social consensus on the question of capital punishment.

Of particular interest are the rules that exclude adolescents from participation in public life. A judge might reasonably infer from the statutory incapacity to vote that society considers young persons not sufficiently mature for self-government. After all, their voices are excluded from that of the sovereign people, which sets the social agenda for legislation, including legislation that vastly curtails their own rights, freedoms, and responsibilities. Moreover, perhaps because society views their insights, priorities, and life experience as an inadequate foundation for judgment, statutes routinely exclude them from juries that determine the guilt or punishment of others, even those in their age cohort.

Expert opinion confirms the view of adolescent maturation implicit in the assorted statutory incapacities. The social science literature reveals that adolescents are generally more vulnerable, impressionable, and subject to peer pressure than adults. They are thus more impulsive and less self-disciplined; more open to experiment, risk-taking, and bravado than to rational deliberation; and unlikely to think deeply about the future consequences of their acts. Moreover, adolescents have a strong sense of their own omnipotence and immortality.[30]

Justice Scalia refuses to draw from the common ground underlying the legislative provisions and the social scientific material any inference whatsoever as to prevailing social attitudes toward juvenile responsibility for their actions. In his view, the individuated criminal process authorized under statute supplants any protective stance that social policy might otherwise accord to minors in other contexts, based on a presumption of immaturity. When that process determines guilt and punishment it deals with an individual, not with the group. It can therefore select out the individuals whose moral blameworthiness merits the ultimate punishment. Therefore, the psychological profile of adolescents presented in the scientific literature and reflected in the statute books is simply not relevant.[31] But does the individuated criminal process single out the most blameworthy for execution?

Justice Scalia's confidence in the individuation process is so strong that it even displaces more specific expert findings that the trial process does not in fact single out the most blameworthy youths for the ultimate punishment.[32] The juvenile felons on death row are, however, distinguishable in other respects. They are the ones, for example, who have suffered from various kinds of extreme abuse and neglect and led exceptionably troubled lives. Moreover, compared to others in their age group, they are exceptionally immature. The criminal justice system condemns them to death, despite the factors that should militate against their moral blameworthiness, because its individuated process does not focus exclusively on moral blameworthiness. It considers other factors as well, such as the seriousness of the offense, prior delinquency, and past failure to respond to treatment.

Justice Scalia easily dismisses these findings as well as any implications they might pose for standard criminal concerns, such as deterrence and proportionality of punishment. He has his own views about moral culpability.[33] In a revealing passage, he condemns as "absurd" any attempt to introduce into the death penalty context, as constitutional stricture, an age proxy for maturity at the level customarily stipulated by statute for careful driving, responsible drinking, and intelligent voting. The level of maturity he considers sufficient for the imposition of the ultimate penalty is quite basic. It is the ability to restrain one's actions according to "that most minimal of all civilized standards"—the understanding that "murdering another human being is profoundly wrong."[34] This moral stand is reflected in Justice Scalia's detailed description of the horror and brutality of the petitioners' crimes as well as their earlier criminal activities at the beginning of his opinion.[35] In contrast, Justice Brennan in dissent focuses on their tragic lives, personal limitations, and failed efforts at rehabilitation.[36]

The metamorphosis is dazzling. Where once stood the nuanced and evolving Eighth Amendment doctrinal test—"civilized standards"[37] of "decency that mark the progress of a maturing society"[38] as judicially elaborated and applied in the light of new insights, theory, and some comparative reflection—now stands a simple moral precept. Those who breach the "most minimal of all civilized standards," that is by committing murder, merit the ultimate penalty. Justice Scalia offers no specific, reliable, objective foundation for this value judgment.

Analysis of the first and second interpretative questions reveal that subjective, substantive values enter into Justice Scalia's judicial method, despite their purported illegitimacy under his conception of the U.S. Constitution. The third question raises a different aspect of this conception: the contention that elected representatives are better able to appreciate the "evolution in views of the American people" than judges carrying out a constitutional mandate. Since judges must identify societal consensus objectively from the statute books and the activities that statutes direct, one might assume that Justice Scalia would insist that the American people, or their elected representatives, provide some indication in statute of their consensus on such an important question as he did in the first example.

Although Justice Scalia's conception of the U.S. Constitution emphasizes respect for statute law as a reflection of public consensus, he registers no concern at the possibility of inadvertent extension of the death penalty to adolescents. In some states juvenile felons stand liable to capital punishment in such circumstances. New laws authorize their transfer into the adult criminal process, where they become subject to preexisting statutes enacted to authorize the death penalty for some crimes without juveniles in mind. Social consensus in favor of this possibility is discernible to Justice Scalia in the clear result produced by these interlocking statutes, which seems to mean only that the result is not actually a fluke or an accident.[39]

Justice Scalia expresses the view that judges would exceed their mandate if they insisted upon a higher standard of legislated clarity or specificity, even when the issue is juvenile execution. Judicial insistence upon some concrete indication of social consensus would "nullify rather than effectuate the will of the people," interfering with the legislative processes so acutely as to strike at the "heart of their sovereignty."[40] In any event, executive clemency would stop the execution of any particular juvenile to which the public seriously objected.[41]

To support this assertion, Justice Scalia equates a fairly traditional interpretative technique—that legislatures clearly express their will when they act against fundamental interests, such as the right to life or freedom from cruel and unusual punishments—with much more invasive interference with legislative process and powers. For judges to insist on a clear legislative directive, he opines, would be tantamount to imposing the requirement of a supermajority vote in the legislature or a referendum.

Once again, the analogies offered are unsatisfactory. Judges do not alter the legislative process or function when they determine that the legislature has not provided an adequate directive.[42] Interpretative rulings of this sort merely establish the necessary common standards that are to prevail for the writing and reading of statutes. Thus, in common law systems retaining full legislative supremacy, judges have stipulated that "basic rights are not to be overridden by the general words of a statute since the presumption is against the impairment of such basic rights."[43] The judiciary uses this technique "to require a clear and unambiguous legislative statement, sometimes in fact a restatement, of its wish to offend against a fundamental principle of fairness within the society."[44]

The context that precipitates judicial insistence upon more explicit legislative authorization in other legal systems prompts Justice Scalia to require less. Legislatures, he observes, find it "difficult" to pass laws visiting the death penalty specifically on "appealing groups," such as white-haired grandmothers, mothers of 2 year olds, and the blind.[45] Consequently, one infers, the social consensus in favor of allowing such executions may not be served by a requirement that they be specifically authorized. This must be one of the rare situations in which judges can discern the social consensus without the aid of reliable, objective legislative markers.

The result is clear, but the reasoning is not. Cold-blooded, vindictive, or uncaring, incorrigible killers evoke no public sympathy. Is Justice Scalia concerned that public and legislative debate on the specific question of juvenile executions might focus on the social science analysis that has depicted juvenile felons as tragic victims of their own inadequacies and/or the toxic combination of familial and social dysfunction? Political sensitivity to the personal characteristics of advanced or tender age, gender, reproduction, family roles, and disability—the characteristics that his examples highlight—are not incidental in the formation of public policy. Rights-protecting instruments often cite these characteristics to trigger special judicial attentiveness to the possible taint of ignorance, prejudice, and ill will in the formation of public policy, as well as the need for special accommodation. Justice Scalia seems to assume that the legislative timidity he observes signifies an excusable legislative incapacity to reflect the social consensus in favor of juvenile execution that the judiciary should indulge. He perceives no reliable objective indication of an emerging social consensus against juvenile execution that further public deliberation—abstracted from any particular killing or killer and illuminated by statistics and expert analysis as well as comparative reflection—might crystallize.

Justice Scalia's conception of the U.S. Constitution requires vigilance to ensure that judges do not influence the "manner" or "form" in which the people's representatives embody their policy preferences.[46] Interpretation must mediate carefully between statutory text and social consensus to avoid this intrusion. Where extension of the death penalty is at issue, Justice Scalia infers a social consensus in favor of juvenile capital punishment from the combined operation of two statutes, even though the result may have been unintended and undesired. Legislatures may not have the political fortitude to produce that result directly. In contrast, in the first example, he reads the absence of capital punishment in the punishment regime of a state as conveying no social consensus against execution of adolescent felons, even though the clear intent and result would be to preclude such executions. To register such a social consensus, the legislature would have to ban juvenile execution expressly, political timidity notwithstanding.

In practice, the circumscribed and mechanical methodology designed to preclude any imposition of substantive values by the judiciary, personal or imported, ventures at will beyond the confines of the reliable, objective legislated record. It rests on questionable analogies, inconsistent approaches to statutory interpretation, and unsupported and nonlegitimated value judgments. Ostensibly to preclude the judicial subjectivity that would undermine popular sovereignty, federalism, and legislative supremacy, Justice Scalia denies the relevance, and even the usefulness, of the more standard elements of modern constitutional method. He thus rejects legal and social science expertise, as well as the comparative material and analysis that have become the standard judicial reference points under modern rights-protecting instruments. Consequently, the doctrinal test that recognizes an evolving standard of decency in civilized society as the Eighth Amendment's promise loses its capacity to evolve. This may not be an undesired consequence for Justice Scalia: "The very objective of a basic law, it seems to me, is to place certain matters beyond risk of change, except through the extraordinary democratic majorities that constitutional amendment requires. . . . The whole *purpose* of a constitution—old or new—is to impede change, or, pejoratively put, to 'obstruct modernity.' "[47]

Justice Scalia's constitutional conception presents such a stark contrast to the postwar conception that cross-fertilization between the two systems is difficult to imagine. In the opinions reviewed, he reads the Bill of Rights as a collection of miscellaneous clauses, not as a rights-protecting instrument with the status of higher law. This understanding makes it possible to read the text of the Eighth Amendment without regard to the standard meaning of the words "cruel" and "unusual." Criminal policy under the Eighth Amendment therefore amounts to nothing more than, and in application something less than, social consensus translated into statute law. Judges who purport to elucidate and apply the normative content of the amendment as a constraint on legislative engage in an illegitimate, entirely subjective, exercise. Consequently, in the absence of constitutional amendment, social change becomes the exclusive product of jury deliberation and the political processes at the state level.

While the postwar constitutional paradigm is not yet a fully developed or adequately theorized practice, it affirms modernity. Nonetheless, it does not activate the judicial subjectivity so abhorrent to Justice Scalia's conception of the U.S. Constitution. It supports societal change by vesting in the judiciary a strong but highly constrained constitutional authority. In Jürgen Habermas' words: "The development of the constitutional state can be understood as an open sequence of experience-guided precautionary measures against the overpowering of the legal system by illegitimate power relations that contradict its normative self-understanding."[48] The postwar conception of constitutionalism marries judicial objectivity to constitutional substance by recognizing the normative content of constitutional text and history informed by expertise and comparative insight. The judiciary as guardian of the constitutional order imposes the discipline of rights protection on the ordinary political process without servicing its own political preferences or importing alien values. It is to that conception that we now turn, first for a general exposition and then for a more detailed critique of Justice Scalia's analysis in *Thompson* and *Stanford.*

III. THE POSTWAR CONCEPTION OF THE CONSTITUTION

The rights-protecting instruments adopted in the aftermath of the Second World War invite comparative reflection and analysis because they rest on a shared constitutional conception that, by design, transcends the history, cultural heritage, and social mores of any particular nation-state. The rejection of a nation-based constitutional conception has two aspects. First, looking back on the tragedy of the Second World War, it builds shared concern for rights protection into the basic law of all nations. Second, looking forward, it characterizes the postwar nation-state as the state of its citizens, transcending ancestry, ethnicity, and religion. This conception has given purpose and institutional structure to new constitutional instruments and influenced the transformation of existing legal systems, with and without formal amendment, under the influence of the international human rights protecting instruments.

The shared conceptual foundation of these instruments is to secure democratic government, the rule of law, and protection for equal human dignity. These instruments recall Immanuel Kant's idea of "cosmopolitan right"—the individual's entitlement to civilized behavior at the hands of all governments, even foreign governments. Kant's premise was the recognition of rights embodying the individual's freedom as a human being and equality as a citizen. He envisaged a "universal community" made up of the "peoples of the earth," which would make possible a law of human rights that transcended both civil and international law, so that "a violation of a right on *one* place of the earth is felt in *all*. . . ."[49] Remarkably, these ideas have proved to be malleable and resilient. They have adapted to civil and common law political systems as well as to new and old constitutional arrangements, written and unwritten. Wherever they have made a home, they invite rigorous and extensive comparative engagement.

The postwar rights-protecting instruments establish the primacy of rights protection as higher law, displacing any presumption of constitutional validity. Accordingly, rights guarantees make up one aspect of the variety of constraints that together constitute limited government. They discipline every exercise of state power whether by elected officials or under their auspices. These guarantees stand as the crystallization of the abstract idea of equal human dignity. They require the state to treat each person over whom it holds power as an end, not a means, and to respect his or her full and equal humanity and opportunity for self-fulfillment. No fixed idea of morality or dedicated social role justifies the failure to respect human dignity, whether its source lies in national or religious tradition, in the majority's calculation of the common good, or in approval by democratically elected bodies.

Human dignity has both universal and particularized meanings. It operates both as an organizing principle within postwar rights protection generally and as a more specific idea in domestic application. Respect for human dignity is a general, abstract principle that informs the analysis of the scope and strength of rights claims. It does not function as a specific concrete rule that mechanically dictates uniform results for similar questions wherever they arise. Indeed, given the considerable diversity in the historical, cultural, and social contexts in which respect for human dignity must flourish, different results are both expected and welcome, as long as there is no denial of the central application of the basic concept. Comparative analysis supports the legitimacy of such differentiation.

Thus, for example, the foundation of the German Constitution is the idea, expressed in its initial article, that human dignity is inviolable. The German Constitution also specifically guarantees freedom of expression as an aspect of that dignity. Nonetheless, German history provides a strong justification for upholding laws that prohibit Holocaust denial that may not obtain in other domestic contexts:

> The historical fact itself, that human beings were singled out according to the criteria of the so-called "Nuremberg Laws" and robbed of their individuality for the purpose of extermination, puts Jews living in the Federal Republic in a special personal relationship vis-à-vis their fellow citizens; what happened [then] is also present in this relationship today. It is part of their personal self-perception to be understood as a part of a group of people who stand out by virtue of their fate and in relation to whom there is a special moral responsibility on the part of all others, and this is part of their dignity. Respect for this self-perception, for each individual, is one of the guarantees against repetition of this kind of discrimination and forms a basic condition of their lives in the Federal Republic. Whoever seeks to deny these events denies vis-à-vis each individual the personal worth of [Jewish persons]. For the person concerned, this is continuing discrimination against the group to which he belongs and, as part of the group, against him.[50]

The courts are the special guardians of the higher law guarantees, which are understood to stand at risk under the majoritarian process by which elected representatives acquire and exercise their temporary electoral mandates to govern. Sir Stephen Sedley, a British High Court justice, perceives the emergence of a new constitutional paradigm that, in his view, may not even require a written constitution or a higher law bill of rights:

> we have today both in this country and in those with which it shares aspects of its political and judicial culture a new and still emerging constitutional paradigm, no longer of Dicey's supreme parliament to whose will the rule of law must finally bend, but of a bi-polar sovereignty of the Crown in Parliament and the Crown in its courts, to each of which the Crown's ministers are answerable—politically to Parliament, legally to the courts. That the government of the day has no separate sovereignty in this paradigm is both axiomatic and a reminder of the sharpest of all the lessons of eastern-Europe: that it is when state is collapsed into party that democracy founders.[51]

Postwar rights-protecting instruments do not, however, authorize the judiciary to treat rights as absolute negations of otherwise plenary state authority. Nor do they simply transfer to the courts the political power or prerogatives denied to elected representatives. They presuppose limited government through a separation of powers that maximizes the complementary institutional strengths of legislatures, the executive, and the courts. Elected representative bodies continue to act as responsible policy-makers, both empowered and disciplined by the constitutional instrument. The executive acts in compliance with the rule of law. The judiciary oversees this compliance as well as fidelity to the substantive strictures created by higher law; rights guarantees. It employs traditional judicial methodology, modified as necessary to higher law, constitutional analysis, including reasoned doctrinal development; and analysis of argument, supported by whatever expertise and data are both relevant and reliable. Especially helpful when fresh questions arise in a domestic context are insights and analysis derived from the parallel operation of other rights-protecting systems.

The judicial role does not usurp the political function. It does not entail an open-ended imposition of the personal views of the judges. Nor does it invite importation of ideas foreign to the domestic system as either authoritative or substantively appealing. It is tightly constrained by an established methodology that reflects the higher law status of the system of rights protection. In respect to the rights themselves, the interpretative method is purposive, delving into text, doctrinal and statutory development, history and theory at home and elsewhere to determine the way in which equal human dignity is forwarded by the particular guarantee in a variety of contexts.[52] If this analysis leads to a determination of state violation, the story is far from over. The state is invited to bear the burden of establishing in a court of law that its impugned legislation or action is, despite the breach of the particular right or freedom, nonetheless justified. This opportunity requires the state to participate in the reasoning process that sustains the values that inform the rights-protecting instrument.

This justification analysis has two parts, the second contingent upon satisfaction of the first. The first requires an examination of legality and the second of legitimacy. The principle of legality is a formal concern. In most instances the legality stricture requires the state to have authorized the encroachment through the regular channels of law-making, so that it is the product of a representative, accountable, deliberative public process and embodied in an accessible and intelligible legal instrument.[53] In common law jurisdictions, the principled elaboration of the common law also satisfies this formal standard. What is excluded is an exercise of power, by legislatures or officials, that does not enable the rights-holder to acquire a reasonable understanding of the rules applicable to a particular situation or course of action. The interpreter does not usurp the legislative role by requiring the legislative body to perform it.

This first and formal stage of the justification analysis in effect vests in all members of the political community a right to the protection of the rule of law when fundamental rights are at issue. This formal stage may indirectly provide a significant measure of protection against rights infringement. It motivates the state to fulfill the formal strictures generally to ensure that, in any later constitutional challenge, it will not find itself precluded from reaching the second stage of justification, which is contingent on satisfaction of the first. The increased measure of deliberation and public attention entailed may result in policies that reflect a wider range of interests, rest on deeper understanding of expert opinion and social data, and offer more respect to the rights implicated.

The second stage of justification focuses on the question of legitimacy. It inquires into the substantive justification of the state encroachment on the guaranteed right or freedom. Here the judge works out any conflicts between the various guarantees, for example freedom of speech and equality, and ensures the equal enjoyment of any particular guarantee. True to the constitutional conception that animates the postwar rights-protecting instruments, analysis restricts itself to normative grounds.[54] The range of arguments that support a ruling of justified limitation exclude those that entail the full abrogation of the guarantee. The state does not satisfy the burden of substantive justification if it puts forward no more than an assertion of its political authority to create or authorize the impugned measure. Similarly inappropriate are arguments that demonstrate only that the state acted to further the common good, to maintain traditional moral values or social roles, or to contain expenditures.

While the concerns are substantive, the adjudicator does not enter into the actual merits of the impugned measure. To this end, the methodology entails a sequence of analytic steps that maintain the primacy of respect for human dignity, even when its crystallization in the particular guaranteed right or freedom must cede. The compendious name for this methodology is "proportionality analysis."[55] The first consideration is the actual objective of the impugned enactment or action. The primacy of the guarantee means that the state must, at the outset, establish that the objective of its democratically approved encroachment is of sufficiently high importance to warrant superseding a constitutional guarantee. Next, the state must establish that the impugned law or decision forwards this special objective directly. This step weeds out measures that do not enjoy a rational connection to their purported objective. The primacy of the right is further enforced by the stipulation that the encroachment may intrude on the right only to the extent necessary to meet its objective. Finally, even when the state has established a sufficiently important objective, rationally pursued with minimal impairment of the right, it must demonstrate that the desired and actual benefit of the impugned measure exceeds the detriment effected by the infringement.

This complicated frame of legal analysis, which reflects the constitutional conception that informs the postwar rights-protecting instruments, stands in stark contrast to Justice Scalia's conception of the U.S. Constitution, as applied to the question of juvenile felons. Where he places democratic process and/or its product (and its extended federal arrangements) above the Bill of Rights, the postwar conception respects these three constitutional elements as coordinate and mutually informing. He reads the Eighth Amendment as a freestanding provision endorsing the self-binding of a diverse set of plenary legislatures deriving no central concept or normative purpose from the Bill of Rights.[56] The postwar rights-protecting systems, in contrast, regard respect for human dignity as the abstract value that informs each specific guaranteed right and freedom. Courts, in Justice Scalia's conception, have no independent constitutional stature; they operate as the agents of the plenary powers accorded to the democratic process. In the postwar systems, courts exercise a separate, coordinate constitutional authority to act as guardians of the constitutional order over the legislatures, the executive, and the administration.

The interpretative methodology and arguments employed by Justice Scalia in *Thompson* and *Stanford* would not fare well in the postwar model. Its overarching concern is the protection of human dignity. Its basic structure requires separate and sequential consideration of content of the right, its possible breach, and then justification for limits on those rights by proportionality analysis with the onus on the state. This value structure and methodology leave no point of entry for specious analogies, unduly flexible modes of statutory interpretation, or fixed moral preconceptions. The analysis rests instead on supporting expertise, legal and otherwise; fidelity to prior doctrinal analysis unless departure is demonstrably warranted by constitutional principle; and relevant comparative research and analysis. The postwar conception does not prioritize public consensus, whether derived from statutory text or presupposed as the traditional social mores of the nation. Nor does it defer to a strong presumption of constitutionality based on democratic enactment, historical practice, or fixed moral imperatives.

The purposive analytic method probes the relationship between human dignity and the specific guarantee. When the issue is juvenile execution, the relevant provisions would be the right to life itself or to equality, or freedom against cruel and unusual punishment. A judge working under the postwar conception would take the words "cruel" and "unusual" as embodiments of fundamental constitutional principles applicable to every political unit. The trend against capital punishment, in practice and as supported by principled adjudicative rulings under rights-protecting instruments elsewhere, as well as the even stronger trend against execution of juvenile felons, would alert the adjudicator to the strong possibility of a breach of a constitutional norm. Social science data and expert opinion would elucidate the particular concerns that arise in the execution of juvenile felons. In contrast, Justice Scalia reads the text of the Eighth Amendment as devoid of substantive content deriving from its text or its place in the Bill of Rights. He would constrain legislative prerogatives only when the legislatures had, in effect, bound themselves by espousing a social consensus so extensive as to exceed the common ground necessary for constitutional amendment in a large and diverse federal state.

Turning to the first interpretative question, it would be unlikely that a judge under the postwar framework of analysis would have occasion to consider whether a general ban on the death penalty reflected a social consensus against the execution of juvenile felons. Constitutional stricture prevails, in terms of substance and process, over both statute and social consensus, however ascertained. A judicial ruling based on statute that excluded from a general rule something particular intrinsically related to it would suggest the impermissible operation of impermissible presuppositions, extraneous to the constitutional text, values, and prescribed methodology.

Justice Scalia's approach to the second of the three interpretative questions would also lie outside the range of accepted judicial method. Recall that he determined that the individuated criminal process provides a reliable apparatus for determining the appropriate punishment for adolescent felons, having set aside the social science statistics and expert opinion. This approach would not satisfy a judge under the postwar constitutional conception. She would reach this contention at the legality stage of justification analysis, when considering the state's substantive arguments to justify breach of a constitutional guarantee—to life, against cruel and unusual punishment, or to equality. The state would presumably argue that the individuated criminal process as applied to juvenile felons meets the standard purposes of the criminal justice system, that is punishment, deterrence, and proportionality as between penalty and moral blameworthiness. The test for a strong rational connection between the objectives and the actual practice and then for minimal impairment of the protected interest would apply, as they do in the analysis of justified limits on all the guarantees. The adjudicator would thus not be in a position to dismiss considerations of rational connection and proportionality as inapplicable to the particular guarantee under review, as did Justice Scalia.

An individuated process that ignored the state's stipulated objectives or that mixed these objectives with considerations that did not have overarching constitutional importance would fail these tests. The general policy of sheltering adolescents from full adult duties and responsibilities, supported by social science explanations of the rationality of such practices at home and in other democracies, would suggest a disjuncture between the constitutionally informed objectives of punishment and the individuated process by which punishment is imposed. The more focused studies reporting the social and psychological profile of young offenders whom the individuation process sends to death row would raise other concerns. They would demonstrate that juvenile offenders face a sentencing process that impairs their rights excessively in failing to give priority to the overriding principles of moral blameworthiness, deterrence, and proportionality as applied to their age, psychological problems, and social deprivation. The subjective individual right against deprivation of life or equality, or against cruel and unusual punishment, would thus not cede to a criminal process, however individuated, that subordinated the distinctive aspects of human dignity that pertain to juvenile offenders to a fixed moral precept.

Justice Scalia's treatment of the third interpretative question would also find no place within a legal system based on respect for human dignity. He read extension of the death penalty to juvenile offenders as the clear effect of a statute that in terms authorized the transfer of some juvenile offenders to the adult justice system where some offenses attract the death penalty. By ruling otherwise, he opined, judges would encroach upon plenary legislative authority.

Moreover, they would impose a specificity requirement in a politically sensitive context. In the postwar conception, in contrast, the judge must interpret legislation to conform to constitutional norms. Consequently, a statute that merely authorized transfer of some juvenile felons to the adult criminal process would not be considered a clear authorization of their eligibility for execution. Thus, the state would have difficulty satisfying the legality stage of justification because the statute did not embody a sufficiently clear legal directive.

In addition, any legislative reluctance to impose the death penalty on juvenile offenders expressly would operate to their benefit. Legislatures must, in addition to conforming to constitutional strictures, take full political responsibility for carrying out their law-making function. Judges would therefore not hesitate to issue interpretative rulings that in effect imposed on legislative bodies the need to delineate their policy preferences clearly when fundamental interests, such as the right to life or the freedom against cruel and unusual punishments, were implicated. The focused deliberation that might follow, however politically difficult for the legislators, would exemplify the appropriate coordination of judicial and political functions, both subservient to the constitutional requirement to respect human dignity.

The postwar constitutional conception thus demands more from democracy and federalism than mere reflection of social consensus. It constrains the legislative function to constitutional norms by recognizing the judiciary, as the guardian of those norms, as a separate and independent constitutional actor. The framework for adjudication of rights claims includes both the determination that an infringement has occurred and the opportunity for the state to justify that infringement. Rights guarantees therefore do not function as absolute countermajoritarian negations of otherwise plenary state power. They intensify the democratic engagement by taking it beyond majority rule at the ballot box and in the legislative chamber. Those who hold a temporary mandate to exercise public power must respect all members of society as right-holders in every stage of law-making and law application.

Comparative elements enter the postwar model in many ways. They provide direction as to the substantive content of the specific guarantees. They shape the interaction of courts and legislatures as well as the responsibilities of those who act under statute. They also structure and exemplify the justification analysis. The material drawn from other systems varies with the purpose of the comparison. Material might include legal strictures set out in constitutional text and international rights-protecting instruments, or statutes drawn under the auspices of such instruments. Such references might provide a single example ripe for emulation. On a larger scale, a general account might demonstrate an established or emerging pattern. More extensive engagement would draw upon the foreign material in a less descriptive way, invoking judicial analysis of text, of institutional role, or of remedial authority. For example, a judge might analyze conflicting material drawn from different constitutional systems as a prelude to determining the appropriate ruling in her own jurisdiction. Or she might invoke foreign examples or analysis to fill in gaps in the text or development of the domestic system.

The comparative engagement is so pervasive and so important that its characterization as comparative reference or analysis is inadequate and awkward. In the early decades of this practice, we see a variety of separate and disparate legal systems cross-fertilizing each other; later generations will perceive the decentralized operation of cognate legal systems.

The reference to foreign material to which Justice Scalia objected in the juvenile death penalty cases would have been unobjectionable under the postwar model. In fact, it would have been notable only in its thinness given the overlap of two exceptionally important concerns—the legitimacy of the death penalty and the rights of children. One might have expected some effort to describe or analyze the reasons for the prevailing international pattern in normative terms. Instead, Justice Scalia swept away both the doctrinal test and the comparative reflection it invited. He could hardly do less. If the doctrinal invocation of societal maturation and civilized standards of decency were left in place, the striking pattern reflected in the legal position in other democracies would be unanswerable. While Justice Scalia is prone to pressing his position to its extremities, it is inconceivable that he would cite with approval the practices of Saudi Arabia, Pakistan, Yemen, Iran, or Nigeria as maturing standards of civilization or decency.

The vehemence of Justice Scalia's rejection of the relatively restrained comparative exercise in these cases is intriguing. It may reflect his insight into the relationship between constitutional conceptions and comparative engagement. His concern may be that any openness to the rich resources of a wide range of persuasive, sophisticated foreign legal material bodes ill for his conception of the U.S. Constitution. The danger goes beyond the possibility of increased validation for modes of constitutional thinking that he repudiates. More serious is the possibility that the claims he makes to legitimate his conception—as intrinsic to an American idea of popular sovereignty, democratic legitimacy, and judicial objectivity—may lose their credibility when released into a larger constitutional universe.

IV. THE NEW COMPARATIVISM AND TRANSFORMATION OF CONSTITUTIONAL CONCEPTIONS

Like other elements that make up a system of constitutional law and practice, comparative analysis must accord with one's conception of the constitution. That is, it must have a consistent, intelligible connection to the value structure, institutional roles, and interpretative methodology of this conception. Different constitutional conceptions generate different approaches to comparative analysis. In the postwar conception of the constitution, shared commitment to human dignity, as the highest aspiration of political community, shapes the comparative engagement. This value structure dictates certain institutional arrangements and, in particular, a special mode of judicial analysis. It does not merely offer a treasure trove of interesting examples or a quick fix for deeply rooted, substantive, or procedural failings.

The nationalist, positivist, and fixed moral conception of the U.S. Constitution exemplified by Justice Scalia's opinions in the juvenile death penalty cases precludes comparative engagement. This closed system offers no shared value structure, no similar institutional arrangements and no sense of organic development in response to common challenges in cognate rights-protecting systems. Comparative reference or analysis would have no intelligible purpose or function. Moreover, given the available comparators, foreign references would add no luster. It is not surprising, therefore, to discover that Justice Scalia has observed:

> we judges of the American democracies are servants of our peoples, sworn to apply, without fear or favor, the laws that those peoples deem appropriate. We are not some international priesthood empowered to impose upon our free and independent citizens supra-national values that contradict their own. If "international norms" had controlled our forefathers, democracy would never have been born here in the Americas.[57]

This passage illustrates the unbridgeable gulf that lies between Justice Scalia's conception of the U.S. Constitution and the postwar conception. His historical starting point is the American Revolution, revered as the historical act that ended subservience to "supranational values" and ushered in popular sovereignty. The historical account prompts the striking assertion that the continued enjoyment of freedom and independence in America today depends on vigilant judicial resistance against domination by cult-like foreign thinking. Like the "modern" school of German jurisprudence in the nineteenth century, Justice Scalia resists the rationality and generality of law. He prefers the view, described by Habermas, that law "as the expression of the spirit of the people, must assume a different form in each nation . . . [T]he acceptance of foreign law would *per se* destroy a legal culture rooted in the ethical life of a people."[58]

The transplantation of legal systems in the twentieth century, including the pervasive adoption of the postwar conception of rights protection, undermines the cogency of this view of law.[59] Justice Scalia acknowledges this phenomenon in a limited way. He concedes the importance of comparative borrowing for the creation of new constitutions, but insists that comparative engagement has no ongoing function: "comparative analysis [is] inappropriate to the task of interpreting a constitution, though it was of course quite relevant to the task of writing one."[60] Modern constitutions belie this distinction as well.

The new South African Constitution, for example, expressly stipulates strong continuity between the comparative work that informed the drafting process and later interpretation.[61] Its opening provision sets down the basic elements for a conception of the constitution. First, it stipulates the values that lie at the foundation of the Republic of South Africa as a sovereign democratic state. These include human dignity, the achievement of equality, and the advancement of human rights and freedoms, as well as nonracialism and nonsexism. This list provides not only the most abstract formulation of the value structure of rights protection—human dignity—but also sets out some of the particular aspects of human dignity that the regime of apartheid notoriously rejected.

Second, this provision sets out the institutional arrangements by which these values are to be fostered and sustained. Thus, the text formulates in some detail the basic features of modern democratic processes, such as universal adult suffrage, regular elections, and political parties. Democratic government marks a great achievement in the aftermath of a regime of apartheid that was systematically undemocratic. The architects of the new Constitution did not, however, regard democratic process as a sufficient institutional framework for the new constitutional order. Accordingly, S.1 stipulates that the Republic is founded on the supremacy of the constitution and the rule of law as well.

S.39 provides the third conceptual element—interpretative methodology. It directs that interpretation of the Bill of Rights:

a) must promote the values that underlie an open and democratic society based on human dignity, equality, and freedom;
b) must consider international law; and
c) may consider foreign law.

This section actualizes the foundational aspirations enumerated in the opening provision of the Constitution by constraining constitutional interpretation to the value structure stipulated. It also directs that interpretation of statute (as well as development of the common law and customary law) must promote the "spirit, purport, and objects" of the rights protection provided. Distinctive here is the detailed delineation of the judicial role, including express reference to comparative analysis, which is specifically constrained to the value structure and the institutional arrangements. Comparative analysis is thus specified as an activity internal to constitutional adjudication.

These textual elements identify the South African Constitution as a postwar, rights-protecting instrument, adapted to the specific needs and challenges of the domestic context. One would be surprised, therefore, to find the South African Constitutional Court citing with favor the type of reasoning contained in Justice Scalia's opinions on the juvenile death penalty in a case raising similar issues. Indeed, one would be surprised to find this type of reasoning employed by judges under the South African Constitution at all. Since the conception of the U.S. Constitution articulated in these opinions rejects the idea of substantive constitutional values and subordinates courts to subservience to popular legislatures, this type of reasoning would not transplant well. In fact, the South African Constitutional Court's decisions on punishment follow the patterns of analysis under other postwar instruments, as does the jurisprudence generally.[62]

The South African constitutional text is exceptional in its detailed specification of its conceptual structure and receptivity to comparative analysis. The constitutional conception it sets out so clearly is the product of extensive comparative study of the incremental creation of this conception in other rights-protecting regimes. This pattern is not exceptional. In the postwar model, the texts of new instruments often gather, amalgamate, and rationalize various strands from older rights-protecting systems. What is new is the express stipulation that comparative analysis, consistent with the normative commitments of the constitution, is to nurture and sustain the transformation of the South African legal system.

While the South African Constitution leaves little to the constitutional imagination in terms of constitutional conception and the comparative method appropriate thereto, other systems have had to work these issues out. Canada's experience demonstrates some of the difficulties that this process generates. Formal constitutional amendments to incorporate a bill of rights based on the postwar model has produced starkly contrasting constitutional conceptions in the Supreme Court of Canada, each supported by the appropriate understanding of institutional role, including comparative method.

After decades of fruitless debate on constitutional renewal, the *Canadian Charter of Rights and Freedoms, 1982* added a bill of rights to a federal, parliamentary system based on legislative supremacy.[63] Members of the Supreme Court remain divided on the constitutional conception appropriate to the renovated constitutional order. This division perseveres despite strong textual directives that reflect the basic elements of the postwar conception of rights protection, adopted at the culmination of a prolonged public debate informed by comparative analysis.[64]

A number of Canadian justices immediately accepted, even welcomed, the postwar constitutional conception embedded in the Charter's text and political genesis. They realized that it would be inappropriate to apply traditional modes of analysis or rely on pre-Charter precedents. Accordingly, they sought out comparative material that illuminated the new value structure, institutional roles, and methodology. They had no difficulty finding what they needed, although regrettably they often did not note their sources. It was readily available in the workings of the postwar, international human rights-protecting instruments, domestic instruments that operate under the umbrella of these international instruments, older constitutional systems based on the same constitutional conception, and—closer to home—in dissenting positions under the pre-Charter constitutional arrangements. This material had in fact provided the actual models for the Charter in its final form.

Other justices resisted this transformation, clinging to various features of the pre-Charter legal order. They purported to protect an abstract notion of the common good delivered by the unrestrained democratic function and the objectivity of judicial function. Many of their opinions, however, seemed motivated to preserve traditional social mores and entrenched political power. They ignored the textual indicia of the postwar model of rights protection, as well as its structural features. Thus, they did not read the rights purposively and substituted benchmarks of reasonableness for justification analysis. Their search for foreign supporting material led to theory and case law in which the constitutional order was either devoid of substantive values or vested no special status or priority in the values espoused within institutional models that subordinated the work of the judiciary to that of the legislature. Their favored sources for comparison were American constitutional theory, case law, and academic writing consistent with Justice Scalia's constitutional conception.

Ironically, Charter analysis has replicated, in the Supreme Court of Canada, opposing constitutional conceptions quite similar to those exemplified in the juvenile death penalty cases in the U.S. Supreme Court. This parallelism has emerged despite a long debate in which comparative models of rights protection competed, and the Canadian public, in effect, determined the winner. This general pattern, evident in many constitutional systems, suggests that the postwar conception stands opposed to a deeply rooted, general conception of the constitutional order, whether it is justified in the particular domestic context by appeals to federalism, a national *Volkgeist*, separation of powers, or traditional moral values understood to encapsulate the common good.

The competition between these two constitutional conceptions has significance beyond the doors of the courtroom. It has the potential to transform the political landscape both at home and in international relations. Recent developments in Canada demonstrate that departure from evolving norms of respect for human dignity can carry a high political cost.[65] This experience is not exceptional. In a brief recently filed with the Supreme Court, in the case of Ernest P. McCarver, nine retired U.S. diplomats describe the impact upon U.S. diplomacy of the practice of executing retarded persons: This execution "will strain diplomatic relations with close American allies, provide diplomatic ammunition to countries with demonstrably worse human rights records, increase U.S. diplomatic isolation, and impair other United States foreign policy interests."[66] This phenomenon reflects Kant's view of the cosmopolitan character of the right to respect for human dignity. Infringements of rights reverberate beyond national borders because they supersede the positive law of national governments. The supranational character of the postwar constitutional conception in effect constructs a "global public sphere."[67] It is this sphere that makes it possible for Amnesty International's brief to enter into the deliberations in *Thompson*.

There are high stakes, therefore, in the battle between constitutional conceptions and the comparative engagement that they invite. For countries such as South Africa and Canada, where formal constitutional change has taken place, there are strong, objective factors that should dictate the primacy of the postwar conceptual paradigm, including new constitutional text, recent political history, public support, and expressly chosen foreign models. For the United States, where no formal change has taken place or is foreseeable, the confrontation between the value structure of the postwar model and more traditional approaches is more open-ended. It may include increased attention to the propriety and scope of comparative analysis.

In a recent concurring opinion, Judge Calabresi demonstrated what may lie ahead. In dismissing an equal protection challenge to sentencing guidelines that imposed disproportionate punishment on drug offenses associated with racial minorities, he turned to comparative analysis to alleviate an injustice. Unlike Justice Stevens and Justice Brennan in the juvenile death penalty cases, he had no doctrinal test inviting comparative reflection on the substantive question in other rights-protecting systems. Thus, he was precluded from noting that modern rights-protecting instruments recognize breaches of equality upon proof of racially discriminatory impact alone, without proof of discriminatory intent at the time of enactment. Lacking any means to restructure the authoritative judicial reading of equal protection, he suggested a different type of adjustment. He invoked a practice of "constitutional Courts of some cognate countries," which informally puts legislatures on notice that changed circumstances and/or newly available information might in the future support a ruling of invalidity.[68]

On a superficial reading, his comments may be seen to recapitulate the standard preoccupation with the primacy and exceptionalism of American constitutional law. Thus, he identifies the roots of the notice technique used by European Constitutional Courts in Alexander Bickel's work on "mediating techniques." In addition, he observes that the postwar constitutional developments in Europe, although different in (unspecified) particulars, "unmistakably" draw their "origin and inspiration from American constitutional theory and practice."[69] Why not benefit from the useful problem-solving record of America's "constitutional offspring," just as wise parents learn from their children?[70] The inference is that exploitation of foreign material does not necessarily challenge a constitutional conception sheltering a distinctively national ethos.

This preoccupation melts away upon closer examination, however. Judge Calabresi's real concern lies in the limited protection afforded by equality rights circumscribed by an assessment of the benign intention of the legislature at the time of enactment. The notice requirement he admires expands that protection somewhat by enabling judges to prompt legislatures to take account of altered circumstances and additional information, even if it includes analysis of the impact of their policies.[71] Although Judge Calabresi presents his suggestion as if it were a minor technical adjustment, his analysis draws on notions of basic constitutional structure. He finds the notice mechanism attractive because it does not reward legislative inertia, but rather calls upon the legislature to engage in "sober reconsideration."[72] It reflects the high normative status of constitutional rights, which legislatures must respect and courts must protect without any prerequisite finding of intentional fault.

This authority would be illegitimate in a system where legislatures do no more than mirror public consensus (or moral tradition), indifferent to any insight that social science analysis might shed on the impact of their policies, and statute law therefore enjoys an almost insurmountable presumption of constitutionality.

Justice Scalia would regard this technique as an illegitimate judicial interference with the people's prerogative to set the agenda for change. Where Justice Scalia sees European modes of government through the eyes of eighteenth-century American revolutionaries, Judge Calabresi sees developed and sophisticated cognate constitutional orders that have much to offer to those who are willing to learn.[73]

American judges like Judge Calabresi will admire the workings of foreign courts working within the postwar constitutional conception if at all, because of their intelligible integration of constitutional value structure and attendant institutional roles. This conception strives to establish respect for human dignity by empowering courts and legislatures to bring their particular strengths to the practice of government. Since the Second World War, this conception has become the prevailing paradigm for a wide variety of legal systems, including those that have undergone extensive formal constitutional transformation and those that have retained traditional systems of legislative sovereignty. Extensive comparative engagement comes naturally to this conception of constitutional ordering, because national borders, history, and legislative prerogative do not define the parameters of human dignity. As Judge Calabresi notes, America no longer holds a "virtual monopoly on constitutional judicial review."[74]

When formal constitutional renewal ushers in the postwar paradigm, comparative reference and analysis help establish and guide the development of its value structure, institutional roles, and judicial methodology, as in the South African and Canadian examples. Comparative analysis has also guided the transformation of legal systems without formal change by fostering respect for human dignity in the interstices of the common law, public and private, as well as constitutional and statutory interpretation.[75] England and Israel stand as examples of such incremental transformation, leading recently in both countries to more formal change.

The U.S. Constitution may also stand on the brink of similar transformation. Justice Scalia's constitutional conception, as exemplified in the juvenile death penalty cases, seems increasingly less plausible. Its judicial objectivity is questionable and its deference appears remarkably detached from the complex and evolving society that the U.S. Constitution serves. In contrast, the constitutional conceptions of some of the Supreme Court justices during the past half-century, much admired and emulated elsewhere, have been open to the postwar conception of constitutional structure and practice. These justices did not believe that the freedom and equality of American citizens depended on characterization of the U.S. Constitution as exceptional, historically fixed, and conceptually isolated. Nor did they consider it appropriate for courts to read the Bill of Rights as a framework sustaining local social consensus against the information and expertise offered by modern social science. It remains to be seen whether, in an increasingly interconnected world of postnational states, the theoretical richness, deep rationality, and institutional legitimacy of this constitutional conception will gain strength in the United States, as it has elsewhere, in response to increased comparative reflection and analysis. While such a prospect may appear revolutionary—or even counter-revolutionary—the U.S. Constitution has undergone transformation as extensive in the past.[76] Indeed, the pattern is as old and well established as one might want: "[l]egal borrowings have been the 'most fertile' source of legal change in the Western world."[77] As Roscoe Pound observed in 1921, reflecting on the influence of Roman law and of continental European law on the development of early American common law specifically and the close link between comparative law and legal development generally:

> In legal history, periods of growth and expansion call for and rely upon philosophy and comparative law. Periods of stability, striving for perfection of the form of the law rather than for development of its substance, rely upon analysis and history. . . . We may be confident, therefore, that the revival of serious use of comparative law in our legal literature is a significant sign of the times. . . . The need for comparative study of law in this country did not come to an end with Kent and Story.[78]

NOTES

1. Immanuel Kant, *Toward Perpetual Peace, in* IMMANUEL KANT: PRACTICAL PHILOSOPHY 317, 330–331 (Mary Gregor and Allen Wood eds., 1996) (emphasis in the original text).

2. Anne-Marie Slaughter, *A Typology of Transjudicial Communication*, 29 U. RICH. L. REV. 99 (1994); Mark Tushnet, *The Possibilities of Comparative Constitutional Law*, 108 YALE L.J. 1225 (1999); George Fletcher, *Comparative Law as a Subversive Discipline*, 46 AM. J. COMP. L. 683 (1998); Christopher McCrudden, *A Common Law of Human Rights? Transnational Judicial Conversations on Constitutional Rights, in* HUMAN RIGHTS AND LEGAL HISTORY (Katherine O'Donovan and Gerry R. Rubin eds., 1999); Christopher McCrudden, *A Part of the Main? The Physician-Assisted Suicide Cases and Comparative Law Methodology in the United States Supreme Court, in* LAW AT THE END OF LIFE (Carl Schneider ed., 2000).

3. 487 U.S. 815 (1988).

4. 492 U.S. 361 (1989).

5. In *Printz v. United States*, 521 U.S. 898, 921 (1997), Justice Scalia objected to Justice Breyer's use of comparative analysis to determine whether other federal systems of government permit federal delegation to state officials: "our federalism is not Europe's. It is 'the unique contribution of the Framers to political science and political theory,' " citing *United States v. Lopez*, 514 U.S. 549, 575 (1995) (Kennedy, J., concurring) (citing Friendly, *Federalism: A Forward*, 86 YALE L.J. 1019 (1997)). A comprehensive account of Justice Scalia's conception of the U.S. constitution would present a more complex model than that reflected in his death penalty opinions. In that model, the purported aversion of the strong comparative engagement would remain constant.

6. Amnesty International (AI) reports nine executions between 1990 and 1994 of persons who were under age 18 at the time of the offence: six in the United States and one each in Saudi Arabia, Pakistan, and Yemen. AI, JUVENILES AND THE DEATH PENALTY: EXECUTIONS WORLDWIDE SINCE 1985, AI Index: ACT 50/05/95. The website of the National Coalition to Abolish the Death Penalty, citing executions back to 1990,

expands this list to include Iran and Nigeria (*at* http://www.ncapd.org/SKK-Background.html (last visited June 20, 2001)). Victor L. Streib describes the execution of juvenile felons as "a uniquely American practice," abandoned by other nations in accordance with the United Nations Convention on the Rights of the Child. He states that the United States has not ratified this Convention in order to preserve this practice (*at* http://www.law.onu.edu/faculty/streib/juvdeath.htm (last modified February 2001, last visited June 20, 2001)). *See also* WILLIAM A. SCHABAS, THE ABOLITION OF THE DEATH PENALTY IN INTERNATIONAL LAW (2d ed. 1993); Roger Hood, *The Death Penalty: The USA in World Perspective*, 6 J. TRANSNAT'L L. & POL. 517 (1997).

7. Antonin Scalia, *Commentary*, 40 ST. LOUIS U. L.J. 1119, 1122 (1996).

8. *Trop v. Dulles*, 356 U.S. 86, 101 (1958).

9. 487 U.S. 815 (1988).

10. *Ibid.*, at 823, n.4, citing *Weems v. United States*, 217 U.S. 349, 373–74 (1910).

11. *Ibid.*, at 823, citing *Ollman v. Evans*, 242 U.S. App. D.C. 301, 326–27 (1984).

12. *Ibid.*, n.4, citing *Weems*, 217 U.S. at 373–74.

13. *Ibid.*, at 830, citing *inter alia, Trop*, 356 U.S. at 102 and n.35, where Chief Justice Warren noted that banishment is "a fate universally decried by civilized people" and statelessness a condition "deplored in the international community of democracies"; and *Coker v. Georgia*, 433 U.S. 584, 596, n.10, (1977), where it was considered "not irrelevant" that a 1965 survey revealed only three of sixty major nations applied the death penalty for rape alone. More recently, in *Knight v. Florida*, 528 U.S. 990 (1999), Breyer J., dissenting, noted that the Supreme Court "has long considered as relevant and informative the way in which foreign courts have applied standards roughly comparable to our own. . . ."

14. For the view that the execution of juvenile felons breaches the U.S. international obligations, *see* C. Hull, *Enlightened by a Human Justice: An International Law Argument Against the Juvenile Death Penalty*, 47 KAN. L. REV. 1079 (1999), and E. Templeton, *Killing Kids: The Impact of Domingues v. Nevada on the Juvenile Death Penalty as a Violation of International Law*, 41 B.C.L. Rev. 1175 (2000).

15. Annex to G.A. Res. 2200, 21 U.N. GAOR Res. Supp. (No. 16) 53, U.N. Doc. A/6316 (1966), Article 6(5), *reprinted in* 6 INT'L LEGAL MATERIAL 368, 370 (1967).

16. O.A.S. Official Records, OEA/Ser. K/XVI/1.1, Doc. 65, Rev. 1, Corr. 2 (1970), Article 4(5), *reprinted in* 9 INT'L LEGAL MATERIAL 673, 676 (1970).

17. August 12, 1949, [1955] 6 U.S.T. 3616, 3560, T.I.A.S. No. 3365, Article 68.

18. *Thompson*, at 830.

19. The footnote references quote from the American Bar Association and American Law Institute's rejection of juvenile execution, but not from the language of the rights-protecting instruments referred to or to judgments rendered thereunder, *see Thompson*, n.32–n.34.

20. Patrick Glenn, *Persuasive Authority*, 32 MCGILL L.J. 261 (1987).

21. *Supra* note 4 at n.1.

22. *Id.*, at 377.

23. *Thompson*, at 815.

24. *See id.*, at 869. This concession to foreign material seems to raise the standard for constitutional protection by requiring not only an extraordinary degree of domestic consensus, but also a sustained consensus over time. Social attitudes need to have changed "so clearly and permanently as to be irrevocably enshrined in the Constitution." Thus, a seventeen-year trend, such as the one that had occurred by 1927, would presum-

ably not suffice to establish the requisite "new societal absolute." That was a period which included no juvenile execution, even though the adult execution rate was high. This period presumably was transformed into a temporary trend when ten juvenile executions followed in the next seventeen years. *Id.*, at 870.

25. *Id.*, at 869.

26. *Id.*, at 392.

27. *Id.*, at 872, "the plurality is inappropriately acting in a legislative rather than a judicial capacity"; *id.*, at 873, "the evolving standards appropriate for our consideration" are "those entertained by the society rather than those dictated by our personal consciences" because the Court is a "small and unrepresentative segment of our society." *See also Stanford*, at 380.

28. *Supra* note 7.

29. *Stanford*, at note 2.

30. *Stanford*, at 395–99.

31. *Id.*, at 397.

32. *Id.*, at 398, cited by Justice Brennan in dissent.

33. *Id.*, at 379 and 392.

34. *Id.*, at 374.

35. *Id.*, at 365.

36. *Id.*, at 399.

37. *Thompson*, at 830.

38. *Supra* note 7.

39. *Id.*, at 876.

40. *Id.*, at 876–77.

41. *Id.*, at 876.

42. *Id.*, at 875.

43. *Ex p. Pierson* [1998] A.C. 539 at 575C. *See also* Sir John Laws, *Judicial Review and the Meaning of Law, in* JUDICIAL REVIEW AND THE CONSTITUTION 173, 188 (Christopher Forsyth ed., 2000).

44. PAUL WEILER, IN THE LAST RESORT: A CRITICAL STUDY OF THE SUPREME COURT OF CANADA 212 (1974).

45. *Thompson*, at 875.

46. *Id.*, at 876.

47. Justice Antonin Scalia, *Modernity and the Constitution, in* CONSTITUTIONAL JUSTICE UNDER OLD CONSTITUTIONS (E. Smith ed., 1995) (emphasis in the original text).

48. J. HABERMAS, BETWEEN FACTS AND NORMS: CONTRIBUTIONS TO A DISCOURSE THEORY OF LAW AND DEMOCRACY 39 (1996).

49. *See supra* note 1. "The point of cosmopolitan law is . . . that it bypasses the collective subjects of international law and directly establishes the legal status of the individual subjects by granting them unmediated membership in the association of free and equal world citizens." J. Habermas, *Kant's Idea of Perpetual Peace: At Two Hundred Years' Historical Remove, in* THE INCLUSION OF THE OTHER: STUDIES IN POLITICAL THEORY 181 (1998).

50. 90 BverfGE 241, Judgment of April 13, 1994, *in* DONALD P. KOMMERS, THE CONSTITUTIONAL JURISPRUDENCE OF THE FEDERAL REPUBLIC OF GERMANY 386 (2d ed. 1997).

51. Stephen Sedley, *Human Rights: A Twenty-First Century Agenda*, PUBLIC LAW 386, 389 (1995). *See also* Sir Robin Cooke, *Fundamentals*, NEW ZEALAND L.J. 158

(1988); Sir Owen Dixon, *The Common Law as an Ultimate Constitutional Foundation*, 31 AUSTRALIAN L.J. 240 (1957).

52. *Hunter v. Southam*, 2 S.C.R. 145; 11 D.L.R. (4th) 641 (S.C.C.) (1984) citing *Minister of Home Affairs v. Fisher*, A.C. 319 (1980). The Constitutional Court of South Africa in *S v. Makwanyane*, (6) BCLR 665 (1995) and the Supreme Court of Israel in *United Mizrahi Bank Ltd. v. Migdal Cooperative Village* 49 P.D. 221(1995) cite the Supreme Court of Canada's purposive interpretation of the Charter with approval. These cases are exemplary models of the new comparativism in that they expressly model the analysis of rights claims in South Africa and Israel on the Canadian structure of purposive rights and then a shift in onus to the state to justify limitation on the basis of proportionality analysis.

53. Mireille Delmas-Marty, *The Richness of Underlying Legal Reasoning*, *in* THE EUROPEAN CONVENTION FOR THE PROTECTION OF HUMAN RIGHTS: INTERNATIONAL PROTECTION VERSUS NATIONAL RESTRICTIONS 319, 323–24 (Mireille Delmas-Marty ed., 1992). Accessibility (to the citizen), sufficient precision, and clarity (so that the citizen can foresee the consequences of given action) are the "three qualitative requirements" necessary for democratic legality.

54. *See, e.g.*, *The Syracusa Principles on the Limitation and Derogation Provisions in the International Covenant on Civil and Political Rights*, E/CN.4/1985/4 Annex, nos. 15-18; René Marcic, *Duties and Limitations Upon Rights*, INTERNATIONAL COMMISSION JURISTS 59, 61(1968); JOHN RAWLS, POLITICAL LIBERALISM 358–59 (1993); Alexandre C. Kiss, *Permissible Limitations on Rights, in* THE INTERNATIONAL BILL OF RIGHTS: THE COVENANT ON CIVIL AND POLITICAL RIGHTS 290, 310 (Louis Henkin ed., 1981); PAUL SIEGHART, THE INTERNATIONAL LAW OF HUMAN RIGHTS 88, 91 (1983).

55. The proportionality principle has become the central analytic feature in judicial review of rights-protecting instruments and emerging systems of common law rights protection. *See* EVELYN ELLIS, THE PRINCIPLE OF PROPORTIONALITY IN THE LAWS OF EUROPE (1999), NICHOLAS EMILIOU, THE PRINCIPLE OF PROPORTIONALITY IN EUROPEAN LAW: A COMPARATIVE STUDY (1996); Gráinne de Búrca, *Proportionality and Wednesbury Unreasonableness: The Influence of European Legal Concepts on U.K. Law* in 3 EUROPEAN PUBLIC LAW 561 (1997); J. SCHWARZE, EUROPEAN ADMINISTRATIVE LAW 5 (1992). For a comparative analysis from the American vantage point, *see* Vicki Jackson, *Ambivalent Resistance and Comparative Constitutionalism: Opening up the Conversation on "Proportionality," Rights and Federalism*, 1 U. PA. J. CONST L. 583 (1999).

56. *Stanford*, at 378; *Thompson*, at note 4.

57. *Supra* note 7 at 1122. Contrast Thomas Paine's view that the ideas driving the American and French Revolutions moved government away from "national prejudices" to promote "universal society." Like Kant, Paine associated these changes with peace. *See* Thomas Paine, *Rights of Man [1971-2], in* RIGHTS OF MAN, COMMON SENSE AND OTHER POLITICAL WRITINGS 83 and 266 (Mark Philp ed., 1995).

58. J. HABERMAS, THE POSTNATIONAL CONSTELLATION: POLITICAL ESSAYS 12 (2001).

59. J.M. KELLY, A SHORT HISTORY OF WESTERN LEGAL THEORY 320–25 (1992).

60. *Prinz v. United States*, 521 U.S. 898, n.11 (1997).

61. CONST. OF THE REPUBLIC OF SOUTH AFRICA (1996) (as adopted by the Constitutional Assembly on 8 May 1996, and as amended on 11 October 1996).

62. *S v. Makwanyane*, (6) BCLR 665 (CC) (1995); 1995 SACLR LEXIS 218 and *S. v. Williams*, (7) BCLR 861 (CC) (1995), 1995 SACLR LEXIS 249. Outside the punish-

ment context, *see S v. Solberg*,(10) BCLR 1348 (CC) (1997), 1997 SACLR LEXIS 30, n. 89 and 90; *Soobramoney v. Minister of Health*, 1997 (12) BCLR 1696 (CC) (1997), 1997 SACLR LEXIS 41; and *Prince v. President of Law Society* (8) BCLR 976 (CC) (1998), 1998 SACLR LEXIS 16 at 18.

63. For a more detailed discussion, *see* Lorraine Weinrib, *Canada's Charter of Rights: Paradigm Lost?*, REV. CONST. STUD. (forthcoming).

64. Lorraine E. Weinrib, *The Supreme Court of Canada in the Age of Rights*, 80 CAN. BAR REV. 699–749 (2001); *The Activist Constitution, in* JUDICIAL POWER AND CANADIAN DEMOCRACY (Paul Howe and Peter H. Russell eds., 2001).

65. Section 33 of the Canadian Charter permits both the national Parliament and provincial legislatures to override selected Charter rights by simple legislative majority, for a maximum, renewable period of five years, if they do so expressly (by invoking the override authority in statute) and specifically (by specifying the Charter right superseded). In domestic federal politics, the premier of Alberta has refrained from using the override against the interests of the disabled, gays, and lesbians in response to strong political opposition in the rest of the country. Similarly, the separatist premier of Quebec has refused to use the override to suppress minority language rights that the Supreme Court of Canada recognized as falling within the Charter's guarantee of freedom of expression. The premier noted that, while such a step would be popular in Quebec, it would attract strong criticism in the rest of Canada and undermine international support for Quebec's aspiration for independence from Canada. *See* Lorraine Weinrib, *Trudeau and the Canadian Charter of Rights and Freedoms: A Question of Constitutional Maturation, in* TRUDEAU'S SHADOW 282 (Andrew Cohen and J.L. Granatstein eds., 1998); *The Notwithstanding Clause: The Loophole Cementing the Charter*, 26 CITE LIBRE 47 (1998).

66. Raymond Bonner, quoted in *Veteran U.S. Envoys Seek End to Executions of Retarded*, N.Y. TIMES, June 10, 2001, A3.

67. *Supra* note 58, at 176. Thus, in *U.S. v. Burns and Rafay*, [2001] 1 S.C.R. 283, the Supreme Court of Canada ruled that the Canadian Charter requires that the Minister of Justice seek assurances against imposition of the death penalty when extraditing persons for trial in the United States, except under exceptional circumstances. The Court's ruling took into account a wide range of concerns, including the following: Canada's commitment to the abolition of the death penalty at the international level in concert with most other democratic countries, the acceptance of leniency for youth as a principle within the administration of justice in Canada, and the high priority given to avoidance of punishment of the innocent and the trauma produced by long periods on death row awaiting execution.

68. *U.S. v. Then*, 56 F.3d 464, 468–9 (1995).

69. *Id.*, at 469.

70. *Id.*

71. *Id.*, at 468.

72. *Id.*, at 469.

73. *Id.*, at 468

74. *Id.*, at 469.

75. Ernest J. Weinrib and Lorraine Weinrib, *Constitutional Values and Private Law in Canada, in* CONSTITUTIONAL RIGHTS IN PRIVATE LAW (Daphne Barak-Erez and Daniel Friedmann eds., 2002).

76. Morton J. Horwitz, *Foreward: The Constitution of Change, Legal Fundamentality without Fundamentalism*, 107 HARV. L. REV. 30 (1993); Howard Gillman, *Preferred*

Freedoms: The Progressive Expansion of State Power and the Rise of Modern Civil Liberties Jurisprudence, 47 POL. RES. Q. 623 (1994); *The Collapse of Constitutional Originalism and the Rise of the Notion of the "Living Constitution" in the Course of American State-Building*, 11 STUD. AM. POL. DEV. 191 (1997).

77. William Ewald, *Comparative Jurisprudence (II): The Logic of Legal Transplants*, 43 AM. J. COMP. L. 489, 498 (1995) (with reference to ALAN WATSON, LEGAL TRANSPLANTS: AN APPROACH TO COMPARATIVE LAW 95 (2d ed. 1993).

78. Roscoe Pound, *Forward to "The Valuation of Property in the Roman Law,"* 34 HARV. L.R. 227, 228–9 (1921).

2

Why Do We Study Constitutional Laws of Foreign Countries, and How?

Kazuyuki Takahashi

We commit ourselves to constitutionalism, which, we believe, is the strategy for freedom, designed to ensure that political power is exercised in conformity with the constitution, guaranteeing fundamental rights and the separation of powers. The Constitution of Japan enumerates various rights of the people, structures government based on the separation of powers, and stipulates in Article 99 that "The Emperor or the Regent as well as Ministers of State, members of the Diet, judges, and all other public officials have the obligation to respect and uphold this Constitution." However, official commitment alone is not enough for constitutionalism to govern the day-to-day behavior of government. Taking root in the minds of the people is indispensable.

The problem is that the idea of constitutionalism is a foreign concept to us Japanese; that is, it is not endogenous to our own soil. Before we learned the idea from Westerners, we did not know the idea of imposing law on rulers. Law had always come from rulers; obedience to the law had been a virtue of the people; rulers had ruled by law instead of being ruled by law.

Of course, rulers were not totally free. They were bound by a moral code that decreed, among other things, that rulers should govern the state as fathers govern their homes. Paternalism was a virtue in rulers. While fathers are supposed to act in the best interest of children, this is a moral restraint lacking organized sanction. We did not know the idea of organizing legal sanctions against rulers. And this mentality dies hard.

In our daily narratives, parents teach children to obey the parents' rules, and teachers teach children to obey the teachers' rules. That is the reality in which children live and grow. It cannot spontaneously occur to them that adults (or rulers) should obey the rules that children (or the ruled) set forth or consent to. That idea has to be taught consciously. This task is not easy because it has to be carried out against the background culture, which is not favorable to the idea. Daily life often contradicts the idea. Yet if the idea fails to come to grips with reality, it cannot take root. In order to succeed in the enterprise, we have to know better not only the spirit of constitutionalism itself, but also the Western culture that generated the spirit from its own soil as well as our own culture, in particular the part of our culture that tends to work against constitutionalism.

Accordingly, Japanese scholars have been studying constitutions of Western countries ever since constitutionalism was first introduced into the design of our governmental structure, in an effort to anchor the spirit of constitutionalism in the minds of our people, with necessary changes in our own culture. We cannot afford the luxury of asking whether comparative study is useful at all. Our sense is, rather, that we have no other choice than to undertake comparative study unless we come to the conclusion that we do not need constitutionalism. We believe constitutionalism is important and yet, because we failed to establish it in pre–World War II Japan firmly enough to contain anticonstitutional sentiment backed by the nationalism that stressed the uniqueness and superiority of Japanese culture, we are always haunted by the idea that what we understood as the spirit of constitutionalism is not in fact the real one. This may be one of the driving forces that are at work behind our study of comparative constitutional law.

My plan here is the following: in Part I, I will outline the history of constitutionalism in Japan, focusing on the way we tried to reconcile it with Japanese culture and under the influence of which countries' constitutional theory; in Part II, I will sketch the framework I use when I study the concrete pictures of the constitutionalism of foreign countries; finally, in Part III, I will take up the issue of constitutional transformation in relation to the guarantee of constitutionalism and present my analysis on a certain aspect of the issue.

I. INTRODUCTION AND DEVELOPMENT OF CONSTITUTIONALISM IN JAPAN

(1) Meiji Constitution and Comparative Study of German Constitutional Law

We have been, and still are, in the long process of learning constitutionalism. Our encounter with the idea of Western constitutionalism dates back to the time when American Commodore Perry visited a Japanese port (now Yokohama) in 1853 and forced the Tokugawa government to cease its long-held policy of isolation and open the country. Under the threat of colonization, Japan accepted unequal treaties with the United States, England, and France. The dispute over the new policy triggered civil war. Feudal clans led by Choshu and Satsuma challenged the legitimacy of the Tokugawa Shogunate, obtaining the Emperor's authority to support their claims. After a decade of inner struggles, Tokugawa finally abandoned power, and the regime of the Emperor was restored in 1868 under the reign of the Emperor Meiji.

The tasks falling on the Meiji government were extraordinarily difficult ones: to centralize political power by dissolving the feudal system and to introduce constitutionalism at the same time. In European history, these two tasks were achieved step by step. It took hundreds of years for the absolute monarch to centralize power. Modern constitutionalism was instituted by limiting the absolute power. The Meiji government needed strong, centralized power to preserve independence against the colonization threat, but at the same time was required to introduce constitutionalism in order to negotiate the revision of unequal treaties.

Centralization generated the armed rebellion of dissatisfied warriors who lost feudal privileges. After suppressing that rebellion, the Meiji government came to face the problem of designing a new regime. Japanese intellectuals have studied the political theories and institutions of European states since the opening of our country, and some works of Montesquieu, Locke, Rousseau, and the like were translated into Japanese. Opponents of the government, realizing that it was no longer possible to continue armed resistance, changed their strategy and demanded the establishment of a parliament, borrowing their arguments from European thought. The government expressed its intention to take gradual steps for constitutionalizing the regime. An Imperial Rescript dated September 7, 1876, and addressed to the chairman of the Senate, stated as follows: "I hereby express my wish to enact a constitution on the base of the original form deriving from the foundation of this polity, with due consideration being paid to varieties of foreign constitutions. You shall give me your advice with drafts of constitution, upon which I will choose."

However, there was a dispute within the government over the time schedule of constitutionalization. The radical faction wanted an earlier, if not immediate, establishment of a parliament, whereas the conservative faction wanted to delay it as much as possible. The dispute surfaced in 1881, triggered by a bribery scandal involving the selling off of a national enterprise, leading to the expulsion of the radicals from the government. But the conservatives, winners as they were of the power struggle, were so weakened in their power-base that they had to make concessions by promising that a parliament would be convened in ten years, that is, in 1890.

In preparation for constitution-making, Ito Hirofumi was sent to Europe on a mission to survey the different European constitutions. He found that the German constitutions, especially the Prussian Constitution, would be most suited to the original form of the Japanese polity. German constitutional theories at that time taught that the sovereign king granted the constitution by voluntarily consenting to limit his power; the king needs to obtain the consent of parliament when, and only when, he enacts a law that restrains the rights of the people or imposes new obligations on them; with this stipulation, law is free to limit people's rights—in other words, there is no judicial review.

Returning from Europe, Ito set to work on drafting the constitution with the aid of a few bureaucrats close to him. The final draft was reported to the Emperor in 1888, who submitted it to the Privy Council, which assembled influential persons to discuss important issues of the state, including the draft of the constitution. During the Privy Council's discussion, one of the extremely conservative members voiced objection to the idea underlying chapter 2 of the draft, which declared that the subjects of the Emperor shall be granted certain enumerated rights. He argued that the idea that the subjects could assert rights against the Emperor was not in harmony with Japanese tradition, even though the draft provided that the rights granted were subject to restriction by laws. Ito retorted sharply that if we wanted to introduce constitutionalism into our system at all, we could not totally deny the rights of the subjects. This episode is indicative of how Western constitutionalism and Japanese tradition were understood by the governing elite at that time.

The Constitution of the Empire of Japan, commonly called the Meiji Constitution, was sanctioned by the Emperor and promulgated in 1889. Its distinguishing characteristics are as follows: with respect to the rights the guarantee of which is the central theme of constitutionalism, the Meiji Constitution enumerated such rights as freedom to choose and change residence (Article 22), freedom from illegal arrest or punishment (Article 23), the right to trial by legal judges (Article 24), freedom from illegal search of one's home (Article 25), secrecy of letters (Article 26), right of property (Article 27), freedom of religious belief (Article 28), freedom of speech (Article 29), and right to petitions (Article 30). But all these rights were subject to restriction by law. This is what the German scholars called the regime of *Vorbehald des Gesetzes*. The underlying premise is that rights not existing before and outside the constitution are to be granted through the enactment of the Constitution by the Emperor, who holds the sovereign power that is the sole source of all legal constructs. In other words, people do not have the status of citizens, but of subjects according to the Rousseauian terminology. Therefore, rights do not precede the constitution and are subject to the conditions prescribed by the constitution. Besides, even if the constitution had not left the fate of rights to the discretion of legislators, it would have been of no use without judicial review.

As for the governmental structure, the Meiji Constitution appears to have paid due respect to the principle of separation of powers. The Imperial Diet was established, and all the laws had to be approved by it (Article 37). Judicial power was to be wielded by the courts in accordance with law (Article 57). Independence of the judiciary was said to be fairly secure. Exercise of the executive power by the Emperor required obtaining countersignature by his ministers (Article 55). This structure appeared to resemble that of England. But here again, the central principle is that the Emperor originally holds all the powers of the government, which he promised to exercise in accordance with the Constitution (Article 4). Thus, he exercises legislative power with the consent of the Imperial Diet (Article 5). He gives sanction to laws, and orders them to be promulgated and executed (Article 6). Ministers who are charged with giving advice to the Emperor are individually responsible and accountable only to the Emperor (Article 55). Judicial power is exercised by the courts in the name of the Emperor (Article 57). So, if one put emphasis on the central principle in interpreting the Constitution, one finds a construction close to absolutism; whereas, if one emphasizes the separation of powers principle, one can come up with a limited monarchy, and possibly even with a dualist parliamentary government. The permissible scope of interpretation is quite extensive, ranging from virtually absolute monarchy to representative democracy. How it functions depends on how the system is understood, and the latter depends on the pre-constitutional concept of the regime the interpreters embraced, that is, the constitutional theory or framework of constitutional thinking with which one performed the interpretative work. And that framework came from Europe, mainly from Germany.

Many constitutional scholars went to Germany to study constitutional law. German constitutional theory at that time was dominated by positivist legal thinking. German constitutionalists such as Paul Laband and Georg Jellinek were the leading figures, and their theories exerted great influence on Japanese scholars. There are several reasons for that. First, since the Meiji Constitution was largely inspired by German constitutions, it was natural to seek German theories to explain our constitution. Second, when the national goal of the time was to modernize the country by overcoming the ancient feudal regime and to strengthen state power in order to maintain independence, legal positivism, which sees law as enforced by state and gives priority to the positive law, was most suited to the task. Third, scholars who wanted to operate the constitutional scheme in as democratic a way as possible thought they could find the best method in the German positivist theory of state. Although the Meiji Constitution did not explicitly state the sovereignty principle, it was obviously not based on popular sovereignty. All that those scholars in favor of democratic construction could expect was to avoid clear presentation of the Emperor as sovereign, and the German theory of "state sovereignty" seemed to pave the way to that end. According to the German positivist theory of the state, the state is regarded as a legal person, the will of which is expressed by state organs; sovereignty belongs neither to the king nor to the people, but to the state as a legal person. In Germany, this theory was said to be elaborated to guard the king's prerogatives against the claim of popular sovereignty, whereas in Japan the same theory was expected to play the role of guarding the Diet's position against attack from the Emperor's sovereignty. Minobe Tatsukichi, a constitutional law professor at the University of Tokyo and a leader of the democratic school, fought the scholars of the autocratic school who advocated the Emperor's sovereignty, claiming that the Emperor is no more than an organ of the state, albeit the supreme organ, just as the Diet is an organ of the state.[1] Evidently Minobe's aim was to raise the relative status of the Diet vis-à-vis the Emperor by explaining their difference not as in kind or nature, but as in degree.

Minobe's interpretation was predominantly accepted among academics, and even among bureaucrats who wielded real power under the Meiji Constitution. But what was taught in primary and secondary school and in the military was different. Official dogma for the purpose of educating the people was the mythology that told of the original foundation of Japan by the Goddess and her descendants (the Emperors), derived from the ancient books called Kojiki and Nihonshoki and compiled by the Emperor's ancestors to justify their rule. According to the myth, Japan has been continuously ruled from its original foundation by an unbroken line of the Emperors, and that is our "Kokutai," the distinguishing form of the Japanese polity.

If you translate this story into European legal terms, you will get the expression "the sovereignty of the Emperor," but those people who emphasized the things typically Japanese did not like to clothe it with foreign legal formulation. In fact, when Minobe's theory was suppressed under pressure from militarists and ultranationalists in the 1930s, the reason advanced was not that he advocated an erroneous theory that denied the sovereignty of the Emperor, but that he called the Emperor an organ, which sounded to them disrespectful and defamatory of the Emperor and Kokutai, nearly amounting to lese majesty.

The word *Kokutai* is not found in the Meiji Constitution. It was created to express the nature of the existence of the Japanese polity, which was presumed to preexist the Constitution. The Constitution reflects the distinguishing feature of Kokutai to the extent that the legal terms can give expression to it, but there is more to Kokutai than what can be translated into legal terms. The word is heavily loaded with emotion, and it is extremely difficult to confine it to the legal sphere. So, in an effort to obtain the clearest possible legal theory, Minobe refused to bring the word and concept into his constitutional theory; he regarded Kokutai as belonging to fields other than law. But most of the constitutional scholars tried to domesticate the term in the field of law by tailoring it to fit into the framework borrowed from German theories. For example, Sasaki Soichi, professor at the University of Kyoto and a rival of Minobe within the same democratic school, translated Kokutai into the concept of "form of state" as distinguished from "form of government" (*Seitai*); the form of state refers to the question of who holds the state power (the king or the people), whereas the form of government refers to the question of how the power is exercised (in a constitutional manner or in a despotic manner); under the Meiji Constitution, Sasaki taught, Japan is to be categorized as a constitutional monarchy.[2]

(2) The Constitution of Japan and Comparative Study of the U.S. Constitution

The Constitution of Japan, which is our current constitution, was established as an amendment to the Meiji Constitution. In order to understand the implication of this statement, we have to go back to the final stage of World War II. The Potsdam Declaration was issued on July 26, 1945, demanding that Japan, as terms of surrender, remove all obstacles to the revival and strengthening of democratic tendencies and establish freedoms of speech, religion and thought and respect for other fundamental rights (section 10). The Declaration promised to terminate occupation upon Japan's fulfillment of its terms and establishment of a peace-loving and responsible government, in accordance with the freely expressed will of the Japanese people (section 12). What the rulers of Japan at that time were most concerned about was the preservation of Kokutai. So they returned with an answer to the effect that Japan accepted the terms of the Declaration with the understanding that it did not imply any demand which prejudiced the prerogatives of His Majesty as a Sovereign Ruler. In their reply, the Allied Powers evaded a direct answer and simply repeated the phrase in the Declaration that the ultimate form of the Japanese government would be decided by the "freely expressed will of the Japanese people." Not assured of the preservation of Kokutai, the cabinet members were divided over whether to accept the Declaration and left the decision to the Emperor. The Emperor, determined to end the war, issued the Imperial Rescript, which called upon the armed forces to surrender, assuring as it did that Kokutai had been preserved.

The government took the position that the fulfillment of the terms of the Potsdam Declaration required neither a change in Kokutai nor a constitutional amendment. Not only the government, but also many constitutionalists thought it possible to make the regime of the Meiji Constitution operate in a democratic way without touching the core structure of the regime. After all, they reasoned, there was a period called "Taishou Democracy," during which the dualist parliamentary government was practiced under the scheme of the Meiji Constitution, with the prime ministers being appointed from among party leaders who commanded majority support in the Lower House, and the Potsdam Declaration talked about the "revival" of democratic tendencies. But the staff of the General Headquarters (GHQ), headed by General MacArthur, had different ideas and "advised" the Japanese government to amend the Constitution.

The Shidehara government reluctantly started preparations by setting up the survey committee on constitutional amendment, headed by Minister of State Matsumoto Joji. GHQ patiently waited for the Japanese government to come up with an approvable draft until *Mainichi Shinbun*, one of the major daily newspapers in Japan, published on February 1, 1946, one of the drafts discussed by the Matsumoto committee, the contents of which did not depart much from the principles of the Meiji Constitution and deeply dissatisfied GHQ.

Judging that the Japanese government would not live up to his expectation, MacArthur decided, under time-pressures coming from a pending relocation of the Far Eastern Commission, to have the draft written by his staff. The so-called MacArthur draft was drawn up in less than ten days and was handed to the Japanese government on February 13, 1946. To the surprise of the Japanese government, the draft clearly stated the principle of popular sovereignty; it retained the Emperor, but only as the symbol of the state and the unity of the Japanese people, without the political powers his position had derived from the will of the people, which meant that the people would have the ultimate power to decide whether to continue the Emperor system because they could abolish the system at any time through constitutional amendment. The Japanese government was told that unless the draft was accepted, it would be very difficult to defend the Emperor against increasing outside pressures to subject him to war crimes investigation, and that if it did not accept the draft, MacArthur would go over their heads, directly to the people and ask them to decide.[3] The Japanese government yielded to the threat and accepted the MacArthur draft as the basis of the new constitution. Its outlines were announced to the public just before the general elections of the Lower House, which were held on April 10, 1946, under the new election law providing for universal suffrage of men and women.

The making of the new constitution proceeded through the amendment procedure of the Meiji Constitution, in accordance with a request from GHQ, which hoped to give the appearance that the process was being carried out voluntarily by the Japanese government. According to Article 73 of the Meiji Constitution, only the Emperor had the right to submit to the Imperial Diet a proposal for amendment, and a two-thirds majority of both Houses was required to pass it. The Emperor submitted the proposal prepared by the government to the Imperial Diet, convened on June 20, 1946.

Two issues drew particularly wide attention among members of the Diet as well as among legal scholars. One was whether the amendment implicated a change in Kokutai. The other was whether the amendment went beyond the limits on constitutional amendments.

As said above, preserving Kokutai was a top priority for the government. Questions and answers in the discussion of the Diet centered around this issue: if the sovereignty rests with the people, doesn't it entail a change in Kokutai? Pressed for an answer, Kanamori Tokujiiro, the minister of state in charge of the amendment, came up with a subtle interpretation: Kokutai in its true sense connotes the character of the form of our state that distinguishes it from others, the essence of which is that the people are spiritually united through adoration of the Emperor; the locus of sovereignty and governmental power is no more than an artificial and phenomenal matter which takes different shape from time to time; Kokutai is the feature which shares the fate of the state, supporting its identity and continuity; Kokutai in this sense never changes in the new constitution. Although Kanamori had to concede during debate that Kokutai in its legal sense, based on Articles 1 and 4 of the Meiji Constitution, would undergo change, he tried to downplay the significance of the change by stressing the emotional aspect of the term.

Contemporaneously with the debate in the Diet, there were several interventions on the part of legal scholars. The most famous was the controversy engaged in between Odaka Tomoo, professor of legal philosophy in the Faculty of Law at the University of Tokyo, and Miyazawa Toshiyosi, professor of constitutional law and Odaka's colleague. Odaka framed the issue in terms of the ultimate force that gives law its validity, and whether the ultimate force was "might" or "justice." He argued for the latter, which he called *nomos*. Under this view, the question of who wields power, of who holds "might," is not a real issue because whoever holds might has to exercise it according to justice, or nomos. If sovereignty means the ultimate authority of law, it rests with the nomos, and the essence of our Kokutai lies in the rule of the nomos. Odaka argued that this would never change even if sovereignty transferred from the hands of the Emperor to the hands of the people.[4]

Miyazawa attacked this apologia for Kokutai. For him, the real issue was who holds and wields governmental power, the Emperor or the people. If nomos has, as Odaka argued, the ultimate authority, then the question is who decides the contents of the nomos—the Emperor or the people—and the principle of sovereignty is there to determine this. Kokutai changes because sovereignty transfers. This is of the utmost importance when we begin to interpret the constitution. Odaka's way of framing the issue served an ideological goal of hiding the real change by downplaying its significance, according to Miyazawa's criticism.[5]

This controversy was caused mainly by different definitions of the term *Kokutai*. Miyazawa's definition was widely accepted by constitutionalists. Odaka's defeat was due, in my opinion, to his failure to point out the existence of the institutions in the Meiji Constitution that were designed to ensure the rule of justice he claimed and that really functioned to that effect. The concept that lacks institutionalization degenerates into ideology.

The second issue concerned the theoretical limit of constitutional amendment. The question was whether it was legally possible to amend the core principles of the constitution. The predominant theory under the Meiji Constitution taught, under the influence of German theories at that time, that amendment power deriving its legitimacy from constituent power is incapable of abolishing the provisions that express the principles closely tied with the constituent power, even if rules for amendment procedure are strictly observed, and there is no doubt that the principle of sovereignty is one such core principle. According to this theory, the Diet went beyond the limit of constitutional amendment, and consequently the new constitution was invalid, in violation of the Meiji Constitution, which still continued to rule.

To this argument Miyazawa responded with the theory of "August Revolution."[6] He maintained that it is legally true that a revision of the sovereignty principle cannot be effectuated through the amendment process, but the use of the amendment procedure was only for the sake of convenience. Its real nature was a revolution in a legal sense. The revolution had taken place when the Emperor decided in August to accept the Potsdam Declaration, which demanded the democratic principle contradicting the Emperor's sovereignty, and the Japanese people, newly becoming sovereign, exercised the constituent power by borrowing only the formality of amendment procedure.

Miyazawa's theory has become orthodoxy among constitutional scholars, but this does not mean that Kokutai finally lost all its influence. For one thing, the Liberal Democratic Party, which has long held power in post–World War II Japanese politics, has never committed itself wholeheartedly to the Constitution for reasons closely related to the values of Kokutai, as I will explain below. People overwhelmingly welcomed the new Constitution, which gave a feeling of freedom after a long life of austerity. But tradition dies hard, and Kokutai represented for traditionalists the quintessence of Japanese tradition. *Kokutai* as a word lost its credit and attraction in postwar Japan because of its abusive use in the prewar period, but it survived difficult times under the guise of "Japanese Culture." When Japanese people newly began to seek their identity in face of the globalizing international society after having recovered self-confidence through economic growth, things traditionally Japanese loomed as something in which they could take pride. Emperor, kimigayo, hinomaru, Yasukuni, and the like—which consituted symbols of Kokutai in prewar years and, for that reason, tended to be looked at with suspicious eyes—are now making comebacks.

The strategy of those who took seriously the lesson of the prewar oppressive regime of Kokutai was to inquire into the "infrastructure" that supports Kokutai and to propose reform plans that would lead to overcoming or destroying that structure. In comparison with the occidental mentality combined with a socioeconomic structure that generated constitutionalism, a Japanese mentality and socioeconomic structure were elucidated that did not seem to go well with modern constitutionalism. Those features that seemingly contradicted the idea of constitutionalism were labeled as vestiges of feudalism to be surmounted. From these studies, we began to know the real meaning of Western constitutionalism and the conditions for its emergence and maintenance. But accumulation of this knowledge does not necessarily work in one direction. To be sure, it guides us in an effort of establishing constitutionalism on solid ground in Japan, but at the same time, it inevitably accentuates awareness of differences in culture.

The distinction between vestiges of feudalism and enduring features of Japanese culture is often difficult. Isn't it true that what remains after modernization of industry, which is supposed to wipe out feudal vestiges, should be regarded as distinguishing features of Japanese culture? Take, for example, so-called groupism. The Japanese tend to attach greater importance to the harmony of group than to the autonomy of individual members. Post–World War II intellectuals taught us that this characteristic derives from the fact that Japanese society lingers at the stage of rural community where individuals are submerged in the collectivity. But even after economic development dissolved rural communities, "liberated" individuals found substitutes in new—albeit pseudo—communities, such as workplace associations, and continued the mentality and behavioral patterns of groupism. Since something that persists through structural changes of society must constitute an enduring characteristic of the society, cultural nationalists argue, we may not be able to do away with groupism without losing our cultural identity. If that is the case, do we have to choose between

Western constitutionalism and Japanese groupism? Is it possible for constitutionalism to take deep, solid roots in Japan without a change in groupism culture? It seems that the spirit of constitutionalism based on individualism conflicts desperately with the spirit of groupism, which gives priority to the harmony of group at the expense of individual autonomy.

Traditionalists who felt nostalgia for the ancient regime of Kokutai abhorred the individualist ideas and ideals they sensed the new constitution embodies. Hiding their real sentiments, they pointed out the legal defects seen in the procedure of constitution-making, as well as in the substance of the constitution, closing their eyes to the fact that the Japanese people enthusiastically welcomed the new constitution. They complained that the constitution was imposed on our government by GHQ with a threat against the very person of the Emperor, it was made under occupation by a foreign army, due respect was not paid to Japanese culture, and so on and so forth. It came as no surprise that, as soon as Japan recovered independence in 1952, traditionalists launched a movement to revise the constitution. Their goals can be summarized in the following three points:

First, the constitution should clearly stipulate that duties of people precede their rights. People live and flourish in groups. Without belonging to groups, people are incapable of fulfillment. Happiness of individual members depends on the thriving of groups. So the first thing you should do is to contribute to the development of your groups, to help your group flourish, to carry out your share of burdens for your group's flourishing; in sum, to fulfill your duties. Then you can enjoy your share of the fruits, that is, your rights. From this perspective, the current constitution is wrong in giving priority to rights at the expense of duties.

Second, the Emperor should be clearly recognized as the head of state. For traditionalists, things typically Japanese are condensed in the Emperor system. The Emperor is not only the symbol of the state and of the unity of the people as stated in the current constitution, but also the symbol of the Japanese culture as a whole, of what Japaneseness is all about. In short, the Emperor represents Japan in its real sense and deserves the legal name indicating the role he actually performs, that is, the head of state. The current constitution does not say who is the head of state. Our government set forth the interpretation that the Emperor is the head of state and asked foreign countries to so treat him in diplomatic protocol. But most constitutionalists dispute this interpretation, saying that our Emperor, having no power except literally a nominal one, lacks the minimum power ordinarily required for a head of state. Traditionalists want to resolve the doubt by strengthening the Emperor's power and recognizing the Emperor explicitly as the head of state.

Third, Article 9, which forbids Japan to maintain any war potential, should be revised so that Japan can maintain a self-defense force. Despite Article 9, Japan has built up so-called Self-Defense Forces of considerable capabilities. The government justifies this, reasoning that every state has the right to self-defense and that the constitution does not forbid a self-defense potential as a means by which to exercise the right, as opposed to a war potential that exceeds the minimum level necessary for self-defense. The problem of this stretched interpretation is that it is impossible to draw a line between a war potential and a self-defense potential. Most constitutional scholars find the Self-Defense Forces unconstitutional. Therefore, the constitutional revisionists want to clear the doubt and make the Self-Defense Forces legitimate.

As the constitution of Japan was originally drafted by Americans, many parts of it reflect ideas of American constitutionalism, especially chapters of the Bill of Rights and the system of judicial review. In contrast to the rights of subjects in the Meiji Constitution, the current constitution guarantees various rights and freedoms conceived as innate rights deriving from natural law concepts. Even the legislators are bound by them, and judicial review was introduced as a guardian.

The problem was that most lawyers and bureaucrats who were to operate the scheme had been trained in German law thinking and there were not sufficient numbers of people who were familiar with the U.S. Constitution. Disputes arose over the nature of new institutions developed in the United States. Quite a few scholars tried to understand them through the lens of German legal thinking, and the system of judicial review was not an exception. Article 81 provides that "the Supreme Court is the court of last resort with power to determine the constitutionality of any law, order, regulation or official act." If you read this Article with the U.S. system in mind, you think this is the provision granting courts the power of judicial review, just like the one practiced in the United States. But if you approach this Article with the system of constitutional court discussed in German law literature in mind, you may get a completely different picture and claim that the Article instituted the Supreme Court as a constitutional court. And this dispute was not a case only for law class discussion. It was brought before the Supreme Court, which ruled in favor of the American style, although it left room, according to one reading, for ordinary law to constitute our Supreme Court into a constitutional court.

Since the establishment of the current constitution, many constitutional scholars, especially the younger ones who entered their careers after the war, have engaged in the study of American constitutional law, and there are quite a few who visited and stayed in the United States for constitutional law research and study. We now know pretty well what the U.S. system is like. We frequently use that knowledge for interpretation of our constitution. Of course, constitutional theories elaborated in the United States do not control or govern our disputes, but the United States Supreme Court decisions and the arguments developed by respectable American scholars are abundantly cited in our articles.

The field most influenced by American law is that of constitutional litigation: issues of case or controversy, standing, standards of review, judicial restraint and activism, and the like have been popular topics for our comparative study. But we explore those topics having in mind the particular issues arising in Japan that do not arise in the same contexts nor reflect the same interests as in the United States. So it often occurs that we approach the topics from different angles. For example, the problem of the countermajoritarian nature of judicial review interested quite a few Japanese scholars, and many articles dealing with American theories designed to resolve or dissolve this difficulty have been published in Japan. But curiously enough, we have never faced the problem of judicial power actively striking down legislation. On the contrary, our Supreme Court is so restrained that we have so far only five Supreme Court decisions that struck down laws during the fifty years of its existence.[7] We are concerned not about a radical court, but also about a court so subdued as to deprive judicial review of all its significance. What we intend to learn from American constitutional law is not how to confine courts in the proper role consistent with democratic principles, but how to justify, even to mandate, a more active role of our courts in order to encourage and push them to perform strict review. But even though the purpose and interest of theories are different, the logic is useful so long as it justifies an active role of the Supreme Court at least in certain areas. Thus, American theories that seek to confine an active role of the Court into specific areas, for example the guarantee of the democratic process, are transformed into theories advocating an active role. This shows that even if we, the scholars of different countries, face different issues in different contexts, we can learn and profit from comparative study by finding common ground that might rest on a higher level of abstraction.

II. FRAMEWORK OF COMPARATIVE CONSTITUTIONAL STUDY

In this section I will discuss how we in Japan explore constitutional laws of foreign countries. I do not mean to claim that there is a special method for the comparative study of constitutional law. All I can tell you is how I pursue my comparative study.

There are two purposes for comparative study. One is to look for possible solutions to the constitutional problems with which we are confronted. Other countries might have confronted the same problems and have found good solutions, which would be a great help to us. To be sure, before we are motivated into studying foreign constitutional law, we need to have the perception that the foreign states we intend to examine are at the same developmental stage as ours and have faced the same kinds of problems or are facing them. Otherwise, if we think, for example, that the states to be examined are too far behind us to be faced with the same kinds of problems, or we are so different from other states that the problems confronting us are unique to us, we will find no interest in comparative study. But, as I said, we have always thought that occidental states are more advanced than ours in terms of the realization of constitutionalism. Admittedly, we sometimes feel that some issues confronting our constitutionalism are unique, but that does not go so far as to prevent us from finding some common ground or common level of abstraction on which to conduct comparison. Of course, comparative study does not always bear fruits in an effort to find a solution to our problems, but even when the very solutions which work well in other states do not seem to work in our state for various reasons, studying them gives us deeper insight into the difference in legal cultures. This brings us to the other purpose of comparative study, which relates to a more detached and objective manner of observation.

Sometimes we engage in comparative study not directly motivated by a specific problem-solving interest, but with general curiosity about foreign constitutional laws. Knowing constitutional issues and theories discussed in foreign countries is always stimulating and fascinating. It helps us widen our perspectives about other possibilities of constitutional thinking. It provides us with new ways or frames of looking at constitutional law. It enables us to become aware of constitutional issues we have missed and of potential issues sure to arise in the near future in our own country. It enables us to articulate our understanding not only of foreign countries' constitutional laws, but also of our own, through raising awareness of similarity and difference in respective laws. Being less affected by an inner drive to justify the claims we intend to advance in case of problem-resolving enterprises, this approach is in a better position to contribute to developing more balanced and objective knowledge, to the extent that the distance it maintains from the immediate interests permits it to avoid the risk of distorting facts in favor of those interests. By saying this I do not mean to advocate the possibility of engaging in research totally free from personal interest. Any research starts with personal interest, and the frame of thought with which to perform the enterprise necessarily affects the way of constructing facts. It's a question of degree.

In addition, we should not forget that a problem-solving approach and an objective-understanding approach are interdependent. Without prior general knowledge of constitutional law of the foreign country, it is very difficult to understand and evaluate the real meaning of the experiments from which to draw lessons for our problem-solving. The real meaning will be revealed when the concrete practices are located in, and assessed against, the whole structure of the constitutional law, the knowledge of which is provided by general study. On the other hand, exploring issues with a view to drawing concrete lessons deepens the knowledge of the general structure.

I, myself, have been more interested in the latter approach, the more detached and objective approach, and have developed a method and framework for the approach. I will present that method and framework below in a brief sketch.

(1) Grand Principles of Modern Constitutionalism

The concept of modern constitutionalism is best expressed in Article 16 of the 1789 French Declaration of the Rights of Men and of Citizens, which states, in effect, that any society in which the guarantee of rights is not assured, or in which the separation of powers is not determined, has no constitution. The constitution implied by modern constitutionalism must include the guarantee of rights and the separation of powers. But the principles that constitute modern constitutionalism are not limited to these two. There are other indispensable principles that these two principles themselves imply or take for granted, the most important of which are the principles of rule of law and popular sovereignty. Thus, we can break down the components of modern constitutionalism into four grand principles: guarantee of rights, separation of powers, rule of law, and popular sovereignty. How each principle is conceived, institutionalized, and operated, and how these four principles are combined differ from state to state and from time to time. The general study of comparative constitutional law aims to inquire into the development of the concepts and combinations of these principles for each state in historical and comparative perspective and to elucidate the distinguishing characteristics of each state's constitution. I note below the points of each principle.

(a) Guarantee of Rights

What is important here is to clarify the nature of guaranteed rights from various angles and on various levels: relation with state power, scope of guarantee, remedies, and so on. For example, as to the relation with state power we can distinguish three categories of rights: freedoms from the state (negative rights), freedoms to the state (rights to participate in state politics), and freedoms by the state (positive rights). In the nineteenth century (the era of modern constitutionalism as distinguished from contemporary constitutionalism), emphasis was put on the freedom from the state, and the most important rights were property rights, which were molded into freedom from the state. But with the progress of universal suffrage, people began to conceive of state power as their own, and the strategy of substantiating rights through state intervention set in. The twentieth century saw positive rights heightened to constitutional rights. In this regard, the United States stands out as an exception, leaving the realization of welfare rights to statutory law alone. The Japanese Constitution declares "the right to maintain the minimum standards of wholesome and cultural living" as a constitutional right. But our Supreme Court grants the political branch so wide a discretion in implementing this right that judicial review relying on this right is hardly conceivable.

(b) Separation of Powers

The principle of separation of powers as I understand it is designed to enable the institutionalization of rule of law. The rule of law requires the enactment of "just" law and observation of the law by state agents. For the purpose of preventing rule of law from degenerating to rule of men and of making state agents observe the law, it is better to separate law-executing agents from law-making agents. If both powers reside in the hands of the same agents, laws will risk being easily amended, resulting in instability, or being distorted through interpretation, resulting in unpredictability. But the separation of law-making and law-executing is not enough. If the dispute over the conformity to law is adjudicated by either agent, either of them will resolve the issue in his or her own favor and make the separation insignificant. In order to avoid this risk, adjudicating agents must be separated from law-making and law-executing agents. Thus, institutionalizing the observation of law by state agents requires the separation of three agents (functions): law-making, law-executing, and law-adjudicating. But this separation does not secure by itself the enactment of "just" law, and if enacted law is not just in its content, it is no use to observe it. How, then, do we obtain the enactment of just law? This depends on how we conceive "justness." For instance, Rousseau saw it in "volonté generale," that is, in that all the people participate in enacting law which applies to all the people. In contrast, Montesquieu saw it in the equilibrium resulting from checks and balances at work in the law-making function. There are many ways to devise checks and balances in law-making, combined with a certain degree of participation by people. Not only the presidential system, but also the parliamentary system can be analyzed as models of the separation of powers.

(c) Rule of Law

The rule of law as a principle governing governmental structure requires a mechanism for verifying the conformity of government acts with law by an independent agency. In modern constitutionalism the rule of law focused on the legal control of executive power by the court. England established a system of control by common law courts, which was described by Dicey. But France produced a different system, whereby an administrative court, called the *Conseil d'État*, controls the legality of administrative acts, giving birth to the French version of rule of law, called *principe de legalité*. The German version, called *Rechtsstaat*, was inspired by the French system, but, failing to establish strong parliaments, it degenerated in its actual operation into a regime of formalistic control without regards to the contents of law. What is worth mentioning is that in modern constitutionalism the ultimate guardian of liberties was a parliament, and there was no system of control of constitutionality of law by courts, except in the United States. After World War II, some of the continental European states introduced the system of control by constitutional courts. Germany, for example, adopted it and transformed its prior "formalistic *Rechtsstaat*" into "substantive *Rechtsstaat*." Even France, which had long maintained the principle of supremacy of law, set up the Constitutional Council in the Fifth Republic, which assumed an active role in ensuring liberties in the 1970s, transforming in its own way the prior *État legal* into the *État de Droit*. After the fall of the Berlin Wall, we saw the proliferation of the control system among the former socialist states, and now some constitutionalists talk about the "constitutionality control revolution." In this respect England stands out as an exception, persisting in parliamentary sovereignty and refusing the introduction of judicial review.[8]

(d) Popular Sovereignty

I find it very interesting that the coverage of this principle differs in the United States and France. For French constitutionalists, the principle of popular sovereignty governs two issues of different levels. One is about who holds the right to make the original constitution. Here American and French constitutionalists share common ground. Popular sovereignty justifies the power of the people to make the original constitution. Of course, as the making of the original constitution takes place prior to and outside of the positive constitution, the justification argument belongs to the level of natural law. The other issue relates to the nature of the relation between representatives and voters. The question is how to explain the denial of the people's right to instruct their representatives. For this purpose French constitutionalists make a distinction between national sovereignty and popular sovereignty. Article 3 of the French Declaration of the Rights of Men and of Citizens stipulates that sovereignty rests with the "nation," which came to be distinguished from the people. The nation is the people seen in its totality by making an abstraction of each member. Since the nation is an abstract entity, it needs an agent who acts on its behalf. The nation does not have its own will other than the one expressed by the agent. Therefore, the nation cannot instruct its agent, parliament, or anything else. Representatives who compose the parliament express the nation's will for the interest of the whole nation, not for the interests of their constituents. If the sovereignty rests with the people, individual members hold the sovereignty and have the right to participate in its exercise. Universal suffrage is mandatory, and when the people elect their representatives instead of making law by themselves, they have the right to instruct their representatives. As you can easily see, U.S. constitutionalists utilize similar arguments in the framework of republicanism. I do not mean to claim that the American framework of republicanism and liberalism and the French framework of national sovereignty and popular sovereignty deal with the same issues, although there is a certain overlap. But I feel that the facts that Americans do not know the distinction between national and popular sovereignty and that the terms republicanism and liberalism are used in very different meanings in the United States and France might reflect one of the distinguishing characteristics of the constitutionalism developed in both countries.

So far I have sketched the general framework that guides me in my comparative research. I had to confine my comments to some general suggestions, but what is important is to realize that the four principles are so closely interrelated that it is impossible to understand the in-depth meaning of each principle without knowing the others. When you observe any one principle, you inevitably see through it all the other principles working and taking their own forms, dovetailed with each other. Studying the concrete shapes of respective principles in comparative perspective, we can hope to grasp distinguishing features of each country's constitutionalism.

(2) Institutionalization of Ideas and Functioning of the Institutions

Major principles constituting constitutionalism break down into many minor principles or conceptions that produce various institutions for their realization. For example, popular sovereignty may be conceptualized as republicanism, which calls for a mechanism designed to put into practice such conceptions as representation and deliberation. There is, in general, more than one way to institutionalize an idea. The same idea or concept can be put into reality by virtue of various institutions differing in the degree of their adaptability to the idea. Some institutions are better adapted by their inherent logic to the realization of an idea. For example, democracy conceived as decision according to the popular will is better institutionalized by initiatives or referenda than by elections of representatives. So we need to explore how well particular institutions fit the purpose of materializing an idea by clarifying the institutional logic driving their operation. In addition, since one institution can serve several ideas, knowing the relationship an institution possibly holds with each idea is important, too. Furthermore, the same institution does not necessarily produce the same result in different countries. Institutions often malfunction or dysfunction in terms of the ideas they are designed to materialize. Therefore, it is necessary to pay attention to how they are functioning and analyze the factors conditioning the way they function.

Comparing requires common ground. The framework of analysis schematized above as an idea-institutionalization-functioning complex serves to locate the common ground. You can search for the commonality to start with anywhere in that complex. If you find it on the level of an idea, you can proceed with comparing its institutionalization and functioning in each country. If you find an institution which looks alike in both countries you observe, you can survey what idea that institution is designed to serve and how it is serving it in each respective country.

What is important in setting the common ground is to formulate the question for research in a well-balanced way, not biased by expected results or hoped-for conclusions. A helpful illustration is provided by a problem involving school textbook screening by the Ministry of Education in Japan. Japanese law requires that school teachers use as textbooks only those books that are approved as such by the minister of education. Authors and publishing companies submit drafts of textbooks to a panel of reviewers, appointed by the minister, that screens their contents in accordance with the teaching guidelines set forth by the ministry to implement the laws on education. The panel is legally authorized to issue advice or orders to revise the contents, and if drafters do not comply with the orders, the panel can refuse to recognize the drafts as qualified textbooks. In general, several textbooks are available for each subject, and teachers choose one for use in classrooms on an individual school level or on an upper level grouping of several schools.

Controversies often arise during the screening process, most often concerning the descriptions of history, particularly of World War II. A university professor of Japanese history who authored a history textbook that was not approved sued the ministry three times, demanding withdrawal of the orders and seeking damages on the grounds that the screening constitutes censorship forbidden by Article 21 (the free speech clause). Many constitutional scholars supported the historian and conducted comparative surveys with the purpose of backing up the historian's arguments. They came up with the research result that there is no other state but Japan that practices such screening of textbooks. For example, in the United States, they said, the writing of school textbooks is totally free. Yes, this is true. But this misses the point. The real issue is whether the contents of education are controlled by the government, and if the answer is yes (it is yes, there being no state that totally leaves free to teachers what to teach), the next question is how and to what extent they are controlled by the government. Textbook screening is only one way of achieving this end. Its absence does not mean there is no control, as the example of the United States shows. There, state authorities or local school boards delegated by the state compile the list of allowable textbooks out of those freely written textbooks, and teachers choose one book from the list. I am not here to argue the superiority of either approach. What I want to point out is that we should have focused on the idea or concept of textbook control and have compared various ways to put it into practice instead of focusing on the particular system of screening.

III. CONSTITUTIONALISM AND TRANSFORMATION OF CONSTITUTIONAL LAW

Constitutionalism requires conducting politics in compliance with the constitution, which guarantees fundamental rights and rests on the principles of rule of law, separation of powers, and popular sovereignty. The legitimacy of government actions derives from their conforming to the constitution. Then, where does the legitimacy of the constitution itself come from? If we do not admit that a constitution can provide its own justification, the legitimacy of the constitution must come from something outside the constitution. When a constitution is newly enacted (written), the constitution is legitimate if it is made by someone who has the right to do so. The principle of sovereignty is designed to decide who has that right. Under popular sovereignty, the right belongs to the people. But this is not a constitutional right. It precedes the constitution. In that sense it belongs to the dimension of natural law. Sovereign people, acting in a state of nature, by newly making the original constitution, create the new dimension governed by that positive constitution. The question is how we should understand the relation of the two dimensions.

E.J. Sieyes, the French revolutionary who wrote a pamphlet entitled "What is the Third Estate?" and exerted tremendous influence at the beginning of the French Revolution, distinguished the constituting power (*pouvoir constituant*), which is the power to make constitution, from the constituted powers (*pouvoirs constitués*), which are the powers created by the constitution, such as legislative, executive, and judicial powers. He argued in that pamphlet that the people (the nation) with whom the sovereignty resides in the state of nature have the inherent power to make the constitution. The power of the nation is supreme and is never bound by positive laws, including constitutional law. Whatever the nation wills has the force of law and its only limit is natural law. In contrast, the constituted powers have only the competence delegated by the constitution. They are limited by the constitution. Believing in natural law, Sieyes claimed that the nation persists even after the establishment of a constitution and can intervene anytime by newly starting the venture of constitution-making.

Because the aim of Sieyes was to justify the revolution and the making of a new constitution outside of the existing Fundamental Laws of the Kingdom, he had to present the constituting power as not bound by the existing constitution. This led him, I presume, to avoid talking about the constitution-amending procedure. The result is the absence in his argument of the power to amend the constitution. But the 1791 French Constitution provided in the First Article of Title VII for the procedure of constitutional revision. The article stipulates:

> The Constituting National Assembly declares that the nation has the imprescriptible right to change its constitution, and yet, considering that it is more conformable to national interest to exercise only through the means taken from the Constitution itself the right to reform those articles the inconveniences of which shall have been made clear through experience, decrees that it will proceed by an Assembly of Revision in the following manner.

In short, the constitution created the power to amend or revise the constitution, which I shall call hereafter the "amendment power." The question is the nature of this power: is it the constituting power wearing the positivist clothing only for the sake of convenience without losing its essence as preconstitutional power, or is it one of the constituted powers created and bound by the constitution as postconstitutional power? If it is the same in its essence as the constituting power, metamorphosed as it is in the amendment power, it admits no other limit than that it imposed on itself, that is, the procedural limits, and even this insofar as it does not amend the procedure through that same procedure. But why does the almighty sovereign have to comply with procedural limits? Because it promised that compliance by transforming itself into the positive amendment power. Otherwise, what's the use of conceiving of it as a metamorphosed constituting power? If it wants to stay free of any limit, it can establish amendment power as a constituted power and distance itself from any constituted powers. But then, the logic of unlimited constituting power shares the fate of natural law thinking.

As natural law loses persuasive power, the unlimited power of the people to make the constitution has to fade out. In other words, the metamorphosis thesis is a strategy for the constituting power to survive with minimum loss in the positivist world by abandoning the advantages that natural law promised but cannot deliver. We can save the values of natural law by reading them into the suitable positive provisions. Reading the constitution-making power of the natural law dimension into the amendment power, we rescue or preserve some of the values that can be reflected through interpretation in the amendment provision, at the minimal cost of accepting the procedural limits. The flip side is that the value of constitutionalism is constricted to the minimum.

If you want to protect the value of constitutionalism in wider scope, you had better commit yourself to the strategy of considering the amendment power as being in the category of constituted powers. In this case, you can argue that the amendment power is subject not only to procedural limits, but also to a certain kind of substantive limitation: since the amendment power derives its legitimacy ultimately from the constituting power, it cannot do anything that amounts to the negation of the principles underlying the constituting power, such as popular sovereignty and guarantee of rights; such acts as amending the sovereignty principle or abolishing guarantee of rights will be regarded as destruction of the source of its own legitimacy. Thus, popular sovereignty and fundamental rights can be shielded from constitutional amendment, and this is a good strategy when you want to entrench certain principles, even against the amendment power. Admittedly, the principles, even if so entrenched against the amendment power, cannot resist an attack coming from the constituting power, which remains free of any constraint of positive law. But now that natural law thinking has lost considerable support, this threat to constitutionalism seems very thin. Preconstitutional values serve only as premises from which all the positivist arguments start. They will not regain their original dynamics except in extraordinary circumstances. Of course, we can bring them into the positive world by reading them into constitutional texts, but this is possible only to the extent that they do not contradict the texts.

So far I have limited my analysis to the case where a constitution is enacted, that is, the case of a written constitution. But as was seen in England, a constitution can emerge as a result of long-standing practices. Here there is no single act of constitution-making. The manner of producing constitutional law is assimilated to that of customary or common law, as opposed to statute. Customs are formed everywhere, and there is no good way to prevent them from obtaining normative force. All the state can do is give priority to statutory law and refuse to apply customary law whenever it contradicts a statute. Viewed in relationship with statute, there are three kinds of customary laws: *intra legem*, *praeter legem*, and *contra legem* customary laws. The most debated question is whether *contra legem* customs can be considered valid, and to what extent. On a constitutional level, the question is whether a *contra constitutionem* custom can claim legal force, replacing the contradictory rule contained in a written constitution. Here we are not confronted with the question of whether we can pass an act, constitutional amendment, or whatever may be in violation of an existing written constitution. If we take constitutionalism seriously, the answer has to be *no*. But in the case of an unconstitutional custom, we are confronted with a different question. Here we stand not at a starting point where an unconstitutional act is taking place, but at the end point, so to speak, where an unconstitutional norm—generated by an act that took place a long time ago and was followed repeatedly after that, often without awareness or challenge of its unconstitutionality—is now overwhelmingly supported as having legal force by the people. We have to decide whether to deny its legal force and protect the written constitution or to deny the legal force of the relevant provision and accept the customary law as part of the valid constitutional law. The latter solution means to admit the possibility of a constitutional change outside the amendment procedure provided in the written constitution. To be sure, constitutionalism is not comfortable with that solution, but the damage might be minimal in view of the fact that this logic would be used only to confirm the new reality long after the act in question took place without being challenged and was built up to form that new reality. If the act in question is challenged at the time it is done, it should be judged as null and void even if it is done by the people themselves or by the government under the overwhelming support of the people.

The theory which deals with the permissibility of constitutional change outside of the amendment procedure is called the "theory of constitutional transformation," (*Verfassungsverwandlung*) in Germany. Under German influence, the theory is also discussed in Japan, mainly with the issue of Article 9 in mind. The Constitution of Japan in Article 9 forbids the maintenance of land, sea, and air forces, as well as other war potential, and yet we have long built up the so-called Self-Defense Forces of considerable scale. When the question of whether Article 9 can be interpreted to allow the maintenance of forces exclusively aimed at self-defense was discussed at the Constituent Diet, Yoshida Shigeru, prime minister at that time, explicitly ruled out the possibility. When the National Police Reserve was established in 1950, demanded by MacArthur at the outbreak of the Korean War, Prime Minister Yoshida justified it by saying that it was essentially a police force, not an army. When the National Police Reserve was reorganized into the National Safety Force in 1952, and further into the Self-Defense Force (SDF) in 1954, each time with the increased capabilities that made the former justification impossible, the Japanese government tried to offer various new justifications. The current position of our government is effectively this: the fact that Japan has the right to self-defense, which is recognized by international law and has never been abandoned by the Constitution of Japan, implies that Japan can maintain some kind of self-defense potential necessary to exercise the right and that the SDF is just that self-defense potential, as distinguished from the war potential forbidden by the constitution. Most of our constitutionalists are not persuaded by this far-too-stretched interpretation, finding problematic the impossibility of distinguishing self-defense potential from war potential except in words. According to the interpretation prevailing among constitutionalists, the SDF is in conflict with Article 9. There were a few suits that challenged the constitutionality of the SDF, but the Supreme Court has avoided deciding them on the merits, resorting to various legal technicalities. Under this situation, some scholars came up with the idea of applying the theory of constitutional transformation to Article 9. After more than forty years of existence, they argue, the SDF has come to be supported now by more than 70 percent of the population; in view of this fact, we should confirm that the meaning of Article 9 has changed, giving birth to a new norm that allows Japan to maintain the SDF.

As the constitutionality of the SDF has been, and still is, one of the most disputed issues in Japan, the theory of constitutional transformation that tried to justify the SDF has been seen with caution and skepticism. But apart from this unfortunate association, the theory itself deserves scholarly treatment. I found at least theoretical interest in it in terms of reconciling constitutionalism and constitutional change, and several years ago I undertook an in-depth study of it. My interest in the theory was awoken again when I came across the arguments Professor Bruce Ackerman advanced with respect to the New Deal reformation.[9] My point is that comparing Ackerman's theory with the theory of constitutional transformation as I understand it might be very fruitful. It makes more sense to me to understand Ackerman's theory within the framework of the theory of constitutional transformation than with the theory of constitutional amendment outside of Article V.

IN LIEU OF CONCLUSION

The Article 9 issues in Japan are serious ones upon which our constitutionalism might founder. If a large majority of Japanese now support the SDF, it is not because they believe the SDF is constitutional, but because they believe it is a necessity. But if necessity can justify the unconstitutional, what is the use of a constitution? It is no wonder that these issues have been among the most important and most contentious ones ever since the current Constitution was promulgated.

In view of the fact that the constitutional policy of the nonmaintenance of war potential is quite unique to post–World War II Japan, you might presume that it would not occasion much comparative study. Quite the contrary! There have been abundant comparative studies conducted in an effort to analyze and clarify the issues relevant to Article 9. Some constitutionalists who argued that constitutionalism would necessarily require pacifism, were led to studying the ways the constitutional laws of other countries regulated war. These scholars found that, in a historical perspective, a move toward nonretention of an army is a realistic choice worth pursuing. Others who wanted to refute or defend the legitimacy of the official interpretation of Article 9 or the avoidance of the issues by the Supreme Court surveyed the methods of constitutional interpretation adopted by other countries' courts and examined doctrines or theories of justiciability, such as standing and mootness, as well as political questions. Still others, trying to rescue constitutionalism from the head-on clash with the unconstitutional *fait accompli*, looked to the constitutional theories of other countries for a way of accommodating or recuperating constitutionalism. The theory of constitutional transformation is just one such example.

NOTES

I am grateful to our colleague Daniel Foote for his comments and advice.

1. For a discussion of Minobe's view of the Emperor as an organ of the state, see Kenzo Takayanagi, A CENTURY OF INNOVATION: THE DEVELOPMENT OF JAPANESE LAW, 1868–1961 (A. von Mehren ed., 1963), *reprinted in* THE JAPANESE LEGAL SYSTEM 621, 628 (Hideo Tanaka ed., 1976).

2. Like Soichi, Yatsuka Hozumi, chair of constitutional law at Tokyo Imperial University, made the distinction between "form of state" (*Kokutai*) and "form of government" (*Seitai*). Takayanagi, *supra* note 1, *reprinted in* THE JAPANESE LEGAL SYSTEM 621, 627–28. For further discussion of the definition of *kokutai*, see Richard H. Minear, JAPANESE TRADITION AND WESTERN LAW 64–71 (1970).

3. Tetsuya Kataoka, THE PRICE OF A CONSTITUTION: THE ORIGIN OF JAPAN'S POSTWAR POLITICS 38 (1991).

4. Yoichi Higuchi, *The Constitution and the Emperor System: Is Revisionism Alive?, in* JAPANESE CONSTITUTIONAL LAW 57, 62–63 (Percy R. Luney & Kazuyuki Takahashi eds., 1993).

5. *Id.*

6. Toshiyoshi Miyasawa, KEMPO (CONSTITUTIONAL LAW) (rev. ed., 1962), *reprinted in* THE JAPANESE LEGAL SYSTEM, 681–84 (Hideo Tanaka ed., 1976).

7. For additional discussion of judicial review in Japan and a description of the five cases in which the Supreme Court of Japan has denied the validity of legislation on constitutional grounds, see Yasuhiro Okudaira, *Forty Years of the Constitution and Its Various Influences: Japanese, American, and European, in* JAPANESE CONSTITUTIONAL LAW 1, 20–21, 35 n.51 (Percy R. Luney & Kazuyuki Takahashi eds., 1993).

8. Editor's note: For description of the recent Human Rights Act in Britain, see Geoffrey Marshall's essay in chapter 7.

9. See Bruce A. Ackerman, *Discovering the Constitution*, 93 YALE L.J. 1013 (1984).

BIBLIOGRAPHY

Ackerman, Bruce A. "Discovering the Constitution." *Yale Law Journal* 93 (1984): 1013.

Inoue, Kyoko. *MacArthur's Japanese Constitution: A Linguistic and Cultural Study of Its Making*. Chicago: University of Chicago Press, 1991.

Kataoka, Tetsuya. *The Price of a Constitution: The Origin of Japan's Postwar Politics*. New York: Taylor & Francis, Inc., 1991.

Koseki, Shoichi. *The Birth of Japan's Postwar Constitution*. Boulder, Colo.: Westview Press, 1998.

Luney, Percy R., Jr., and Kazuyuki Takahashi, eds. *Japanese Constitutional Law*. Tokyo: University of Tokyo Press, 1993.

McNelly, Theodore. *The Origins of Japan's Democratic Constitution*. Lanham, Md.: University Press of America, 2000.

Minear, Richard H. *Japanese Tradition and Western Law*. Cambridge, Mass.: Harvard University Press, 1970.

Overby, Charles M. and Kazuma Momoi. *A Call for Peace: The Implication of Japan's War-Renouncing Constitution*. Trans. Masao Kunihiro. Tokyo: Kadansha International, 1997.

Tanaka, Hideo, ed. *The Japanese Legal System: Introductory Cases & Materials*. Tokyo: University of Tokyo Press, 1976.

3

Comparative Constitutional Law: Its Increasing Relevance

Donald P. Kommers

I. INTRODUCTION

Let me begin by congratulating Vicki Jackson and Mark Tushnet on the publication of their marvelous course book in comparative constitutional law.[1] This is an important publishing event for three reasons. First, it represents a healthy shift from the overwhelming emphasis among comparative legal scholars on private law, with its focus on the traditional distinction between civil and common law, to a broader, internationalist, public law perspective. As Mathias Reiman noted in a recent symposium on comparative law, "we should look beyond the traditional topics of private law to those areas that present the most urgent and interesting problems today."[2] These most urgent and interesting problems focus heavily on *constitutional* issues arising out of the vast expansion of the modern regulatory state.

Second, the 1999 Jackson-Tushnet book affirms the value of comparative constitutional law as a subject of advanced research and analysis. It legitimizes the efforts of academicians who have been struggling to develop the field into a legal discipline of valid current applicability. The field's development has been made possible not only by the explosion of constitution-writing around the world in recent decades,[3] but also—and mainly—by the rich and voluminous jurisprudence of certain postwar constitutional courts, especially those of Germany, Austria, Italy, and Japan.[4] Enriching this jurisprudence even further is the work-product of more recently created tribunals, such as the Spanish, Hungarian, and South African constitutional courts,[5] not to mention Canadian judicial opinions under the relatively new Charter of Rights and Freedoms or the spiraling case law of the European Court of Human Rights.[6]

Third, and relatedly, the Jackson-Tushnet course book acknowledges the cosmopolitan character of modern constitutionalism and its relevance to the interpretation of domestic constitutions. Constitutional ideas have been floating unimpeded across national boundaries as fast as trends in pop music or art. There are numerous signs of this global phenomenon. One is the increasing frequency with which constitutional courts around the world are citing one another,[7] just as constitutional court judges around the world are talking with one another about their mutual problems and experiences in various fora;[8] another sign is the routine practice of some tribunals, such as the European Court of Human Rights, Canada's Supreme Court, and South Africa's Constitutional Court, to seek guidance in international and comparative law for the resolution of constitutional conflicts;[9] still another sign is the extent to which international human rights norms have influenced constitution-makers around the world in recent decades.[10]

II. DIFFERENCES AMONG CONSTITUTIONS

In this chapter I attempt to do two things: I underscore critical differences between the U.S. Constitution and recent constitution-writing around the globe and then offer a set of reflections on the uses Americans might make of foreign constitutional case law.

As for the first, Tushnet and Jackson ask whether "the category of domestic constitutions [is] an appropriate category for comparative study." As a purely academic exercise, the comparative study of national constitutions—independent of how these documents have been interpreted—has a number of benefits. First, such study has an obvious enriching value, certainly as enriching as the study of comparative literature or comparative religion, and for the simple reason that comparison exposes students to a range of models that illuminate the meaning or foundation of constitutional justice in our time.[11] Second, comparison enhances our power of discernment by enjoining us to differentiate the accidental, particularistic, or autobiographical elements of constitutions from their more general, inclusive, or universalistic components. Third, there is a comforting element in comparing constitutions, for comparison shows that we Americans are not altogether exceptional and that, with respect to human rights and democratic governance, we have much in common with other constitutional democracies. Finally, we compare to observe differences, and here I refer to many contrasting constitutional currents in the light of which Americans might wish to reassess our own fundamental law.

Writing in 1996, Giovanni Sartori reported that "[o]f the 170 or so written documents called constitutions in today's world, more than half have been written since 1974,"[12] not to mention the remodeling in recent decades of some post-1945 Western European constitutions.[13] These new constitutions include those of Greece (1975), Portugal (1976), Spain (1978), and Brazil (1988), along with Canada's Charter of Rights and Freedoms, adopted in 1982. Equally notable is the cascade of constitution-making that took place in post-Communist Eastern Europe.[14] A comparison of these documents with the American Constitution reveals a common core of basic rights and liberties, both substantive and procedural. Although many of these constitutions are still on trial, especially those adopted in Eastern Europe's transitional democracies, they nevertheless incorporate an emerging constitutional morality in tension with certain basic precepts of American constitutionalism. Whether this should give Americans pause or disturb their self-certainty is an issue worthy of discussion and debate.

Can Americans extract anything of value from these rich deposits of foreign constitutional precepts, values, and principles? Initially, one would think "yes." After all, the American founders were themselves students of comparative constitutionalism. They looked to the experience of Sparta, Athens, Rome, and Carthage for guidance in crafting a new constitution for the United States, but they had no body of knowledge about constitution-making comparable to what we have today. In fact, today's constitution-makers face the daunting challenge of picking and choosing from a bewildering variety of constitutional arrangements and principles.

One finds that many of the constitutions drafted since 1974, particularly those of Eastern Europe and Latin America, not to mention Spain, Greece, Portugal, and South Africa, have been heavily influenced by Germany's Basic Law. Institutional structures such as dual executives, specialized constitutional courts (including abstract judicial review), and systems of proportional representation largely imitate their corresponding German models. They also imitate the Basic Law in combining rights with duties and in their incorporation of state objectives.[15] It is no exaggeration to suggest that Germany's Basic Law is the preferred model of constitutional governance today, a reality that should prompt Americans to take stock of their constitution by assessing its capacity to meet the aspirations and needs of a society of a new millenium.

In recent decades, accordingly, the U.S. Constitution has served mainly as a negative model of constitutional governance around the world, not only with respect to governmental structures and relationships, but also, and more importantly for present purposes, with respect to certain guaranteed rights. The positive influence of the United States on the development of constitutionalism abroad during the nineteenth century, especially in Latin America and Europe, has been well documented.[16] American influence was also important in the reconstruction of democracy in Europe and Asia after World War II.[17] Since then, however, the world's constitution-makers have been disinclined to follow the lead of American constitutionalism. Rather, as noted, they are more inclined toward the model of constitutional governance and morality represented by Germany's Basic Law.[18]

Three interrelated themes, conspicuous for their absence in the U.S. Constitution, distinguish many of the world's new constitutions. First, they unite liberal constitutionalism with a strong commitment to social solidarity. Second, they speak in the language of individual duties as well as rights. Finally, they impose on government an obligation to foster and protect the dignity of persons.[19] As with Germany's Basic Law, these constitutions celebrate negative liberties against government but qualify them with an overlay of positive rights and institutional guarantees that the state is required to honor, defend, and promote.

The most significant feature of this new or emergent constitutionalism is its emphasis on human dignity, an emphasis that draws its primary inspiration, once again, from Germany's Basic Law as well as from the dignitarian jurisprudence that informs the meaning of the Basic Law's provisions. The notion of dignity inherent in the new constitutionalism of the postwar era has a core meaning that seems to differ from the core meaning of what we Americans understand by liberty, and these meanings are often found in the different images of society and personhood that they project.[20]

In this respect, I have often differentiated between German and American constitutionalism by describing the Basic Law as a constitution of dignity and the American document as a constitution of liberty[21] and, despite the skepticism of some Canadian scholars, I have described the Charter of Rights and Freedoms as a constitution which celebrates fraternity as its highest value. Liberty and dignity, of course, are interrelated, and their commonality is greater than their disjunction. In American constitutional law liberty is often justified by reference to dignity, just as in Germany dignity is often founded in the exercise of liberty. Yet liberty in the United States often qualifies—and occasionally trumps—claims rooted in dignity, just as dignity in Germany often qualifies—and occasionally trumps—claims rooted in liberty.[22]

III. LESSONS FOR THE UNITED STATES

With these differences in mind, and in the second part of this brief commentary, I'd like to focus more directly on constitutional case law and mention the approach that I have found useful in my advanced seminar in comparative constitutional law. The seminar's emphasis is on American constitutional law, viewed in comparative perspective.[23] The seminar singles out problematical areas of American fundamental rights jurisprudence and then examines—sympathetically—the equivalent decisional law of other countries as an aid to critical reflection on the work of our Supreme Court. In short, foreign decisional law is deployed as a heuristic stimulus for the purpose of rethinking aspects of American constitutional law.

The areas regularly covered in my seminar are right-to-life issues, freedom of speech, religious liberty, equality, and social and economic rights. Except perhaps for socioeconomic rights, these are topics on which our Supreme Court is deeply—even hopelessly—divided, and where neither constitutional history, structure, nor text provides convincing answers to the questions under review. It is precisely here—in the presence of case law marked by fundamental disagreement and lacking convincing support in text, structure, or history (in short, where judicial discretion is at its greatest)—that the comparative perspective seems most illuminating, particularly when the foreign courts under study are charged with interpreting provisions and defining concepts similar to, or functionally equivalent to, language found in the U.S. Constitution.[24]

This, of course, is not the only way to approach the subject. One of the questions addressed in the 1999 Jackson-Tushnet book is "what is comparative constitutional law?" One answer is that it constitutes a repository of substantive principles, of a transcultural and universalist kind, that offers judges and commentators "objective" standards for determining the content of contemporary constitutional jurisprudence.[25] This conception of the enterprise, however, is a hard sell. One of its difficulties is the probable unwillingness of a national tribunal to follow universalist principles or policies—to the extent that they can be identified and explained—if these principles or policies contradict language that a court must interpret.

As for geographical coverage, my seminar focuses on the highest constitutional tribunals of Canada and Germany, together with the European Court of Human Rights, but I also include selected decisions from the highest courts of judicial review in Hungary, South Africa, India, and Japan. The comparative enterprise seems most challenging when it combines common and civil law jurisdictions, along with Western and non-Western legal cultures, which is the reason I include cases from Japan and India. The point is to have a sufficient combination of similarity and difference to make comparison intelligible and useful. Japan is particularly interesting because it is not a religious society in any Western sense of the term "religious," yet Japanese constitutional law contains elements of natural morality, which, if incorporated into American law, would be questioned on religious grounds. One objective of comparing Japan with Western jurisdictions is to explore whether a transcultural, normative value system is beginning to emerge, and if it is, whether it is wise, prudent, or reasonable for the United States Supreme Court to insulate itself against this emerging moral consensus.

Foreign judicial decisions are most challenging when they are found to critically engage the principles and policies of American constitutional law. The South African Constitutional Court's exacting scrutiny of *Gregg v. Georgia*[26]—a virtual line by line refutation—is a thing of beauty to behold.[27] The opinions in the case not only scrutinize practical problems left largely unexamined by the Supreme Court, but also include a detailed and rich examination of the meaning of terms such as "dignity" and "life," providing other jurisdictions with a public philosophy most worthy of imitation and respect. As an imaginative exercise, the seminar tries to bring the various sets of justices into conversation with each other and, in this way, to underscore the strengths and weaknesses of their respective arguments or philosophical positions.

Our treatment of cases on freedom of speech and abortion is particularly fruitful. When American students find foreign constitutional courts rejecting the moral vision found in the American abortion cases or consciously refusing to follow American precedents in the fields of pornography and hate speech,[28] they must ask themselves why when faced with the realization that in each case judicial review is being consciously exercised to vindicate the constitutional values of liberty and dignity.[29] In exploring and explaining these interpretive differences, the seminar is forced to drive constitutional doctrine back to its foundation in social, political, and moral theory. Dealing with the cases at this level helps to provide students with the normative tools of analysis that they might not possess in the absence of the comparative perspective.

I hope it is clear that the comparative enterprise, as I'm trying to define it, is less concerned with who wins or loses a constitutional case than in the general way courts approach constitutional conflicts. Another major focus of my seminar is the comparison of judicial methodologies, which is important in any effort to see how the courts try to resolve the perennial tension between competing claims to individual liberty and those based on the moral claims of the community, on the one hand, and between the values of constitutionalism and democracy, on the other. In a nutshell, and at the risk of oversimplification, the two approaches are distinguished by their respective libertarian and dignitarian impulses. One approach—the American—is marked by a tendency to interpret particular words and phrases in absolute or categorical terms, often sacrificing one value in the interest of another (e.g., using the "establishment clause" to defeat a claim to the "free exercise" of religion). The other approach—dominant in Europe, Canada, and South Africa—emphasizes balance and equilibrium in constitutional interpretation, the harmonization of conflicting rights and values, and a perspective that envisions the constitution as a unified structure, requiring a holistic approach to interpretation.[30] These differing methodologies are important because they project alternative visions of the human person, society, community, equality, and democracy, visions that may help students to a greater self-understanding of American constitutionalism and its possibilities.

Briefly, and finally, comparison allows American students to judge their constitutional jurisprudence by norms other than what is familiar to them, and this can have a transforming effect. So students are amazed when they see one of the most powerful and respected constitutional courts in the democratic world rejecting every proposition about the meaning of life and personhood advanced in *Roe v. Wade*,[31] and they marvel at how several of these tribunals have struggled to honor the values of both personality and life instead of awarding total victory to just one of the players on the field. Some of them are puzzled as to why the United States Supreme court cannot at least *permit* what some of these courts require.

Students are dazzled when they learn that the courts of other liberal democracies advance conceptions of equal protection, human dignity, cruel and unusual punishment, freedom of religion, and even concepts such as rationality and right reason considerably at variance with the way in which these concepts are treated in the work of the United States Supreme Court. They are intrigued by an understanding of fundamental rights that requires the state to establish the conditions essential for the enjoyment of familial, marital, social, political, and religious life. They light up when comparing the absolutism and bold assertiveness of the Supreme Court's definitional approach to First Amendment freedoms to the "reasonableness," "proportionality," and "necessity" standards used in other constitutional democracies, and they wonder whether the judicious use of these standards leads to a better settlement between constitutional and democratic values than we see in the United States.

Last, students are impressed with the contrast between the relative consensus that marks foreign judicial approaches to interpretation and the presence of deep division on the United States Supreme Court, particularly with respect to the topics I've mentioned. If American jurisprudence is as unsatisfactory as many commentators have suggested—some of them going so far as to characterize the Court's work in some areas as unprincipled, incoherent, and simplistic—here is where the comparative perspective could be most illuminating, to scholars and judges alike—especially when no right answer is to be found in the text, structure, or history of the American Constitution.

NOTES

1. *Comparative Constitutional Law* (New York: Foundation Press, 1999).

2. "Stepping Out of the European Shadow: Why Comparative Law in the United States Must Develop Its Own Agenda," 46 *Am. J. Comp. L.* 645 (1998).

3. For a short summary of these developments, see Donald P. Kommers, Book Review Essay in 9 *East European Constitutional Review* 92–97 (2000).

4. See, for example, David P. Currie, *The Constitution of the Federal Republic of Germany* (Chicago: University of Chicago Press, 1994); Donald P. Kommers, *The Constitutional Jurisprudence of the Federal Republic of Germany*, 2d ed. (Durham, N.C.: Duke University Press, 1998); Robert Walter and Heinz Mayer, *Grundriss der Österreichischen Bundesverfassungsrechts* (Vienna: Manzsche Verlags-und Universitätsbuchhandlung, 1992); Livio Paladin, *Dritto Costituzionale* (Padova: Cedam, 1991); Mary L. Volcansek, *Constitutional Politics in Italy* (New York: St. Martin's Press, Inc., 2000); and Lawrence W. Beer and Hiroshi Itoh, *The Constitutional Case Law of Japan, 1970 through 1990* (Seattle: University of Washington Press, 1996). For a general survey of the development of constitutional jurisdiction around the world, see A.R. Brewer-Carias, *Judicial Review in Comparative Law* (Cambridge: Cambridge University Press, 1989). See also Mauro Cappelletti, *The Judicial Process in Comparative Perspective* (Oxford: Clarendon Press, 1989), esp. 115–181.

5. With respect to Hungary, see Laszlo Solyom and Georg Brunner, *Constitutional Judiciary in a New Democracy: The Hungarian Constitutional Court* (Ann Arbor: University of Michigan Press, 2000). Much of the South African Constitutional Court's work is discussed and cited in Johan de Waal et al., *The Bill of Rights Handbook*, 2d ed. (Kenwyn, South Africa: Juta & Co. Ltd., 1999). The decisions of the South African Constitutional Court are reported in *Butterworths Law Reports: Constitutional Law*.

6. See Peter W. Hogg, *Constitutional Law of Canada*, 4th ed. (Toronto: Carswell, 1997), esp. 779–1338; R.A. Lawson and H.G. Schermers, *Leading Cases of the European*

Court of Human Rights (Nijmegen: Ars Aequi Libri, 1997); and Mark Janis et al., *European Human Rights Law* (Oxford: Clarendon Press, 1995).

7. For an introduction to these practices, see Sujit Choudhry, "Globalization in Search of Justification: Toward a Theory of Comparative Constitutional Interpretation," 74 *Ind. L. J.* 819–892 (1999); Vicki C. Jackson, "Ambivalent Resistance and Comparative Constitutionalism: Opening up the Conversation on 'Proportionality,' Rights and Federalism," 1 *University of Pennsylvania Journal of Constitutional Law* 583–639 (1999). See also Ulrich Drobnig and Sjef van Erp, *The Use of Comparative Law by Courts* (The Hague: Kluwer Law International, 1999)(dealing in part with the employment of comparative legal and constitutional materials by national courts of judicial review).

8. At their 11th biennial conference, for example, European constitutional court justices dealt with contemporary issues of freedom of conscience and religion. See opening remarks of Marek Safjan, President of the Polish Constitutional Tribunal, "Introduction to the 11th Conference of the European Constitutional Courts," *Bulletin on Constitutional Case-Law* (Strasbourg: Council of Europe [Venice Commission], 1998), No. 3, 495–499. For two other examples of such fora, see "Justice at Work," 18 *Cardozo L. Rev.* 1609–1873 (1997) (featuring arguments and opinions in an international moot court case on religious freedom heard by a panel of constitutional justices from France (Justice Noelle Lenoir), Germany (Justice Dieter Grimm), Hungary (Chief Justice Laszlo Solyom), Israel (Justice Itzhak Zamir), Italy (Chief Justice Antonio Baldassare), United Kingdom (Lord Slynn of Hadley), and United States (Justice Ruth Bader Ginsburg), and Yale's Global Constitutionalism Project. The Yale Law School's project for the year 2000 focused on criminal procedure, campaign finance, and judicial independence. See Paul Gewirtz, Karen Johnson and Jacob Katz Cogan (eds.), *Global Constitutionalism: Criminal Procedure, Courts, and Politics* (Yale Law School, collected printed materials, August, 1999). See also Stephen Breyer, "Changing Relationships Among European Constitutional Courts," 21 *Cardozo L. Rev.* 1045–1061 (2000) (describing the results of meetings between a delegation of American federal judges and various transnational and national constitutional courts in Europe).

9. With respect to South Africa, see Choudhry, *supra* note 7, 841–846. See also Rudolf Bernhardt, "Comparative Law in the Interpretation and Application of the European Convention on Human Rights" in Salvino Busuttil (ed.), *Mainly Human Rights: Studies in Honour of J.J. Cremona* (Malta, 2000), 33–40, and Gerard V. La Forest, "The Use of American Precedents in Canadian Courts," 46 *Me. L. Rev.* 211–220 (1994).

10. For several studies of the relationship between international human rights standards and the new constitutions of Central and Eastern Europe, see Rein Müllerson et al. (eds.), *Constitutional Reform and International Law in Central and Eastern Europe* (The Hague: Kluwer Law International, 1998), 151–254. See also David Weissbrodt, "Globalization of Constitutional Law and Civil Rights," 43 *J. Legal. Educ.* 261–270 (1993), and Bruce Ackerman, "The Rise of World Constitutionalism," 83 *Va. L. Rev.* 771 (1997).

11. Several essays devoted to a discussion of these models are included in Irena Grudzinska Gross (ed.), *Constitutionalism and Politics* (Bratislava: International Symposium on Constitutionalism and Politics, 1993), 61–112.

12. *Comparative Constitutional Engineering*, 2d ed. (London: Macmillan Press, Ltd., 1997), 197.

13. For a discussion of these changes see Joachim Jens Hesse and Nevil Johnson,

"The Agenda of Constitutional Change in Europe: Adaptation, Transformation, and Internationalization," in Joachim Jens Hesse and Nevil Johnson (eds.), *Constitutional Policy and Change in Europe* (Oxford: Oxford University Press, 1995), 371–392.

14. See Müllerson, *supra* note 10; Rett K. Ludwikowski, *Constitution-Making in the Region of Former Soviet Dominance* (Durham, N.C.: Duke University Press, 1996); and Herman Schwartz, *The Struggle for Constitutional Justice in Post-Communist Europe* (Chicago: The University of Chicago Press, 2000).

15. For a detailed account of Germany's influence on constitution-writing abroad, see Juliane Kokott, "From Reception and Transplantation to Convergence of Constitutional Models with Particular Reference to the Basic Law," in Christian Starck (ed.), *Constitutionalism, Universalism and Democracy* (Baden-Baden: Nomos Verlagsgesellschaft, 1999), 71–134.

16. See Andrzej Rapaczinski, "Bibliographical Essay: The Influence of the U.S. Constitution Abroad," in Louis Henkin and Albert Rosenthal (eds.), *Constitutionalism and Rights: The Influence of United States Constitutional Rights Abroad* (New York: Columbia University Press, 1989), 405–462.

17. See Albert Blaustein, "The Influence of the United States Constitution Abroad," 12 *Okla. City U. L. Rev.* 435–467 (1987).

18. See Kokott, *supra* note 15. For a detailed description of German influences on the development of constitutional law in Middle and Eastern Europe, see Andreas Zimmermann, "Bürgerliche und politische Rechte in der Verfassungsrechtsprechung mittel- und osteuopäischer Staaten unter besonderer Berücksichtigung der Einflüsse der deutschen Verfassungsgerichtsbarkeit" in Jochen Abr. Frowein and Thilo Marauhn (eds.). Grundfragen der Verfassungsgerichtsbarkeit in Mittel-und Osteuropa (Berlin: Spinger, 1998), 89–124.

19. See Donald P. Kommers, "Can German Constitutionalism Serve as a Model for the United States?" 58 *Zeitschrift für ausländisches öffentliches Recht und Völkerrecht* 790–791 (1998).

20. For a comparative study of the different meanings of liberty and dignity found in German and American constitutional law, see Edward J. Eberle, "Human Dignity, Privacy, and Personality in German and American Constitutional Law," 1992 *Utah L. Rev.* 963–1056 (1992). See also Mary Ann Glendon, *Abortion and Divorce in Western Law* (Cambridge: Harvard University Press, 1987) (comparing different images of personhood and society that emerge from different constitutions).

21. *Id.; supra* note 18.

22. These differences are most prominent in constitutional cases dealing with freedom of speech and abortion. See Eberle, *supra* note 20, 1009–1024, 1034–1045.

23. For one attempt to present American constitutional cases in a comparative perspective, see Donald P. Kommers and John Finn, *American Constitutional Law: Essays, Cases, and Comparative Notes* (Boston: West-Wadsworth, 1998).

24. For an exceptional discussion of how comparative constitutional analysis might contribute to the interpretation of the U.S. Constitution, see Mark Tushnet, "The Possibilities of Comparative Constitutional Law," 108 *Yale L. J.* 1225–1309. See also Donald P. Kommers, "The Value of Comparative Constitutional Law," 9 *J. Marshall J. Prac. & Proc.* 685–695 (1976).

25. See Choudhry, *supra* note 7, 833–835.

26. 428 U.S. 153 (1976).

27. *State v. Makwanyane*, 6 BCLR 665 (1995).

28. Translations of the German Abortion Cases appear in Kommers, *supra* note 4, 336–355. See also *Regina v. Keegstra*, 3 C.R.R. (2d) 192 (1990)(upholding a statute punishing the promotion of hate speech against Jews) and *Regina v. Butler*, 89 D.L.R. (4th) 449 (1992)(sustaining an antipornography statute as a reasonable measure for protecting women and society against the harms associated with pornographic materials).

29. See Donald P. Kommers, "The Constitutional Law of Abortion in Germany: Should Americans Pay Attention?" 10 *J. Contemp. Health L. & Pol'y* 1–32 (1994).

30. For an example of a holistic approach to constitutional interpretation in the area of religious freedom, see Mary Ann Glendon and Raul F. Yanes, "Structural Free Exercise," 90 *Mich. L. Rev.* 477 (1991).

31. 410 U.S. 113 (1973).

4

Modern Constitutional Developments in the Arab World: The Case of Judicial Review in Egypt and Its Impact on Other Arab Countries

Adel Omar Sherif

Many constitutional developments have taken place in the Arab world in recent years. Constitutional reforms have enabled some Arab countries to achieve greater political liberalization and acquire effective protection of human rights. Contemporary studies, however, have shown that democratization and constitutionalism are still lacking under most systems within the region.

This should not undermine the fact that democratic practices, including judicial review, do exist in some Arab countries as a result of modern constitutional developments. Judicial review is one such development that has played a fundamental role in Egypt in restricting state powers and effecting greater protection for human rights through the implementation of constitutional rights. Following a protracted struggle between the executive branch of government (which monopolizes the greatest authority in the state) and a suppressed public will to protect individual rights and freedom, judicial review emerged in Egypt in the twentieth century to strike a balance between the government's interests and citizens' rights. It has developed gradually, assisted largely by steady movement towards political liberalization—however limited this may sometimes appear—as well as by a solid judicial tradition that seeks to protect individual rights and freedoms.

Egypt's modern legal culture has been largely influenced by the civil law tradition since the last century—when new codes and new court systems for both Egyptians and foreigners were introduced—with legal interpretation essentially founded on civil law bases and its devices. New approaches to constitutional interpretation, however, have arisen under the jurisprudence of the Supreme Constitutional Court since its very inception. The Court is particularly influenced by the jurisprudence of the United States judiciary on constitutional issues and increasingly employs American standards. We can therefore see that three powerful legal traditions—civil, Anglo-American, and Islamic—have all come together to shape the unique character of Egypt's legal system as it exists today.

The Egyptian model is closely observed by other judicial systems and governments within the region, undoubtedly due to the pioneering role of Egypt's legal system. Attempts by other Arab countries over the years to adopt the Egyptian system—either to achieve the same goals, or, alarmingly, to serve and authorize the rulers rather than inhibit them—have met with varying results. What may have been overlooked is the historical context within which this experience was able to flourish in Egypt in particular. Perhaps the greatest force can be attributed to the country's trend towards political liberalization, which set the stage for judicial review to emerge and develop.

Although the Egyptian experience is available for other Arab systems to derive from, its success in other environments cannot be guaranteed unless judicial independence and a more liberal political atmosphere prevail.

CONSTITUTIONS, CONSTITUTIONAL LAW, AND CONSTITUTIONALISM

Constitutional developments in the Arab world have increased dramatically in recent years. While they have often occurred as a response to public pressure, at other times they have been voluntarily introduced by the ruling authorities themselves. When discussing these developments within the context of Arab systems, terms such as "constitutions," "constitutional law," and "constitutionalism" are left generally undefined, although they are accurately viewed as interrelated concepts. Today, more than ever, these terms reverberate throughout the entire political and legal structures of these countries. Deference to the rule of law, respect for human rights, and adherence to constitutional commandments now appear as essential elements in the official policies of almost all systems of governments throughout the Arab region.

FAILURE OF ARAB GOVERNMENTS TO JOIN THE GLOBAL TREND TOWARD DEMOCRATIZATION

However, many scholars believe that constitutional order and democratic participation within most Arab countries is noticeably weak, and it is not anticipated to have a promising future.[1] This viewpoint is usually supported by the argument that Arab governments alone were absent from participating in the recent worldwide movement toward democratization. Within the last three decades, many countries from different geographic regions of the world—with varying levels of social and economic development and different religions—have managed to undergo successful democratic transitions. Contrary to this, however, Arab societies in general—including some countries that meet and satisfy the preconditions for democratic transition—have not participated in this movement.

This detectable lack of interest in democratization by Arab states is frequently attributed to cultural or historical factors. Some suggest that Islamic culture, which unifies religious and political authority, provides for an authoritarian political system within which state power can hardly be restrained. The historical explanation adds that modern Arab states were formed during the colonial period in a way that did not permit them to acquire public support; rather, the colonial power was keen on having these states dependent on them and on limiting their ties to their own citizens. This autonomy of the state from society continued even after the Arab states had gained their independence, and continues to impede efforts towards democratization to this day.[2]

REFUTING THE CLAIMS OF AN ALLEGED FAILURE OF ARAB DEMOCRACY

On the other hand, there are many opponents to the previous view who disagree with both its reasoning and its final outcome.[3] They argue that modern history has proven that most of the Arab states have undertaken profound constitutional reforms and political liberalization in recent years. A trend toward political liberalization, though limited, does, in fact, exist. The alleged gap between the state and its citizens is gradually diminished as a logical outcome of modern constitutional reforms. The Islamic system of government, they add, does not prevent the citizens from actively participating in their state's affairs, nor does it preclude constitutional reforms or democratic transition. Rather, it allows for a highly sophisticated mechanism that, as for any democratic government, respects the individual's rights and freedoms. Islamic values and traditions seek justice, equality, and mutual respect and therefore are not different from those of other divine revelations, as they are all derived from the same value base. This can easily be observed by examining the history and evolution of law in its various cultural contexts. Here one clearly finds parallel tracks, and can trace the migration of legal traditions and ideas from one civilization to another. At the same time, there are some parallel ideas which may not necessarily have migrated, but because they emerge from the same value base, have necessarily found their expression in the same ways.

Therefore, neither the cultural nor the historical justifications for the absence or weakness of Arab democratization are totally correct, and hence we should not be pessimistic when evaluating the recent efforts of Arab governments in moving toward constitutionalism and democratization. We are aware that the Arab democratic experience is imperfect—and perhaps not progressive by nature—but we should not undermine these real efforts, nor be suspicious of them.

RECENT EFFORTS TOWARD CONSTITUTIONALISM AND DEMOCRATIZATION IN THE ARAB WORLD

Today, the efforts exerted by different Arab systems of governments to cope with the prevailing international trends toward democratic government and constitutionalism are similar to those performed by many other of their counterparts from the Third World countries. They are all keen on establishing and maintaining a constitutional order that justifies their legitimacy (especially before the international community), and that also allows for greater democratic participation of their citizens in public life (as a response to the increasing outside pressure for democratization).

CONSTITUTIONAL REFORMS

With these goals in mind, many constitutional reforms have taken place in recent years in different parts of the Arab world. Such constitutional reforms are plainly visible from the active steps being taken in many of the Arab countries toward adopting a written, rigid basic law or constitution that is superior to state legislation and regulations, and thus restricts state powers in their actions and behaviors by prefixed constitutional ordains.[4]

Unfortunately, the constitutions and basic laws being put forward in some Arab countries, and their mechanism for democratic government and protection of human rights, can occasionally be seen as a hypocritical phenomenon. Such is the case when the concerned government does not adhere to the state constitution, or when constitutional texts are either silent or vague to the extent that they authorize the ruler, more than restrain his powers. However, this fact should not lead us to a final conclusion that the Arab world, in general, lacks constitutionalism and respect for basic laws. There are still systems of governments within the Arab world that have been restricted in their authority by constitutional commands.

CONSTITUTIONAL GUARANTEES IN ARAB CONSTITUTIONS

It is not only theoretical, but also sometimes practical, to notice that valid constitutions in the Arab countries do, for the time being, pay great attention to individual rights and freedoms. Almost all basic political, civil, economic, social, and other fundamental rights and freedoms have been included, and therefore become constitutionally guaranteed, by virtue of these constitutions. In addition, many of the agreed-upon constitutional principles—such as separation of powers, multiplicity of political parties, freely elected parliament, representative and responsible government, as well as judicial independence—are also recognized. Furthermore, there are various mechanisms to guarantee the checks and balances among the state's powers to ensure that none of them will ever exceed their constitutional mandate or infringe upon individual rights and freedoms. One of these guarantees is judicial review, which is the focus of this chapter.

With limited platforms for public opinion, and parliaments dominated by the executive, the only hope for democracy and liberalization, if there is any, would be an independent judiciary—a body that is not dominated by the government and therefore can implement the constitutional commands and maintain the constitutional order through judicial review.

JUDICIAL REVIEW IN THE ARAB WORLD

For those critical of Arabic democracy, it might be surprising to learn that judicial review is now widespread in most parts of the Arab world. It has even, on occasion, been known to exist in the absence of a constitutional text allowing for its exercise, as was the case in Egypt before 1971.[5]

But this should not come as a surprise, for two reasons. First, the spread of judicial review within the Arab world coincided and ran parallel to its global acceptance in other parts of the world following World War II. Second, in most cases judicial review has spread without becoming politically important. The presence and importance of judicial review today varies from one Arab country to another.

WHY DO ARAB SYSTEMS OF GOVERNMENT ACCEPT JUDICIAL REVIEW?

There have always been many theoretical and practical justifications as to why Arab systems of government, especially those known for being undemocratic, would adopt, or indulge the emergence of, the constitutional mechanism known as judicial review. How could the judiciary, the weakest branch of government, be trusted and be able to limit the ruler's powers, and therefore reshape the state's policies?[6] Perhaps rulers have instituted this mechanism, or tolerated its emergence, in order to serve and sustain their powers rather than democratize the system of government. The preferred explanation is that logical democratic evolution in the region has required, and therefore brought into being, judicial review as both a method and a technique to protect human rights.

THE EMERGENCE AND ADOPTION OF JUDICIAL REVIEW IN ARAB CONSTITUTIONAL SYSTEMS

Whatever explanation we accept, the fact is that judicial review in the Arab world has become the norm rather than the exception. What is noteworthy here is that some of the cases in which judicial review was instituted in the constitution are not that rare or recent—some go back as early as the 1920s.[7] Different forms of judicial review can be found in the Syrian Constitution of 1920, the Iraqi Constitution of 1925, the Jordanian Constitution in 1952, the Kuwaiti Constitution of 1962, and the United Arab Emirates Constitution in 1971. Specialized constitutional courts were created in Yemen in 1970, in Sudan in 1973, and in Syria also in 1973. A constitutional judicial council, similar to the French model of the Constitutional Council, was created by the Moroccan Constitution in 1962. Algeria, Tunisia, and Lebanon all adopted the Constitutional Council model as well, with somewhat different applications.[8]

JUDICIAL REVIEW IN EGYPT

The case of Egypt is unique and has been a remarkable influence on other Arab systems and their attitudes toward judicial review. This is not only because the Egyptian legal system is the most influential in the region, but also because its many constitutional reforms and increasing political liberalization have encouraged a bolder approach to judicial review, therefore achieving more protection for human rights.

SOLID JUDICIAL TRADITIONS FACILITATED THE EMERGENCE OF JUDICIAL REVIEW

Although once considered the weakest of the state's powers, the judiciary in Egypt has an admirable history as to the enforcement of constitutional commands and protection of human rights. The Egyptian judicial tradition insists that the judiciary should not be a political actor. Courts are there to settle disputes, not to be involved in them. Therefore, this tradition necessitates isolating the judiciary from any political debate and minimizing its direct role in political life. Adhering to this solid tradition has, in fact, helped the judiciary to build and develop its professional, independent character. It has also promoted a sense of security within executive circles that the judiciary is neither aiming at nor interested in playing a direct political role. Political and executive powers in the Arab world, including Egypt, have always been sensitive to the scope and limits of their political authority, preferring to exercise this authority exclusively without interference from any other bodies, including the parliament and the judiciary. It is uncommon for them to tolerate or accept any limitations on their power. The judicial tradition hindered the judiciary from directly breaking into the areas designated by the executive as, either directly or indirectly, falling under its direct control.

Consequently, adhering to this tradition meant that judicial activities concentrated, to a large extent, on the protection of individual rights and freedoms, either among the individuals themselves or vis-à-vis the state. Within this formula, judicial review emerged due to a bold judiciary with a primary objective of protecting individual rights and freedoms. This formula also allowed the judiciary to become generally immune to political intrusion and attacks from the political wing. But, with the passage of time, the exercise of judicial review did not prevent the necessary, indirect political consequences of many judicial decisions, which at times were not to the advantage of the executive. The reaction of the executive was in some cases aggressive. Although less common now, history provides many examples of attacks upon the judiciary following certain judicial decisions that were not appreciated by the executive. Even today, indirect political consequences of many judicial rulings have continued to arouse concern, and the attacks on the judiciary have not ceased.[9]

THE EMERGENCE OF JUDICIAL REVIEW BY A JUDICIAL ACTION

As already mentioned, judicial review first emerged in Egypt early this century, and as a result of judicial action rather than constitutional provision. Certainly, there was some hesitation at first, even within the judiciary itself, to assert the principle of judicial review. This was, on the one hand, because of its potential threat to the separation of powers—and on the other, because of its envisioned contradiction with the democratic principle that gives supremacy to the will of the people over that of the judiciary. Such hesitation, however, did not continue for long. As early as 1948, decisive rulings, initially from the State Council, then from the ordinary courts, began to affirm the right of judicial review.[10] It was argued in these ruling that the first duty of a court of law, when it finds two contradictory laws applicable to a dispute, is to determine which of them should be applied. The court should give supremacy to the highest law over all other laws, and thus disallow the application of any law that contradicts the constitution. Within a very short time it was definitely settled that courts have the power of judicial review.

THE MAIN OBJECTIVE OF JUDICIAL REVIEW

It was never the intention, however, that judicial review should intrude upon executive or legislative affairs, nor was it intended to prove judicial authority over prevailing executive policies—rather, it was first exercised as a technique to settle cases and controversies in a professional manner. The main concern of the courts was to engender respect for the legislative legal hierarchy. This required that courts enforce the highest textual provision in the hierarchy whenever a lower provision attempted to contradict a higher one. In this way, constitutional provisions were enforced when they were violated by legislative acts. In consequence, formulating judicial review within this framework did, in fact, secure its peaceful emergence and led to its flourishing later on.

THE DECENTRALIZED REVIEW

In the following two decades (1948–1969), all courts, irrespective of their level and regardless of the nature and scope of their jurisdiction, had the power to exercise judicial review in its form known as "abstention control," and disallow the application of any legislation they deem unconstitutional. The main disadvantage of the abstention method, however, was that the provisions considered unconstitutional by any given court would still be in existence and could have been upheld by the same court or other courts in future cases. This flaw was not rectified until a centralized mechanism for judicial review was adopted in 1969.[11]

THE SUPREME COURT AND CENTRALIZED REVIEW

In this same year, 1969, a Presidential Decree Law was passed to create the Supreme Court of the country vesting it, among other competencies, with the exclusive power of judicial review in constitutional issues.[12] The creation of the Court was one of the many steps in the modern constitutional reform of Egypt, although it was seen at the time by some as motivated by, and perhaps cloaking, other political objectives.

From the inception of the Supreme Court, judicial review has become centralized in a single court, with the role of other courts in this process becoming diminished. This centralization has, in fact, helped unify judicial opinion in constitutional issues by recognizing the supremacy of the Supreme Court's rulings.

JUDICIAL REVIEW IN THE 1971 CONSTITUTION: THE CREATION OF THE SUPREME CONSTITUTIONAL COURT

Another constitutional development took place in 1971 when the current constitution was promulgated. It was the first constitution in Egyptian constitutional history to regulate the exercise of judicial review in constitutional issues through a specialized, independent judicial body. The constitution created the Supreme Constitutional Court to replace the Supreme Court and to exercise exclusively the power of judicial review, statutory interpretation, and jurisdictional conflict between judicial bodies. The details of how to carry out this task, however, were left to implementing parliamentary legislation.[13]

Practically, the original Supreme Court continued to function until 1979, when the implementing legislation was passed, allowing the Supreme Constitutional Court to become a reality. By virtue of this law, all cases, controversies, and claims that were pending before the previous Supreme Court were referred to the Supreme Constitutional Court.

MECHANISMS OF JUDICIAL REVIEW

In the Egyptian model, bringing a constitutional claim before the Supreme Constitutional Court requires the parties to a dispute on the merits to establish standing, that is, to demonstrate that they are directly and personally affected by the application of the legislation in question. The court on the merits (lower court) is then required to pass a *prima facie* ruling on the constitutional question and prescribe a time limit within which the parties may bring their constitutional arguments to the Supreme Constitutional Court. The proceedings before the court on the merits are suspended, and new proceedings before the Supreme Constitutional Court come into being. The party raising the constitutional issue is required by the Court to define the issue in the most precise of terms—however, the Court has never restricted itself to the question raised if a broader constitutional violation exists. This reflects a trend of judicial activism that begins at the level of the court on the merits, which is entitled to, *ex officio*, bring a constitutional issue to the Supreme Constitutional Court, where, in any proceedings, it appears that there is a *prima facie* violation of the constitution that bears on the subject matter of the case at hand, and the party to the original case either does not have the interest or cannot see the violation to bring the case on their own.

This jurisdictional power of courts on the merit compensates for their lack of power to consider the constitutional issues on their own, and establishes throughout the judiciary the principle that constitutional violations are grave and will not be tolerated, even in cases where there does not appear to be a test case ready to try the particular issue. Here, the Supreme Constitutional Court is empowered, in the course of exercising its mandate, to face the violation. The only restriction on this principle is that of linkage—wherein the Court must show some relatedness between the constitutional issue it is ruling on and the original question brought before it.[14]

JUDICIAL ACTIVISM

The history of judicial review in Egypt reveals that the Supreme Constitutional Court has played a fundamental role in establishing the principles of constitutionalism, the rule of law, constitutional guarantees, and human rights. Although the Court is a relatively new organ in the Egyptian judicial system, its rulings have been progressive in defining the rights accorded to all Egyptian citizens under the constitution and under current notions of human rights.

The fact that the power of judicial review is reserved for the Supreme Constitutional Court has placed the Court at the forefront of the battle to maintain constitutional order and to preserve human rights, which are guaranteed to the Egyptian citizen under the constitution, as well as international legal instruments to which Egypt is bound.

EXAMPLES OF THE COURT'S DECISIONS

Despite a limited number of attacks on the Court in recent years—including a notable example in the form of a Presidential Decree Law restricting the retroactive effect of the Court's decisions—the Court has never surrendered its deep belief in constitutionalism and rule of law. The Court is in a constant struggle to strike a balance between the stability of the country and the protection of human rights. It has managed to widen the scope of its power by eliminating, or at least easing, jurisdictional impediments, such as Acts of Sovereignty, and hence guarantee a wider scale of judicial remedy. There are many examples that demonstrate how the Court manages to guarantee constitutional rights and freedoms:

In addressing political rights, for example, the Court twice struck down the electoral laws and necessitated new parliamentary elections. In both cases the Parliament was dissolved.[15] This was also the case for the *Shura* Council,[16] and the local assemblies.[17] The Court struck down many restrictions on political parties,[18] and enforced restrictions on the President's power to issue emergency decrees with the force of law.[19]

Regarding civil rights, the Court struck down many legislative provisions that allowed to confiscation of private property, or to its restriction, without fair compensation. [20] It restored a long-absent balance in the tenant/landlord relationship by striking down several laws creating a disparity in power.[21] Legislation violating constitutional criminal guarantees such as fair trial,[22] the presumption of innocence,[23] double jeopardy, and personal criminal liability were also struck down by the Court,[24] as was legislation affecting a person's right to freely choose his/her attorney.[25]

Economic, social, and public rights were impeded by many legislative provisions affecting the right to work, voluntarily and in return for fair payment—and these too were found unconstitutional.[26] Legislation restricting the person's right to receive a pension upon retirement was ruled null and void,[27] and the Court also invalidated a considerable number of laws affecting individual rights to join syndicates and participate in their activities.[28]

THE COURT'S APPROACH TO JUDICIAL REVIEW

When assessing the increasing activism of the Court in recent years, it becomes quite clear that the Court's approach to judicial review is derived from several essential principles, the following three being the most important:

1. Judicial Self-restraint. The Court believes in judicial self-restraint and exercises it, especially when the case under review carries undesirable political consequences. This fact may explain why the Court abandoned the Acts of Sovereignty in favor of the American theory of Political Questions, which is a basic component of the concept of judicial self-restraint. The Court does not flaunt its power, and usually does its best to implement the constitutional commands without agitating the executive. It is, in fact, the Court's desire to ease tensions with the executive, especially when the Court's decisions lead to fundamental changes. The Court is keenly attentive to the potential for political or public anarchy in reaction to its rulings, and frequently includes in the decision itself solutions to deal with any possible undesirable consequences. This was the case when the Court struck down the electoral law upon which the parlia-

ment was elected. In this decision, the Court pointed out that, based on the general retroactive effect of its judicial decision in constitutional issues, the configuration of the parliament whose members had been elected in an unconstitutional election was, as a result, unconstitutional.[29] Nevertheless, the laws passed by this parliament are, and will continue to be, valid and in force, unless they are amended by the legislature or declared unconstitutional by the Court on other grounds. Such a conclusion undoubtedly facilitated the acceptance of the Court's ruling by the executive power.

2. Implementing Islamic *Shari'a*. Constitutional protection provided by the Court should always be rendered within Islamic *Shari'a* standards. This is a logical consequence for the constitutional provision that provides that Islamic *Shari'a* is the principal source of legislation.[30] The Court's language usually merges Islamic rules and principles with contemporary constitutional principles while deciding the case at hand.

3. Standards of International Human Rights. The Court always affirms that the state must respect the international treaties to which Egypt is a party, including international human rights instruments. This understanding has been laid down by the Court, through its interpretation of the Constitution, in a number of recently decided cases. Unlike Article 55 of the 1958 French Constitution, in which the duly ratified or approved treaties and agreements are accorded authority superior to that of parliamentary statute, in Egypt, under Article 151 of the 1971 Constitution, duly ratified treaties are part of internal law. Although the Egyptian Constitution does not indicate at what level of the internal legal hierarchy such treaties take effect, the Supreme Constitutional Court gave treaty law that concerns human rights a special status as a constitutional principle. Furthermore, the Court insists that the human rights clauses of the constitution are to be interpreted in accordance with norms generally recognized and applied by democratic states, including international standards applicable in those states.

CONCLUSION: THE IMPACT OF THE EGYPTIAN EXPERIENCE ON THE ARAB WORLD

The rulings of the Court are not only binding on all the courts in Egypt, but also are closely observed by judicial systems and governments throughout the Arab world. This is, undoubtedly, due to the pioneering position the Egyptian legal system occupies, in general, in the region. At the moment, the Egyptian experience is copied to some degree in different parts of the Arab world. What helped this experience to flourish in Egypt in particular was the country's recent movement toward political liberalization. It was this factor, more than any other, that allowed judicial review to emerge and develop so successfully in Egypt. Although the Egyptian experience is available to other Arab systems to derive from, its success in other environments cannot be guaranteed unless a liberal political atmosphere prevails.

Even so, the Egyptian experience is still in its primary stages and needs to be advanced. Continued political liberalization that enhances judicial independence and strengthens public opinion is essential to developing a bolder judicial mechanism. What the future will hold for constitutional order and the role of the Supreme Constitutional Court in implementing constitutional commands will ultimately depend on the growth of democratic liberalization in the coming period.

NOTES

1. Bruce K. Rutherford provides an intensive explanation for the lack of Arab democracy and the failure of Arab countries to join the "Third Wave" of democratization in the twentieth century, in chapter 1 of his unpublished thesis, "The Struggle for Constitutionalism in Egypt: Understanding the Obstacles to Democratic Transition in the Arab World" (1999) (Faculty of Graduate Studies, Yale University).

2. *Ibid.*

3. The movement of political development in the Arab countries during the twentieth century is rich and has attracted many scholars. With regard to Egypt, for instance, see JOHN WATERBURY, THE EGYPT OF NASSER AND SADAT: THE POLITICAL ECONOMY OF TWO RÉGIMES (1983); RAYMOND A. HINNEBUSCH, EGYPTIAN POLITICS UNDER SADAT: THE POST-POPULIST DEVELOPMENT OF AN AUTHORITARIAN-MODERNISING STATE (1985).

4. Rigid, written constitutions have lately become the norm in the Arab world. During the twentieth century, Egypt, for example, adopted a number of constitutions (1923, 1930, 1956, 1958, 1964 and 1971, amended in 1980, the existing one) and one constitutional declaration (1953).

5. For more details see ADEL OMAR SHERIF, CONSTITUTIONAL ADJUDICATION IN EGYPT, *AL-QADDA AL-DOSTORY FE MISR* (1988).

6. Nathan J. Brown discusses this phenomenon in his book THE RULE OF LAW IN THE ARAB WORLD: COURTS IN EGYPT AND THE GULF (1997). See also James H. Rosberg, Roads to the Role of Law: The Emergence of an Independent Judiciary in Contemporary Egypt (1995) (unpublished thesis, Massachusetts Institute of Technology).

7. For more details and an interesting coverage of the topic of judicial review in the Arab world see chapter 5 of NATHAN J. BROWN, CONSTITUTIONS IN A NONCONSTITUTIONAL WORLD: ARAB BASIC LAWS AND THE PROSPECTS FOR ACCOUNTABLE GOVERNMENT (2001).

8. Texts of these constitutions are published in Arabic. See YUSUF QAZMA KHURI, CONSTITUTIONS IN THE ARAB WORLD 1829–1987 (1989).

9. Adel Omar Sherif, *Attacks on the Judiciary: Judicial Independence—Reality or Fallacy, in* THE YEARBOOK OF ISLAMIC AND MIDDLE EASTERN LAW, VOLUME 6, 1999–2000, 3 (Eugene Cotran ed., 2001).

10. Abdel Rahman Nossier, *The Supreme Constitutional Court of Egypt and the Protection of Human Rights* (1992).

11. For general revision of the power of judicial review in Egypt, see Awad Mohammad el-Morr, Abdel Rahman Nossier, and Adel Omar Sherif, *The Supreme Constitutional Court and its Role in the Egyptian Judicial System, in* HUMAN RIGHTS AND DEMOCRACY: THE ROLE OF THE SUPREME CONSTITUIONAL COURT OF EGYPT 37 (Kevin Boyle and

Adel Omar Sherif eds., 1996). See also Abdel Rahman Nossier, *The Supreme Constitutional Court of Egypt and the Protection of Human Rights*.

12. Presidential Decree Law No. 81 for 1969, issued by President Gamal Abdel Nasser.

13. Article 175 of the 1971 Constitution.

14. Constitutional Case No. 38 for the 17th Judicial Year, decided on 18 May 1996 (Decisions Collection).

15. Constitutional Case No. 131 for the 6th Judicial Year, decided on 16 May 1987; Constitutional Case No. 37 for the 9th Judicial Year, decided on 19 May 1990 (Decisions Collection).

16. Constitutional Case No. 23 for the 8th Judicial Year, decided on 15 April 1989 (Decisions Collection).

17. Constitutional Case No. 2 for the 16th Judicial Year, decided on 3 February 1996 (Decisions Collection).

18.Constitutional Case No. 56 for the 6th Judicial Year, decided on 21 June 1986; Constitutional Case No. 44 for the 7th Judicial Year, decided on 7 May 1988 (Decisions Collection).

19. Constitutional Case No. 28 for the 2nd Judicial Year, decided on 4 May 1985; Constitutional Case No. 25 for the 8th Judicial Year, decided on 16 May 1992 (Decisions Collection).

20. Constitutional Case No. 26 for the 12th Judicial Year, decided on 5 October 1996 (Decisions Collection).

21. Constitutional Case No. 11 for the 16th Judicial Year, decided on 3 July 1995 (Decisions Collection).

22. Constitutional Case No. 13 for the 12th Judicial Year, decided on 2 February 1996 (Decisions Collection).

23. Constitutional Case No. 5 for the 15th Judicial Year, decided on 20 May 1995 (Decisions Collection).

24. Constitutional Case No. 25 for the 16th Judicial Year, decided on 3 July 1995 (Decisions Collection).

25. Constitutional Case No. 6 for the 13th Judicial Year, decided on 16 February 1992 (Decisions Collection).

26. Constitutional Case No. 16 for the 15th Judicial Year, decided on 14 January 1995 (Decisions Collection).

27. *Ibid.*

28. Constitutional Case No. 22 for the 17th Judicial Year, decided on 3 February 1996 (Decisions Collection).

29. Constitutional Case No. 37 for the 9th Judicial Year, decided on 19 May 1990 (Decisions Collection).

30. Article 2 of the 1971 Constitution stipulates that principles of Islamic *Shari'a* are the principal source of legislation.

REFERENCES

Boyle, Kevin and Adel Omar Sherif, eds. *Human Rights and Democracy: The Role of the Supreme Constitutional Court of Egypt*. London: Kluwer Law International, 1996.

Brown, Nathan J. *Constitutions in a Nonconstitutional World: Arab Basic Laws and the Prospects for Accountable Government.* Albany: SUNY Press, 2001.

Brown, Nathan J. *The Rule of Law in the Arab World: Courts in Egypt and the Gulf.* Cambridge: Cambridge University Press, 1997.

Brown, Nathan J. "Constitutionalism and Judicial Review in the Arab World." Paper Presented at the Annual Meeting of the Middle East Studies Association, 1996.

Brown, Nathan J. "Law and Imperialism: Egypt in Comparative Perspective," *Law and Society Review* 29 (1995) 103–125.

Brynen, Rex, Bahgar Korany, and Paul Noble, eds. *Political Liberalization and Democratization in the Arab World, Theoretical Perspectives.* London: Lynne Rienner Publishers, 1995.

Brynen, Rex, Bahgar Korany, and Paul Noble, eds. *Political Liberalization and Democratization in the Arab World, Comparative Experiences.* London: Lynne Rienner Publishers, 1998.

Cannon, Bryon. *Politics of Law and the Courts in 19th Century Egypt.* Salt Lake City: University of Utah Press, 1988.

Cotran, Eugene and Adel Omar Sherif. *The Role of the Judiciary in the Protection of Human Rights.* London: Kluwer Law International, 1997.

Hill, Enid. *Mahkama! Studies in the Egyptian Legal System: Courts & Crimes, Law & Society.* London: Ithaca Press, 1979.

Magnarella, Paul. *Middle East and North Africa: Governance, Democratization, Human Rights.* Brookfield, Vt.: Ashgate, 1999.

Mallat, Chibli. *Constitutional Law in the Middle East: The Emergence of Judicial Power.* London: School of Oriental and African Studies, Working Papers, 1993.

Mallat, Chibli. *Islam and Public Law.* London: Graham & Trotman, 1993.

El-Morr, 'Awad. "The Supreme Constitutional Court of Egypt and the Protection of Human and Political Rights" in *Islam and Public Law.* London: Graham & Trotman, 1993.

El-Morr, 'Awad. "Human Rights in the Constitutional Systems of Islamic Countries" in *Human Rights and Democracy: The Role of the Supreme Constitutional Court of Egypt.* London: Kluwer Law International, 1996.

Reid, Donald. *Lawyers and Politics in the Arab World, 1880–1960.* Chicago: Bibliotheca Islamica, 1981.

Rosberg, James H. "Roads to the Role of Law: The Emergence of an Independent Judiciary in Contemporary Egypt." Ph.D. diss., Massachusetts Institute of Technology, 1995.

Rutherford, Bruce. "The Struggle for Constitutionalism in Egypt: Understanding the Obstacles to Democratic Transition in the Arab World." Ph.D. diss., Yale University, 1999.

Sherif, Adel Omar. *Constitutional Adjudication in Egypt, al-Qadda al-Dostory fe Misr.* Cairo: Dar el-Shaab, 1988.

Tate, C. Neal and Torbjorn Vallinder, eds. *The Global Expansion of Judicial Power.* New York: New York University Press, 1995.

Vallinder, Torbjorn. "The Judicialization of Politics—A World-wide Phenomenon," *International Political Science Review* 15 (1994).

Ziadeh, Farhat J. *Lawyers, the Rule of Law and Liberalism in Modern Egypt.* Stanford: Hoover Institution on War, Revolution, and Peace, 1968.

5

Reflections on Continental European Public Law in the Tradition of Hobbes and Napoleon

Thomas Fleiner

STATE AS BIG BANG

Continental and civil law countries have a different perception of the "state." Europeans see the state as the "Leviathan," which is, by its authority or sovereignty, the only source of law and justice.[1] The "pouvoir constituant" instituting the state can be compared to the Big Bang out of which develops the universe of justice, law, and legitimate state authority, including the rule of law and human rights, this universe being limited, however, to the territory of the state. The perception of the state as a collective unit containing all elements of justice and law and established by the social contract does not correspond to the understanding familiar to the American legal and cultural tradition.

CITIZENS AS SUBJECTS

According to the European tradition, public law can be perceived as a hierarchy of norms developing out of the constitution by statutes and bills, decrees and ordinances, or agency rules, depending each on its mother-statute and all of them depending again on the constitution, which can be compared to the first "Galaxy" developed out of the Big Bang. This idea of the *Stufenordnung*, the hierarchical order of legal norms (*see* Kelsen), was the basis for the establishment of constitutional review in continental Europe.[2] According to this understanding, the source of the law is the authority of the sovereign and not the reason nor the wisdom of court precedents.

THE FUNCTION OF PUBLIC LAW ACCORDING TO NAPOLEON

Napoleon constructed a very new realm of legal norms, which he called "public law" to distinguish from traditional private law. Napoleon's decision has probably had the most far-reaching consequences for the different developments and different legal cultures of countries with common law and countries with civil law systems. By separating public from private law, Napoleon aimed at an efficient administration, which he installed as the state instrument to change the feudal into a liberal society.[3] The state, according to his opinion, could only be an *efficient instrument for social engineering* if the administration would not be under the jurisdiction of the traditional and conservative courts. Thus, the construction of public law had a very pragmatic and political reason; that is, to give more power to the executive and the administration. Although administrative courts have been established in different civil law countries since Napoleon they still have very limited power with regard to the administration. They do not have remedies at their disposal in order to enforce their decisions. They can only quash administrative acts of administrative authorities. There is no contempt of court possible with regard either to administrative authorities or to civil servants. On the other hand, citizens are still subjects and not partners of the administration, as the "public law" gives administrative authority the power to issue unilateral decisions or administrative acts with almost the same obligatory force and authority as court judgments.[4]

STATE AS INSTRUMENT TO CHANGE SOCIETY

Napoleon's perception of the status and function of the state was that it could be used as an instrument to change society, and this perception has strongly influenced legal thinking within liberal, and even socialist, Europe. According to continental European constitutionalism, constitutions are not only conceived as instruments to limit governmental power, but they are also tools to set up, organize, and empower the governmental branches to develop the liberal state, and later the social welfare state.

ARISTOCRATIC LEGAL SYSTEMS

Rooted in medieval Church law, which was based on the ideology of the "King by the Grace of God," the notion of hierarchy in the sense that *higher authorities decide better, know better, understand better, and judge more justly* became crucial for the European legal culture. Thus, the level of authority issuing norms, administrative decisions, or even judgments is more important than the content of these adjudications. It is not the procedure that guarantees legitimacy, good law, and justice; it is the higher authority, which is closer to the roots of justice. This has only slightly changed since the French Revolution, namely in that the "King by the Grace of God" has been replaced by the "Sovereign Nation or People," which has been enabled as the highest authority to decide what is just, good, and correct. Thus, the democratic sovereign has become the only source of the law, and the parliament, as legislature, has received a monopoly on law-making within the nation-state. The realm of the law is limited to general, democratically approved legislative norms. The judge as authority to create law has been abolished. Thus, the common law idea of democracy to be guaranteed by the jury trial has become strange to the European legal culture. From this results a different understanding of democracy as legitimacy of the legislature and not as legitimacy of the courts.

INALIENABLE RIGHTS

The American Declaration of Independence is based on a Lockean concept of natural law, right of resistance, and right of self-determination. This understanding of human rights as being preconstitutional still has difficulty finding roots in European constitutional thinking. The reluctance of the constitutional court in Karlsruhe to accept international rulings with regard to human rights is an example.[5]

CONSTITUTION OF A NEW UNIT OR A NEW LEGITIMACY

In 1787, the American Constitution did indeed *constitute* a new unity composed of several sovereign states and members of the confederation. In general, European constitutions are the result of the French Revolution (except for Switzerland). They did not constitute a substantially new state entity or national unity. They changed the government, the legitimacy of the state, and, in some instances, the society. Thus, constitutions constituted only new governments, not new state-units. But the new democratic state was organized for the same subjects living in the same territory. Today, the making of Europe as a new unity is a challenge of historically new dimension.[6]

CALVINIST IDEOLOGY

It is well known that American society is much more competitive than European society. The ideology behind this tendency is not only the *invisible hand*, but also the Calvinist conviction that competition guarantees not only the selection of the fittest, but also the selection of the most valuable.[7] This has consequences for the understanding of the function of a trial in court. According to the civil law perception, the party that is in its rights should win the case. According to the American perception, as I understand it, the one who wins the case, has the right.

LEGAL EDUCATION

This has concrete consequences for legal education. According to the European tradition, we have to teach students what the law is and how they can find the law with regard to concrete cases. The American law teacher seems, in my perception, to be much more a trainer who gives the students the training they need to win a case.[8]

DIFFERENT PERCEPTIONS OF JURISPRUDENCE

The different positions of the court also have different consequences for our understanding of jurisprudence, and specially the strong influence of law and economics in the United States, which has almost (with the exception of Italy) no counterpart in Europe. Jurisprudence or legal philosophy in Europe is a science that deals with a better understanding the law made by constitution and legislation. In the United States, the law is also made by the judge. Judges use tools like the assessment of costs and benefits to make law. A judge who applies and interprets legislative norms does not need any such kind of tool. And with regard to the legislature, such economic concepts are part of the political decision-making process influenced by the different party ideologies.

LEGITIMACY OF THE JUDICIARY

The legitimacy of the judiciary based on preconstitutional rights, very often invoked in discussions with American judges, certainly does not correspond to the traditional European understanding. According to our understanding, the court's legitimacy stems from the constitution and statutes. A decision of a court to establish constitutional review, as in *Marbury v. Madison*,[9] is unthinkable within the continental tradition.

DIFFERENT UNDERSTANDINGS OF THE RULE OF LAW

Finally, we also have to be aware that the very principle of the rule of law so often invoked by the international community has different meanings in the European and the common law traditions.[10] The rule of law, according to the European perception, limits the government to the normative decisions of the sovereign established in the constitution. According to *Marbury v. Madison*, the American government is a "government of law and not of men," so that the rule of law has preconstitutional meaning. This goes far beyond the European understanding of the *Rechtsstaat*, which only guarantees the correct application of the constitution by the state authorities.

By no means would I propose that one or the other of these understandings is more valuable. But we have to be aware that globalization requires cooperation, which needs a better understanding of the very roots of the different legal traditions. Only by knowing those roots can misunderstandings be avoided and a real dialogue established.

NOTES

The author thanks Alexander Misic, Research Fellow at the Institute for Federalism in Fribourg (Switzerland), for his help.

1. J.M. Broekman, *A Philosophy of European Union Law* (Leuven: Peters, 1999), p. 3; Thomas Fleiner, *Hobbes' Lehre vom Gesellschaftsvertrag und die Tradition der Schweizerischen Volkssouveränität, in* Otfried Höffe (ed.), ANTHROPOLOGIE UND STAATSPHILOSOPHIE (Freiburg, Switzerland: Universitätsverlag Freiburg Schweiz, 1981), pp. 79–91.

2. *See* H. KELSEN, *Reine Rechtslehre* (Vienna: Österreichische Staatsdruckerei, 1992), pp. 228–282.

3. Alexis de Tocqueville characterized Napoleon's administration as a walking headless body (*"un corps qui marche après que la tête en a été séparée"*). *See* J-J. Chevallier, *Histoire des institutions et des régimes politiques de la France*, 7th ed. (Paris: Dalloz, 1985), p. 122.

4. Thomas Fleiner, *General Remarks on Some Principles of the Cantonal and Federal Administrative Law of Switzerland, in* Dessemontet and Ansay (eds.), INTRODUCTION TO SWISS LAW, 2nd ed. (The Hague: Kluwer, 1995), pp. 27–45, 31.

5. *See, inter alia*, P. Kirchhof, *Das Maastricht-Urteil des Bundesverfassungsgerichts, in* Hommelhoff and Kirchhof (eds.), DER STAATENVERBUND DER EUROPÄISCHEN UNION (Heidelberg: C.F. Muller, Juristischer Verlag Heidelberg, 1994), pp. 11–25.

6. *See* Thomas Fleiner, *The Yugoslav Crisis: Challenge for a New Theory of Federalism*, 6 CARDOZO J. INT'L COMP. L. 85–97, n.1 (1998).

7. *See* R.M. Kingdon, *Althusius' Use of Calvinist Sources in his Politica, in* Duso, Krawietz, and Wydunckel (eds.), KONSENS UND KONSOZIATION IN DER POLITISCHEN THERIE DES FRÜHEN FÖDERALISMUS, Rechtstheorie (Berlin: Beiheft, 1997), pp. 19–29.

8. *See* David Kennedy, *A Rotation in Contemporary Legal Scholarship, in* C. Joerges and D.M. Trubek (eds.), CRITICAL LEGAL THOUGHT: AN AMERICAN-GERMAN DEBATE (Baden-Baden: Nomos, 1989), pp. 353–396.

9. *Marbury v. Madison*, 5 U.S. 137 (1803).

10. *See* Lidija Basta, *Quelques considérations sur la relation conceptuelle entre la "Rule of Law" et le "Rechtsstaat," in* DROIT CONSTITUTIONNEL (MÉLANGES P. GÉLARD) (Paris: Montchréstien, 1999), pp. 9–11.

FURTHER READING

Damaska, Marian R. *The Faces of Justice and State Authority, A Comparative Approach to the Legal Process*. New Haven: Yale University Press, 1986.

De Tocqueville, Alexis. "De la Démocratie en Amérique." In *Oeuvres Complètes II*. ed. Pléiade, Paris: Gallimard, 1992.

Fleiner, Thomas. *What are Human Rights?* Leichhardt, NSW, Australia: The Federation Press, 1999.

Jackson, Vicki C. and Mark Tushnet. *Comparative Constitutional Law*. New York: The Foundation Press, 1999.

Häberle, Peter and Jörg Paul Müller, eds. *Menschenrechte und Bürgerrechte in einer vielgestaltigen Welt.* Munich: Helbing & Lichtenhahn, 2000.
Hart, H.L.A. *The Concept of Law*, 2d ed. New York: Oxford University Press, 1994.
Solomon Robert C. and Mark C. Murphy, eds. *What is Justice? Classic and Contemporary Readings*. New York: Oxford University Press, 1990.

Part II

Constitutions, Courts, and Legitimacy

6

European Integration and the Ideal of the Common Good

Winfried Brugger

I. INTRODUCTION: THE COMMON GOOD AS THE GUIDING IDEAL OF A WELL-FUNCTIONING LEGAL ORDER

Legal orders are subject to analysis and evaluation in manifold dimensions. The well functioning of a particular legal order, here the European Community (EC or Community), may be assessed through its degree of consonance with the common good. Reference to the common good as a guiding ideal is as old as the notion of legal order. Many scholars doubt the usefulness of such a vague and open-ended standard. However, when viewed in light of the following two conditions, the common good constitutes an apt and sensitive guiding ideal. (1) The notion should be developed enough to capture the main features of a well-functioning modern legal system. (2) The standard should not be used as a tool to determine specific details of the organization under consideration, but rather serve as a conceptual framework for guiding the legal analysis.

The common good should be construed by means of three components, or, in more visual terms, three pillars—legal certainty, legitimacy, and practicality.[1] Each pillar is subject to further differentiation. Thus, legal certainty consists of four elements, or goals: certainty of meaning, certainty of obedience to law, certainty through stability, and clear institutional responsibilities. The second pillar, legitimacy, comprises the two goals of the good and the right, or, expressed differently, the goals of pursuing good purposes within the confines of the requirements of justice. The third pillar, practicality, is well constructed if it exhibits several characteristics. The actions of legal institutions should be based on valid empirical assumptions. Moreover, all interests associated with a

Table 1

Elements of the Common Good		
1. Legal Certainty	***2. Legitimacy***	***3. Practicality***
Formal Rationality	Material Rationality	Instrumental Rationality
Legal Coherence	Ethical Coherence	Empirical Coherence
• certainty of meaning • certainty of obedience to law • stability • clear institutional responsibilities	• good purposes • just regulations (especially through policies at appropriate level and protection of basic rights)	• validity of empirical assumptions; analysis of interests affected • means-end efficiency; analysis of consequences • consideration of "nature" or structure of area to be regulated
• emphasized in legal positivism	• emphasized in legal idealism	• emphasized in legal realism and law and economics
Procedures of the Common Good		
Legal Processes	***Political Processes***	***Scientific Processes***
especially within the separation-of-powers scheme	especially formation of public opinion and democratic elections	especially to obtain scientific support for or against regulation through law

proposed action should be considered and appropriate means-end efficiency pursued. Finally, consideration should be given to the peculiarities of the sphere of life or course of action subject to planned regulation by law. This brief explanation already illustrates the complexities involved with the concept of the common good in a modern legal system.

With respect to a particular problem or institutional arrangement, the criteria thematized in the three pillars may support each other and facilitate the installation of the proposed action or arrangement. However, they may also collide. For example, the requirements of legal certainty, legitimacy, and practicality conflict when a binding court decision is actually based on wrong or doubtful evidence, such as in a criminal conviction. Then the three components of the common good have to be balanced against each other. Similar observations may be made for the internal divisions of the three guiding lights of a well-functioning legal order. The constitutive elements of certainty, legitimacy, and practicality can be in a relation of support, indifference, or tension.

This article highlights[2] the guiding ideal of a well-functioning legal order in the context of the EC legal order.[3] Table 1 summarizes and visualizes the elements and processes of the common good described hereafter.

II. LEGAL CERTAINTY IN THE EUROPEAN COMMUNITY

The first pillar of legal certainty includes the subelements of intelligible meaning, legal compliance, sustained stability, and delineated and transparent institutional tasks and responsibilities.

1. The first subelement of legal certainty consists of the goal to provide circumscribed and intelligible meaning. EC institutions meet this challenge when creating secondary Community law that clearly communicates the binding law to state actors and citizens. According to Article 249 of the Treaty Establishing the European Community (ECT) (formerly Article 189), they can make use of regulations, directives, and decisions: "[a] regulation shall have general application. It shall be binding in its entirety and directly applicable in all Member States" (para. 2); "[a] directive shall be binding, as to the result to be achieved, upon each Member State to which it is addressed, but shall leave to the national authorities the choice of form and methods" (para. 3); "[a] decision shall be binding in its entirety upon those to whom it is addressed" (para. 4). Controversies over the specificity of law-making measures are adjudicated by the European Court of Justice (ECJ), which, in Art. 220 ECT (formerly Article 164), is tasked with ensuring "that in the interpretation and application of this Treaty the law is observed." These cases reach the ECJ through precisely circumscribed "direct actions,"[4] which are brought by EC institutions, Member States, or natural and legal persons or, indirectly, through "reference proceedings," which may or shall be initiated by courts or tribunals of the Member States when deciding domestic cases that involve questions of Community law.[5] The structure of the legal review system is intended to secure a clear and uniform interpretation and application of Community law.

2. Legal compliance standards, the second subelement of legal certainty, serve to secure obedience to the binding law. Here, a first difference to a national legal order opens up. In the United States or Germany, for example, multitudes of executive agencies, including marshals and police forces, make sure that binding legal orders or judgments are being followed. This may involve the use of force. Since the EC does not have similar organs, Community law is implemented within the national legal orders through domestic institutions and procedures. In this sense, it constitutes the "least dangerous branch."[6] This characteristic is compensated through the duty of sincere cooperation imposed by Article 10 ECT (formerly Article 5) upon the Member States and the Community. The Member States are held to take all appropriate measures for the attainment of EC objectives and to abstain from jeopardizing these goals. The ECJ views this obligation as a constitutional lever. In addition, the ECT and the Treaty on European Union (TEU) provide for sanctioning schemes when the Member States violate certain duties. Examples include fines imposed for defiance of ECJ judgments in Member State actions[7] or suspension of rights for disregard of the European Union's foundational principles.[8] The rise of direct

effect and Member State public tort liability fall into the same context of securing supranational compliance interests.[9]

3. Sustained stability is the third element of legal certainty. Stable laws that are valid and applicable over a long enough period are anchored in the customs and legal traditions of a people. They become matters of reciprocal, settled, and, at times, deep-seated expectations. The almost five decades after the signing of the treaty establishing the European Coal and Steel Community may not constitute a sufficient time frame for creating deep-seated expectations in the populations of all Member States. European integration has always been an incremental process. However, the various stakeholders have been affected over the years in different degrees. Most provisions of EC law address economic questions that primarily affect the specialized clientele of economic operators, including companies and organizations. These actors may be assumed to have adapted to the new legal regime quite rapidly. With respect to the consumers in general, most substantive changes in EC law may not yet have transformed into well-settled traditions because new frameworks have only recently been established, or are still arising. Examples include the euro and the concept of a "passport-free" Europe without frontiers. It remains to be seen whether the next ten or twenty years will achieve firm expectations of European citizens with respect to money and open borders.

On a more general level, while almost fifty years of European integration have witnessed various crises (e.g. the delayed accession to the EC of the United Kingdom, the constitutional issues involved with unanimity voting in the Council and resolved through the Luxembourg accords, and the European posture in the Balkan Wars,[10] no development has really threatened to bring down the whole enterprise. To a substantial degree, the EC has been able to steer a firm and stable course, thus ensuring legal certainty on this more general level.

4. The existence of delineated and transparent institutional tasks and responsibilities constitutes the final subelement of legal certainty. The ideal is directed at establishing institutional actors who know their reciprocal rights and duties. As a consequence, sound balance of control and cooperation can be expected. Have the main actors, the European Parliament, the Council, the Commission, and the Court of Justice lived up to this standard?[11] Their tasks and responsibilities have been established by primary Community law. Although certain changes (in the case of the European Parliament, to a significant extent) were accomplished through grand revisions of the Foundational Treaties, the core institutional powers have been preserved, and thus remain clear. When disputes among the European organs arise, the ECJ delineates the "institutional balance." If, for example, the ECJ finds, in an action for annullment, that a European institution has acted without the requisite competence, infringed an essential procedural requirement, violated the ECT or any rule relating to its application, or misused powers,[12] the Court shall "declare the act concerned to be void" and, in the case of a regulation, shall, if considered necessary, state "which effects of the [voided] regulation . . . shall be considered as definitive."[13] The institu-

tions concerned "shall be required to take the necessary measures to comply with the [ECJ's] judgment."[14] The same consequences attach if the corresponding action for failure to act succeeds because Community institutions, in infringement of the ECT, fail to act.[15] Translated into the terms of a national constitution, these scenarios captured by these two sister actions may be characterized as separation-of-powers conflicts. The ECJ has full power to adjudicate the "institutional balance," however, the Court's jurisdiction is one of attribution (compétence d'attribution).[16] The ECJ has repeatedly been criticized in academic circles for arrogating powers to itself that are not covered by the Treaties.[17]

The advantage of installing European organs, instead of different national organs, to adopt binding legal decisions, lies in the much greater level of uniformity or certainty signaled to the national legal systems and their members. In the spirit of greater uniformity, the EC institutions themselves in 1957 and 1965 were subject to a two-stage fusion establishing common institutions for the three Foundational Communities (European Economic Community, European Atomic Energy Community, and European Coal and Steel Community).[18] While the scope of the three Communities differs, a single set of institutions leads to more consistent, certain, and predictable policies.[19]

On a conceptual level, legal positivism addresses the combination of these four components of the ideal of legal certainty.[20] Independent of the legitimacy of the substantive goals (pillar two) and the means-end rationality (pillar three) of the whole enterprise, the principal actors and their procedures for establishing clear legal commands must at least be transparent and predictable. Analyzed solely from this important, albeit one-sided, goal of a well-functioning legal order, the EC structure does strongly resemble a nation-state; however, a robust and strong executive branch with a police force and an army at its center and a full-fledged foreign affairs power are missing. These features are currently organized in different international frameworks (e.g., NATO) or supplemented by other, nonintegrated, purely European arrangements (e.g., TEU, pillars two and three of the EU). In this sense, fully developed European organs have not yet emerged.

III. PRACTICALITY IN THE EUROPEAN COMMUNITY

Practicality constitutes the third pillar of the common good.

The institutions of the European Community as well as their national counterparts employ specialized staffs who are tasked with ensuring that governmental actions are based on valid empirical assumptions, consider means-end efficiency, and listen to all interests affected. It is hard to compare the performance level in the EC with the record of national legislatures, executives, or courts. If EC institutions are characterized as performing poorly, increased funding and staff may present the answer. However, this is a conclusion that not many national governments are willing to accept and implement at the present time.

One area of EC activities exhibits a substantial, some might say *dramatic*, shift from the arrangement in the U.S. and German constitutions. This relates to the question of whether a constitution should set up a particular economic order. The U.S. Supreme Court, in the first third of the twentieth century, answered this question in the affirmative, having a free market system in mind. The seminal case is *Lochner v. New York*.[21] In the post-Lochner era, the Supreme Court emphasized that it was not the task of the U.S. Constitution to bind itself to a particular economic philosophy. The German Federal Constitutional Court (FCC) made similar statements in the Investment Aid Case of 1954. The Court said: "The Basic Law's neutrality in economic matters consists . . . in the fact that the 'constituent power' has not adopted a specific economic program. This omission enables the legislature to pursue economic policies deemed proper for the circumstances, provided the Basic Law is observed."[22]

For Germany and the other EC Member States, this stance has been supplanted by the rise of the Community legal order that enjoys supremacy over conflicting domestic law. The ECT announces "the principle of an open market economy with free competition"[23] and states that the "Member States and the Community shall act in accordance with the principle of an open market economy with free competition, favoring an efficient allocation of resources, and in compliance with the principles set out in Article 4."[24] The principle, which, in many instances, has been implemented into specific common policies, aptly emphasizes the rationale for relinquishing a posture of neutrality with respect to the economic system of choice. The EC embraces and secures free market postulates because, in contrast to other philosophies, this economic system is deemed to facilitate increased material wealth and competitive strength for the Community's population. Reformulated in the terms of the third pillar of the common good, the EC views the decision for a free market order as a path toward optimal attainment of the ideal of practicality and efficiency in the economic sphere. Thus, securing free markets also is good policy. This leads to the second pillar, the ideal of legitimacy.

IV. LEGITIMACY IN THE EUROPEAN COMMUNITY

Actors in a legal order, when ordaining their laws, try to convince the public that they are pursuing the good and just, or, in one word, legitimate purposes. Legitimacy as a guiding ideal plays an important role because no legal order can survive in the long run only through using its police and army. Indeed, in a system like the EC, which has no police or army, legitimacy apparently assumes increased significance. In this context, legitimacy becomes more complex and intricate, because it is not a fixed or all-or-nothing ideal. Instead, it exhibits several facets that may change over time. These challenges are present in the process of European integration. The following passages provide the major battlegrounds.

1. Legitimacy embraces substantive and procedural aspects. One substantive

goal has already been mentioned. The ECT views open markets and competition among economic actors as good policy because this approach strengthens Europe's position in global competition and leads to greater material well-being than other economic regimes. But what about those groups in the European population that do not have the intellectual and educational capacities to secure their position in the marketplace? Most national constitutions of the Member States accept in their social welfare provisions an institutional responsibility to look after those who are unable to cope in the economic competition of economic spaces previously confined to national borders. Since national economies have become subsystems of the European economic order, the question arises whether the institutional responsibility for the social welfare should be extended to all unemployed workers. In the preambles of the TEU and the ECT, reference is made to "economic and social progress."[25] This can lead to the false impression that the powers of the EC are equally strong in both fields. The ECT allows for some social activities on the European level but still leaves the core responsibility for supporting the weak and needy to the national legal systems.[26] Nevertheless, new European powers in the field of social welfare will arise.

As a consequence of the revisions made by the Treaty of Amsterdam, the ECT in Article 137 (3) now grants the Community coordination and supplementation powers to act in the field of "social security and social protection of workers" on the supranational level, subject to the heightened threshold of unanimity voting in the Council. Yet, the contours of a European social order are progressively emerging.

2. A second legitimacy challenge concerns the source of regulation. Should legal precepts be determined on the national or the European level? The answer to this question obviously lies in selecting the best level for taking the action. This depends first upon the nature of the problem, which can be national, European, or global. Second, it is contingent on the ability of a particular level of government to resolve the problem. Both aspects form part of practicality, which includes the consideration of the character of the problem at hand. In addition, a legitimacy concern arises because many members of the public expect and believe that decision-making powers should generally be exercised close to their world, which they can understand and influence. And this world, in their—possibly already outdated—point of view, means the national and local legal orders. In response to this issue, the TEU introduced the subsidiarity principle into the ECT. Article 5 (2) (formerly Article 3 b (2)) requires that, outside the sphere of exclusive competences, "the Community shall take action, in accordance with the principle of subsidiarity, only if and insofar as the objectives of the proposed action cannot be sufficiently achieved by the Member States and can therefore, by reason of the scale or effects of the proposed action, be better achieved by the Community."[27]

Determining the level of the legal order for tackling a problem is not an easy task. A common point of view or action may be achieved in several ways. The legislator may opt for a uniform Community regulation, use the less intrusive

EC directive to approximate laws, or choose "mere" intergovernmental cooperation.

3. The firm commitment to the protection of constitutional rights constitutes another aspect of legitimacy. When the legal actors pursue their goals, they shall not proceed in a way that violates the constitutional rights of the population. These rights represent the requirements of justice and impose limitations on European policy decisions. Unlike the U.S. Constitution or Germany's Basic Law, the ECT does not include a bill of rights or a comprehensive chapter of fundamental rights. However, the Community is mainly predicated upon the four basic economic freedoms of "free movement of goods, persons, services and capital."[28] These freedoms are the normative equivalent of the professional liberty, the right of property, and the freedom to contract in Art. 12, 14, and 2 (1) of Germany's Basic Law. The ECT also prohibits discrimination on the ground of nationality.[29] In addition, the Treaty incorporates the "principle of equal pay for male and female workers for equal work or work of equal value."[30]

Pressures forcing the adoption of European constitutional rights have led to several important developments. The following three appear most pertinent. Since 1969, the ECJ has distilled European constitutional rights out of the common constitutional traditions of the Member States.[31] These "general principles," which constitute primary Community law, include "a right of legitimate expectation, a right to be heard, the duty to respect fundamental rights, a right to equality of treatment, and a duty to employ means that are proportional (not excessive) to the end sought."[32] This jurisprudence provides one of the major sources for comparative research in the constitutional rights area. Moreover, the TEU commits the EU organs to respect the European Convention for the Protection of Human Rights and Fundamental Freedoms.[33] Neither the EC nor the EU is a formal member of this regional human rights regime, however nothing prevents them from imposing upon themselves a binding constitutional rights standard. Finally, the Community has tasked a commission with formulating a bill of rights for insertion into the treaty framework through a future revision. The commission in the meantime has proposed a Charter of Fundamental Rights of the European Union. This Charter has been proclamated by the European Commission, the Council, and the European Parliament, and it has been welcomed by the European Council in Nice (7–9 December 2000). It has not been made into binding law yet.[34]

Where is the existing European human rights standard positioned in relation to the protection of constitutional rights in the Member States that are guarded by national constitutional courts? Which legal system is paramount? As the case of Germany illustrates, this is an intricate and delicate question. The issue arises when national authorities execute Community law—which is increasingly the case due to the accelerating law-making activity on the EC level—and a plaintiff alleges that the implementation by the German agency violates a right secured in the German constitution. The German FCC has gone through several stages in addressing this "supremacy" and preemption question. In its first decision of

1974,[35] the FCC held that so long as the Community had not developed a constitutional rights regime roughly equivalent to the German level of protection, the German constitutional rights were the standard for scrutinizing European legal provisions implemented in Germany. The FCC emphasized that it retained the requisite jurisdiction to engage in that analysis. In the second decision of 1986,[36] the FCC adjudged the jurisprudence of the ECJ and the institutional pronouncements in the constitutional rights field as basically equivalent to the German standard. The FCC, while not permanently retracting control, suspended its exercise as long as the Community stayed this firm course. In the third decision, the Maastricht decision of 1993,[37] the FCC even further scaled back its own jurisdictional powers, however the Court stopped short of totally and permanently renouncing its prerogative to adjudicate conflicts between European acts and German constitutional rights. The new formula may be expressed as follows: As long as the European organs stay within the broad but circumscribed powers conferred upon them by the TEU, the FCC will refrain from claiming jurisdiction in constitutional rights conflicts. However, if, in the assessment of the FCC, European institutions act ultra vires, beyond the confines covered by the assent of the German constitutional organs, the FCC would view this as a violation of the German sovereign power and reclaim jurisdiction.

All three decisions are in Germany known as "so-long-as decisions numbers 1, 2 and 3" (Solange-Entscheidungen). The specific requirement expressed through "so long as" in the three decisions, however, has shifted over the years in the way described—from claiming primary jurisdiction over Community law implementation in Germany even against a prior ECJ judgment, to a reactive guardian role to be actualized only when EC organs act ultra vires. This last stage in the development of the supremacy question may be described as a German dormant sovereignty doctrine.

In addition to its substantive aspects, legitimacy also exhibits procedural aspects. The processes used for creating law lead to the question of democracy. The democratic principle forms a constitutive part of the constitutions of the EC Member States. It is also incorporated in the Community fabric, albeit in a more indirect and complex manner than in the nation-states. In the Member States, the parliament is the main repository of democratic legitimization. For the EC regime the same does not (yet) hold true for the European Parliament (EP). The EC legislative process is driven by various players. The Commission is the initiator of legislation. The Council serves as the main decision-maker. Under the ECT, the EP enjoys different degrees of participation rights, including consultation, cooperation, codecision, and full assent.[38] The Single European Act, the TEU, and the Treaty of Amsterdam have incrementally strengthened the EP's prerogatives; however, they still fall short of the powers held by the national parliaments.

The reason for this power distribution lies in the persisting reluctance of the Member States to weaken their national parliaments to the point of marginalization. They still seek to retain substantial decision-making power for the national governments elected in the domestic arena. In parliamentary systems, the national governments represent parliamentary majorities. The national governments send their respective ministers to the Council of the EU, where they vote for or against proposed Community legislation. Thus, the Council derives its democratic legitimization in an indirect fashion.

The democratic legitimization of the EP occurs more directly. Since 1979, its members have been elected by universal suffrage, albeit subject to national voting procedures.[39] The EP's layered participation powers are weaker than those of a national parliament. Under no participation mode is the EP enabled to outvote and replace opposing decisions of the Council. This so-called legitimization deficit of the Community is often deplored by scholars. However, this characterization seems simplistic. The counterargument advances that giving the EP full-fledged legislative participation powers would lead to a legitimization deficit in the second theater of operations, the national parliaments. Most voters in the Member States project the main legitimization of power into their national parliaments. Most voters still—more or less—know their representatives. Moreover, in the national parliaments, the political discourse is conducted in the native language of the electorate. In addition, voters know the political customs, believe that they can assess the quality of political decision-making, and feel responsible for the weal and woe of their compatriots.

Strengthening the democratic decision-making power on the European level is thus a tricky business. The avenue of conferring more powers on the EP, according to many observers, presupposes that some or most of the criteria just described can successfully be established on the European level. Thus, the argument runs, before moving from the national parliaments as the primary source of democratic legitimacy to the EP, a stronger European mentality or identity has to arise. This may be accomplished through finding a common language or understanding in conjunction with the political conversations currently conducted in twelve languages. In addition, a full-fledged European political party system that deserves its name needs to develop.

The unresolved problem of democratic legitimization has a substantive counterpart that involves the clear identification of the final goal of European integration. This is the big question. It is no coincidence that the TEU and the ECT engage in a *Formelkompromiss*, the German term for semantic obfuscation, through use of the catchphrase "ever closer union."[40] The rise of a European Federal State with strong European powers vis-à-vis the responsibilities of the Member States resides at the consequential end of the spectrum. However, this message cannot currently be sold to the populations of the Member States without delegitimizing existing political loyalties. Yet no Member State takes the position that the status quo reflects the final stage of European integration. The economic and political elite in the Member States tends to believe that many problems, including environmental pollution, military security, and human rights, could be better solved on a continent-wide basis comparable to the U.S. federal framework.

In light of this ambivalent posture in the Member States, this tension between national sovereignty and European interests finds expression in the three-pillar structure of the EU conceived by the TEU. The three supranational Communities are integrated in the first pillar, while the Common Foreign and Security Policy and the Police and Judicial Cooperation in Criminal Matters are organized in pillars two and three, where intergovernmental processes of coordination dominate.

The subject matter governed by pillars two and three, as well as the defense and security frameworks of NATO or the TEU,[41] involves prerogatives that form traditional aspects of national sovereignty. Certain activities also belong to deep-seated home-country loyalties held by the people in the Member States. Who should be(come) a citizen? Who should be allowed into the country and who should be extradited? Whose well-being should be secured within the social welfare system, which, in Germany and several other Member States, is rather generous? How should the police proceed? Whose vital interests—life or living standards—are important enough for a country to go to war and risk the loss of lives on the battlefield? Despite these strong local and national underpinnings, as well as the close nexus to notions of nation-state sovereignty, no standstill is in sight. Even in the extremely sensitive area of military confrontation, an increasing number of voices advocate a more prominent role of the EU in regional conflict management (for example, in the Balkans). The idea consists in creating a defense identity that, without eliminating or marginalizing national armies or the responsibilities of NATO, is able to secure peace and respect for human rights on a Europe-wide level. The exact form of a potential intervention force and the design of the legal umbrella for carrying out its mission are not yet clear. But this latest policy plan vividly illustrates that European integration, although advanced in many respects, has not yet reached its final stage.

NOTES

I would like to thank William Vukowich and Markus Puder, Georgetown University Law Center, for their reviews of the manuscript.

1. For an exposition of this concept, see Winfried Brugger, *Concretization of Law and Statutory Interpretation*, 11 TUL. EUR. & CIV. L.F. 209 (1996); Winfried Brugger, *Verfassungsstabilitaet durch Verfassungsgerichtsbarkeit? Beobachtungen aus deutsch-amerikanischer Sicht*, 4 STAATSWISSENSCHAFTEN UND STAATSPRAXIS 319 (1993); WINFRIED BRUGGER, LIBERALISMUS, PLURALISMUS, KOMMUNITARISMUS ch. 2 (1999); Winfried Brugger, *Gemeinwohl als Ziel von Staat und Recht, in* STAAT, SOUVERAENITAET, VERFASSUNG. FESTSCHRIFT FUER HELMUT QUARITSCH 45 (Dietrich Murswiek et al. eds., 2000).

2. *See also* Winfried Brugger, *Gemeinwohl als Ziel von Staat und Recht an der Jahrtausendwende. Das Beispiel Europaeische Gemeinschaft, in* RECHT UND RECHTSWISSENSCHAFT. SIGNATUREN UND HERAUSFORDERUNGEN ZUM JAHRTAUSENDBEGINN. FESTSCHRIFT DER JURISTISCHEN FAKULTAET DER UNIVERSITAET HEIDELBERG 15 (Peter-

Christian Mueller-Graff and Herbert Roth eds.) (providing a more comprehensive, German-language version of this comment).

3. The provisions referenced in this article are governed by the Treaty Establishing the European Community (ECT), Mar. 25, 1957, O.J. (C 340/03) 173, as amended by the Treaty of Amsterdam amending the Treaty on European Union and the Treaties Establishing the European Communities (Treaty of Amsterdam), Oct. 2, 1997, O.J. (C340/01) 1 (1997) and by the Treaty on European Union (TEU), Feb. 7, 1992, O.J. (C340/02) 145, as amended by the Treaty of Amsterdam. In parentheses, reference is made to the articles of the ECT and TEU before the Amsterdam revisions, which either are identical in content to, or form the functional equivalent of, the new articles of the ECT and TEU.

4. Art. 226 *et seq.* ECT (formerly Art. 169 *et seq.*).

5. Art. 234 ECT (formerly Art. 177).

6. *See* ALEXANDER BICKEL, THE LEAST DANGEROUS BRANCH (1962) (applying this proverbial title to the judiciary).

7. *See* Art. 228 (2) ECT (formerly Art. 171 (2)).

8. *See* Art. 7 TEU.

9. *See* THOMAS OPPERMANN, EUROPARECHT 82–3, 212–13 (2d ed. 1999).

10. For a historical overview of European integration, *see* GEORGE A. BERMANN, ROGER J. GOEBEL, WILLIAM J. DAVEY, & ELEANOR M. FOX, CASES AND MATERIALS ON EUROPEAN COMMUNITY LAW, ch. 1 (1993).

11. *See* Art. 7 ECT (formerly Art. 4).

12. *See* Art. 230 ECT (formerly Art. 173).

13. Art. 231 ECT (formerly Art. 174).

14. Art. 233 ECT (formerly Art. 176).

15. *See* Arts. 232 and 234 ECT (formerly Arts. 175 and 177).

16. *See* Art. 46 TEU (enumerating the ECJ's areas of jurisdiction). While in the second pillar the ECJ exercises limited control, its jurisdiction is excluded in toto in the third pillar.

17. *See* OPPERMANN, *supra* note 9, at 152–3.

18. *See* OPPERMANN, *supra* note 9, at 102.

19. Certainty also helps reach means-end efficiency, an aspect of the third pillar of the common good, practicality.

20. *See* PHILIP SELZNICK, THE MORAL COMMONWEALTH: SOCIAL THEORY AND THE PROMISE OF COMMUNITY 50 (1992) ("The most striking feature of the ethos of positivism is a quest for determinacy. . . . The precise meaning, the operational indicator, the definite objective—these are watchwords of a positivist program").

21. 198 U.S. 45 (1905).

22. Federal Constitutional Court, Decision of 20 July 1954, 4 BVerfGE (Official Reports) 7 (1954). For the English translation, *see* DONALD KOMMERS, THE CONSTITUTIONAL JURISPRUDENCE OF THE FEDERAL REPUBLIC OF GERMANY 244 (2d ed. 1997).

23. Art. 4 (1) ECT (formerly Art. 3 (a) (1)).

24. Art. 98 ECT (formerly Art. 102 (a)).

25. The TEU preamble confirms the signatories' "attachment to fundamental social rights as defined in the European Social Charter . . . and the 1989 Community Charter of the Fundamental Social Rights of Workers."

26. *See* Part 3 Title XI ECT.

27. *See also* Art. 2 TEU (formerly Art. B) and ECT (formerly Art. 3 (b)).

28. Art. 3 (1) (c) ECT (formerly Art. 3 (c)).

29. *See* Art. 12 ECT (formerly Art. 6).

30. Art. 141 ECT (formerly Art. 119).

31. *See* Case 29/69, *Stauder v. City of Ulm*, Sozialamt, E.C.R. 419 (1969) (providing the leading case).

32. RALPH H. FOLSOM, EUROPEAN UNION LAW 71 (2d ed. 1995).

33. *See* Art. 6 (2) TEU (formerly Art. F (2)).

34. For the text of the Charter, see the Official Journal of the European Commission, 2000/C 364/01; and http://europa.eu.int/abc/cit1_en.htm.

35. Federal Constitutional Court, Decision of 29 May 1974, 37 BVerfGE (Official Reports) 271 (1974). For the English translation, *see* Decisions of the Bundesverfassungsgericht-FCC-Federal Republic of Germany, published by the members of the Court, vol. 1 I: *International Law and Law of the European Communities 1952–1989*, at 270 (no. 19).

36. Federal Constitutional Court, Decision of 22 October 1986, 73 BVerfGE (Official Reports) 339 (1986). For the English translation, *see* preceding note, vol. 1 II, at 613 (no. 35).

37. Federal Constitutional Court, Decision of 12 October 1993, 89 BVerfGE (Official Reports) 155 (1993). For excerpts in English, *see* KOMMERS, *supra* note 22, at 108, 182.

38. *See* Art. 249 *et seq.* ECT.

39. Prior to 1979, the Members of the EP were appointed by the national parliaments of the Member States. *See* OPPERMANN, *supra* note 9, at 19.

40. *See* Art. 1 (2) TEU and the Preamble of the ECT.

41. *See* Art. 17 TEU.

7

The United Kingdom Human Rights Act, 1998

Geoffrey Marshall

In 1998 the British Parliament enacted its Bill of Rights a mere three hundred years after its first experiment in rights legislation.[1] Since the Bill of Rights of 1689 was in its essentials an assertion of parliamentary rights against the Crown, rather than of the rights of citizens against Parliament, the current legislation is the United Kingdom's first attempt to give itself a bill of rights in the modern sense. The Human Rights Act's main features deserve examination in an international context since they raise some important general issues of constitutional engineering. One such issue is whether the provisions in a bill of rights should be fully justiciable and prevail over ordinary legislation, present and future. A second issue is whether rights legislation should be designed to protect citizens against governmental or public acts exclusively or whether they should directly or indirectly operate in a so-called horizontal fashion to impose obligations on other citizens and private bodies (and if so, what criteria are to be used to distinguish public from private bodies). A third issue is what rules should be adopted by (or imposed upon) the judiciary for interpreting statutes to which the new rights legislation is relevant and for assessing or reviewing the compatibility of such statutes with the Bill of Rights. Finally, can the content of these rules be prescribed conclusively by legislation, or is their determination an inherently judicial function? (Or is that just a superstition deriving from the separation of powers?)

The genesis of the United Kingdom Human Rights Act was in a Labour Party commitment to adopt or incorporate the European Convention on Human Rights into United Kingdom law. Prior to its enactment, the proposal was explained in a government White Paper, "Rights Brought Home"[2]—perhaps an imprudent title, since it prompts the question, "Where have our rights been all this time, and who was responsible for letting them get away from us in the first place?" The new legislation can for analytic purposes conveniently be placed in a tripartite ordering of Human Rights Acts. We might distinguish them as follows:

1. The Full-Blown Version. This is exemplified by the bills of rights that form part of the constitutions of the United States, Germany, Ireland, and South Africa. All legislation, whenever enacted, is subject to judicial invalidation if determined to be inconsistent with a provision of the Bill of Rights.
2. The Half-Loaf Version. The best example is Canada. All legislation enacted before the bill of rights (the Canadian Charter of Rights and Freedoms in the Constitution Act, 1982) is subject to invalidation, but all legislation enacted after the adoption of the Charter (with some exceptions) may have its validity preserved by the enactment by the federal or provincial legislatures of an express provision overriding the Charter rights.[3]
3. The Enfeebled Version. The New Zealand Bill of Rights of 1990[4] and now the United Kingdom Human Rights Act are examples. This version has been dubbed an "interpretive" measure. The courts may not strike down legislation, whether enacted before or after the enactment of the bill of rights, but may seek to give it, wherever possible, an interpretation that preserves rights.

Since British governments are ex officio disbelievers in bills of rights, they were glad to hear about the New Zealand enfeebled version and have faithfully reproduced its essential features.

"INCORPORATION" OF THE EUROPEAN HUMAN RIGHTS CONVENTION

The claim that the Human Rights Act incorporates the European Convention on Human Rights into United Kingdom law can be seen on inspection to be either a wilfull deception or a disingenuous misrepresentation. In fact, the Act does not incorporate the Convention, as the Lord Chancellor conceded very clearly in the debate in the House of Lords in November 1997. If it did, it would, on the normal rules of statutory construction, supersede existing law that was inconsistent with it—a result that the Human Rights Act is designed to prevent. The Lord Chancellor admitted that the Convention rights would not "become part of our domestic law."[5] But if the Convention rights are not part of the domestic law of the United Kingdom, it cannot be the case that they have been incorporated into it. It therefore constitutes a clear breach of the government's election manifesto commitment.

In this respect the crucial provision of the Act is section 3, which provides that the duty to interpret legislation in the light of Convention rights "does not affect the validity, continuing operation or enforcement of any incompatible primary legislation." The section is closely modeled on the comparable provision in the New Zealand Bill of Rights. Neither statute allows the judges to disregard or invalidate any statute whose meaning is clear and that is consistent with Convention rights. Thus the more blatantly an Act of Parliament violates human rights, the more clearly it is protected by the Human Rights Act. This is in the name of protecting parliamentary sovereignty. It has not previously been supposed, however, that there is any diminution of the sovereignty of Parliament in a statutory bill of rights that supersedes (being a later statute) earlier inconsistent legislation. But a bill of rights that is subservient to all legislation hardly deserves the name. Some of its supporters have said without shame that it is an ingenious and elegant compromise between the sovereignty principle and the rights principle. But sovereignty and rights are all-or-nothing principles, one of which must prevail. You might as well claim to have found an elegant compromise between chastity and fornication.

This seems a good point to mention the mystery of Article 13 of the European Convention on Human Rights. The Convention articles, if not exactly incorporated, are at least loosely attached in a schedule to the Human Rights Act, which says that the scheduled articles are "to have effect for the purposes of this Act." Article 13 is an important article. It guarantees to everyone an effective remedy before a national authority when their rights are infringed. A skeptic might argue that section 3, which prevents a court from giving an effective remedy when rights are infringed by unambiguous primary legislation, fails to provide litigants with such a remedy and is inconsistent with Article 13. That argument may indeed have been anticipated, since the Convention articles scheduled to the Act comprise Articles 2 to 12 and Article 14. The important thing about Article 13, like the dog that never barked in the night, is that there is no Article 13. It has gone missing. Why so? No convincing explanation is on offer. Moving shiftily from foot to foot, ministers have said that the whole Bill is intended to satisfy the requirements of Article 13. But if so, why be so keen not to acknowledge or reinforce that fact by including the Article? The Lord Chancellor had a different explanation—namely, that the inclusion of Article 13 might give the judges the idea that they could fashion some new form of remedy not foreseen by the Act.[6] So the suspicion lingers that the Article was omitted precisely to forestall the possibility that the courts might discern a clash between its guarantee and the provisions of section 3 and perhaps of some other central provisions of the Act. Disappointed litigants may indeed advance this argument before the Human Rights Court at Strasbourg.

THE PARLIAMENTARY-JUDICIAL DIALOGUE

In promoting the Human Rights Act the government has said that it introduces a dialogue between Parliament and the judges. That seems to leave out of account the citizen for whose benefit the legislation was enacted. Still it may give us a simple framework for outlining the processes envisaged by the Act. The dialogue begins with the parliamentary initiative outlined in section 19.

At this first stage the minister in charge of the bill makes a statement that, in his view, the provisions of the bill are compatible with the Convention rights. Alternatively, he may make a statement that he is unable to make such a statement. It is just possible that in that case someone may ask him why he is introducing legislation of so dubious a character. Various answers are possible here, such as "Well, you never can tell," or, "The Cabinet have decided to ram it through." None of this, of course, is part of the serious dialogue, which starts later. The minister does not, at this point, have to give his reasons one way or the other and, provided his statement is in writing, he can publish it in any way he thinks appropriate. Presumably he could put it in *Exchange and Mart* (a specialized newspaper) or announce it on breakfast television. A conceivable constitutional question may arise here as to whether these announcements are now for the human rights acts a mandatory part of the manner and form of legislation, which, if omitted, would allow the legislation to be judicially challenged. Probably not. So stage one seems a harmless form of entertainment and little more.

Stage two occurs when, in the course of litigation, or on an application for judicial review, a superior court makes a so-called declaration of incompatibility in the terms of section 4 of the Act—namely, that provision in a statute (or in some kinds of secondary legislation) is incompatible with a Convention right. Such a declaration is the nearest the courts may come to judicial review of legislation, but it does not affect the validity of challenged legislative provisions or provide litigants with any legal remedy. The position of secondary legislation (generally, administrative regulations but sometimes more than that) is incidentally somewhat obscure. In general, unlike primary legislation, it is subject to judicial review and invalidation for inconsistency with Convention rights.[7] But section 3 protects the validity of incompatible secondary legislation if primary legislation prevents removal of the incompatibility. What primary legislation must say to do this is unclear. Under section 6 of the Act it would be unlawful for a public authority to act in a way which is incompatible with a Convention right. But it would not be unlawful so to act either if primary legislation leaves the authority no choice ("if the authority could not have acted differently") or if the authority is acting to give effect to, or enforce, secondary legislation that is made under the terms of any incompatible primary legislation.

A litigant who appeals to the Convention and gains a declaration of incompatibility has clearly gained a pyrrhic victory. The court is telling him that his argument won the day. The legislation that he is challenging violates his rights and is incompatible with the Convention. Perhaps what the courts should tell him is that the provisions he is challenging are incompatible with the Convention and would have violated his rights if Parliament had not chosen to authorize the violation. But an authorized or lawful violation is a contradiction in terms, so perhaps the appropriate judicial conclusion should be that there has been a lawful deprivation or restriction of his rights by an exercise of legislative sovereignty. At any rate, the court has in these cases no remedy to offer other than its good wishes and the hope that the relevant minister will see him right.

This takes us into the final stage of the dialogue or dialectical process. In Marxist terms it can be seen perhaps as the synthesis or final stage of the dialectic, which moves the argument on to a higher, or at least a different, plane—in this case, Parliament. The declaration of incompatibility has been said to be, amongst other things, a trigger that precipitates parliamentary action. The Human Rights Act, in fact, speaks in section 10 of "remedial" action. Remedies certainly imply faults. Indeed, in the Lords' debate on the Bill, Lord Lester, the Founding Father—or, at any rate, father-in-law—of the legislation, said that every declaration of incompatibility will represent a systemic failure, in that our courts will be unable to provide a remedy, and inconsistencies will have to be remedied by Parliament under the fast-track remedial procedure.

There may be room for doubt, nevertheless, about the efficacy of the remedial trigger and the speed of remedial measures along the fast track. No one knows how many declarations of incompatibility there will be, or how long a queue of wronged litigants, suffering from systemic injustice, will be waiting in the sidings. Section 10 states that when a legislative provision has been declared to be incompatible with the Convention, a minister may by order make such amendments as he considers necessary to remove the incompatibility. But this action is dependent on a further requirement, namely that the minister must consider that there are compelling reasons for proceeding. So it is open to the minister to find that some systemically damaged litigants' claims are less than compelling. Conceivably the minister may disagree with the decision of the court. Or the members of his party may disagree and be reluctant to vote for an amending order. Or the minister may think that there are more pressing demands on parliamentary time. So the dialogue between courts and Parliament—which in reality is a dialogue between courts and party politicians—will not necessarily have a happy ending or lead to the withering away of perceived injustice. The outcome will depend upon whips and partisan majorities, as it did before we had a Human Rights Act. Justice under the remedial procedures is dependent on the good will of politicians who have been responsible for the injustice in the first place. So the declaration of incompatibility may be not so much an elegant device for securing rights as a clumsy recipe for provoking disenchantment.

PUBLIC AND PRIVATE BODIES

We are told that the judiciary, or selected portions of it, are being limbered up by the provision of appropriate training courses in preparation for the coming human rights regime. They will certainly need some help in sorting out the various puzzles to be found in the wording of the Act. One such puzzle is the intended scope of the legislation. The effects on administrative law will be potentially far-reaching since a new head of illegality has been created by the obligation on all public authorities, imposed by section 6, to conform their actions to the requirements of the Convention rights. But, as in Canada and New Zealand, the Act does not on its face create new causes of action against private persons. So the difference between public and private bodies is of some importance. But what is it? Parliament, for example, sounds like a public authority, but the Act decrees that it is not. The Scottish and Welsh assemblies sound like public bodies, and indeed they are (their legislative output being secondary and not primary legislation). Courts and tribunals (whatever they are) are also public authorities. For general guidance on the nature of public authorities, one must look to section 6(3) and 6(5) of the Act. That section tells us that a public authority includes any person "certain of whose functions are functions of a public nature." But if such a body or person acts in a nonpublic way, his, her, or its acts will not be public. Subsection 5 determines the circumstances in which this will be so by telling us that in these circumstances a public authority will not be a public authority when the nature of the act in question is private.

In the House of Lords some fears were expressed about the vagueness of the public-private distinction. One peer said that Safeway stores were exercising a public function because they dealt with members of the public, and another peer put down an amendment, later happily withdrawn, to define a public authority as any person concerned with the provision to the public, whether for payment or otherwise, of any goods, services, or facilities—a provision that would have made any streetwalker or pizza seller a public authority. In the end it may be that private persons will find their obligations affected by Convention rights, since the inclusion of courts and tribunals as public authorities who must conform their conduct to the Convention is thought by some to mean that, in developing the common law in actions between private persons, courts must take account of Convention rights. The extent of such "horizontal" effects of the Human Rights Act is a major source of indeterminacy that is likely to present some tricky discussion topics for the judicial training sessions.

THE "INTERPRETIVE" OBLIGATION

Of all the provisions of the Act, section 3(1) is the most puzzling. It provides that, "So far as it is possible to do so, primary legislation and subordinate legislation must be read and given effect in a way which is compatible with the Convention rights." This injunction is deeply obscure and can be variously understood. Reading and giving effect to a statute in the context of human rights legislation arguably relates to two separate enquiries, one of which should be prior to the other. In the first place, it is always necessary to decide what the statutory words as enacted mean. In some circumstances it may then be necessary to assess or characterize the statutory provision in the light of the limitations imposed by the relevant human rights provisions—that is, to decide whether the statute can be given effect and stand alongside them or whether it infringes or is incompatible with them. The most obvious way in which a statue can be given effect compatibly with a constitutional limitation is by way of a judicial holding that it does not infringe but can be characterized as a proper limitation on or valid restriction of the individual right in question (especially where it can be held to fall within specific limitations or exceptions set out in the rights provisions themselves). If, therefore, judges strive to obey the injunction in section 3 when considering whether to make a declaration of incompatibility, it would seem that they should endeavor, wherever possible, to find that legislation that is challenged as an infringement of a Convention right that cannot be given effect compatibly with it is, on a proper construction, a legitimate limitation compatible with the right. The litigant in such circumstances will fail to gain a declaration of incompatibility. So the more faithfully the courts follow the instructions of section 3 to find that legislation is compatible with the Convention, the more unsuccessful human rights claimants there will be (since successful applicants for a judicial declaration under section 4 have to show that the primary or secondary legislation they are challenging is incompatible). This is clearly not the "compatibility" situation envisaged by the human rights legislation's proponents. What they have in mind is that courts should avoid the necessity to consider the question of constitutional compatibility by reinterpretation of apparently inconsistent statutes. They see section 3 as urging the courts to protect individual rights by reading down or rereading legislation so as to remove any meaning that would prejudice the relevant rights claim.

In a public lecture Lord Irvine, the Lord Chancellor, commended European techniques of interpretation as adaptable to the human rights regime. Interpretive techniques might be used, he said, to make the domestic legislation comply with community law, even where this required straining the meaning of words, or "reading in words which are not there."[8] If, in order to make a claim under the Convention prevail it is regarded as permissible to read words in or out of statutes, then the normal rules of statutory construction are being crudely abandoned.

Of course, "possibility" is a broad category. In some sense or other anything is possible. But there is nothing in section 3 of the Human Rights Act to provide parliamentary authority for a radical change in the rules of statutory interpretation. In this respect, the Act differs from the European Communities Act of 1972. It may well be argued that that legislation authorizes a presumption that Parliament intends its legislation in all cases to be consistent with community law, so that a court may legitimately appeal to that evident legislative purpose. But in the case of the Human Rights Act, whose provisions are differently drawn, and which expressly preserves the right to legislate inconsistently with the European Convention rights, the only legislative purpose or intention that can be attributed to Parliament is that it intends its legislation to conform to the Convention unless it decides that it should not. Where the issue is whether in a particular case Parliament has so decided, the appeal to legislative purpose is empty. There are, of course, many who say that where human rights instruments are concerned, interpretation should be guided by principles that are large, broad, liberal, or generous. But this encourages a dangerous tendency. As Lord Hoffman remarked in a recent Privy Council appeal, "If the language used by the lawgiver is ignored in favour of a general resort to 'values' the result is not interpretation but divination."[9] It is symptomatic of the confusion of principles in the 1998 Human Rights Act that its proponents—who, in the supposed interest of preserving the sovereignty of Parliament, stubbornly refused to allow the judges to apply the Convention rights directly and straightforwardly—should be happy to encourage them to subvert the intentions of the legislature by a process of judicial massage or sleight of hand.

To sum it up, one can see the Human Rights Act as combining a confused attachment to parliamentary sovereignty with a dangerous lack of concern for the integrity of the judicial function. If one adds that it suffers also from vagueness, obscurity, and unclarity of purpose, we are forced to the conclusion that, of all the bills of rights we might have hoped for, this is not one that makes the best of all provisions in the best of all possible worlds. Even Dr. Pangloss would have found it a disappointment.

NOTES

1. Human Rights Act, 1998, c. 42 (Eng.).
2. Rights Brought Home: The Human Rights Bill, 1997, Cm. 3782.
3. Can. Const. (Constitution Act, 1982) pt. I (Canadian Charter of Rights and Freedoms).
4. Bill of Rights Act, 1990 (N.Z.).
5. PARL. DEB., H.L., Committee Stage, November 18, 1997, col. 508–9.
6. PARL. DEB., H.L., November 18, 1997, col. 475.
7. [Editorial note: The phrase "secondary legislation" here refers to what in the United States would be called "regulations".]
8. Lord Chancellor Irvine, The Development of Human Rights in Britain Under an Incorporated Convention on Human Rights, Keynote Address to the Solicitors' Annual Conference (The Tom Sargant Memorial Lecture) (Dec. 16, 1997), [1998] Public Law 221, at 228.
9. *Matadeen v. Pointu*, Minister of Education and Science, [1999] 1 AC 98, [1998] 3 WLR 18 (quoting Kentridge AJ in *State v. Zuma*, 1995 (4) BCLR 401, 412).

8

Judicial Systems: Challenges for the Twenty-First Century

Roberto G. MacLean

He chose capable men. . . . They served as judges for the people at all times. The difficult cases they brought to Moses, but the simple ones they decided themselves.

Exodus 18:25–26

I. INTRODUCTION

The World is filled with light!

—Mevlana Jalaluddin Rumi, Sufi Poet XIII Century

It is not the sound of victory, it is not the sound of defeat, it is the sound of singing that I hear.

—Exodus 32:18

At the beginning of the twenty-first century, the world is moving at an increasing pace toward the goal of a global community. Trade, finance, investment, multinational organizations, and, unfortunately, even crime has become global. Lawyers have reacted to this stimulating phenomenon through individual research and the work of entities like United Nations Organization (UNO), Human Rights Watch, and Amnesty International (in developing the fields of human rights and international crimes), or United Nations Commission on International Trade Law (UNCITRAL), International Criminal Court (ICC), or International Institute for the Unification of Private Law (UNIDROIT) (in developing a growing body of uniform laws or uses and customs in subjects like international sales, bills of lading, air transport, and money transfers). Some global mechanisms to solve disputes arising from these globalization developments have been created by the World Trade Organization (WTO), the North American Free Trade Agreement (NAFTA), Personal Communications Industry Association (PCIA), and the Andean Community, among others; but still the substantial body of conflicts, and even international conflicts, in the world is dealt with in national judicial systems.

The problem with a growing body of uniform laws applied by national judicial systems around the world is that the differences in quality and efficiency of courts of law, and even of legal systems, is so staggering that multinational organizations like the World Bank, the United Nations, the Inter-American Development Bank, the European Union, government agencies for foreign aid like the United States Agency for International Development (USAID), and countless national governments have stepped in with programs of reform to shape up judicial systems to meet the challenges of globalization in the twenty-first century and to promote democracy and respect for human rights. In a global community struggling to achieve better levels in quality of life, freedom, comfort, self-realization, and, ultimately, happiness, it is not much good if judicial systems work well in New Zealand, Norway, France, or the United States but at the same time the judicial systems in Peru, Indonesia, Russia, and Albania create serious concerns.

Globalization demands not only a comparative approach to the old and the new problems, but also a comparative approach that goes beyond the traditional comparisons of context, sources of information, sources of the law, language and terminology; categories and classifications; and reasoning processes. This approach submerges into, and looks for the common denominators in, the elementary and essential needs of communities around the world while respecting differences and allowing room for unavoidable contrasts. That is the bounty that can be retrieved by experiencing the successes and shortcomings of the projects of the World Bank. The success of these activities depends on far more than the name we put on the project. Success depends, first of all, on what standards we fix to measure progress or achievement; second, on the methodology we adopt to accomplish real progress, not merely to fix bureaucratic and formalistic landmarks; third, on how successful we are in involving judges in the process, so that they assume their responsibility as leaders; and fourth, on how well we develop and grow a sense of duty, responsibility, and solidarity beyond the pure formalities of behavior and beyond political boundaries.

We have to face that almost anything can go under the heading of judicial reform projects: from buying computers, photocopiers, and faxes to increasing salaries and building new courtrooms; from changing laws of procedures to training judges. And yet these projects might be undertaken and still change nothing. What is required is that the minimum standards of valid field projects and academic studies be articulated. Otherwise, certain common concepts like independence, efficiency, effectiveness, access, honesty, impartiality, promptness, fluidity, due process, and fairness can take on some unreal tones when contrasted with the bizarre realities found in some countries. The question is which standards we use to measure progress and accomplishment.

II. THE STANDARD OF SOCIAL EFFICIENCY OF LAWS

> The law is only a shadow . . . not the realities themselves.
>
> —St. Paul, Hebrews 10:1

> Like love we don't know where or why,
> Like love we can not compel or fly,
> Like love we often weep,
> Like love we seldom keep
>
> W. H. Auden, *Law like love*

A. The Social Efficiency of Laws

One feature of developing countries and economies in transition around the world is the gap between laws as they are enacted and the way in which communities conduct their daily political, economic, and social affairs. To perform their role of solving disputes in society, judges are restricted to acting within the frame of possibilities set up by laws. But at the same time, laws are the tools with which judges are to face the challenges of our time and place. One of the main challenges that judges have to confront, especially in developing countries and economies in transition, is that of the social efficiency of laws. When 10 percent of the population of a country disobeys or ignores a law, it is a problem of law enforcement. But if the group that disobeys the law comprises 40 or 50 percent of the population, then the problem is one of social efficiency of the law and cannot be solved by police action and sanctions of the courts alone. The latter situation represents the biggest challenge that legal systems face in the third millennium. Authoritarian and elitist legal systems and governments have nourished a culture of indifference and skepticism about the law in the developing world, where the general belief is that nothing can be changed except by paternalistic gift from the government or by the use of physical force and violence. Thus, laws are obeyed formalistically, but important sectors of the population try to circumvent their real objectives by breaking their monolithic rationality with either inertia or corruption. This syndrome, although deeply rooted in many parts of Latin America, is by no means limited to it. Nations in Asia and Africa are also suffering from the same symptoms, as are many Central and Eastern European countries that are in transition from state-run economies to competitive and open markets.

In most of Latin America, as in many nations of Asia and Africa, when it becomes necessary to write a new law, the main difficulty is usually that there is not enough information about the subject requiring legislation. If a legislator does not have enough information about the facts of the matter to effectively legislate, then a foreign law, a uniform model law, or even an international treaty can become quite a convenient source from which to draw inspiration.

As a result of this practice, many developing countries have the best laws that money can buy. As one Belgian professor puts it, referring to the laws of civil procedure: "the best civil procedural codes in the world are in Latin America." During the debates in the United States about the signing of NAFTA, when those who opposed the treaty claimed that Mexico did not pay as much attention to the environment as it should, proponents answered that Mexican laws on the environment were, perhaps, even more complete than those of the United States. The same is true with civil and commercial codes, antitrust laws, constitutions, by-laws governing the functioning of restaurants, and many other regulations. And yet, in all of these examples, there is something that is not working; there is a spark of life that has not been summoned.

The purpose of this section of the chapter is to explore some aspects of this phenomenon, as perceived mainly from the Latin American experience; to reaffirm how this experience coincides with others observed in other parts of the world; to identify what, if any, is the common denominator to all of them that should not be taken for granted and bypassed by governments, law reformers, and international institutions; and to explore their impact in the economy and political system of a country.

B. The Natural Limits of Power

Laws enacted in the way we have mentioned are, without a doubt, acts of authority and, as such, have behind them all the coercive and sanctioning strength of the police force and the courts of law, but little else. They lack the respect and the observance of the community. If they have any life in them, it is by chance or coincidence and not by any conscious and deliberate effort of drafters or legislators. However, laws, like languages, are not only the rules or the words, but also what those rules or words are intended to convey, and without which they have very little, if any, meaning at all. What laws are trying to convey is the social compromise between two or more existing interests in conflict: providers and users, buyers and sellers, landlords and tenants, employers and workers, citizens and the state. In a functioning democracy, laws are the expressions or records of these compromises. They may last for centuries, as is the case with the American Constitution; or nearly as long, as the Napoleonic Code; or only for a short time, as the Exchange Control regulations or landlord and tenant laws in some countries. Laws are good or bad to the degree to which they adequately reflect real conflicts and draw an equilibrium into society. To legislate without that in mind, by a pure act of authority, is as blind an act as is a doctor prescribing a medicine to a patient without a previous exam and based on what a sibling took in a similar case, or as an engineer building a bridge without taking the measure of the span and simply being guided by a more or less similar bridge. We should not be surprised if the result is not what we expected and, of course, does not work efficiently.

Nevertheless, it is still possible to go a long way with pure acts of authority. Criminal law is one example. In Latin America, during the authoritarian and dictatorial regimes of General Pinochet in Chile and General Stroessner in Paraguay, order prevailed and crime was reduced to an impressive extent. Chile and Paraguay were then very safe countries as long as you did not disagree with the government.

But pure power has its limits, even in the field of criminal law. In the upper Huallaga Valley, in Peru, around 17,000 soldiers and policemen, with support from the air force, have not been able to curtail significantly, in more than ten years, the growing of coca, the production of the basic paste of cocaine, or its export to Colombia for refinement. Even in such a great world power as the United States, the laws prohibiting the sale and consumption of alcohol could not be effectively enforced. The problem is as critical in commercial and civil law. In Lima, Peru, in public transport, strong leftist military governments, powerful right-wing regimes, and civilian centrist governments have not been able to impose the use of meters by taxi drivers in spite of repeated announcements by each of these governments that they would do so in a short time. And in Mexico City; Rio de Janeiro, Brazil; Lima, Peru; Caracas, Venezuela; and, to a lesser extent, Santiago de Chile, Chile, and Buenos Aires, Argentina, there are extensive housing developments, most of them really shanty towns, completely outside of the regulations and procedures established by official laws and the Civil Code. The answer to the question of social efficiency of laws has to be somewhere else. What does make a law work? What are the qualities that make a good law?

C. The Model of What a Law Should Be

Drafters, legislators, and commentators frequently take for granted, and consciously or unconsciously skip, the question of what a good law is or should be. Looking at many examples of legislation in Latin America, one is tempted to think, sometimes, that the objective of laws is not to regulate real life, but to be a pure act of authority and power to be taught rationally at law schools. That is how perfectly drafted they are.

When we visit a country and talk to lawyers, law professors, jurists, and even judges, we can listen to one perception of the legal system. But if we talk to entrepreneurs, businessmen, human rights workers, trade union leaders, housewives, mechanics, or butchers, we get quite a different version. Several writers have pointed out this contrast and the varied reactions of society to the artificiality of laws interwoven in a political and economic system of privileges and discriminations.[1] We tend to think of laws as intellectual and academic pieces of work, not as social tools, and we say that laws should be simple, clear, predictable, transparent, equally applicable to everybody, accessible, implementable, and enforceable.[2] And so they should be, because all of this definitely helps our task. But it is not enough to make a law work and make it socially efficient.

D. Laws as Compromises of Interests in Conflict

What makes a law work, the life and heartbeat that are to be found in laws, consists essentially of the conflicting interests it assembles in a workable whole. Its architecture is that of the structure and organization of ambitions, fears, hopes, toils, weaknesses, virtues, and vices into a free and livable environment. In modern societies, these compromises are made with the participation of bodies in which other interests that may be affected are also represented. Besides the interests of landlords and tenants, for example, the overall interests of the community are also taken into consideration and, in some cases, may influence the final outcome. Usually laws are compromises that represent the situation that conflicting interests have reached in their relation at a given time and a given place. There is nothing static or universal about it, although drafters try, and can achieve, a certain degree of generality and permanence in order to embrace the multitude of possibilities that the simplest of statements may involve, especially in a changing environment. That is what a good law is.

What drafters and legislators usually do in many countries is to resort to the best-reputed foreign legal models and adapt them without understanding very well how or why they work successfully in their countries of origin and taking them out of their natural context. For example, the political success of the American Constitution does not lie, even mainly, in how well it was drafted or the language in which it was written, but in how well it represents the interests of the federal government, the states, and the individual and how well it balances the different perspectives of the relationship. It reflects the reality of political development and practice in the United States of America with its virtues and shortcomings. When that Constitution is taken out of its habitat, it ceases to be alive and it becomes literature. Legislators in Latin America, as well as in other societies in transition in other parts of the world, take what is seemingly the easiest and most expeditious way to legislate, and in the process lose perspective of what they are really doing and the reasons for which laws need to be enacted.

When a foreign element is introduced in a relationship, sometimes it may fit well into the whole. All languages—and, for that matter, all legal systems—have been importantly enriched that way. It can be a healthy process in order to become inserted into a wider international and global perspective. But even then we cannot afford to lose sight of the fact that the only meaning that a law has is as a compromise between real and representative interests in a community. Outside of that context, law has no significant meaning at all, except, perhaps, as a subject of academic study or erudite knowledge. If the foreign component helps to articulate an existing situation or describe an intricate relationship taken from reality, it should by all means be used, provided that, as with a wild animal, we keep it fastened close, in this case, to real life. Now, how do we achieve this in changing and uneven societies? To keep rules close to life implies that we understand the particular segments of life that we are trying to put in order, for the purpose of making exchanges and intercourses easier. The way we understand things depends to a great extent in how accurately we perceive them through the information we receive.

E. Public Opinion as the Foundation of Social Efficiency

The essence of law, as of language, is not the rules or the words, but what those rules or words are trying to convey—without that they have little or no meaning. It is not possible to change the rules or meanings of a language or word without the consent or acceptance of those who speak it. That is why in authoritarian and elitist societies, where the law is considered as a pure act of authority and power, the law commands so little respect, and I do not mean by criminals and outlaws, but by those who are otherwise decent, hard working, honest, and respectable individuals. The social efficiency of a law, as of a word or phrase, depends on its observance or use by an immense majority of the members of a community.

Why are Bolivar and San Martin such important figures in the Latin American pantheon, when other "successful" leaders like the Somozas or Duvaliers are not? The difference is that Bolivar and San Martin represented not only high personal qualities and virtues, but also carried the mainstream of the public opinion of their time. It is informed public opinion that ultimately legitimizes a political or legal action.

Language and laws are social tools: one to communicate with each other and the other to live together in order and peace. So their value is not in their beauty or excellence, but in their being useful, in their acceptance and observance by the community, and in their use not by the elites, but by the overwhelming majority of ordinary people. For both of them—law and language—to have any meaning and use, they must be full not only, or even mainly, of ideas and concepts—not of logic, as Justice Holmes said—but also of life.[3]

F. The Shaping of Opinion: Access to Information

Access to information plays a central role in the way we perceive things and, consequently, in shaping public opinion. But in most developing countries at least two obstacles are almost invariably found: the absence of adequate information and, even when that information exists, the unwillingness of those in government who have it to share it with the rest.

Drafters and legislators face an almost impossible task: trying to draw, blindfolded, a three-dimensional chart of the geography of a problem-fixing boundaries, assigning rights and obligations, and inventing a whole plot. At its best these efforts are an amazing feat of pure imagination. At its worst, as is frequently the case, they are a prelude to social fracture and miscommunication, frustration, and error.

The other side of the problem is that, probably on account of these deficiencies, governments and government officials become very secretive about the process of decision-making and very defensive about providing the little information they have. In most Latin American countries there is no equivalent to the Freedom of Information Act of the Unites States by which any citizen can obtain information about any public document. Ordinary citizens take no part in decision-making and do not understand how decisions are reached or how laws are passed. Consequently, citizens cannot criticize what they do not understand.

G. The Shaping of Opinion: Alternative Sources of Information

If adequate information about a problem reached the citizenry, discussions could take place among those with different tendencies of opinion. But the problem, as we have seen, is that information does not reach the citizens, or even drafters and legislators. Such information lacking, the second best option seems to be to listen to the testimony of the stakeholders, of those affected in one way or another by the piece of legislation under consideration, so as to learn what is happening to the different actors. Unfortunately, this almost never happens. New laws and regulations are issued profusely by executive branches and parliaments, and very little attention is paid to alternative sources of information like these.

1. Legislation Issued by the Executive Branch

By far, the largest proportion of legislation in most countries is issued by the executive. In developing countries, this is usually the governmental body most removed from public participation. In a personal interview held some years ago, a Minister of Industry and Trade in a South American country candidly confessed that his ministry lacked information about the problem, but that he had consulted some of his friends for advice. These friends, who knew a great deal about the problem, were all local tire manufacturers. The Federation of Truck Drivers had not been consulted, nor had the Association of Car Assembly Plants, not to mention others. It is easy to imagine how they feel about a legal system that deals with their interests so lightheartedly and what respect and observance they feel those rules might deserve from them.

In another South American country, the government issued a regulation for the functioning of restaurants. There was actually nothing wrong with the rules themselves, except that of the thousands of restaurants that the country has, no more than twenty would have been capable of complying with them. The regulation seemed to be one issued for Switzerland, Japan, or Norway, because it had not taken the least consideration into what the diverse groups affected thought. It is also easy to imagine what all those affected might think about that rule.

There is, however, a sign that things might begin to change. In Peru, a private think tank, Institute for Liberty and Democracy (ILD), has been sponsoring since the early 1980s a process of democratization of decision-making by the executive through consultations and hearings. Entities were created and commissioners were appointed, but, at the last crucial moment, three different governments got cold feet, and the attempts failed. In Mexico, however, as a result of NAFTA, a rule was introduced[4] by which any new rule affecting industrial standards to be issued has to be prepublished in order to allow those affected—directly or indirectly—to offer their opinions and suggestions. In those cases, the attitude is going to be quite different toward the regulation.

2. *Legislation Issued by Parliaments*

Legislatures are not much better in this respect. Bills are prepared and discussed in committees that very rarely invite interested parties to full hearings. Lobbying is considered to be an almost secret and illegal activity, resulting in only those with connections being heard. It is interesting to examine the minutes of the committees that draft and approve important pieces of legislation, like codes or organic laws, and to see what have been the sources of information on what is really happening in the community. Most of the sources are academic writings or foreign models. Very rarely are the opinions of interest groups cited. It is not uncommon that whole parts of civil codes, and even constitutions, are not put into practice for years and are mostly decorative. The difference between law and reality, in many areas of the law, is already an accepted feature of Latin American legal and civic culture. Nobody turns head at it, particularly lawyers. The ones who raise their voices are usually economists, sociologists, anthropologists, and representatives of nongovernmental organizations (NGOs).

H. The Shaping of Opinion: Debates About Perceptions and Options

Even if information reaches its targets, that is not enough to have an informed opinion. Very frequently the same data can be interpreted in different ways according to the particular perspectives from which it is examined, analyzed, and judged. It is important to provide opportunities to oppose and discuss the different possible solutions. Consider the question of whether to impose a prohibition on importing foreign car and truck tires. It would be important to counterbalance the interests of tire manufacturers, drivers' associations, assembly plants, rubber planters, and peasants' unions and also the opinion of economists and planners as to the overall cost to the community of the measure proposed. All sectors must be heard and all possibilities discussed. For that purpose, there must be a functional freedom of assembly and a reasonable and acceptable freedom of the press. Meetings and written debates must take place openly in order to identify if not a consensus, at least a mainstream opinion. These debates will provide an amazing richness of information about reality, an extraordinary creativity in solutions, and an enthusiastic civic involvement and commitment to the solutions. As an additional bonus, it is a school and training ground in leadership and social responsibility.

I. Transparency in Decision-Making

In order to create an effective process in decision-making, all steps from the assembling of necessary information to the last stages of producing the norm have to be absolutely transparent. This involves a summary presentation of the relevant facts and the reasons to issue the norm, the findings of the hearings, the different options available, and the reason or reasons to choose the one enacted. This apparently basic and simple set of principles very often presents a gigantic obstacle to those who have to work with legal rules in most of the developing world. Frequently legislators are not interested in explaining the reasons behind a norm. Also, legislators frequently do not want to assume full individual responsibility for what they do, and hide behind an anonymous consent because it is common in developing countries that the votes in the legislatures are not individually recorded. As a consequence, legislators are not even politically accountable.

J. The Effects of the Social Inefficiency of Laws

When laws do not meet the expectations of those interested, several things happen. First, people gradually begin to become skeptical about laws, indifferent to their mandates, and disrespectful in their observance. When this practice persists for a long time, those feelings become part of a culture, a way of living in which citizens no longer ask "who" or "how." The condition is simply there, and that is how it is. The result of this situation is the loss of prestige of legal and judicial systems; they become useless, irrelevant, and purely formalistic. The second consequence is that, since the official legal system is useless, society develops alternate rules that govern the true and real conflict of interests that exists. Some years ago, Keith Rosenn, in his already classic article on the Brazilian "Jeito," showed how society begins to cope with these situations.[5] Kenneth Karst[6] and Rogelio Pérez Perdomo[7] did something similar for Venezuela, and, in perhaps the most exhaustive and analytical book on the subject, Hernando de Soto unveiled the rich experience of the Peruvian "informal" economy.[8] Thus, a form of Latin American common law is developing under a decaying body of many socially inefficient laws. To make the picture more complicated, Latin American judges do not know what to do with this situation: whether to ignore the socially inefficient laws and apply the living rules or to adhere firmly to the official laws and ignore what is happening around them. All of these are causes of duplication and unnecessary cost, effort, and delay.

The problem is that the "official" laws do work efficiently sometimes and are observed by the elites, but they keep large majorities of the population unrecognized and outside the system. The paradox of it all is that, at a time in which Marxism is waning in the world, its doctrine about law as an instrument of domination fits surprisingly well into the situation of how legal systems still work in many places on the continent. All of this contributes to the existing big differences in income and opportunities and to a feeling of social injustice and unfair deprivation. Cuba, Guatemala, Peru, and Bolivia are examples of countries where violent revolutions, civil war, or terrorism developed out of this situation. It is surprising, under the circumstances, that these movements did not succeed, except in Cuba, and propagate to other countries. And all of this can also be applied to many countries in Eastern and Central Europe, Asia, and Africa.

K. The Role of Public Opinion in Law-Making

There are two ways in which this critical gap between legislation and reality can be solved. The first one is the absorption by law-makers of the prevalent opinions of those concerned or affected by the proposed norm. Surveys, interviews, hearings, and discussions should be encouraged as a way of supplementing the existing deficiencies. No one will know better than these people the true nature of problems. Promoting active participation will lead to the following advantages:

a. legislators will call the attention of the community to the importance of proposed legislation by informing the public about the purposes and objectives of the norm;
b. legislators will hear the true nature of the situation as it actually is in the respective field from the different actors directly affected and holding different perspectives of the problem;
c. legislators will have the opportunity to listen to suggestions coming from those involved, rather than from intermediaries with secondhand knowledge who may fall into the temptation of being unrealistic, utopian, and academic;
d. the process will encourage civic duty to participate in the analysis, discussion, and solution of problems and promote commitment from civil society;
e. legislators will gain as allies those participants who feel that they are part of the solution and that the new law belongs to them, breaking in this way the traditional indifference toward rules; and
f. legislatures will legitimize the whole process by promoting participation and transparency.

Only then can all the technicalities, logical structures, clear language, conciseness, precision, and other qualities achieve a meaning, become socially effective, and create a fluent two-way relationship between law-makers and citizens. Only then can laws become living expressions of what is actually happening in society: the conflicts, the issues, and the compromises.

But, as Portia says in *The Merchant of Venice*: "If to do were as easy as to know what were good to do, chapels had been churches, and poor men's cottages prince's palaces." Governments and officials are not always happy to provide access to information. Law-makers are not always happy to share with other citizens the prerogative of exercising the authority to make rules. Law-makers are not always happy to discuss publicly the different options available when facing a particular problem. Therefore, before going much further in any process of law reform it is necessary:

a. to ensure that all interested parties have access to available information;
b. to ensure that all interested parties have the opportunity to give their opinion and make their suggestions for the law;
c. to enure that there is the opportunity to publicly discuss the different opinions, suggestions, and options;
d. to ensure that there is enough transparency in the process resulting in the final outcome.

The second way of filling the gap between law and reality involves judges. It is necessary for them to understand that the service they provide for society is not the intellectual and academic interpretation of the laws, but the solving of social, political, and economic conflicts. The purpose of laws is to create a framework to solve those problems efficiently, and judges must fulfill, within that framework, the same function in individual cases. Judges, therefore, must not be automatic bureaucrats, but leaders in defusing conflicts, experts in crisis resolution, and promoters of dialogs and understanding.

L. How All of This Affects Political and Economic Development

The main and more lasting effects of the social inefficiency of laws are the loss of credibility in the legal system that it generates, the distrust and skepticism that it causes about its application and enforcement, and the indifference it produces in the citizens about their own power to influence events in public life. These conditions affect the working of democracy, the possibility of planning future business and investments, the predictability of the outcomes of possible disputes, the reliance on a judicial system to protect the individual against the state or large economic interests, and the confidence that government is free from corruption and abuses of power.

M. The Role of Judges in Making Laws Socially Efficient

But all of this is not enough, because, in spite of our best efforts, reality is richer in possibilities than the abstraction of a general rule can cover; and, for the reasons mentioned above, this is even more true in developing societies or societies in transition. So the endeavors of legislators have to be coupled with the assumption by judges of their full powers in order to keep laws alive by filling the interstices, ambiguities, and ambivalences of the law with the social, political, ethical, personal, and economic values held by the public of our time.[9] Judges could not be replaced by computers for the automatic application of statutes. Judges are not to merely repeat the text of the law. They make numerous decisions that involve value judgments every day. But those values must not be their personal ones only, and sometimes judges must even set apart their individual values when they are not representative of the system of values held by the community.[10] The role of judges in society is to defend the set of values held by society at a particular time and place within the framework of possibilities established by the law and to make easy the process of transition when it is necessary.

III. THE STANDARD OF JUSTICE AS A SERVICE

> We must look at the past with infinite gratitude,
> We must look at the present with infinite service,
> We must look at the future with infinite responsibility.
>
> —Zen-Buddhist saying

A. Introduction

Pedro Sanchez, a small garage owner in a South American country, is turned down by a bank when he asks for a loan backed by a mortgage on his business. The chairman of the Bank Association in that country, in an interview, explains that the judicial process to recover a debt, even with a mortgage, is so lengthy, expensive, and complicated that bank directors have adopted the policy of making loans only within a small circle of trustworthy friends and relatives. "We do this," he says, "despite our interest in making loans to every reasonable and interesting operation that is presented to us. In that way both the borrower and the bank could grow. But we can't because of the inefficient judicial system."

Fredericka Koychevska, a young technician starting a small enterprise in a Central European country, wants to purchase insurance to protect herself and her family from unexpected hazards. The insurance company's premium is so forbiddingly high that she has to give up on the idea. The president of the company, when interviewed, complains that his business is not growing because he cannot reduce the costs of premiums due to the high legal costs and length of time his company has to spend collecting damages from the parties responsible.

In Southeast Asia, Sarv Macaya has been looking unsuccessfully for a modest job for more than a year in order to pay for his studies and get married. The president of a U.S. company doing business in that country explains in a regional seminar that his company would like to increase investment by at least 50 percent, which would create more jobs as well as profits. However, an unreliable, ineffective, and inefficient judiciary in that country prevents the company from doing so. As the company president further explains, "without an effective judiciary, companies are unable to adequately enforce contracts, protect property, and recover debts and damages."

As these examples illustrate, an inefficient judiciary has enormous impact on most of our daily lives, expectations, and hopes for change and social justice; however, this impact is often not perceived by ordinary citizens or understood even by lawyers. Fortunately, this "invisible" impact has been highlighted by economists like Douglass North and de Soto, who have shown that economic growth, trade, investment, transaction costs, and the distribution of wealth are closely linked to the environment created by the legal system and its institutions.[11] The recognition of this link is what led the World Bank, decades back, to propose the establishment of the International Centre for Settlement of Investment Disputes (ICSID) as an alternative to the national courts for the solution of investment disputes. More recently, the World Bank has turned to the domestic sphere, establishing a program to support legal and judicial reform in Latin America, Asia, Africa, and Central and Eastern Europe.

The main purpose of this more-recent program is to achieve social change and growth, increase investment and trade, reduce poverty, and eliminate corruption through an adequate, efficient, and effective mechanism for the solution of social conflicts.[12] The challenge is that this has to be achieved at a time when many countries are going through a period of transition from closed to open societies and from planned, state-run economies to free market economies where great majorities are beginning to have access to property, markets, and effective political power.

The basic ideas from which the World Bank starts the development of its strategy and methodology are as follows: First, the administration of justice is essentially a service, delivered by the state to the community in order to keep social peace and facilitate economic development through the resolution of disputes. The final beneficiary, therefore, is not the judge, but the citizen. The purpose of reform is to enable the judiciary to better serve the citizen and economic agents in society.

Second, there is a major obstacle to judicial reform, which is the gap, prevalent in most developing countries, between the law as it is enacted and the ways in which society and the economy behave. Of all the legal actors, only the judge can solve the contradictions involved in this situation. How she responds to this challenge is critical. However, in most developing countries the machinery of justice is not prepared to face this challenge and adequately fulfill its role in society. As a result of this fact and other interrelated sociopolitical factors, the confidence and esteem of the community in the laws, the legal system, and the administration of justice are critically low.

Finally, financial and political support will never be sufficient to carry out effective judicial reform unless a leading group of judges and a core of the important elements of the legal community are committed to carry it out.

The starting point to evaluate and identify the problems in a given judicial system is to examine at least the following elements: (1) the legal context, (2) the administration of the system, (3) the economic cost of the system, (4) training and legal education, (5) legal procedures, (6) methods of alternative dispute resolution, (7) physical facilities, (8) the community's perception of the administration of justice, and (9) the impact of court decisions in society.

I will explore in this part of the chapter the culture of service in the administration of justice. I will present the case that the culture of service is a required perspective to begin work on the nine elements listed above. I will look at how the culture of service can be perceived, where or what are its roots, what is its nature, and what are the main obstacles for its achievement. I will present the judicial system as a service organization operating in a competitive environment; therefore, the administration, cost, performance, quality, and independence of the judicial system should emulate any efficient service organization. I will also suggest that the judge's critical role is leadership: judges are leaders who, within the framework of possibilities determined by the law, should try to reflect and help to express the main trends of the public opinion of their time and community as well as certain universal standards that are gaining ground in this age of globalization, such as the protection of minorities and the basic principles of human rights.

B. The Culture of Service

1. *A Story of Two Flights*

Some time ago, as I boarded an airplane taking me from the United States to an Eastern European country, I crossed paths with the captain in the aisle. As I moved aside to let him pass, I said, "You go first, because without you, we can't fly." To that he answered, "No, you go first, because without *passengers*, there's no reason to fly." A few days later, when I took a local flight within that Eastern European country, I recalled this seemingly insignificant exchange. The plane carried over 170 passengers, and my seat was in the first row. When I stood up to go to the rest room, the flight attendant informed me that the rest room directly in front of me was exclusively for the crew. He then directed me to the passengers' rest room at the rear of the plane. Upon arriving at our destination, a voice on the overhead speaker informed us that no passengers were to leave their seats until the crew completely deplaned.

These seemingly inconsequential exchanges graphically contrast the perspectives or attitudes that exist between former socialist countries and the countries of Western Europe, the United States, and some of Southeast Asia. Both planes safely transported me to my destinations and met security and hygiene regulations. However, on the first flight, the airline focused on the needs of the passenger. On the second flight, it seemed as if the airline and the crew barely considered the passenger. In an open economic market, it is not difficult to guess which of the two airlines would win the customers' patronage, trust, and confidence. Although aviation regulations were complied with on both flights, the captain's attitude on the first flight was the by-product of a systemic focus on service that centers on the consumer. The attitudes on the second flight were the by-product of a systemic focus on authority and power. The differences in the attitudes projected are more far-reaching than our first impression.

2. How These Attitudes Apply to Other Developing States

Although in a less transparent manner than the socialist countries, many developing countries also center their systems on authority and power. Even though theoretical, political, and legal discourse in developing countries pays lip service to the importance of users or consumers, when this discourse is translated into practical actions, a strong role for the authority is still present. This results from, among other things, little or no participation outside of the social group in power. This, in turn, explains the prevailing situation where only elite and privileged groups with connections or influence have access to the market and to services.

The members of these elite and privileged groups, who generally have a capacity for leadership and, therefore, a potential to effect positive change, do not seem aware of the shortcomings and limitations of a social system based on authority, power, and a lack of participation by the actors or the community. This is particularly true with regard to the legal systems in which the shortcomings are frequently obscured by a thick mist of formalism, rituals, routine formulas, and abstract postulates. All of this is done to cloud the transparency of the actions, make effective application of the law difficult, lessen accountability of the legal actors, and maintain the system of privileges. This situation, in various degrees, is often found in Latin America, in some Asian states, and in many parts of Africa.

3. Where or What Are the Roots of the Culture of Service?

I believe that there are two roots of this culture of service. The first hypothesis is that the attitude of service consists of a religious conscience that is present in much of Judaism, Christianity, Islam, Hinduism, and Buddhism, as well as Confucianism and Taoism. The second hypothesis is that the attitude of service rests on the realities, practices, and ethics of market economies.[13]

C. The Nature of Judicial Service

1. The Application and Interpretation of the Law

A traditional and widely held view about the role of the judiciary is that it consists primarily of applying and interpreting the law in a reasonable and predictable manner. While this view is technically correct, it is incomplete and partial to the point of distortion: it fails to consider the main objective of the judiciary—the peaceful solution of conflicts. For example, one could correctly maintain in the same way that a firefighter's function is to fill hoses with water, that a physician's function is to prescribe pharmaceuticals, and that an architect's function is to draft blueprints. However, as does the traditional definition of the judiciary's function, these characterizations fail to consider the firefighter's, the physician's, and the architect's ultimate objective, that is, their essential contribution to society.

Moreover, at least in the Judeo-Christian and Islamic traditions, the ideal image of a judge is not that of a learned doctor of laws who merely interprets and applies the law, but rather a King Solomon figure who, when called to solve the situation of two women disputing the motherhood of a child, did not interpret or discern the applicable law, but found a common sense and nonlegal way to solve the controversy. Similarly, in the classical models of Spanish and English literature, Cervantes and Shakespeare design archetypes of justice based not only on the law, but also on something beyond the norms. In fact, my analysis of judges' work in Argentina, Peru, Bolivia, Ecuador, Venezuela, Mexico, Egypt, Indonesia, Germany, Albania, Poland, and Russia reveals that judges dedicate a relatively small part of their time to actually applying and interpreting the law. Interviews with English judges and federal and state judges in the United States have rendered similar observations.

In many cases, the Solomonic figure may be an arbitrator or a mediator. In Peru, Justices of the Peace are the judges that receive the widest community acceptance, yet they have the least amount of formal legal training. I have observed similar situations with the judges in Colombian small claims courts, in councils of elders in Albania and Guatemala, with the lay judges in the Zulu and Xhosa communities in South Africa, and in the Native American reservations of Isleta and Taos in New Mexico.

2. The Law as Only a Frame of Possibilities

Even when a judge is interpreting and applying the law, there is considerable room for judicial flexibility. Even within the limited rules of a civil code, judges have wider discretionary powers than have been traditionally recognized.[14] This is because the law merely sets the stage where issues can be put forward or draws the lines within which debate can take place. Hans Kelsen, the most distinguished positivist jurist in the twentieth century, states that the law is "simply a frame within which various possibilities for application are given, and every act that stays within this frame, in some possible sense filling it in, is in conformity with the norm."[15]

Fernando de Trazegnies illustrates how the legal frame of possibilities should not be restricted by the legislative intent because, in many, if not most, cases, the real intent is impossible to find.[16] But even if this were not the case, the legislator's subjective intent, he says, should not have any role in the objective interpretation of the text of the law—what the legislator thought or meant to say, but did not say directly in the text, must not be taken into account. Legislators should disappear when a law is passed, and if they try to survive with "doctrinal" clarifications or declarations on their intent, they should be ignored.

3. *Conflict or Dispute Resolution Beyond the Law*

Part of the problem consists of considering the law as a model of conduct. The law does not embody a model of conduct any more effectively than a football field embodies a game, a dance floor embodies a modern dance, or a theatrical stage embodies a drama. If life on the edge of the law can—and almost always does—lead people and their families to misfortune, then a life modeled solely on the law is both sad and pitiful. Fortunately, all those who in some way enrich our lives and happiness do not view the law as the goal, but as a means of getting somewhere else. When Jesus Christ was interrogated about why his disciples had done "on the Sabbath day that which [was] not lawful," he answered, "The Sabbath was made for man and not man for the Sabbath."[17] St. Paul, in the epistle to the Galatians, reflects in a similar fashion on the role of law and man. All this is not too distant from what Islamic Sufis have thought about the law since the Middle Ages—that the law was a means to get to what is at the other side of the legal text.

The judge's proper role when resolving disputes consists of organizing the process to resolve a crisis by clarifying arguments, coordinating statements, investigating the veracity of evidence, and rendering decisions, all of which often include the use of discretionary powers. To perform this role effectively, the judge must specifically evaluate documents and oral testimony,[18] scrutinize the truth behind tears and dramatic gestures, handle frustrated parties and witnesses, organize the procedure efficiently and economically, and defuse conflicts and crises at the risk of losing his peace of mind, and even his soul. The judge's main objective is to resolve controversies peacefully, which is what differentiates a judge from other legal players. The sole purpose of the judge's vested authority; the profuse legislative norms, regulations and procedures; the available material resources; and the contribution of professionals is to solve the problems society brings before the courts. The law itself is merely one element among many that helps provide a solution.

4. *Law and Reality*

The ability of the judge to conform the often static law to real and dynamic circumstances is important in every society, but especially in societies and economies in transition—either from state-planned economies or from closed-market systems to open societies and economies. In both situations, the differences between law and reality are so great that only a judge, using all possible resources, can resolve the inherent conflicts within the maladjusted law in a way that conforms with the reality of the times and circumstances. Poland provides a good example. There, judges applied the same commercial code during the

Nazi occupation, the liberation, the communist rule, and Poland's return to a market economy. The judge's response to the challenges of these and similar circumstances is crucial.[19]

D. The Illusion of a State Monopoly of Justice

1. The Illusion of Power

The traditional view of the judiciary (that its work consists primarily of interpreting and applying the law), accompanied by the view that making laws is the exclusive prerogative of the state, leads to the dangerous conclusion that the state has a monopoly over the administration of justice. Those under the illusion that the state has a monopoly of justice are ready to believe that if it does not provide an efficient solution to conflicts, no one else will. However, a closer look at systems throughout the world reveals that when judicial systems begin to function inefficiently, society spontaneously produces a rich variety of alternative solutions. This can occur within the state, the private sector, or the informal sector.

2. Consequences of the Illusion of Power

a. Within the state

In many states, society's alternative solutions occur first in a less-perceptible form that may even receive official sanction. When the state fails to provide just and adequate judicial solutions to societal needs, society will create alternative responses. For example, disputes related to commercial matters (including taxes and customs), the constitution, the electorate, or the military may slowly be removed from the jurisdiction of the Supreme Court and the courts of general jurisdiction and referred to parallel specialized courts. This removal results from the perception that these courts cannot efficiently deal with these disputes. This has happened in varied forms in many countries, including Russia, Indonesia, Egypt, and Peru where, one way or another, the most important matters politically, economically, socially, or legally are removed from the ordinary courts. However, Norway, New Zealand, England, and the United States do not experience this phenomenon because their judicial systems are more efficient.[20] International tribunals provide another example where the state sanctions the removal of a different group of matters from ordinary courts. These tribunals, which decide such things as commercial and investment disputes, are given jurisdiction because the state courts are perceived as providing inefficient service. Some examples of these tribunals include the WTO and NAFTA.

b. In the private sector

The growing popularity of private arbitration, conciliation, and mediation has also eroded the power of the national courts. Shipping companies, banks, and insurance companies often try to settle the disputes between themselves in this way. Notwithstanding, national courts have not viewed this phenomenon as a destructive alternative to ordinary justice. Indeed, in many instances mediation, conciliation, and arbitration complement the national courts and help alleviate the heavy load they frequently carry.

c. In the informal sector

Yet another example of the erosion of state power over judicial administration is the wide variety of "informal justice." Studies of informal justice in Peru, Venezuela, and Brazil show a significant erosion of judicial power.[21] In the Philippines, Guatemala, Egypt, Albania, and Africa, the erosion of judicial power affects not only civil areas of the law, such as commercial, property, and family disputes, but also the administration of criminal justice. For example, citizens frustrated with the criminal justice system may take the law into their own hands and subject thieves and lawbreakers to lynching and other violent acts.

It is surprising how little has been learned about this phenomenon that was first described in the Spanish literature of Lope de Vega and in the English plays of Shakespeare. Upon the system failing, society never fails to take alternative measures to satisfy their own needs. It has reached the point that the state monopoly of justice is merely an illusion. The judicial system's constant, bitter and, for some, invisible battle against other social forces can, at the moment least expected, render the judicial system irrelevant to society. All of this is taking place without the mention of corruption, which takes up most of the discourse of politicians, news reporters, and critics who seem to think that this is the only problem. Even when judges are honest and learned, it sometimes appears as if they have lost their way and do not know what it is really about, this business of the administration of justice.

3. Ways and Methods of Alternative Dispute Resolution

A fact that is usually overlooked in developing nations and in economies in transition is that if the state does not provide a socially efficient and effective system of administration of justice, society, unfailingly, will provide mechanisms for alternative dispute resolution (ADR), either by legal means like negotiation, conciliation, and mediation or by illegal means like intimidation or lynching.

However, ADRs do not have to be, necessarily, a sign of decaying judicial systems that are incapable of meeting the needs of the community. Rather, quite often they are not only very useful to judges overloaded with cases, but also an indispensable instrument whose use should be encouraged by the courts themselves.

One of the common features of countries where the legal system does not meet the needs of society and, therefore, where there is an important gap between law and reality, is that the official system of administration of justice is not used by both the very rich or very powerful *and* the very poor, destitute, or marginalized members of a society. Also, it is not used by groups of people engaged in activities that require specialized knowledge to understand.

The most common reasons why the administration of justice does not meet the needs of society in developing countries or economies in transition are, first, the inadequacy of the legislative tools that the judge is given to work; second, the lack of administrative organization of the court system that, for a wide variety of reasons, results in overloaded judicial dockets, great backlogs, and long delays in cases; third, the lack of developed skills in judges to organize their own work in an efficient way in order to be more productive and dispose of a larger number of cases; fourth, the lack of training in new issues and developments in the law, which causes judges to postpone cases for long periods of time until they learn how to solve the issue; fifth, the neglect or low priority given to the material and logistic needs of the judiciary; sixth, the high costs of litigation; and, finally, corruption that, unfortunately, in some cases, interferes with the just expectations of the citizens.

The reactions to this situation are varied. One of the answers is to write off debts or claims below a certain amount. A second common reaction is to exhaust negotiations; a popular saying goes "better a bad settlement than a good judgment." A third reaction is to resort more and more, particularly in the business community, to conciliation, mediation, or arbitration. But ADR also has its dark side, and not just in settling disputes between rival criminal gangs. Impatient citizens in the informal urban developments of Lima, facing an uncontrolled upsurge in crime, have several times taken justice into their own hands to punish a rapist, thief, or murderer. In Jakarta and other localities of Indonesia, unsatisfied creditors engage gangs of "debt collectors," who bully and threaten the physical integrity and health of overdue or careless debtors.

But, well-understood ADR can be a very useful component of and assistance to the official system. Practically everywhere in the world, dockets are overcrowded and any form of licit relief is welcome by those who monitor the performance of courts. Also, judges who understand that their real role in society is not necessarily to apply the law by writing learned and long judgments, but is rather to solve disputes, can encourage the parties to conciliate and can even compel them to settle the dispute when, in the judgment and understanding of the court, such a process is workable and when the litigation is going to be costly and time-consuming both for the parties and for the court. Mechanisms for conciliation have always existed in the codes of procedure, but have rarely been used by judges because of a lack of understanding of their real roles or simply because they don't know and have never been trained in the techniques required to carry it through. In the United States, these techniques of negotiation reach even the field of criminal law in "plea bargaining," which is flatly rejected by countries in the civil law legal system. However, when push has come to shove in Latin America for instance, in Colombia, Peru, and Bolivia—legislatures have passed various plea bargaining methodologies to induce drug traffickers and terrorists to surrender to the police.

A danger looming over the judicial systems of many developing nations is that of becoming irrelevant to the society over which they exercise at least theoretical jurisdiction. Over the past fifty years—and in some cases even longer—a gradual and progressing erosion has deprived these high institutions of justice of an important part of their real jurisdictional realm. When developing nations become independent from their colonial powers, or when former socialist or state-controlled economies enter the market economy, foreign companies, foreign partners, foreign financiers, and foreign investors become the main actors in the new organization of the economy. Almost invariably they have resorted, and still resort, to arbitration in order to settle their disputes with the host states, partners, or counterparts. ICSID and the Permanent Court of International Arbitration are among the dozens of arbitration centers dealing with these matters. Each international trade treaty or organization brings with it its own mechanism of solving disputes beyond the reach of national courts, whether it be the WTO, the European Court, NAFTA, or the Andean Common Market (even though the latter has kept a role for national courts). In the Americas, human rights matters must ultimately be examined by the Inter-American Court of Human Rights. Even in commercial disputes of a certain magnitude within one country, it is the exception rather than the general rule that they are decided by ordinary courts. Many countries have created special courts outside the system to deal with constitutional matters involving the most delicate political problems. Military courts have invaded the normal jurisdiction of ordinary courts in serious criminal matters like drugs and terrorism in view of the incapacity of ordinary courts to handle the cases in an acceptable manner.

At the other extreme of the spectrum—and for mostly different reasons, like excessive formalism, red tape, unaffordable cost, inefficiency to recognize the reality in front of them, the presence of indigenous populations and peasant communities, and what has been called "the informal economy,"—cities like Lima, Caracas, Rio de Janeiro, Cairo, and Jakarta have all developed spontaneous ways and methods to peacefully solve their differences. Most of these mechanisms do not have to face the problems of judgment enforcement that ordinary courts have, because they usually reach a high degree of acceptance.

Last, there is one more reason why people resort to arbitration: when the issues in the dispute require such a degree of specialized knowledge and cultural mind-set that the matter is outside the professional reach of ordinary judges; instances of maritime matters, insurance adjustments, securities, stock exchange, air transport, and banking are common examples. These disputes are either referred to arbitration by expert lawyers or businessmen or to foreign courts with expertise in the field, like the courts of New York for financial, banking, and investment matters; the courts of London for banking, insurance, and maritime matters; and other similar courts of other countries.

In most cases of ADR, the whole process takes place with no intervention whatsoever by judges or the courts. Even though disputes are unavoidable in communities of any sort, the fact that most of them never reach a court of law should not be a matter of distress, or even necessarily of concern. And if the settlement of the matter is peaceful, equitable, fair, and satisfactory no more should be said about it. But in some cases the losing party refuses to comply with the award, and courts of law must provide enforcement, as is also true when a foreign award has to become effective locally. Courts of law should also provide assistance when due process has not been observed to correct the omissions or distortions. Courts of law could also act more directly to assist the parties in selecting a third-party arbitrator or in cases when an appeal to ordinary courts has been agreed upon.

A second occasion when courts act in this manner is based on the fact that, when exercising discretionary powers or when authorized by legislation, judges can encourage or even compel the parties to refer one, some, or all of the issues in dispute to negotiation, conciliation, mediation, or arbitration. The judge should even act as a conciliator whenever possible and according to the rules of the legal system to settle the matter before judgment, because the service provided by the judge is conflict resolution and the objective is social peace and economic growth.

A third way in which objectives could be achieved by alternative methods but within the system is by promoting the participation of lay persons in small claims courts; misdemeanor courts, like those provided by the justices of the peace in Peru, are very much rooted in the community and enjoy more social prestige than any other judge—lawyer or not—in that country. Over 63 percent of decisions made by these courts are not appealed.

E. The Judicial System as a Service Organization

Those who want to collect a debt, recover damages, protect their property, or execute a contract should be able to resort to a judicial system with the same confidence and ease with which they pick up a telephone, write a check, or call a taxi. However, with the administration of justice, it happens that the service providers have chosen to cover themselves with a thick robe of rhetoric that has created a language of religious, academic, and protocolary symbolism. This rhetoric leaves the users of judicial services unable to value the excellence of individuals who work conscientiously, intelligently, and creatively to solve real conflicts; it also leaves them unable to expose the inadequacies of those individuals without the vocation of service who are true bureaucrats, are unimaginative, and have the most timid relationship with the law, forgetting that the object of the law is to serve and protect human beings. To the extent of this particular approximation to the law, Stendhal, who besides being a novelist was also a lawyer and sometimes a judge, comments, "Law begins where love ceases."[22] Judges should learn that law only gains full meaning through love, service, and hope.

We must not deceive ourselves that social problems, entrusted to humans with all our faults, virtues, and limited resources, can be solved by the perfect final judgment found in Judeo-Christianity and Islam or in Buddhist nirvana. A similar perspective led the great Scandinavian realist philosopher of law, A. Vilhem Lundstedt, to postulate that true justice does not exist.[23] In a similar vein, it could also be stated to civil engineers that there are no eternal bridges, or to geologists that there are no inexhaustible mines, or to aeronautical engineers that there are no perfect airplanes. Perhaps, in order to demystify justice and to correct the astigmatism with which we are accustomed to examining problems, we should promote the idea to reformists that true justice does not exist. From there, we should modestly attempt to maintain peace, freedom, dignity, life, and health, as well as encourage savings, business, investment, and an equal distribution of wealth, with neither more nor less effort than we put forth to provide water, sewage, electricity, transportation, and communications.

F. How to Administer the Service

As in all public service, dispute resolution should be organized to obtain the most efficient results. This includes the efficient management of funds, the maximum satisfaction of public needs with existing resources, and the rational organization of these resources. In short, the goal is to achieve the maximum benefit at the lowest cost while also striving for the highest level of quality. The administration of judicial services can be considered at three overlapping levels: the administration of the national system, the administration of the courts as units, and case management.

1. The Administration of the National System

When talking or thinking about the administration of the national system, the first problems that often come to the minds of many public officials are the lack of funding, physical facilities, equipment, organic laws of the system, procedural codes, and, to a lesser degree, training. All of these matters are enormously important, but none of them addresses the heart of the problem. The principal and most ignored problem is invariably administrative because, more often than not, it is the channel to solve the most serious structural problems.

Any public service needs an administrator with expertise in organizing resources and designing systems which best serve the user of the service. An effective administrator must realize that the benefactor of this public service is not the judge, but the citizen and the political, economic, and social players. The judges and their staffs are servants whose salaries are paid by the taxpayers, the users of the system, or both. Those who pay for the system deserve the utmost consideration, interest, and respect. Unfortunately, judges are not trained to administer organizations or resources. As a result, until recently, judges have tended to ignore the important overarching problems and instead focus too much time on minute issues, such as paper work, the purchase of office equipment, or the support staff's vacation time. An effective administrator should take responsibility for these minute issues, freeing the judge to focus on more important jurisdictional matters or on questions of general administrative policy.

A lack of strategic planning also contributes significantly to administrative problems. In this age of sophisticated computer programs, it is possible to predict the number and incidence of lawsuits with equal or greater precision than forecasting the weather. Judicial planners should use this technology to acquaint themselves with a knowledge of the frequency and level of damage awards in tort cases. With this knowledge, judicial planners could organize a more efficient approach to the handling of such cases.

It is also possible to predict the societal cost of contractual disputes because of certain constants in the origin of conflicts, such as changes in the economy or government policy. Changes in these factors accompany peaks and valleys in the number of contracts breached or executed. The banks are experts in calculating the bad debt percentage of loans. These examples demonstrate that lawsuits are not an anomaly, but a constant and natural part of our society. This constancy makes judicial administrative pressures and complications almost as predictable as disease, aging, and the changing seasons.

Different countries take different approaches to administering their national judicial systems. In countries such as Poland, Indonesia, Egypt, and Albania, the Ministry of Justice is in charge of judicial administration. The ministry is responsible for the judicial budget; handling the policy of remuneration, incentives, leaves, and sanctions; and, in large part, for making judicial appointments. And, upon consultation, the ministry decides whether to increase or reduce the number of courts and jurisdictions.

In other countries, some organized as differently as the United States and Peru, the judicial branch manages itself through specialized offices and public officials. The United States has developed this field of judicial administration by utilizing specialized administrators in both federal and state courts. Russia has a mixed and very complicated system for administration of courts. And there are states, such as Venezuela, that have successfully created a Judicial Council that acts like a mixed and independent body responsible for the administration of the whole judicial system. It is unrealistic to consider any one of these systems as the absolute best in the abstract. In this matter there are no universal magic formulas, except that in each concrete circumstance the system should be developed by a deliberative process, enriched by the interested parties.[24]

2. The Administration of the Courts as Units

The second level of administration of the judicial branch deals directly with the organization and function of the court as an office. At this level, the foremost concerns are the physical aspects of location, furniture, electricity, water, gas, utilities, hygiene, security, and the functional independence and comfort of the citizenry. The judge's support staff must also be considered. In particular, the number and organization of secretaries, assistants, clerks, court reporters, and bailiffs must be rational and functional.[25]

Regrettably, whether in Kraków, Bandung, or Quito, judges commonly complain of low wages and a lack of financial resources. How can a service function if there are inadequate funds to attract quality personnel, amply equip judicial offices, provide libraries, and provide a fit environment for the judges and the users? The problem is critical in various parts of the world. The most recurrent problem is that many countries lack an adequate system of information, or even basic libraries. There are, however, many other problems. In Egypt, the summer heat is so extreme that, due to the lack of air-conditioning, the courts have to close down for a few months each year. In Central Asia the cold is so severe that courts are also closed for long periods each year. Similarly, in Colombia, Italy, and Peru, the lack of security is sometimes a serious predicament. Any private entrepreneur would find it inconceivable to function under these circumstances.

At this level, the model of efficiency should be that of an efficient private enterprise. There are various examples around the world of judicial branches that are efficiently and functionally organized. The United States, Great Britain, Canada, France, Spain (particularly in the Basque region), and Singapore are clear examples of courts having good results in this area; that is, they function efficiently in a manner similar to service offices in the private sector. In general, they are physically accessible, clean, orderly, technically equipped, and service-oriented.

3. Case Management

The third level of administration deals with the administration of the cases themselves—case management. This takes into account various considerations, such as registration of complaints, case distribution, case loads, case flow, archives, group dynamics for hearings and conferences, and time management. At this level, procedural efficiency, which at the same time protects the rights of parties, is the best way to serve the users of the judicial system.

It is important to consider the organization of the judge's work as well as the judge's workload. In some countries the workload is so heavy that judges are unable to do anything other than look at papers. A greater return is expected from a judge than from an engineer or a surgeon. Due to this rigorous demand, the goal must continue to be that of obtaining the best service at the lowest cost with the highest quality. Ultimately, the number of judges should be in proportion to the demand for judicial services as forecasted by experts.

G. The Cost of the Service

1. Are We Paying Enough Attention to the Problem?

Despite the problems encountered in the administration of the judicial service, few people—either in government administrations, courts, or the private sector—have conducted an economic analysis of operating in this manner. The few who have conducted such analyses propose solutions without a sufficient financial and economic basis. Some studies have made cost-benefit analyses based solely on the percentages of the budget allocated to the judicial branches in various countries. The flaw in this type of analysis is similar to judging the status of a bank solely on deposit receipts. Effective judicial reform, however, requires an accurate assessment of all costs and benefits of the judicial system.

2. How Are the Costs and Benefits of Justice Distributed Within Society?

The first question that must be asked when analyzing the costs of justice is how are these costs distributed to the various sectors of the community? The answer to this question may differ from country to country. In some countries, the costs are borne by the taxpayer. In others, they are directly borne by the users of the system. And in all countries, to varying degrees, the transaction costs are borne by the society in general. Previous studies have failed to take into account all of the relevant costs and benefits, or, if they were considered, their interrelation was ignored.

a. The Taxpayer

For the most part, if not always, in Latin American countries general tax revenues (i.e., from the taxpayer) provide the principal source of funding. Costa Rica sets aside 6 percent of its annual budget for the judicial branch, perhaps the highest percentage in the world. In countries with highly efficient judicial systems, such as Japan, the United States, and Germany, the percentage set aside is less than, or around, 1 percent.

The percentage of the budget allotted to the judiciary does not demonstrate much unless one considers how a country taxes its citizens. In a country that directly taxes rents and property, but has few indirect taxes, the budget is funded predominantly by the affluent class. Thus, the most affluent sectors of society, such as corporations, banks, and insurance companies, finance the judiciary. And, because the affluent sectors are the primary users of the court system (e.g., for debt collection and breach of contract cases), the users of the courts provide the ultimate financing for the judiciary. However, one must consider that non-users also benefit from the certainty and low transaction costs resulting from a well-financed, efficient, and effective system.[26]

If most of the taxes are indirect and the country has large economic differences within the population, it is the poor who might be financing the judicial system used primarily by merchants, companies, and property owners. Obviously then, the percentage of a state's budget spent on the judiciary and the costs incurred by those using the judicial system only becomes meaningful within a complete fiscal and socioeconomic context. Therefore, this aspect, as with other service industries, should be studied by those who recognize whether a certain sector of the economy is being unduly subsidized.

b. The users of the system

In other countries, the users of the system bear the costs of the judiciary directly in the form of various fees, fines, and other charges. In Russia, those that use the commercial courts pay for a large part of the costs. In Egypt, the user pays about 80 percent of the costs. Preliminary observations indicate similar percentages in Poland and Indonesia. In the state of Tennessee, court fees and fines *more* than cover the cost of justice.

These fees and fines are certainly not the only costs incurred by the users of the system. It must be remembered that the net benefit for the users of the judicial system who appear in court to protect a property right or a possession, execute a contract, collect on a debt, or seek damages for an injury is calculated by subtracting the total cost incurred individually from the resulting benefit. In most judicial systems, those who seek to use the system must retain the services of an attorney. In most cases, these attorneys do not compete in an open market; they belong to an oligopoly that operates on a schedule of minimum fees and a closed shop. The high costs resulting from such arrangements are reinforced by professional organizations, such as bar associations, which wield considerable power over their membership.[27] In other service industries, maximum tariffs are fixed under price controls. However, attorneys are an exception; often they are the only service industry where minimum fees are set.

In addition to the fixed costs—fees, fines, the costs to hire an attorney, and other charges that users of the system incur when going to court—other costs, not to be forgotten, are paper, photocopies, transportation, meals, and lodging when a case is tried at a site away from home. Finally, there is time lost due to the inability to work on given days. This is a composite of the costs that an individual incurs in pursuing justice. Given the many costs, the person who pays for this service rightfully expects to be treated as if the judiciary were any other service industry, such as an airline, where a passenger expects courteous and high-quality attention.

An inefficient judicial system can drastically increase the user's incurred costs. In a South American country that I visited, each time users of the judicial system inquired as to the status of their case, they had to wait patiently in a line for two hours, often only to reach the window of the office and be rudely told that the person they were looking for was not available. In another country in Eastern Europe, to commence a lawsuit individuals must file the lawsuit themselves and submit all materials to the judge. Because judges will only receive new complaints twice per week, it is very difficult to start a suit. Citizens must stand in line from the early morning hours, and in some cases overnight, to have their requests honored. Often, those who have connections receive preferential treatment, which creates resentment. The public as a whole feels mistreated by such activity. There is not a bank, investment company, or consumer-oriented business that would survive operating in such a manner.

c. Society in general

Determining who directly finances the judicial system is not the end of the problem. As North, and then Sherwood, Geoffrey Shepherd, and Celso Marcos de Souza observed, society in general incurs the costs of an inefficient judicial system in at least two ways.[28] First, since an inefficient legal system increases the risks of doing business with strangers, business opportunities are limited to a close circle of friends and associates.[29] Second, transaction costs are increased by inefficient systems. For example, an appellate judge who annuls a judgment for a debt because of a superfluous formality can cause a one- to two-year delay and, by a chain effect, cause higher transaction costs, reduce opportunities, and discourage investment. It has been calculated that inefficient systems affect the growth rate by no less than 15 percent.[30] As Justice Anthony M. Kennedy once said, courts of justice are one of the most important economic assets of a country.[31]

H. Physical Facilities

Security, if not a higher value than justice, is at least a more pressing and urgent one. Indeed, it is the cornerstone of the administration of justice. There is a deceptive aspect about physical facilities in developing countries and that is that, eight times out of ten, when someone begins to talk about judicial reform or modernization of the administration of justice, the response will be that the solution or, at the very least, the highest priorities are buildings, computers, and Xerox machines. Sometimes salaries, law reform, and training will be added. In fact, most of these first reactions to the problem miss the real nature of the issues, but, in certain cases, buildings and computers can be really essential to the very delivery of the service of conflict resolution.

The type of ill-treatment illustrated by the examples of long lines and closed offices seriously damages the performance of the courts, the feelings of the users, and the image of justice. While talking to a judge in his office in a northern province of Peru, an attorney for one of the parties was seriously concerned because a cow was poking its head through a window and licking the papers on the judge's desk. In Kraków, several judges have to share the same office without privacy to work or to make telephone calls because there are not enough rooms for them; many times they have to work out of their homes.

The problem of buildings in some countries is a matter not only of better conditions for the judges to work in, but also of security for the people (I hate to think what would happen if a fire or earthquake started in that court building in Caracas), the papers (a cow eating an important piece of evidence in Peru), or the judge (several hundred judges were murdered during the drug war in Colombia). Many times, as during hearings of a trial, quietness is required in a courtroom while evaluating a piece of evidence or listening in concentration to an oral argument. Yet, in Albania, for example, judges have to work while listening to arguments in the hallways of public buildings. A minimum of dignity, comfort, and cleanliness is also due to any public function.

On the other hand, in centers with great concentrations of population and, consequently, with great concentrations of work, the use of automation for several of the courts' activities not only makes a great deal of sense, but can also help enormously for simplification of procedures, organization of work, and reduction of the time required to obtain information. It can also help to make more transparent the process of assigning and distributing cases to judges. Some successful experiments have been conducted in Argentina to simplify procedures and reduce delays, and there is ample room for improvement in a very visible way. However, many times there is the danger of overemphasizing the importance of automation, especially in countries that lack the most elementary facilities in which to operate.

One common dearth in practically every developing country is that of adequate libraries and archives. After the human aspect, it could be said that the quality of a court can be measured almost totally by the quality of its library and archives. Both are the sources, storehouses, and memory of judges. When Lord Denning became eighty years old, someone asked him to what did he attribute the fact that he was considered the greatest English judge since Lord Mansfield, to which he answered that he had the best law library of all judges. However modest he was in his answer, there is a good deal of truth in what he said. Judges must, at least, be able to know what the law is. This is perhaps the most urgent common need in courts around the world.

I. The Performance of the Service

The price that society or the user of the judicial system pays must correlate to the service given. Three common problems in the execution of the judicial service, usually connected to corruption, are (1) delays, (2) the secrecy of many acts and lack of information, and (3) the ineffectiveness of judgments due to a lack of adequate enforcement.

1. Delays and Corruption

Long delays are ultimately a source of corruption.[32] Poland is a country where the judicial system is well known for its honesty and high morals. Litigants and attorneys attest to the high independence, trustworthiness, and honor of Polish judges. Nevertheless, some tribunals may experience delays of up to nine months for even relatively simple matters. This has caused corruption to surface among support personnel, who alter the strict order of the case admissions for some kind of payoff. Even if only through the influence of a friend or a relative, this type of corruption breaks down the solid nature of the service and opens up avenues for more corruption that is even harder to control or track. In Jakarta, for example, "justice" belongs to the party with the largest bid. In many countries this is the primary problem.

2. *Secrecy and Corruption*

Secrecy breeds corruption. Public scrutiny can prevent much corruption in judicial systems throughout the world. Civil society and NGOs play a critical role in this regard, as does the press. Much has been said lately about the role of the press in regard to the access and secrecy of the judicial procedural system. In Italy and Peru, the identity of some judges has been hidden in some cases to protect them from terrorists.[33] Still, despite the inconveniences that come along with it, the best way to combat corruption, privileges, inequalities, and irregularities is with public exposure. The O.J. Simpson trial is a good example. Despite the debate about the justness of the jury's decision and the effectiveness of the system, the massive media coverage made it difficult, if not impossible, for one of the parties to corrupt the judge or jury. Despite the imperfections, these are the events that restore confidence in a public system.

Secret deliberations and nontransparent decision-making are the hardest characteristics to eradicate in a judicial system that is transforming from a privileged authority to an open and free judicial system. Despite a public audience, hearings, and oral arguments, it is common for opposing lawyers in Latin America to confer individually and separately in private chambers with judges, magistrates, or other mediation officials. This practice, in addition to being illegal, takes up a significant amount of the judge's time and slows down the process.[34]

3. *Effectiveness and Corruption*

In Egypt, Indonesia, Poland, Albania, and Russia, due to the formal system's ineffective enforcement of judgments, troubling developments are appearing. Because reaching a final and firm judgment is so difficult in these countries and only a small part of the legal process, an endless number of "collection agencies" are used to extort payment and kill if necessary. A slow-paying debtor in Jakarta may one night find a basket full of snakes or a box of spiders in his room. Nonpaying debtors in Cairo or Alexandria may awaken to the sound of a brick crashing through their car windshield. Between 1993 and 1995, the Russian Mafia was suspected of eighty-three assassination attempts and forty-five assassinations of bankers in Russia.[35]

The second example is the payment of insufficient compensation for damages. Such small damage awards for breaches of contract, property damages, personal injuries, and other torts create perverse incentives that ultimately discourage investment.[36] Insufficient damage awards have also undermined the integrity of the judicial system. This, in turn, encourages forum shopping. For instance, in a multinational lawsuit, plaintiffs search multiple jurisdictions until they reach one that grants them the most advantages. Besides the Bhopal case in India, many interest groups in Latin America have tried to commence lawsuits in the

United States against U.S. petroleum or mining companies conducting business in their state.

J. The Quality of the Service

1. The Impact of the Judicial System in Society

Even in a judicial environment without delays and corruption, where judgments are adequately enforced and judges produce reasonable and predictable application and interpretation of the law, the judicial system may fail to critically impact the litigating parties or society as a whole. One example illustrates this perspective well: the payment of debts in an inflationary economy. When the rate of legal interest (fixed by statute when the parties have not done so by contract) is relatively small compared to the rate of inflation, the judicial decision to link debt payment to the nominal value (which does not account for the high inflation rate) of the debt, as opposed to the real value (which does account for the high inflation rate), helps the debtor pay off the debt (especially after a judgment has been rendered at the end of several years of litigation) while at the same time maintaining high savings rates. This practice encourages frivolous litigation and appeals and, in the end, leaves the creditor with only a small percentage of his initial capital. All of the most learned citations from cases or legal writers cannot make this an effective or efficient decision.

2. Independence of the Judiciary

A frequent complaint about the judiciary in many developing countries is its lack of independence. Independence of the judiciary may have several meanings: (1) independence from political or governmental influence, whether from the executive or legislative branches;[37] (2) independence from the parties to the controversy;[38] (3) independence of one judge from another;[39] and (4) the independence of the judge from his or her own ideological beliefs.[40]

The state can maintain the independence of the judiciary in several ways. With respect to the first type of independence—independence from political or governmental influence—it is important to select judges on the basis of merit. This will ensure the quality of the judiciary, and, perhaps more important, avoid situations where a judge may feel pressure to return political favors.[41] Another vital point, advanced by Justice Stephen G. Breyer, is that the stability of the judiciary must be maintained.[42] According to Justice Breyer, the United States, for example, has been able to maintain judicial stability because of the protections guaranteed under Article III of the Constitution, which provides that federal judges will "hold their Offices during good behavior" and that they will "receive for their services a Compensation, which shall not be diminished during continuance in Office."[43] Justice Breyer also suggests that the judiciary should be self-administered.[44] Self-administration is an often-overlooked factor for judicial independence; however, the question of who controls the environment in which judges decide cases is critical to judicial independence if one thinks about how environment affects a person's work.[45]

Yet another critical point is that the state must create and maintain a transparent and independent system for the discipline of judges.[46] Moreover, the executive branch must complement and effectively support the judiciary. For example, the judiciaries in Russia, Indonesia, and Egypt lack independence because of the executives' ineffective enforcement of their judgments.[47] Also, a lack of protection in Russia and Colombia has resulted in murdered judges.

The second type of independence—independence from the parties to the dispute—is rooted in the idea of impartiality and is uncompromising in its demands—the more detachment from the parties the better.[48] The U.S. Congress has imposed on judges a statutory duty to disqualify themselves from sitting in a case in which their impartiality may be questioned.[49] Judges have an affirmative duty to investigate whether they or their family members have a financial interest in the case before them. The role of the state in this respect is to make very clear rules with respect to conflicts of interest.[50]

The third type of independence—independence of one judge from another—is threatened when superior judges may exercise control over subordinate judges.[51] In Chile, for example, the Supreme Court must annually rank all the judges in the country. This ranking, which is important for career promotions, gives the Supreme Court justices great power over the lower courts; some rankings by the Supreme Court have been interpreted as punishment of lower court judges who have gone too far in contesting the Supreme Court's holdings on human rights issues.[52]

To maintain the fourth area of judicial independence—independence from ideology—judges must be committed to decide the case on the basis of law, not on their own whims or ideology.[53] Legitimization depends on the public perception that law is something other than the arbitrary configuration of power.[54] I concur with a Ukrainian judge who expressed with deep certainty that a judge's independence lies in his internal mental feelings, that is, within the individual.

3. *Judges as Leaders*

The quality of service in a judicial system depends, to a great extent, on the tools that are used to service the citizen. It also depends on whether the providers understand their role toward the citizen and their contribution to society in ensuring justice. It is of utmost importance that judges be aware that they are more than simple bureaucrats who mechanically apply the law.[55] They are leaders who on a daily basis preside over and mold the economic, political, and business life of the country. Judges should also realize their enormous impact on the family structure, the rights of the individual, and the peace of the community. The future significantly depends on how well judges can fill their function in society.

Of all the instruments that a judge deals with, the law stands out as the most important, whether it is contained within legislative texts, previous case law, or textual doctrines. The nature and quality of the law largely influence what a judge offers, although bad law, except in certain circumstances, does not preclude a judge from rendering good service.[56] In part, the situation of the judiciary in developing countries is due to the transitional state of their societies and economies, the lack of information about events taking place inside and outside the government, and the fact that decision-makers lack the mechanisms or the willingness to perceive public opinion. These factors often lead the legislature to adopt rules that do not fit societal needs. Even beautifully written and internally logical laws may not address the needs and concerns of reality. This leaves an enormous gap, which the judge must bridge to make equitable and effective decisions in spite of inadequate laws. But even with adequate laws, as de Trazegnies has shown us, the intent of the legislator often constitutes an inscrutable mystery.[57] It is left to the judge to cover the gaps between law and reality. Yet there remains the floating question: How and where to go?

I venture to give a personal answer based on my own experience and on what I have seen and heard from learned judges with whom I have had the honor of meeting and talking. I would say that a judge should clearly feel that his or her mission is primarily to resolve social conflicts, if necessary, by going beyond the plain text of the law. This entails maximizing the limits and letter of the law. This does not mean to revolutionize the law, but rather to milk it for all it is worth and go beyond the words to the essential human situations that they involve.[58] They should also salvage and revive the value of hard proof and get the most of it, especially in judicial systems that do not have a jury system. Finally, the judge should utilize all of his intelligence, capacity, intuitive ability, common sense, and social perception to reduce and simplify areas of dispute and then work within an area of the law to induce, stimulate, and, when allowed, force the parties to reach a settlement. There is much to be written on this subject. For those who think that this only concerns civil and commercial areas, I remind you of the use of plea bargaining in the United States and pardon laws used by states like Colombia, Bolivia, and Peru to encourage terrorists or drug traffickers to give themselves up to the authorities. It is not necessary to reiterate that judges need to expand their roles beyond that of simple bureaucrats.

4. Judges and Public Opinion

Many attorneys often say that the judge should not be a politician, but a technician. I believe that a judge who is not a politician does not deserve to occupy such a position. Of course, judges should not be party politicians, but they should have a political concept of the society in which they live and preside and of the permanent values that made their community cohesive. They should fight to protect those values.

A judge, besides having the character qualities of being independent, honest, firm, and compassionate, should also be intelligent, cultured, and constantly investigating surrounding life, circumstances, and public opinion on life and political strife. The judge does not need to share the opinion of the public, which changes from day to day, oscillating from one extreme to another depending on what is reported in the media. A judge should represent the permanent values that reside in the bedrock of the community—values relating to religion, ethics, economics, love of life and liberty, rejection of discrimination and unjust inequalities, desire for peace, and desire to prosper.

Among other things, public opinion exemplifies a social force that changes with time and varies from country to country. Public opinion is often invisible on the surface, but it is omnipresent in the conscience of individuals; in family discussions; in civilized debates taking place in universities; in programs and plans of political parties; and in the minutes and letters of chambers of commerce, trade unions, and cultural associations. When united, this force is what determines and forges history; it is an uncontainable avalanche. In this respect, the judge, besides being a jurist, needs to be a leader who interprets public opinion. It is not on a daily basis that a judge can write an opinion such as that in *Brown v. Board of Education*[59] which, without rewriting the U.S. Constitution or U.S. law, terminated racial segregation in public schools and changed forever many other patterns of conduct in the United States. This way of understanding the judicial function should serve as an inspiration. In this way, the judge should interpret and follow public opinion and, occasionally, with a light but daring pressure, help bring it to light.

What patterns must we look for in the precarious and sometimes irregular constitutional life of Latin American countries; in the struggling and, at times, failing democracies in Africa; in the emerging economies in Asia in conflict with authoritarian regimes; and in the governments and economies in transition in Central and Eastern Europe in order for us to determine that a judicial reform program or activity is viable?

Looking back to different times in history and making a comparative analysis throughout the contemporary world, the best indication has proven to be when the government and laws of a country keep a relatively close relationship to, or at least are not diametrically opposed to, the main trends of current public opinion. World history abounds with instances where the citizens of a country have insisted upon reform—some are remembered as models of freedom and liberty to be imitated, and others are universally condemned as shameful cases of oppression and tyranny. Invariably a key difference between the first group and the second is the role played by the government—the action of the law in relation to public opinion.

IV. THE STANDARD OF PRECONDITIONS FOR JUDICIAL REFORM

> If only I knew—she thought to herself—which was neck and which was waist!
>
> —Lewis Carroll, *Alice Through the Looking Glass*

> Which way I ought to go from here? That depends a good deal on where you want to go to, said the cat.
>
> —Lewis Carroll, *Alice in Wonderland.*

A. The Functional Method of Comparative Law

The family of legal systems a country belongs to is not an element that affects the methodology that should be followed to identify the problems in the administration of justice. Whether the country follows the Roman civil law tradition, the common law, or the *Shari'a*, the steps to be followed are the same. To simplify the account for our purposes, many Islamic countries have adopted, at least for civil and commercial matters, the civil law model; once the socialist legal system is dismantled little by little, what is left is very much a civil law structure. On the other hand, the situation is a bit more complex in a few mixed systems that combine civil or common law elements and some other religious or local customs, but, as has been said, this does not need to affect the methodology. The method is basically the comparative law approach to analyze the function of the courts of law.

B. Perception of Court Decisions in Society

In democracies, as in market economies, what people think can, at certain moments, be even more important than whether they are right or wrong. Eventually, common sense and lasting or permanent values tend to emerge, but the process can sometimes be complicated and confused. However, in many crises, public opinion, with all its defects and limitations, has proven to be the best guide, even though there are at least a couple of very conspicuous exceptions to this assertion. If we consider that the administration of justice is a service provided principally by the state to society, in asking how the service is delivered, it is indispensable to ask directly the users how they perceive it. In order to accomplish this, it is useful first to learn how judges perceive their own function and the general conditions of the job. Then it is useful to ask legal writers and lawyers in law firms, bar associations, and academics. But all of them are the officials or assistants in the task of administering justice. The real users, at least in civil cases, are mainly banks, insurance companies, chambers of commerce, foreign investors, and trade unions. It is they who will give the true and final testimony of how the service is working and whether the courts are independent, efficient, prompt, inexpensive, and effective.

Some judges contend that in a legal suit there is always a loser who tends to blame the courts. The problem that we face in many developing nations is that complaints come not only from the losers, but also from the successful litigants since many of the judicial victories are only paper triumphs that many times have no economic, moral, social, political, or transcendental legal content.

However, even taking into account all the previous elements considered in this paper, they are of no use at all if, at the end of the legal process, the decision of the court does not produce a significant effect in society. Many times lawyers, jurists, judges, and reformers fall into the intellectual temptation of forgetting the real purpose of dispute resolution, which is to serve the needs of the hundreds, thousands, or millions of individuals who seek remedies to situations that they or their lawyers perceive to be wrong. Unfortunately, in many countries the judicial process is a too-painful and too-costly exercise that, at the end of the day, often leaves the litigant in a situation very much like that she was in at the beginning of the suit, or even worse.

One situation of this type is given in economies going through an inflationary process. In Peru, for instance, during the 1970s and 1980s, when inflation once reached 7,000 percent in a year, it was a good business for debtors to go to court and not pay their debts. Judges gave judgments only for the nominal value of the debt. As a result, many debtors deposited the borrowed money in banks and earned interest while trying to delay cases as long as possible. After three years, debtors had earned commercial interest on their deposits and had to repay only a small portion of what they had received plus a very low legal interest. To commercial and private creditors, the judicial process was only a pointless and discouraging exercise.

Another example, unfortunately all-too-common in developing countries, is the low level of monetary compensation for damages, whether tortious or contractual. Judges, with poor or no education even in basic economics, grant damages that do not at all discourage breaches of contract or negligent behavior. As horrible as it sounds, it can be said without exaggeration that in many countries to kill a person is reasonably inexpensive, or even a cheap incident, as far as damages are concerned.

Both examples show instances not only of a poor education about the economics of the law, but also about the role of a judge and about the enormous discretionary powers that, even in civil law systems, judges really have. Not everyday does a judge have the opportunity to write a decision like *Brown v. Board of Education*, but everyday judges have the irretrievable-if-lost opportunity of not becoming irrelevant to the society in which they live and work.

C. Viability of a Judicial Reform

When we have the standards for a judicial reform project, where and how should we begin? Intellectually, it is perfectly possible to think of methods or processes to modernize and make more efficient a court system in practically any given political, economic, or social circumstance appearing in front of us. Indeed, in principle it should not matter how bad a system is in order to begin working on it, because whatever can be done will likely be an improvement.

One of the symptoms of the lack of development in most nations (and perhaps, as North suggests, the cause for not developing) is the lack of institutions or legal rules that not only make economic growth possible, but also promote freedom and democracy. If we contrast the standards of most developing nations against the political standards of Switzerland, Sweden, the United Kingdom, or the United States, most likely very few would pass the test. Moreover, some will be in open contradiction with them. Although the legal systems in developing countries often defy sound thinking, they have stood the test of time for the past fifty years. Should we insistently pursue a model that exists only in developed nations, or should we try to decipher, amid the turmoil and contradictions of political life in the Third World, a pattern to make its work sensible and meaningful? I personally think the correct answer is the second one.

D. Stages of Reform

The situation can be perceived in a clearer way if we become conscious that in the great majority of cases, judicial reform has to be executed gradually and in different stages that, by themselves, help to define the order of priorities, because the second stage requires the support of the first, and the third that of the second. It is senseless to change the laws of procedure of a country if the judges of that country do not see the need for the reform and if they do not even comply with existing laws. Also, it is of no use to try to protect the constitutional rights of a citizen if we have not first solved the problem of the machinery of justice taking between two and three years to reach a decision. To think otherwise is to deceive ourselves as to the types of goals we can achieve realistically.

In most developing countries there are at least three stages in any judicial reform project that can be best achieved following a certain order of priorities.

1. The first stage can be carried out in almost any type of society—democracy or autocracy, military or civilian, progressive or conservative, traditional or reformist. The basic premise at this stage is that the judicial system of a country is like an enterprise of services, and, as any enterprise, it has to be organized efficiently and has to produce its services in a prompt, adequate, and effective manner. For this purpose, it does not matter whether the enterprise produces milk, violins, nylon, contraceptives, or guns. It has to be efficient and work better.

Examples of the tasks that can be undertaken at this stage are varied and numerous. An appellate judge in Ecuador complained that, because she had to spend most her time receiving visits from litigants and attorneys representing clients before her court, she could usually only write one decision a day—which, for the type of statutory appeals seen in Latin American countries is very low. Her court had a heavy backlog, but she neither saw anything wrong in meeting with one of the parties without the presence, or even knowledge of the other—a feature common in Latin American legal culture—nor did she think of the possibility of limiting the visits to certain hours and certain days, since the bar association would not like it.

Another example is a criminal trial court in Peru that called more than seven or eight hearings each afternoon, each one lasting only thirty or forty minutes, resulting in few results being reached and great delays in the disposition of cases. In Argentina, judges are in their courts only in the mornings, and most of the jurisdictional work is performed by legal secretaries or assistants, while the judges have to spend a great deal of time performing administrative tasks related to the budget, appointments, or promotion of court personnel. The content of the reforms needed to be carried out at this stage is very technical in nature and neutral politically. It has to do mainly with organization and administration. It is, above all, a task for an administrator.

Another task at this stage should be undertaken by educators. Judges in most developing countries are imbued with their importance as authorities and with the majesty and solemnity of their appointments, very much with an attitude of nineteenth-century civil servants. Very few of these judges realize that they are offering a service that many times has, in practice, the pretensions of a monopoly. Many of these judges behave with the indifference of a monopoly owner without realizing that this is only an illusion. No reform of the judicial system is possible without educating the judges about the nature of the service they perform, the resources and instruments the law offers to them, and the advantages of continuing legal training. In many countries, most judges are not aware of ways to use the law and its resources to solve extreme, different, or exceptional cases. The tendency is to resort to standard and formal solutions at the expense of justice, fairness, and equity. Many times, when the solution is difficult, they search for procedural causes of nullity in order to get the case out of their way.

For all these tasks, but especially for the educational ones, in extreme cases one can apply priorities, but significant success cannot be achieved unless it is possible to reach a large number of judges, diversified by geography, hierarchy, and specialty, in such a way that the benefits can be spread and felt throughout the system. Without this, law and code reform will remain on paper but never put into practice.

2. The second stage requires some degree of definition that is absent in the first. At least the general outline of an economic model exists that, in this case, is that of a market economy, free trade, private enterprise, and private property. The purpose of this stage is to create a climate that promotes trade, investment, and development and an atmosphere where the merchant, businessman, and banker feel safe and comfortable. One of the main items in the program has to be to eradicate corruption, even though this could also be undertaken in the first stage. Doing so involves undertaking measures making the administration of justice transparent; avoiding ex parte communications; making the judges and staff accountable for their acts; and promoting publication of, comment on, and open discussion about court decisions. A priority can be established for commercial, civil, tax, and customs courts, among others in this field.

Measures must also be adopted to economically discourage frivolous litigation and appeals, measures like raising the monetary threshold to appeal a judgment, making payment of the full amount due into a scroll account a necessary condition for an appeal to be granted, and raising the legal interest payable to a creditor when judgment is granted in his or her favor.

Achieving a proper economic model must take other points into consideration. As Ibrahim Shihata notes, the monetary costs of criminality can be quantified by the cost of insurance to foreign investors.[60] Private insurance covers kidnapping and ransom, hijacking, terrorist attacks, sabotage, and violent strikes.[61] In countries such as Colombia, narcotics cartels are major economic actors, shaping the economy and undermining the government.[62] The drug trade might even have the effect of deterring legal businesses from financing growth from public offerings for fear that a higher profile could make them the targets of kidnappers or blackmailers.[63] The presence of criminality also deters foreign investment.

An interesting development in countries like Peru and Colombia has been the creation of alternatives for dispute resolution. In Peru, the creation of courts of lay judges for small claims, petty offenses, and misdemeanors has produced a popular alternative to the ordinary dispute resolution mechanisms. These judges, who comprise more than 70 percent of the judges of Peru, enjoy more social prestige, and their decisions are better accepted by the community. Around 60 percent of their cases are either settled or not appealed. In Colombia, during the last four years, the government has created 107 conciliation centers, which, in some areas of conflicts like those arising with the police or other offices of the government, have resolved around 80 percent of the cases.

3. The third stage is more comprehensive because, unlike the first and second stages, it can be carried on in almost any type of political and social climate and requires none of the conditions necessary to make development sustainable in the long run. This stage must try to protect freedom, security, and opportunities for the individual in order to defend average citizens from the abuses and excesses of the government and the powerful. Without these conditions, no business community can develop and prosper in the long run. This stage would extend to criminal, constitutional, and administrative courts, but freedom and security would have to be secured by technical, nonpolitical means like freedom of information, transparency in acts of government—especially in the decision-making process—and accountability of public officials, including judges. These are, in fact, the most revealing and effective benchmarks or "conditions" that need to be met within the judicial system for reform to move forward.

E. Judicial Participation in the Project of Reform

One feature I have observed while participating in the reform and modernization of legal systems around the world is that, almost invariably, the strongest resistance to change comes from the judges themselves. Generally their first reaction is to feel threatened in the tenure of their jobs. Administrative and professional inertia in the ways things have been done for years, and perhaps decades, contributes to the resistance, as do their personal lives, which have adjusted to those ways. "Rent-seeking"[64] attitudes and habits, which involve a great variety of benefits that are not written anywhere but have developed in practice over a long period of time, also matter.[65] An additional reason for this resistance is cultural. In many countries, even though the laws and equipment have been modernized, the judges—especially within the countries of the civil law tradition—consider themselves as purely, or mainly, civil servants. This perspective allows them to not feel responsible for what is going wrong in their society.[66]

Another observation I have made during my experiences is that reforms introduced, either from the political power above or from academics or bar associations outside, tend to be ephemeral and short-lived, unless the judges become involved in the process, commit to the reforms, and feel that they own and conduct the whole project. Now, to start a process of modernization, adjustment, or reform of a court system, a great number of things are necessary.

For one, it is necessary to compile factual data that will make it possible to identify where the problems are. The data will also make it possible to measure the real progress and achievements of pilot projects. Further, the data must be organized in a meaningful and accurate manner. The organization of the data should present information in the context in which the judicial system operates: the administrative structure of the courts and the cases themselves; economic aspects of the budget, costs for the litigants and the invisible costs to society; and the availability of training, legal procedures, and ADR methods. Finally, it is necessary to gather information about physical facilities and equipment, the perception of justice by the community, and the real impact of judicial decisions in society. However, all this information is managed by judges, and if they do not participate in its analysis, it is easy to be deceived or become lost in a sea of statistics and trivia. For this reason, it is very useful to get judges involved in these projects as early as possible. This strategy could be carried out by interviewing judges one by one. But apart from the obvious disadvantage of the amount of time this would require, this method would entirely ignore the strong need felt by judges to share and discuss their experiences with their colleague judges. A better technique is to get together in workshops an adequate and significant number of judges, in a convenient location, to discuss common problems freely and frankly.

Such workshops have substantial advantages over both individual meetings and the distribution of written material. Among other benefits, workshops can help motivate judges in developing countries whose loneliness of work, isolation, and inadequacy of compensation should not be forgotten. Workshops can help develop judges' sense of observation and creativity to contribute to solutions, and they can be a morale booster, reinforcing pride in the job and satisfaction with what each judge is doing. At the same time, workshops may give judges a feeling of participation in a national or regional task that fulfills them not only as judges, but also as citizens and human beings. Such workshops, moreover, help involve judges in the process. Listening to their perceptions, experiences, and proposals for solution generally produces the result of judges not feeling that reform is something alien to them, imposed by a Supreme Court or Ministry of Justice or legislature, but is rather a process that involves them directly and that cannot succeed without them. It also makes the judges responsible for the results, and so makes them allies of reform.

Workshops, in addition, help identify those judges who show a better understanding of the nature of the needed changes and who possess the qualities of leadership that will become necessary at the stage when reforms must be implemented. Judicial reform can only be achieved through people with leadership qualities. Finally, workshops help encourage fraternity among judges. In light of the environment in which they work, it can be very helpful to have the opportunity to share experiences and opinions on matters of common interest, especially when judges are from different backgrounds, which in turn encourages socalization and helps form an *esprit de corps* among the judges.

A key point is the nature of the judges' participation in these workshops. Judges should attend to discover from their own experiences things that have always been in front of them but that they often are too busy or too distracted to notice—to discover things that are perceptible only through a perspective brought about by discussions with others. This opportunity to create a deeper consciousness of problems and to open a general debate in order to precipitate beneficial changes can occur in regional, national, or even transnational workshops.

In many places where foreign and international aid has flowed generously lately, judges are becoming indifferent and skeptical. If a very complex problem could be summed up in a couple of words, I would venture to say that those words are "participation" and "leadership." Judges should be allowed to share their experiences, articulate their thoughts about common problems, vent their frustrations and anger, discuss possibilities, suggest solutions, and dream and hope aloud. When this is done, case analysis and discussion of problems bring about astonishing and creative responses. All of these actions are at least as effective as audiovisual gadgets, computers, and the like. Technology is enormously important, but only when it is handled by a thinking, creative, and sensitive human being.

The reason why the World Bank is so optimistic about the future is because we have heard from and spoken with judges in such countries as Venezuela, Guatemala, Peru, Argentina, Mexico, Brazil, Ecuador, Poland, Russia, Egypt, and Indonesia. In all of these countries, the administration of justice is facing gigantic challenges and, in some, even government interference. But the starting point to any change is to find a few judges who are willing to take up the challenge and work hard in silence, for no or little applause, and certainly not for wealth. Training, therefore, must encourage initiative, creativity, and activism instead of passivity and conformism.

V. JUDGES AS SERVICE PROVIDERS AND THE USES OF JUDICIAL DISCRETION

We happy few, we band of brothers.
—W. Shakespeare, *Henry V*, Act IV, Scene 3

I dreamt that life was joy. I woke up and realized that life was service. I served and found that service was joy.
—R. Tagore

What for each of us is inevitable? Happiness.
—The Mahabharata

A. The Ideal of Judges as Servants of Society

A great part of the difficulty that the general public has in relating to law and justice as something relevant to their daily lives—and therefore, an area where governments, parliaments, international organizations, and the private sector should invest resources—is in the process by which statutes and regulations are made and enacted. A look a little below the surface shows us how in developing societies and societies in transition there is a gap between the law and the way in which society really conducts its affairs. This gap also accounts for the lack of credibility, observance, and respect that the legal system receives. This is the situation in many of our societies. Of all the legal actors, judges are the only ones who can help to bridge that gap peacefully and in order. But the judge has to understand how to produce a real impact in society, and judicial academies must prepare the judges for this role. In many countries, this training determines the difference between having a viable future or not, between law and order on the one hand and revolution on the other, and between peace and prosperity on one side and poverty and social decay on the other.

All this drama or tragedy begins in the most harmless and respectable way, when laws have to be passed and enacted. Information and data about most issues, in most developing countries, are either nonexistent or deficient. The state is not organized efficiently to provide ample access to the small amount of information available or to adequately channel the richly diverse points of view that an active and informed public opinion can provide to solve fundamental problems. Instead, by following a tradition from colonial times in some countries, or by way of paying a tribute of admiration to great legislators in others, foreign constitutions, codes, or laws become handy and more or less safe models to follow. Because, after all, who could go wrong following the American Constitution, the French Civil Code, the Swiss *Code Des Obligations*, or the German or Italian Codes? The surprising answer: almost everybody who does not live in the United States, France, Switzerland, Germany, or Italy.

Laws are compromises reached in democratic societies, between different and concrete interests in opposition. Therefore, in principle, laws reflect situations at a given time and place. Even though many transplants work partially, others produce only distorted images. It is exceptional, although it happens, that a country can successfully insert foreign models. Japan is one of several examples in which public opinion has accepted and observed a foreign model. In most other countries, appearances are equal, but the real functioning of laws is quite different. The problem is not one of enforcement but of social efficiency; of making the law really work; of gaining observance, respect, and credibility. General educators and police can help in certain cases and to certain degrees, but in this ocean of contradictions and incoherencies, the only person who has to face, live with, and solve these issues every day of the year is the judge.

To react adequately to this challenge, judges cannot be, as has been said, bureaucrats and formalistic officials. They must learn to decipher the signs of the social, ethical, economic, and political values held by societies in a global age, while still maintaining big internal and external differences. The need to avoid bureaucratic, formalistic approaches extends to all adjudicatory tasks of judges, whether in commercial civil litigation, criminal cases, or constitutional cases. Judges must become leaders of society upon whom, ultimately, depend all of these theories, principles, policies, hopes, and dreams. A judicial education that does not prepare judges to live up to this responsibility and to these expectations from society is not fulfilling its role, notwithstanding all the information, all the philosophy, and all the skills provided to the judges. Judges so trained will have no impact in the community. The beating heart, the breathing lungs, and the dreaming mind of the judiciary will be missing.

Service also implies that, in an age marked by the diversity in faiths, cultures, languages, alphabets, ethnicity, economic standards, education, and ideas and, paradoxically, aspiring to understand civilization, law, politics, and trade in a global perspective, judges must play an important part in dissolving barriers, building bridges, and opening ways. This is a wide gap to fill.

But judges and lawyers also have barriers of their own that may affect legal education. First, there are the obvious differences arising from the various conceptions about what a judge should be according to different common law cultures, civil law traditions, the *Shari'a*, and the systems of socialist countries in transition. In the common law culture, judges usually reach the bench after a long and successful career at the bar. In civil law countries, judges tend to pursue a career that many times begins as court auxiliary staff and later rises to become lower judges only a few years after graduation from law school. Islamic Cadis are closer to the civil law practice, but have a different approach. In socialist systems in transition, the practice is essentially identical to that of civil law systems. Another difference between systems arises out of whether judges are appointed or elected. Judges also differ in that some enjoy tenure for life or until they reach the age of retirement, and others are either appointed or elected for only a limited term. There are still other distinctions in whether or not judges come from cultures in which the judiciary is traditionally held in high social, moral, political, cultural, and intellectual esteem.

Most of those differences, however, come from an intellectual and formal way of understanding the work of the judge as being legalistic. But the true essence of the work of the judge is closer to the warmth of the human heart, in the same basic way in which mothers, teachers, foremen, friends, adjusters, neighbors, and colleagues help us to solve our daily conflicts from early childhood until death. The interpersonal dynamics in a conflict between two lovers in Istanbul or involving a thousand shareholders of a corporation in Chicago is not so different in essence. Conflict in human life is as natural as the seasons. The work of the judge is to help us to solve these conflicts with dignity, fairness, and love. This is clearly understood by judges as different as those on the councils of elders in Maya villages in Guatemala, judges in Zulu towns in South Africa, Justices of the Peace in Peru, elders applying Adat law in Indonesia, and learned and highly sophisticated jurists like Justice William Douglas in the United States and Lord Denning in the United Kingdom. In making human sufferings more bearable, in making dreams become realities, and in engineering hope, judges form a global brotherhood that interprets the system of values held by the public opinion of our time through the use of the terrestrial language of contracts, property, torts, individual rights, and personal freedom. They must be aware that to build a global civilization, it is necessary to go beyond the mere technicalities and formalities of the law to arrive at the essence of human conflict, communication, understanding, and dialogue. One of the most important tools for this purpose is the exercise of judicial discretion. But too many times judges are reluctant to use it. In most countries judges do not use even 25 percent of their powers and real authority.

B. The Uses of Judicial Discretion

In Cervantes' *Don Quixote*, when Sancho Panza is appointed governor of Barataria Island, he is required by the villagers to try a number of cases as judge. One of those cases involves a law requiring every person who enters the village over a particular bridge to declare his purpose for entering the village. If the person tells the truth, he is allowed to go free, but if he tells a lie, as punishment he is hanged at the gallows next to the bridge. One day a man crossing the bridge into the village is asked why he was going there and replies, "I am going to be hanged." Thus, if the man is let go, he would have told a lie and should have been hanged, but if he is hanged, he would have told the truth and should have been let go. In either instance, the solution would be legally unsatisfactory.

Contemporary lawyers are as cunning as the man crossing Cervantes' bridge, and changing social, economic, political, and cultural circumstances place modern judges in situations where there is in the law no express disposition to guide them. In our times, certain factors such as inflation and existing family relations present the judge with everyday problems for which there are no express provisions in the law. The questions that must be resolved are how such changes in social, political, economic, and cultural circumstances should be faced and whether the civil law system—since the common law judge's discretion is well known—is adequately equipped to meet that challenge. One of the most effective ways by which a legal system can do this is through the discretionary powers given to its judges.

In evaluating such powers, one must first determine what the general image of the discretionary powers of the judiciary is in the civil law. One of the leading comparatists in this country, Professor John H. Merryman says:

> In the civil law a judge is a kind of expert clerk. He is presented with a fact situation to which a ready legislative response will be readily found in all except the extraordinary case. His function is merely to find the right legislative provision, couple it with the fact situation, and bless the solution that is more or less automatically produced from the union. The whole process of judicial decision is made to fit into the formal syllogism of scholastic logic. The major premise is in the statute, the facts of the case furnish the minor premise, and the conclusion inevitably follows.
>
> The net image is of the judge as an operator of a machine designed and built by legislators.
>
> Judicial service is a bureaucratic career; the judge is a functionary, a civil servant; the judicial function is narrow, mechanical, and uncreative.[67]

The foundations, if not the justifications, for this image of the civil law judge are of two kinds: historical and structural. Among the historical reasons, traced to Rome, one finds that in the Roman legal system the civil law judge's predecessor, the iudex, was not a prominent man of the law. For a long time the post was filled with laymen who enjoyed rather low social prestige, because the post was often gained through royal or political favors and, in some cases, was even bought by the candidate. This situation gave rise to the attitude that judges were not fair, honest, or hard working and that they rendered their judgments in favor of the most powerful. The code instituted by Frederick the Great of Prussia attempted to be judgeproof; it contained over sixteen thousand articles and left no room for judicial interpretation. In fact, the judge was forbidden to interpret the law. In France, the theory of separation of powers, which arose during and after the Revolution as a reaction to abuses committed by judges, in effect put judges on "probation" in society.

Besides these historical factors, there are certain structural reasons for not granting ample discretionary powers to the judge. Among these reasons is the idea that a code is a self-sufficient, self-contained body of law that needs no discretionary assistance. Related to this idea is the principle that reason must prevail over experience, for one must remember that at one time reason was the goddess of philosophy. The influence of Kant and the rationalist philosophy had reached its height, and there was a strong reaction against the use of mere experience and pragmatism. As a second structural reason, in some civil law countries there exists the crime of prevarication—committed almost solely by judges. Prevarication consists of rendering a judgment that goes against the text of the law; this, of course, creates a serious drawback to granting discretionary powers to the judge. A third structural reason is that some judges are not as creative as others; their case loads and routine are enemies of judicial discretion. When a judge has a large case load and approaches his daily work as routine, he will find it easier to act mechanically and more difficult to exercise his potential discretion.

This image of the civil law judge is exaggerated to the point of distortion. The civil law judge enjoys a wider discretion than is commonly believed. His accepted image has arisen as a result of a different cultural approach. When comparatists examine the civil law judge, they must consider how the judge functions within the general context of the system in which he operates.

One now finds that the judiciary in some civil law countries enjoys increasing prestige and importance. Common and familiar examples of this heightened stature are the importance of *jurisprudence constante* and the rising number of new cases in which court decisions have a binding force in civil law countries. Some examples of this phenomenon in Latin America are the Amparo law of Mexico, the sumulas of the Supreme Court of Brazil, and the decisions of the civil law courts sitting *en banque* in Argentina. These developments reveal that the role of the judge in civil law, in spite of everything else, is not decreasing. On the contrary, the judge is obtaining more power, although the paradox is that he does not like to use it.

Among the structural reasons opposing the accepted image of the civil law judge is the general nature in which many laws are drafted. In *Major Legal Systems in the World Today*, Rene David describes the civil law technique by saying: "To formulate the legal rule in the most general terms means that it is less precise; it means that the judge is given greater discretion in its application."[68] On the other hand, the image of the judge bound by the strictness and rigor of formal logic is not compatible with many of the doctrines of modern times. Two legal philosophers working in Latin America, Professors Luis Recasens Siches and Garcia Maynes, have asserted that the formal syllogism traditionally associated with civil law is no longer applicable; the logic to be applied to the law is not the formal one, but what they call "logic of the reasonable." Likewise, one of the leading philosophers of our time, Professor Kelsen, in his *Pure Theory of Law*, describes the legal rule not as an imperative in the sense that J.L. Austin describes it, but as a frame of possibilities that must be fulfilled by the judge according to the particular characteristics of each case.[69] In view of the fact that these arguments are contrary to the foundation of the accepted image of the civil law judge, it is wise to delve more deeply into the civil law system in order to see how that system works in practice.

One of the main problems that legislation must address is how to capture reality in the few precepts of a legal rule. Many times the information used by the legislator to produce a new rule or a new piece of legislation is insufficient in terms of data or elements of fact to accurately reflect all the richness and variety of the issue regulated. Many times the interests that are actually in conflict in society are different from the apparent conflicts solved by the law; hence, many times the observer of a legal system finds contradictions between laws as they are given and the actual behavior of people in society. Everyone who works in a legal system—legislators, practitioners, professors, and judges—are conscious of these contradictions. Legislators strive to do their best both in gathering maximum information about a problem and in synthesizing that information into a rule of law, but once the legislators have completed their task, their work obtains a life of its own. The legislators can believe justly that they did their job in the best way they could and then turn their attention to another problem. The attorneys for the parties involved in litigation are conscious of the shortcomings of rules of law, but they, too, can only do their best to present their clients' cases. The academicians are conscious of the contradictions between law and reality. They can meditate and conjure up devices for overcoming such contradictions, but they can also postpone solutions until a better occasion for dealing with a particular contradiction arises. The only person who cannot postpone or avoid a contradiction is the judge. He is the one who must solve, here and now, all contradictions that he finds existing between the law as it is given and the actual behavior of people. This is particularly so when the judge tries to be just and is not content with simply applying the mechanics of the law—when she wishes to achieve justice in the judgment she gives.

Contradiction is inherent in the law. The moment that a statute is posited, it begins to age and become inadequate for unanticipated future circumstances. Life never stops. Perhaps some of the characteristics of the civil law system, such as the belief that reason can do too much, have helped to accentuate the contradiction between law and reality. What can a judge do? As Ehrlich says, "There is no excuse, as it were, for squeezing decisions out of a statute with a hydraulic press."[70] There is no easy way out. Even at the height of post-revolutionary France, Article 4 of the French Civil Code provided that the judge who refused to render a decision under the pretext of the silence, obscurity, or insufficiency of the law was liable to prosecution for a refusal of justice. Professor Roger Perrot observes that: "The judge has the immense power to transform a ready-made garment into a tailor-made suit at the price of alterations that may be considerable and sometimes rather unexpected. From this it has often been deduced that the judicial authority is thus able to perform a work of rejuvenation."[71] No legal system can survive in any society without an acceptable degree of judicial discretion. In the civil law, one finds discretion at the following levels: within the civil law as a system, within the civil codes, and within the particular rules of those codes.

Discretion within the system itself is a technique which gives ample leeway to the judge in his characterization or interpretation of facts. When a judge is faced with a particular set of facts, he has the choice of placing those facts under one legal category or another—he has a choice in characterizing the facts according to law. An example of this technique is the decision of the Supreme Court of the writer's own country, Peru, regarding irregular marriages. A large percentage of the people of Peru live under irregular marriages, which means the parties cohabit without having gone through the accepted procedure for contracting a legally valid marriage. The question of the legal effect of these irregular marriages has been the subject of much discussion. Until some time ago, the legislature in Peru refused to give legal effect to irregular marriages, and the Supreme Court, in principle, could do nothing to recognize such unions. However, it was still very difficult for the judges to completely ignore a phenomenon that was occurring among an enormously large percentage of the population. The Supreme Court of Peru then found a solution by characterizing the facts of such a situation in an imaginative and unexpected way. The case was an unusual one in which the "husband" died after living with his "wife" for thirty or thirty-five years and after raising a family together and being, for all practical purposes, like any other family, except for the lack of legal sanction. All of his legal inheritance was to be inherited not by the woman with whom he lived, but by some of his blood relatives. The Court declared, on the basis of the couple's having lived together for so many years, that there existed between the man and the woman a "de facto" partnership that should produce all the effects of such an association. As a partnership ends by the death of one of the partners, so had this de facto partnership ended by the demise of the husband. Hence, the assets and liabilities of the husband were to be liquidated, with half of the proceeds going to the woman and the other half to the man's estate. Like Hamlet, the judge in such cases could say: "I could be bounded in a nutshell and count myself a King of infinite space."

The second technique for exercising discretion within a civil law system is through the interpretation of the law. There are some codes which attempt to be as precise and exact as possible concerning the methods of interpretation to be used, such as literal interpretation, logical interpretation, and exegetical interpretation, but always it is the judge who must choose among the many methods available. One of the great Louisiana jurists, Judge Albert Tate, said on one occasion that the legal problem is not always simple; the meaning of the law may not be clear, hence it must admit of judicial discretion in interpretation in order to produce a just result.[72] Thus, the choice of methods of interpretation to produce a just result is always an exercise of judicial discretion. Professor Julio Cueto-Rua, in *Judicial Methods of Interpretation of the Law*, very aptly notes that, "In choosing the method to which he will turn when a grammatical-logical approach is unsuccessful, the judge will choose that method of interpretation which will yield the most fruitful result in the case. By most fruitful result is meant that result most consistent with justice."[73]

In *The Merchant of Venice*, Shylock insists on specific performance of Antonio's bond, even though Antonio has offered him money in lieu of the pound of his flesh, which he has committed himself to give in case of default. The judge, in exercising discretion, has a choice of several methods of interpretation by which to reach a just result. The decision is that Shylock should have his pound of flesh but is not entitled to a single drop of blood. The judge in this case uses the literal method of interpretation to reach what seemed the most just solution to the case.

Apart from these general techniques present within the codes themselves, the judge in the civil law tradition has sufficient discretion to achieve a justice beyond that granted by the mere words of the law. Professor Merryman, for instance, states:

> That the dogma that a code can be complete and coherent fails to survive even a cursory glance at the jurisprudence. . . . The books are full of decisions in which the court has had to fill gaps in the legislative scheme and reconcile apparently conflicting statutes. Although the text of a statute remains unchanged, its meaning and applications often change in response to social pressures, and new problems arise that are not even touched on by any existing legislation.[74]

However complete a code might seem, there will always be gaps and interstices which require the judge's exercise of discretion.

The gaps in statutes or codes are a reality that must be recognized. How can those gaps be filled? There are several solutions provided in the legislation itself. First, for example, the Civil Code of Switzerland, which dates from 1912, establishes in Article 1 that all gaps left by the code are to be filled in by the judge, who acts as a legislator. Professor Alfred E. von Overbeck notes in this regard that "the Swiss legislator was the first modern legislator to recognize that he needs the judge to achieve his own tasks. . . ."[75] Even though the Austrian code dates from 1811 and its text does not seem to expressly permit the use of the same technique allowed under the Swiss Code, more than one commentator has interpreted Article 7 of the Austrian Civil Code as allowing the judge to act as a legislator in such cases.

Another code technique used for filling gaps is legislation that requires the judge to resort to general principles of law. This is the solution opted for in the Argentine Civil Code of 1869,[76] the Swiss Code of 1912,[77] the Mexican Civil Code of 1932,[78] the Peruvian Civil Code of 1936,[79] the Brazilian Civil Code of 1942[80] and the Italian Civil Code of 1942.[81] The use of such general principles of law allows the judge ample resources from which to draw in deciding cases involving gaps in the law, and some of those codes are even more precise.

The doctrine of abuse of right is a long-standing doctrine in many civil law countries. The doctrine of abuse of right condemns not the exercise of a right, but the abusive use of it in such a way as to damage another person. A good example of the application of the doctrine of abuse of right is found in literature, specifically in Shylock's efforts to exercise his right against Antonio. When

Antonio falls into default and can not pay Shylock, the latter demands the pound of flesh to which he is entitled as a result of his agreement with Antonio. The exercise of that stipulation is, however, an abuse of right because Shylock could have received money for the payment of both the principal and interest due, since Antonio, although late, did offer a repayment in money. Besides this literary comparison, the doctrine of abuse of right has very interesting modern uses in such fields as antitrust legislation, especially in the European Union, where monopolies are not condemned per se, but only insofar as they constitute an abuse of a dominant position in the market.

Another general principle of law to which judges may turn in filling gaps is the principle that condemns undue or unjust enrichment. Unjust enrichment is based upon the tenet that no one ought to enrich himself at the expense of another. An example of unjust enrichment is provided by a case heard by the Supreme Court of Peru in which the facts centered around the credit sale of a secondhand truck. The dealer asked for a 20 percent down payment and, for the remainder of the purchase price, he asked the buyer to sign a number of promissory notes. In the sales agreement, it was stipulated that if the buyer defaulted in the payment of two installments, the dealer would repossess the truck. As could be anticipated, the truck broke down soon after the sale, and the purchaser, unable to work as a result, could not pay the remainder of the price. Consequently, the dealer repossessed the truck and not only kept the down payment, but also sued for the balance due under the promissory notes. Even though the seller had the formal right to sue on the notes, the court rendered judgment in favor of the defendant on the grounds that the seller would otherwise be unduly enriched.

A third widely recognized general principle of law relied upon by judges in filling gaps in the law is that of equity. As it is understood within the meaning of Articles 21, 1903, 1964, and 1965 of the Louisiana Civil Code, equity is based on natural law, on reason, and on the idea that one should not do unto others that which he would not wish others to do unto him. If there are any doubts about how broad the powers of a judge are under Article 21, one need only quote Judge Tate, who says:

> [A] practicing state appellate judge for twenty-five years prior to my federal service, I must confess that instances arise with increasing frequency in the present day in which, with all the judicial good faith in the world, no real legislative intent or text can be found to have intended to govern a particular new conflict of interest. In the past I have spoken of this dilemma, arising in part from rapid changes (which in a new social context deprive the literal legislative text of any functionally-intended application to a "new"—unforeseen or unanticipated—conflict of interest), and also from the legislative preoccupation with social and governmental problems of greater magnitude than the tinkering with private law to keep it current. On those occasions I have suggested that article 21 of the Louisiana Civil Code permits the Louisiana judge, in the unprovided-for case, to formulate the new law-rule or law application on the basis of its fairness and social utility, as would a legislator.[82]

Finally, the judge exercises discretion with regard to particular rules of law. A general survey of the Louisiana Civil Code, for instance, provides numerous examples of such rules allowing the exercise of judicial discretion. The judge in some cases must determine whether an agreement or obligation is against the public order or the public good. For example, Article 11 provides:

> Individuals cannot by their conventions derogate from the force of laws made for the preservation of public order or good morals. But in all cases in which it is not expressly or impliedly prohibited they can renounce what the law has established in their favor, when the renunciation does not affect the rights of others, and is not contrary to the public good.

Likewise, under Articles 217, 1892, and 2031, in cases closely connected with the notion of public good, the judge must decide what constitutes good morals, or *bonos mores*.[83] In other cases, the judge must decide when someone has acted in good faith or with good intention.[84] Conversely, the judge has discretion in determining when a spouse has acted in bad faith in the management of the community under Article 2354.[85] In examining the intention of the parties, the judge at times must not only determine good and bad faith, but must also examine the parties' motives in terms of interest or passion.[86]

A determination of whether an act has or has not been performed in a reasonable manner is also within the discretion of the judge.[87] In other instances, the judge is called upon to evaluate certain circumstances,[88] to examine the nature of a particular relationship,[89] to determine the intention of the parties,[90] and to determine whether something has been done with prudence.[91] The code grants a judge ample discretion to determine whether or not an agreement or act constitutes simple lesion.[92] In other instances, the judge is given even broader discretion as, for example, when he is called upon to determine whether or not an act or agreement is immoral or plainly unjust[93] or when he is given latitude in assessing damages.[94] There are also instances in which the discretion of the judge is expressly established.[95] Finally, to come full circle, paragraph 10 of Article 3556 defines discretion: "When it is said that something is left to the discretion of the judge, it signifies that he ought to decide according to the rules of equity and the nature of the circumstances."[96]

In completing the circle, one can return to the situation in which Sancho Panza finds himself when confronted with the man who, upon being questioned about his entry into the village, replied that he was going to be hanged. In terms reminiscent of Portia's speech on the quality of mercy, or of the text of Article 21 of the Louisiana Civil Code, Sancho Panza allows the man to go free, stating that in cases when justice is in doubt, the judge should be merciful.

VI. CONCLUSION

Laws are not goals to be pursued, but starting points to achieve democracy, peace, progress, development, fulfillment, and happiness. They are not an end in themselves, but an instrument. They are not intellectual academic devices to amaze us, but political tools to make society a better and more livable environment. Laws are not the property of the state, but belong to the community as a whole. Only in such a context will citizens behave as components of a system, and laws, even if not perfect, will be efficient in helping us fulfill our expectations, achieve our projects, and crown our ambitions. For these ends, none are so fit and qualified as the judges, provided that they assume their roles as leaders of society to put the machinery of justice at the service of the community instead of using it as a tool to exercise only authority and naked power.

The culture of service is like a current that runs deep under most of the great legal systems of the world: Roman civil; common law; *Shari'a*, or Islamic law; and the law of countries that were at one time under the socialist legal system. Wherever and whenever it comes to the surface and is met by judges who embrace it and understand their true role as leaders, there begins to appear in societies oases of peace, freedom, dignity, economic growth, development, trade, investment, reduction of poverty, and social justice. This is due mostly to the work of judges, who are, above anything else, hard laborers of hope and quiet craftsmen of the highest dreams.

NOTES

This chapter is dedicated to Roberto, Ana Cecilia, Guillermo and Alicia, in remembrance of the many nights spent breathing the sweet aroma of Huánuco under the sign of Orion. Much of this study is based on interviews with Ministry of Justice officials, court administrators, judges, and lawyers (i.e., the providers of judicial service), as well as ordinary citizens (i.e., the users or consumers of the judicial service). These interviews were conducted around the world in the author's capacity with the World Bank; the author has the notes on file. To ensure an open and accurate dialogue, the author guaranteed many of the judicial officials and others that they would not be named. The chapter recollects the experiences the author gathered as an associate justice of the Supreme Court of Peru and as a member of the Judicial Reform Commission of Peru, where he was involved in a very important program of the American Bar Association (ABA) conducted by Charles Norberg and coordinated by Kathrine L. Ebert. It also reflects the experiences he gathered with Professor Seymour Rubin at the Interamerican Juridical Committee of the Organization of American States and by serving as a Judicial Specialist at the World Bank for several years, working around the world. The author received many suggestions, which greatly improved his observations, from Mr. Ibrahim Shihata, Douglas Webb, Andrew Vorkink, Judge Sandra Oxner, Judge Bertrand du Marais, Teresa Genta-Fons, Reynaldo Pastor, Roberto Laver, Lama Abu-Odeh, Izumi Ohno, Jose Augusto Carvalho, Malcom Rowat, and Waleed Malik. The author also received very useful suggestions from Professor Philip S. James from Buckingham and Leeds; Professor Joseph Norton from Southern Methodist University, London and Hong Kong; Professor Dale B. Furnish from Arizona State University; Professor Luke Nottage from Kyushu University, Japan; Luis Pasara from the United Nations; Diego Garcia Sayán; Javier de Belaunde; German Larrieu; and his students from SMU, Rosario Segovia, Annie Borello, Kirsten Doty, Fallyme Guerrero, and Charles Tardivat. None of these contributors, however, is responsible in any way for the ideas expressed in this chapter, which are entirely the author's, as are the shortcomings. In this chapter the author has reproduced parts of his works previously printed in other publications: much of Part III is drawn from "The Culture of Service in the Administration of Justice," *Transnational Law & Contemporary Problems*, 1996; much of Part IV is drawn from "Judicial Discretion in the Civil Law," *Louisiana Law Review*, 1982. The author also owes his gratitude to Oriana Fretz and Monica Tomasevich.

1. HERNANDO DE SOTO, THE OTHER PATH (New York: Harper & Row, 1991); JOSE MATOS MAR, DESBORDE POPULAR Y CRISIS DEL ESTADO (Lima: Instituto de Estudios Peruanos, 1984); ROGELIO PÉREZ PERDOMO & PEDRO NIKKEN, DERECHO Y PROPIEDAD DE LA VIVIENDA EN LOS BARRIOS DE CARACAS (Caracas: Universidad Central de Venezuela, 1991); TINA ROSENBERG, THE CHILDREN OF CAIN: VIOLENCE AND THE VIOLENT IN LATIN AMERICA (New York: Penguin Putnam, 1992); Kenneth L. Karst, *Rights in Land and Housing in an Informal Legal System: The Barrios of Caracas*, 19 AM. J. COMP. L. 550 (1971); Keith S. Rosenn, *Brazil's Legal Culture: The Jeito Revisited*, 1 FLA. J. INT'L L. 1 (1984).

2. Katarina Mathernova, Presentation at a Law and Judicial Reform Seminar at the World Bank, Washington, D.C. (1997).

3. Oliver Wendell Holmes, *The Path of the Law*, 10 HARV. L. REV. 457, n.8 (1897).

4. Part 3, ch. 9, art. 909 of NAFTA.

5. *See supra* note 1.

6. *See supra* note 1.

7. *See supra* note 1.

8. *See supra* note 1.

9. A.V. DICEY, LAW AND OPINION IN ENGLAND IN THE 19TH CENTURY (London: Macmillan, 1917).

10. MORRIS GINSBERG, LAW AND OPINION IN ENGLAND IN THE 20TH CENTURY (Westport, Conn.: Greenwood Press, 1974).

11. *See* HERNANDO DE SOTO, THE OTHER PATH: THE INVISIBLE REVOLUTION IN THE THIRD WORLD 131–87 (June Abbot trans., New York: Harper & Row, 1989); DOUGLASS C. NORTH, EL MARCO INSTITUCIONAL PARA EL DESARROLLO ECONÓMICO (Lima: Instituto Apoyo/Banco InterAndino, 1995) [hereinafter *El Marco Institucional*]; DOUGLASS C. NORTH, TRANSACTIONS COSTS, INSTITUTIONS AND ECONOMIC PERFORMANCE (San Francisco: Institute for Contemporary Studies, 1992) [hereinafter *Transactions Costs*]; Douglass C. North, *Economic Performance through Time*, 84 AM. ECON. REV. 359 (1994).

12. *See* Ibrahim F.I. Shihata, *Judicial Reform in Developing States and the Role of the World Bank, in* JUDICIAL REFORM IN LATIN AMERICA AND THE CARIBBEAN: PROCEEDINGS OF A WORLD BANK CONFERENCE (Malcom Rowat et al. eds., World Bank Technical Paper No. 280, 1995); Ibrahim F.I. Shihata, *Judicial Reform: Issues Addressed in World Bank Projects* (Oct. 1995) (unpublished paper presented at the Inter-American Development Bank Conference in Montevideo, Uruguay, about Justice and Development in Latin America and the Caribbean: on file with author).

13. In a conversation on this subject, Justice Anthony Kennedy noted that there are several religious societies that do not reveal an attitude of practical service. He also mentioned that this matter received the attention of Alexis de Tocqueville, who considered that this practical attitude of service, in the case of the United States, was the result of the attitude of the first colonizers who sought to sever their links with the Old World

and start anew in an environment that was unknown, difficult, hostile, and aggressive. These circumstances made the colonizers more dependent on one another. *See generally* ALEXIS DE TOQUEVILLE, DEMOCRACY IN AMERICA (Francis Bowen ed. & Henry Reeve trans., New York: Alfred A. Knopf, 1991) (1864).

14. Roberto G. MacLean, *Judicial Discretion in the Civil Law*, 43, LA. L. REV. 45 (1982).

15. HANS KELSEN, INTRODUCTION TO THE PROBLEMS OF LEGAL THEORY 80 (Bonnie L. Paulson & Stanley L. Paulson trans., Oxford: Clarendon Press 1992) (1934).

16. Fernando de Trazegnies, *La Muerte del Legislador*, Acceptance Speech Made to Membership of the Academy of Law, Peru (1995), *in* BOLETIN DEL INSTITUTO DE INVESTIGACIONES JURÌDICAS DE MEJICO (Mexico City: Universidad Nacional Autonoma de Mexico, 1997). These discourses and reflections take full meaning when we realize that de Trazegnies was one of the authors of the Peruvian Civil Code of 1984 and an influential writer on torts.

17. *Mark* 2:24 and 2:27 (King James).

18. In many developing countries, oral testimony is regarded with contempt to the point that judges are not even present when it takes place.

19. This is an important point which we will come back to later. *See infra*, Part. III J 3.

20. I am not referring to specialized courts of general jurisdiction. Admittedly, the United States and other countries have specialized courts to deal with many different issues. But in these situations the actors may ultimately appeal to the courts of general jurisdiction and eventually the Supreme Court. The phenomenon I refer to here is the situation where the actor in the parallel specialized court is precluded from appealing to the courts of general jurisdiction of the Supreme Court.

21. *See generally* works cited, *supra* note 1.

22. MARIE-HENRI BEYLE (STENDHAL), THE RED AND THE BLACK (C.K. Scott Moncrieff trans., New York: Boni & Liveright, 1926).

23. A. VILHEM LUNDSTEDT, LEGAL THINKING REVISED: MY VIEWS ON LAW 53–64 (Stockholm: Almqvist & Wiksell, 1956).

24. It should be noted that personnel is one very important aspect at this level of administration.

25. Different countries exhibit varied judge–to–staff-member ratios. In Russia, for example, the ratio of judges to staff members is one to three, while Guatemala has a ratio of one to eleven.

26. *See supra*, page 127, for specific illustrations of these indirect effects.

27. In some countries, however, such as Chile, Indonesia, or Russia, membership in a bar association is not obligatory for all attorneys.

28. *See El Marco Institucional, supra* note 11; *Transactions Costs, supra* note 11 at at 260–1; *Economic Performance through Time, supra* note 11; Robert M. Sherwood et al., *Judicial Systems and Economic Performance*, 34 Q. REV. ECON. & FIN. 101 (1994).

29. *See supra*, Part II L.

30. *See* Sherwood et al., *supra* note 28.

31. Comment made in a personal conversation with the author.

32. In addition to Hamlet's soliloquy, the more recent Janacek opera titled *The Makropoulos Case* has put music and imagination to judicial delay—the background to the opera is a legal case lasting more than seventy years!

33. This fear of terrorists is not unjustified given that from 1980 to 1990, Medellin

drug traffickers "were presumed responsible for the murders of 300 judges" in Colombia. Rosenberg, *supra* note 1 at 24.

34. Curiously, many attorneys who willingly engage in these ex parte communications are upset when judges interrupt their oral arguments with questions. Attorneys also lose perspective about the service they perform. In this aspect, the participation by the community is essential. There is much more to say about this, but it is beyond the scope of this chapter.

35. BBC SUMMARY OF WORLD BROADCASTS: RUSSIAN BANKERS DEMAND LEGISLATION TO PROTECT THEM FROM ASSASSINATION ATTEMPTS (British Broadcasting Corporation, Aug. 4, 1995), available in LEXIS, News Library, Curnws File. The Russian Mafia has in fact settled down somewhat because, in order to "operate," they demand of the person "hiring" them the production of a valid and conclusive judgment.

36. In the United States, some argue that excessive damage awards discourage investment. Obviously awards should be economically realistic. While in the United States a child kissed by a schoolmate may receive several hundred dollars, in Latin America, a wrongful death action may yield only one thousand dollars in damages.

37. Owen M. Fiss, *The Right Degree of Independence, in* TRANSITION TO DEMOCRACY IN LATIN AMERICA: THE ROLE OF THE JUDICIARY 55–6 (Irwin P. Stotzky ed., Boulder: Westview Press, 1993); Paul W. Kahn, *Independence and Responsibility in the Judicial Role, in* TRANSITION TO DEMOCRACY IN LATIN AMERICA, *supra* at 73, 76–9.

38. *See* Fiss, *supra* note 37 at 55; Kahn, *supra* note 37 at 74–6.

39. *See* Fiss, *supra* note 37 at 55–6.

40. *See* Kahn, *supra* note 37 at 79–81.

41. *See* Fiss, *supra* note 37 at 59.

42. Stephen G. Breyer, *Judicial Independence in the United States* 4 (unpublished paper presented at the Conference of Supreme Courts of the Americas, Washington, D.C., 1995: on file with author).

43. *Id.*

44. *Id.* at 5.

45. *Id.*

46. *See* Fiss, *supra* note 37 at 61.

47. *See supra*, part III I 3.

48. *See* Fiss, *supra* note 37 at 55.

49. *Id.* at 9.

50. *Id.* at 9–10.

51. *See* Fiss, *supra* note 37 at 55–6.

52. *See generally* Edward G. Synder, *The Dirty Legal War: Human Rights and the Role of Law in Chile 1973–1995*, 2 TULSA J. COMP. & INT'L L. 253, 270–5 (1995) (discussing the Chilean Supreme Court's failure "to safeguard the civil and constitutional rights of Chilean citizens"); Robert G. Vaughn, *Articles: Proposals for Judicial Reform in Chile*, 16 FORDHAM INT'L L.J. 578, 594 (1993) (discussing proposals to limit the disciplinary authority of the Supreme Court in Chile).

53. *See* Kahn, *supra* note 37 at 79.

54. *Id.*

55. *See supra*, Part II M for discussion of the use of judicial discretion.

56. Roberto MacLean, *Judicial Reasoning and Social Reality in Peru*, 28 Am. J. Comp. L. 489 (1980) (Dale B. Furnish trans.).

57. *See supra* note 16 and accompanying text.

58. Judges have much to improve in this regard. In most cases, judges do not even use 20 percent of their discretionary powers.

59. 347 U.S. 483 (1954).

60. I.F.I. Shihata, *MIGA and Foreign Investment* 145, note 12 (1988).

61. *Id.*

62. *Colombia: Cali High*, THE ECONOMIST (Dec. 25, 1993).

63. *Colombia's Financial Markets: Opening at Last*, THE ECONOMIST (Dec. 18, 1993).

64. Edgardo Buscaglia & Maria Dakolias, *Judicial Reform in Latin America: Economic Efficiency vs. Institutional Inertia* (Working Paper No. Econ-2377-06-495, School of Business Administration, Georgetown University, 1995).

65. Some of the several examples we have found are that in one country, court support personnel are used by judges to do errands for their wives and families, considering this as an unofficial compensation for the low salaries judges are paid. In another country, judges' salaries are so low that they "moonlight" in order to earn some extra income, even though they are not supposed to work on anything but their activities as judges. In a third country, judges appoint members of their families as paid assistants in order to supplement low income.

66. When judges in several countries are asked about the reasons why their judicial systems don't work properly, their answers include the lack of funds, the lack of political support, the lack of cooperation from the lawyers, the lack of proper and adequate legal education, and bad publicity from the press as well as interference from the political powers in the region or country. Very rarely will judges spontaneously accept that they have a share of the responsibility and that there is a great deal they can do independently from other factors in order to change society.

67. J. MERRYMAN, THE CIVIL LAW TRADITION 37–39 (Stanford: Stanford UP, 1969).

68. R. DAVID & J. BRIERLEY, MAJOR LEGAL SYSTEMS IN THE WORLD TODAY 91, 2d ed. (New York: Free Press, 1978).

69. H. KELSEN, PURE THEORY OF LAW 351 (Berkeley: University of California Press, 1976).

70. E. Ehrlich, *Judicial Freedom of Decision: Its Principles and Objects, in* SCIENCE OF LEGAL METHOD: SELECTED ESSAYS 76 (Boston: Boston Book Co., 1969).

71. Roger Perrot, *The Judge: The Extent and Limit of His Role in Civil Matters*, 50 TUL. L. REV. 495, 496 (1976).

72. Albert Tate, *Techniques of Judicial Interpretation in Louisiana*, 22 LA. L. REV. 727, 754 (1962).

73. J. CUETO-RUA, JUDICIAL METHODS OF INTERPRETATION OF THE LAW 276 (Baton Rouge: Louisiana State University, Law School, Publications Institute, 1981).

74. Merryman, *supra* note 67 at 44.

75. Von Overbeck, *Some Observations on the Role of the Judge Under the Swiss Civil Code*, 37 LA. L. REV. 681, 685 (1977).

76. Codigo Civil de la República Argentina Art. 16 (1869).

77. Code Civil Suisse Art. 4 (1912).

78. Codigo Civil Para El Distrito y Territorios Federales Art. 19 (1932).

79. Codigo Civil Peruano Art. 23 (1936).

80. Codigo Civil Brasileiro Art. 4 (1942).

81. Codice Civile del Regno D'Italia Art. 12 (1942).

82. Albert Tate, *The "New" Judicial Solution: Occasions for and Limits to Judicial Creativity*, 54 TUL. L. REV. 877, 885 (1980).

83. *See* Louisiana Civil Code Art. 217 ("As long as the child remains under the authority of his father and mother, he is bound to obey them in everything which is not contrary to good morals and the laws."); La. Civ. Code Art. 1892 ("That is considered as morally impossible, which is forbidden by law, or contrary to morals. All contracts having such an object are void."); La. Civ. Code Art. 2031 ("Every condition of a thing impossible, or contra bonos mores (repugnant to moral conduct) or prohibited by law, is null, and renders void the agreement which depends on it.").

84. *See, e.g.*, Louisiana Civil Code Art. 1901 ("Agreements legally entered into have the effect of laws on those who have formed them. They can not be revoked, unless by mutual consent of the parties, or for causes acknowledged by law. They must be performed with good faith."); La. Civ. Code Arts. 3006 and 3033.

85. *See* Louisiana Civil Code Art. 2354 ("A spouse is liable for any loss or damage caused by fraud or bad faith in the management of the community property.").

86. *See* Louisiana Civil Code Art. 419 ("He who petitions for the interdiction of any person, and fails in obtaining such interdiction, may be prosecuted for and sentenced by pay damages, if he shall have acted from motives of interest or passion.").

87. *See, e.g.*, Louisiana Civil Code Art. 218 ("An unemancipated minor cannot quit the parental house without the permission of his father and mother, who have the right to correct him, provided it be done in a reasonable manner."); La. Civ. Code Art. 2937.

88. *See, e.g.*, Louisiana Civil Code Art. 160 ("In determining whether the claimant spouse is entitled to alimony, the court shall consider his or her earning capability, in light of all other circumstances."); Louisiana Civil Code Art. 231.

89. *See, e.g.*, Louisiana Civil Code Art. 3006 ("The judge must have regard to the nature of the affair, and the difficulty of communication between the principal and the attorney.").

90. *See* Louisiana Civil Code Art. 3073 ("Transactions regulate only the differences which appear clearly to be comprehended in them by the intention of the parties, whether it be explained in a general or particular manner, unless it be the necessary consequence of what is expressed; and they do not extend to differences which the parties never intend to include in them.").

91. *See* Louisiana Civil Code Art. 2298 ("In managing the business, he [the negotiorum gestor] is obligated to use all the care of a prudent administrator.").

92. *See* Louisiana Civil Code Art. 1864 ("Minors, not emancipated, are relievable against simple lesion in every species of contract. That is called simple lesion, in which the amount to be suffered by it, is not designated by law, as it is in the cases above mentioned of partition and sale between persons of full age.").

93. *See, e.g.*, Louisiana Civil Code Art. 1757(2) ("A natural obligation is one which cannot be enforced by action, but which is binding on the party who makes it, in conscience and according to natural justice."); La. Civ. Code Art. 1758(1).

94. For instance, Louisiana Civil Code Art. 2127 states that "[t]he penalty may be modified by the judge, when the principal obligation has been partly executed, except in case of a contrary agreement."

95. *See* Louisiana Civil Code Art. 2288 ("Presumptions, not established by law, are left to the judgment and discretion of the judge, who ought to admit none but weighty, precise and consistent presumptions, and only in cases where the law admits testimonial proof, unless the act be attacked on account of fraud or deceit.").

96. Although the examples given in the text have been limited to those contained in

the Louisiana Civil Code, comparable examples could have just as readily been provided from codes of most civil law countries.

FURTHER READING

American Bar Association. *The Judicial Administration Division Handbook. The Improvement of the Administration of Justice.* 6th ed. American Bar Association Press, 1981.

Banco Interamericano de Desarrollo. *Justicia y Desarrollo en America Latina y el Caribe.* Seminario patrocinado por el Banco Interamericano de Desarrollo, 1993.

Black, Donald. *Sociological Justice.* Oxford University Press, 1989.

Burton, Steven J. *Judging in Good Faith.* Cambridge University Press, 1992.

Cappelletti, Mauro. *Giustizia e Società.* Milano: Edizioni di Comunità, 1972.

Commission on Trial Court Performance Standards. *Trial Court Performance Standards.* National Center for State Courts, 1990.

Dubois, Philip L. *The Analysis of Judicial Reform.* Lexington Books, 1982.

Federal Judicial Center. *Litigation Management Manual.* Federal Judicial Center, 1992.

Fix-Fierro, Hector. "Courts and Efficiency: A General Investigation with Evidence From Three Continents." Inaugural dissertation zur Erlangung des Grades eines Dr. iur. Dem Fachbereich Rechtwissenschaft der Universitat Bremen vorgelegt von (1998).

Galloway, Russell W. *Justice for All? The Rich and Poor in Supreme Court History 1790–1990.* Carolina Academic Press, 1991.

Goerdt, John A. *Divorce Courts: Case Management, Case Characteristics, and the Pace of Litigation in 16 Urban Jurisdictions.* National Center for State Courts, 1992.

Hanson, Roger A. *Appellate Court Performance Standards.* National Center for State Courts and American Bar Association, 1995.

———. *Handbook for Appellate Judges: Management Information and Court Performance.* National Center for State Courts and American Bar Association, 1995.

Hewitt, William E., Geoff Gallas and Barry Mahoney. *Courts That Succeed: Six Profiles of Successful Courts.* National Center for State Courts, 1991.

Jarquín, Edmundo, and Fernando Carrillo. *Justice Delayed.* Washington, D.C.: Inter-American Development Bank, 1998.

Kramer, Larry. *Reforming the Civil Justice System.* New York University Press, 1996.

Lawyers Committee for Human Rights. *IFI's Judicial Reform, and the Environment—A Preliminary Assessment: Environmental Enforcement in Paraguay.* Lawyers Committee for Human Rights, May 1998 (visited 25 Mar. 2000). <http://www.lchr.org>.

Liu, Nanping. *Judicial Interpretation in China.* Sweet & Maxwell Asia, 1997.

Nance, Dale A. *Law and Justice: Cases and Readings on the American Legal System.* Carolina Academic Press, 1994.

Pastor, Ricardo Leon. *Diagnostico de la Cultura Judicial Peruana.* Academia de la Magistratura, 1996.

Plapinger, Elizabeth, and Donna Stienstra. *ADR and Settlement in the Federal District Courts: A Sourcebook for Judges & Lawyers.* Federal Judicial Center, 1996.

Provine, D.M. *Settlement Strategies for Federal District Judges.* Federal Judicial Center, 1986.

Redish, Martin H. *The Federal Courts in the Political Order: Judicial Jurisdiction and American Political Theory*. Carolina Academic Press, 1991.

Revilla Vergara, Ana Teresa. *Acceso a la Justicia*. Oficina Tecnica de Proyectos de Cooperacion Internacional del Poder Judical, 1997.

———. *Reforma Judicial*. Oficina Tecnica de Proyectos de Cooperacion Internacional del Poder Judical, 1997.

Rhyne, Charles S. *Law and Judicial Systems of Nations*, 3rd ed. The World Peace through Law Center, 1978.

Sagues, Nestor Pedro. *Cuadernos para la Reforma de la Justicia*. Universidad Nacional Autonoma De Mexico, 1998.

Schneider, Andrea Kupfer. "Getting Along: The Evolution of Dispute Resolution Regimes in International Trade Organizations," *Mich. J. Int'l L.* (1999).

Schubert, Glendon, and David J. Danelski. *Comparative Judicial Behavior*. Oxford University Press, 1969.

Shetreet, Shimon. *The Role of Courts in Society*. Martinus Nijhoff Publishers, 1988.

Sipes, Dale Anne. *On Trial: The Length of Civil and Criminal Trials*. National Center for State Courts, 1988.

Stienstra, Donna, and Thomas E. Willging. *Alternatives to Litigation: Do They Have a Place in the Federal Court*. Federal Judicial Center, 1995.

Stone, Alec. *The Birth of Judicial Politics in France*. Oxford University Press, 1992.

Strong, Frank R. *Judicial Function in Constitutional Limitation of Governmental Power*. Carolina Academic Press, 1997.

Tarr, G. Alan. *Judicial Process and Judicial Policymaking*. West Publishing Company, 1994.

Vanderbilt, Arthur T. *The Challenge of Law Reform*. Princeton University Press, 1955.

Wedekind, W. *Justice and Efficiency: General Reports and Discussions*. Dutch Association for Procedural Law, 1989.

9

Constitutional Development: The African Experience

Dullah Omar

I. INTRODUCTION

The development of constitutional democracy and constitutionalism in Africa can only be properly appreciated when approached from a perspective that takes full cognizance of its historical past and experience, in particular its colonial legacy.

The history of Africa is rather complex. It represents an amalgam of Africa's precolonial past, its postcolonial anguish, and its postindependence challenges and achievements. There is often a tendency when discussing the development of constitutional democracy in Africa to be apocalyptic and to ignore the fact that the African communities had, even long before the introduction of modern institutions, a long history of democratic rule and concern for human dignity.

II. AFRICA BEFORE THE SLAVE TRADE

In its precolonial phase (before the advent of the slave trade and colonialism) Africa was characterized by rich and vibrant cultures and civilizations. Many African societies had their own religious and social beliefs, methods of democratic self-government, and ways of keeping the peace and stability. At a social level, the clan and the family provided very good vehicles through which social values were nurtured and mutual respect fostered and reinforced. This is not to suggest that there were no instances of abuse of power. Indeed, there is evidence of high-handedness and authoritarianism among some precolonial African societies. However, whenever such situations arose, they were met with utmost social disapproval and reproach. Given the level of interdependence that characterized the early African communities, tolerance, mutual respect, communal well-being, and social cohesion were the critical pillars around which society found its realization.

Pre–slave-trade Africa was a hive of activity with trade flourishing through the Arab world, the Far East, and Europe.

III. THE SLAVE TRADE

The onset of a long and painful transatlantic slave trade heralded a chapter in Africa which saw the destruction of African civilizations. The slave trade certainly contributed to economic development in England and Europe, but for Africa it spelled ruin, human degradation, and suffering. Africa has yet to recover from the consequences of centuries of slave trade, colonialism, and domination. The middle of the nineteenth century saw the end of the slave trade, mainly for economic reasons, but it also witnessed a revised but equally vicious and obnoxious form of subjugation. The rise of the industrial state in Europe precipitated a relentless search for markets overseas as well as new sources of raw materials. Instead of exporting labor, Europe opted for using labor within Africa itself to produce the much-needed raw materials for the European industrial capitals. However, this could only succeed if Europe were able to take control of the indigenous people in the continent. The Berlin Conference of 1884 largely gave content to these intentions as Africa was invaded, partitioned, and divided among the various colonial powers. The era of colonial domination replaced the era of slave trade.

IV. COLONIALISM AND THE ONSET OF REPRESSION

The onset of colonialism did not only mean loss of independence on the part of African states and communities, but also signified the physical, social, and political disintegration of African communities, some of which found themselves divided among various colonial states. In many instances boundaries were drawn through territories of former states and communities, leaving one part in one colonial system and another in another colonial system. The Somali people, for example, were divided into British Somaliland, Italian Somalia, French Djibouti, and Ethiopian Ogaden. Similarly, in West Africa, the Mandikas were included in the French system, while others found themselves in British Sierra Leone and The Gambia. The effect of partition has been well documented and analyzed by African historians, and it is not the intention of this chapter to go over that ground. What needs emphasis is that, to the extent that partition fragmented African communities and states, it not only laid the basis for future conflicts—some of which persisted even after independence—but also destroyed the very fabric which provided the essence of democratic culture and mutual support.

To overcome resistance to colonial conquest, colonial states became increasingly authoritarian and suppressive, which intensified after the Second World War when nascent forms of nationalism began to take shape. Although the colonial state gradually transformed itself from the military to civilian authorities, the system of governance remained undemocratic, authoritarian, and dictatorial. Power was placed in the hands of governors directly accountable to their governments in Europe. The local population had very little input in the decisions that were made, and where convenient, the local population was employed in auxiliary chores as policemen, servants, and interpreters in local courts. Through bribery and corruption the indigenous elite was made to operate against the interests of their own communities. They abused their positions and acted as bullies toward their own people. The colonial powers wanted collaboration, not partners.

Thus, the importance of the colonial state for our discussion is that it was the antithesis of human rights and democracy. It created an antidemocratic and anti–human rights culture. It was neither guided by democratic principles nor did it set out as a matter of policy to establish democratic institutions and structures which could provide a nucleus for the development of a human rights culture in the postindependence era. What is more, independence was seen by the new political elite as an opportunity to access the power corridors that hitherto had been reserved for the colonial elite. At the same time, the departing colonial powers ensured that colonial domination was secured through other means, what Kwame Nkrumah termed "neocolonialism." In other words, the postcolonial state emerged largely constrained and, in certain cases, determined by the structural values of its predecessor. To the extent that the colonial state was also a bureaucratic and administrative state, it provided very little latitude for participation and public accountability. That is part of Africa's legacy to a great degree. This still remains one of the major challenges to the creation and consolidation of democracy in Africa generally. It is in the context of this historical experience that the failures and challenges of the contemporary democratic processes must be viewed.

V. LEGACIES OF THE COLONIAL STATE AND THE IMPLICATIONS FOR CONSTITUTIONAL DEMOCRACY IN AFRICA

Reference to Africa's historical legacy is not to suggest that the democratic failures of postindependence Africa can be attributed solely to the democratic flaws of the inherited colonial state. The postindependence elites have to take their share of the blame. Indeed, the present leadership must also accept responsibility for the socioeconomic regression ushered in by ill-conceived policies and corruption. What needs to be emphasized, however, is the vulnerability of the new states due to the absence of a strong democratic infrastructure and the lack of development. The absence of strong democratic apparatuses (often part of deliberate strategies to suit powerful interests) made it easier for the postindependence elites and dictators to manipulate and use the state to their own advantage and to the advantage of foreign interests. Thus, the challenges to Africa, and South Africa in particular, lie in our ability to overcome this legacy and to build sustainable but genuine democratic institutions capable of generating and supporting human rights values.

Law as an Instrument of Oppression and Authoritarianism

It is our submission that there are continuities from the colonial state which help define characteristics of contemporary states. While it is not possible to touch on every possible continuity, we would like to mention some of those in the legal order. One of the important legacies of the colonial state is the authoritarian character of the colonial state and its relative autonomy from the people governed. One still finds in criminal law and administrative law, for instance, statutes that insulate the state agencies and administrative officers from accountability. Also, most of our statute books still contain legislation guaranteeing "immunities" to state officials.

Similarly, despite the general commitment to constitutionalism, many constitutions are still replete with strong constitutional provisions dealing with "emergencies" and "emergency powers," laws providing for preventative detention, laws regulating voluntary associations, and laws giving wide discretions to bureaucratic agencies and officials. Besides, the absence of human rights standards and protection in the panoply of inherited law needs to be squarely confronted. The authoritarian nature of these laws and administration cannot be dissolved simply by the overlay of a "bill of rights" and new democratic institutions, but rather through an extensive review of the law, including law creating equitable delictual and criminal remedies for violations of basic rights. In addition, the law reform institutions and processes must also reflect the different interests in society in an attempt to distribute power and enforce accountability and thus change the relationship between the state and the people.

The second important legacy to note is that law was used to service the colonial states so that they could continue acting as surrogates for the metropolitan firms in the European capitals. To the extent that law had a social function, it facilitated and, in certain cases, deepened the process of dependency and imperialist penetration and exploitation. Internally, law was used to create pools of wage labor, spur cash production, develop exports, and provide sources of revenue. Toward the end of the colonial era, the patterns of state intervention were in fact being entrenched, a feature that continues to underscore the state in many instances as the dominant economic enterprise, a major employer of skilled and professional people, and a major access to national resources and opportunity.

A third aspect of colonial legacy that is often uncritically discussed is the role and character of the political elite, which emerged with independence and has continued to shape the nature and the role of the state in the modern economy.

Its significance as a group lies in the fact that, over time, it established norms, ideologies, and practices governing the conduct of politics and the structuring of institutions and administration, and shaped the role of law in these activities. What is of even greater concern is that postindependence competitive politics was often characterized by struggles among these elites to control the state. In the process, they tended to exploit ethnic and regional cleavages to establish or consolidate their political bases. Their concomitant skepticism and suspicion of political opposition and conflict, of parliamentary institutions and competitive politics, and of the media, has provided a poor basis for the development of an infrastructure to support a robust constitutional base, especially one based on human rights and the rule of law. What is more, their lack of grassroots linkages and participatory structures has to a great extent not only influenced the pace of the development of democratic institutions, but also determined the parameters within which they presently evolve.

For the greater part of its independence, the history of Africa has been one characterized by civil wars, military coups, disasters, and economic decline. While the escalation of civil wars has given rise to massive internal displacements and social dislocations, the deteriorating economies dominated by powerful foreign interests have destabilized democratic structures and created authoritarian regimes. The last two decades, for example, have been characterized by serious economic decline as commodity prices have fallen and foreign debt has skyrocketed. If democracy is indeed predicated on observance of civil liberties and a relatively stable middle class, the conditions in postindependence Africa militated against the attainment of that ideal. Continued foreign domination has also played a crucial role in frustrating democratization.

African Renewal

Despite the dim democratic picture that the postindependence analysis seems to paint, the current democratization process is significant. In 1990, only four sub-Saharan African nations—Botswana, Gambia, Mauritius, and Senegal—were multiparty democracies. Today, over twenty African governments have been elected in multiparty contexts, while many more are involved in economic liberalization. These developments are important for understanding Africa's political dynamics. One is inclined to ask why these changes are taking place at this point in time and, change having now begun, what can be expected in the future. In order to answer these questions, one must examine the roots of democratic failure in independent Africa.

There are conflicting explanations for Africa's rather depressing performance. Failure was not preordained from the start, and in fact most African countries achieved their independence under constitutions that enshrined a bill of rights and separation of powers principles. However, the overwhelming factor would seem to be that the newly established states, dominated by powerful foreign interests often encouraging dictatorships, were often fragile structures and faced immense challenges to the development of democratic institutions. Obstacles included, *inter alia*, ethnic strife, low levels of literacy and economic development, and an intensified political culture that contained, at best, an ambiguous commitment to democratic values. Thus, one of the early, daunting tasks of the new leaders was to establish the legitimacy of the independent states themselves. National unity would remain a virtual pipe dream if states were still fragmented by ethnic, religious, or regional interests. The bloody civil wars in Nigeria and Rwanda in the early 1970s and, more recently, in Burundi, Rwanda, Democratic Republic of the Congo, Liberia, and Sierra Leone, are but a few examples of ethnic turbulence and institutional decline in Africa. Of course, apartheid in South Africa was destructive in its consequences at every level.

The challenges facing Africa in the next millennium will be how to transcend these historical and structural distortions in an environment characterized by increased globalization. Africa has to find a way to galvanize its immense resources and, where possible, take advantage of existing goodwill to launch on to the global scene. This will certainly require more than a lip service commitment to the process of social and economic reform. It would engender the consolidation and promotion of truly democratic forms of governance.

VI. HUMAN RIGHTS AND DEMOCRACY IN A HISTORICAL CONTEXT

Like the democracies of Europe, Africa's constitutional development was partly influenced by the democratic reforms that took place in Europe and the Americas during the second half of the nineteenth century. Over the last four decades, many African countries gained their independence under the Westminster constitutional model or via written constitutions with basic guarantees of human rights. The cardinal principles of universal suffrage, separation of powers, bill of rights, and independence of the judiciary invariably provided the epicenter of constitutional development in most African states. Indeed, the inspiration of these principles is clearly noticeable in the constitutions of Nigeria, Ghana, Lesotho, and many other African states.

A number of African constitutions share common characteristics. They provide for united, nonracial, and democratic states; common and equal citizenship and nationality, regardless of color, race, sex, or creed; the right to participate in the government and administration of the country on the basis of universal equal suffrage under a nonracial voter's roll and by secret ballot; and universally recognized human rights, freedoms, and civil liberties, protected under an entrenched bill of rights.

A second important characteristic of African constitutions has been the recognition of the supremacy of the constitution. Most of the constitutions provide for a clear supremacy of the constitution over the activities of all the branches of government including, in certain instances, the judiciary. For example, Section 2 of the South African Constitution provides for the supremacy of the constitution and rule of law. It further provides that the constitution "shall bind all legislative, executive and judicial organs of the State at all levels of government." The effect of this development has been to place the constitution above any other law, including Acts of Parliament. This signifies a departure from the system based on parliamentary sovereignty in terms of which Acts of Parliament were regarded supreme and therefore not susceptible to challenge or review in the courts. One must note in this regard that constitutions also tended to enshrine in a more visible and significant way the principle of separation of powers. They established Parliament, the executive, as well as the judicial power. Legislative power was vested in the Parliament, while national executive authority was usually vested in the President, who would exercise that authority together with the Cabinet.

Most constitutions also recognize the principle of collective ministerial responsibility, which is crucial for governmental accountability. Although the President and his ministers, or members of the Cabinet, are in many instances members of Parliament and remain primarily accountable to Parliament, each minister is individually accountable to the President as well. At the same time, the President would normally be under an obligation to dissolve the government in cases in which Parliament passed a vote of no confidence in the government. In that sense, the relationship between Parliament and the executive has largely been a blend of parliamentary and presidential types of executive government. This arrangement has been further reinforced by the creation of an independent judiciary, which, apart from interpreting the constitution and applying the law of the land, has an additional function, namely that of an arbiter in disputes between the organs of State and the citizens as well as between organs of state *inter se*. The courts would normally have power to declare an executive decision or parliamentary act unconstitutional and thereby invalid if it transgressed, for example, any of the provisions relating to fundamental rights or any other provisions of the constitution. To this end, a number of countries have either established specialized or dedicated constitutional courts or designated their respective highest courts to be final arbiters on constitutional matters.

Apart from the separation of powers, a number of constitutions also provide for the establishment of several watchdog institutions such as officers of the Ombudsman and human rights commission. Although the success of these institutions has been uneven, they were meant to act as checks and balances against abuse of governmental power and discretion. However, their greatest significance lies in the fact that they have created an awareness among the public of abuse of power and thereby laid the foundation for the development of good governance and public integrity.

Unlike many other countries in Africa, South Africa has a rather unique historical past. It is a past characterized by institutionalized racial discrimination, ethnic tension, and hatred as well as unequal access to resources and institutions of decision-making. What makes South Africa's past even more peculiar is the concerted resistance to meaningful change that would facilitate the dawn of a democratic order. However, as apartheid entered its final phase, the debate as to values, structures, and institutions to govern the impending democratic order became less romantic and dealt with real issues of statesmanship. After intense all-party negotiations between various parties, an Interim Constitution was finalized and adopted in early 1994 that provided the framework of the democratic transition. The Interim Constitution that emerged out of the negotiation process had its deep genesis in the concrete experiences of South African society as well as generations of resistance against apartheid and social injustice. Thus, the actual constitutional choices, though principled, were to a considerable degree dictated by the complexity of South Africa's socioeconomic and political mosaic. Consequently, any assessment of South Africa's democratic achievements must be seen against the background of an arduous and sometimes slippery attempt to keep the social tapestry together.

General Principles Underlying South Africa's Democratic Transition

While the constitution is largely a byproduct of a collective will and consensus achieved after a process of arduous negotiations at Kempton Park, its broad parameters are traceable to the Freedom Charter adopted at Kliptown by the Congress of the People in 1955. The charter espoused a free and nonracial South Africa in which all the various racial groups would be able to live together and work collectively toward a common destiny. The principle of nonracialism was always at the center of the African National Congress (ANC) perception of a new democratic order and still represents the minimum standard to be followed if a democratic South Africa is to be built on the destruction caused by apartheid.

Although the Freedom Charter did not deal with the institutions of government or indicate in detail how the rights it proclaimed were to be guaranteed, it did set out a vision for an apartheid-free future. This vision was reflected in subsequent constitutional documents submitted by the ANC to the negotiating process and formed part of the working documents of the ANC Constitutional Committee.

The Interim Constitution, which came into being after the 27 April 1994 democratic elections in South Africa, was thus a constitution that not only consolidated the gains achieved over many years of struggle for liberation, but also represented a blueprint for the future society that was to replace the apartheid era. It marked the beginning of a new phase in the history of South Africa and represented a watershed between the apartheid era and democratic governance.

The Interim Constitution was right from the beginning destined to be temporary, pending the drafting of the final constitution. The main purpose of the Interim Constitution was to facilitate the handover of power to a democratically elected government in an atmosphere that would ensure national unity and reconciliation. This was apparent not only in the general postamble to the constitution, but also in the structures of government that were established as well as the principles underlying their relationships and competencies. The preamble to the constitution clearly stipulates that the constitution was designed to provide for the promotion of national unity and the restructuring and continued governance of South Africa while an elected constitutional assembly drew up the final constitution.

Thus, the constitution made generous provision for power-sharing between various political parties and for continuity of existing apartheid institutions. It also provided for the granting of amnesty in respect of acts, omissions, and offenses associated with political objectives and committed in the course of the conflicts of the past. This was subsequently formalized through the establishment of the Truth and Reconciliation Commission, whose task was to investigate past gross violations of human rights and, where appropriate, grant amnesty to the perpetrators. The constitution in a sense represented a truce between various warring parties and was thus designed to facilitate the normalization of the situation conducive to meaningful change and transformation.

Overview

Our Interim Constitution in large measure shaped our final constitution, which meant we had to take our *interim* constitution seriously, but it was also meant to be an Interim Constitution. We were making compromises, but at the same time we wanted to make a choice that was principled. In our survey of constitutions and constitutional systems in different parts of the world, we learned quickly that we could not be mechanical and simply take over, willy-nilly, aspects of constitutions and systems from other parts of the world. Therefore, in our constitution we adopted measures that are not found in any other constitution.

Further, while we learned from many countries, we did not always follow them. Canada, for example, has no property clause in its Bill of Rights. We adopted a bill of rights that did have a property clause in our Interim Constitution, and our final constitution has a property clause. There is still a great deal of debate as to whether we made the right choice, but here it was not only a question of deliberate choice, but also of compromise.

In terms of the core values of our constitution, we had to take into account our history. The system of apartheid built up massive inequalities between the minority, which enjoyed privilege, and the overwhelming majority, which suffered at the hands of apartheid. Hence, an important component of the core values of our constitution is equality. Dignity assumes a central position in our constitution due to the many indignities suffered by our people over such a long period of time. Liberty is not the main core value of our constitution, rather it is equality and dignity. We deliberately chose the word "freedom" rather than liberty because of the connotation of liberty in the American constitutional jurisprudence.

We also wanted to ensure that we distanced ourselves from the divisions of the past. Apartheid had divided our country. It fragmented our country and our people. Building the unity of our people, and therefore national unity, was an important component of the liberation struggle. And yet, due to the diversity of our people in terms of religion, language, and culture, we had to take care to develop a constitution that made it possible for us to build that nation, and, at the same time, to respect diversity. That is why our constitution includes a specific provision that the state shall set up a special commission to protect and promote the rights of religious, linguistic, and cultural communities. Of course, our new democracy is only five years old, and it is too early to judge success. But thus far I think we have managed to protect both the right to be the same and the right to be different. We also borrowed from the Indian experience. There was great pressure that South Africa should be declared a religious state. But the view of the ANC prevailed that the state shall be a secular state: not an irreligious state, but a secular state with many religions. There we looked closely at the Indian Constitution and modeled ourselves somewhat on that experience.

Again, while building a nation and building the unity of a single country, we wanted to ensure that there was real democracy for our people and that there was an evolution of power. Therefore, we created nine provinces in our country. But to ensure that the apartheid-based racial fragmentation of the past did not persist, we looked at the way Germany dealt with its problem and modeled the second chamber of our Parliament after the German experience. We have a second chamber called the National Council of Provinces, to which each of the provinces sends ten delegates. There is a strong bond beginning to pull the provinces together, but at the same time each province is able to deal with matters of concern to it.

We also paid a lot of attention to what rights should be entrenched in our Bill of Rights. Our Bill of Rights contains civil and political rights as well as social and economic rights. Because of our history, we chose to include social and economic rights in the Bill of Rights itself, not just as guiding principles. Again, we considered majority rule to be important because in our country it is not minorities, racial or otherwise, that were oppressed and suppressed, it was the numerical majority that was suppressed. Even today it is that numerical majority that continues to suffer from the social and economic imbalances created by the apartheid system. It is the numerical minority, classified white according to South African law at the time, that dominated the majority and that continues to benefit from the system. Dealing with the social and economic imbalances of the past is a huge problem, and it will take us many years to deal with them effectively. In the context of South Africa, we should be very careful about how we address the issue of majorities and minorities, because in that context it is the majority that requires to be liberated, not the minority. But, of course, in the process of liberating the majority and creating a nonracial, democratic South Africa, we need to build into the system mechanisms and processes that will ensure that minorities are not dominated or suppressed. Time will tell whether we have successfully found the balance in that respect.

We have an electoral system based on proportional representation, and to ensure that provinces feel comfortable within a framework of building national unity, provinces have representation in Parliament. In addition to the National Council of Provinces, our second chamber, we have a 400-member National Assembly, of which 200 members are sent by the provinces themselves. So, in effect, we have a kind of second chamber in our National Assembly, resulting in the provinces being very well represented in our Parliament.

In sum, I think we benefited from a comparative approach to constitutional drafting. We learned a great deal from the U.S. experience—both positive and negative. For seventy-five years, the United States existed with both a Bill of Rights and slavery. Because we live in a globalized world, South Africa does not have the luxury of time to make our Bill of Rights work. Unlike societies in the late eighteenth and early nineteenth centuries, we have a very different kind of world environment. In the world environment that we have, South Africa, and indeed Africa as a whole, needs to solve its problems of building democracy, building respect for human rights, and effecting transformations of society in the next decade. Insofar as Africa itself is concerned, we are going through a period of democratizing. Many African countries south of the Sahara have been adopting constitutions more or less along the same lines as the one South Africa has adopted. Many of the new constitutions in Africa contain bills of rights. Most of them contain social and economic rights as well. The challenge before us is to make those rights real.

A classical liberal democratic constitutional framework is inadequate to address the problem of democratic transformation and the renewal of the African continent. Civil and political rights are very important, but they are not enough in the context of our continent. While it had the trappings of the Westminster type of constitution, independence ultimately turned out to mean very little for people in African countries. We need to deal with the legacy of the past and with a culture of violence that is the result of the repression that went on for many hundreds of years. We need a developmental state in the countries of Africa. We need to promote nation-building and we need to address the massive inequalities and poverty in Africa, and the state has to play a role in this.

Furthermore, within the context of Africa and South Africa in particular, the notion of empowerment and access to justice are absolutely crucial. We need to pay special attention to this, because while our constitution contains many underlying liberal values and protects individual rights and civil liberties, people will not be able to exercise those rights—or many, many people will not, and the majority will not—because of the massive inequalities. The rich will be able to exercise those rights, and the poor will not. Therefore, there must be special provisions to ensure that people know of their rights as guaranteed in the constitution, that they understand those rights, that they know how to access those rights, and that they have the capacity to exercise those rights.

Structural Parameters

The structural parameters were thus influenced by the principles underlying the transitional process. In the interim phase, the constitution enshrined the principle of power-sharing in terms of which all the political parties that had attained a certain percentage of the vote in the elections would automatically be entitled to representation in the Cabinet. Indeed, the National Party as well as the Inkhata Freedom Party were able to participate in the government under this formula. Although the mechanism did not quite work well in the end, with the National Party deciding to withdraw from the government of national unity two years into the democratic order, it did facilitate a smooth transition and highlight areas of critical concern that had to be catered for in the final constitution. The latter includes, for instance, the principles to govern parliamentary representation, the powers of the executive branch of government, and the powers and competences of provinces and local authorities.

One of the most notable features of the Interim Constitution was also the recognition of the supremacy of the constitution. Section 4 of the constitution provided that the constitution would be the supreme law of the Republic and that any law inconsistent with its provisions would, unless otherwise provided expressly or by necessary implication, be of no force or effect to the extent of the inconsistency. The supremacy of the constitution was also reflected in various other provisions, particularly those relating to fundamental rights, constitutional amendment procedures, and unconstitutional parliamentary acts.

Apart from the separation of powers, the constitution also provided for the establishment of several watchdog institutions. These included the Public Protector (Ombudsman), the Human Rights Commission, and the Gender Equality Commission. Of particular significance was the role of the Public Protector, whose function is primarily to oversee public functionaries and, when appropriate, conduct investigations into alleged abuse of power or maladministration. The Human Rights Commission, on the other hand, has a relatively wider mandate. The competencies of the commission include the promotion and observance of, respect for, and the protection of fundamental rights and the development of an awareness of fundamental rights. If the commission is of the opinion that any proposed legislation may be contrary to the Bill of Rights, to norms of international human rights law, or to norms of international law, it may bring that fact to the attention of the relevant legislature. The commission also complements the work of the Public Protector in that it also has competence to investigate or receive complaints regarding any alleged violation of fundamental rights and assist the aggrieved party to seek redress in the appropriate forum.

However, it must be emphasized that the establishment of safeguards to the exercise of governmental power, while crucial to the evolution of a democratic governance, does not on its own guarantee the consolidation of democratic rule. For democracy to be meaningful, it must involve the people and generate perceptions in terms of which people see themselves as part of the democratic system. The authoritarian rule and culture that arose, characteristic of both the colonial and apartheid regimes, must change. This can only be achieved through the creation of institutions and structures through which ordinary people not only can participate in deciding who goes into positions of power, but also are able to influence day-to-day decisions in matters affecting their lives. The establishment of a democratic Parliament has gone a long way to address this concern. However, one must also recognize that the institutions created by the Interim Constitution, Parliament included, have been conditioned, and to some extent limited, by the need to create a common platform from which meaningful nation-building can take place.

For instance, the system of representation remains largely influenced by proportional representation designed to reassure minorities. A true democracy, while sensitive to minority interest, must ultimately depend on majority rule. This probably remains one of the major challenges of our constitutional development. A formula will have to be found in terms of democratic rule based on the wishes of the majority but without trampling upon the legitimate rights of the minorities.

The Bill of Rights in the constitution partly addresses this matter insofar as it entrenches the nondiscrimination clauses. But the challenge for participatory democracy certainly transcends reforming the electoral system. While the latter is important, there is a need to create grassroots structures to which people can easily relate and in which they can easily participate. Local government structures need to be strengthened and democratized to facilitate easy access and participation. The quasi-federal dispensation enshrined in the constitution will also go a long way to strengthen local institutions and generate the requisite interest in local governments from the grassroot level. This will not only provide a useful participatory mechanism, but will also set in motion a feedback system that is indispensable for any system of government concerned with accountability.

Bill of Rights

One of the most remarkable achievements of the constitution-making process was, *inter alia*, the inclusion of a justiciable Bill of Rights in the constitution. For the first time South Africa had a Bill of Rights that guaranteed basic fundamental rights and freedoms. The inclusion of the Bill of Rights was preceded by political contestation between the two major political parties, namely the ANC and the outgoing National Party. While both parties were agreed on the need to have a bill of rights in the constitution, they had different views on what should be the purpose and the content of a bill of rights. The National

Party and its supporters saw the Bill of Rights as a useful mechanism for the limitation of powers and authority of the new democratic government. Furthermore, by arguing vehemently for the protection of group rights, they hoped that the incorporation of the Bill of Rights would provide a means to secure economic and cultural privileges of the white minority.

The ANC, on the other hand, wanted the Bill of Rights for different reasons and saw it performing different functions in the process of democratic transition. A meaningful bill of rights would have to be a mechanism to redress and, where possible, eliminate the inequities, indignities, and inequalities created by apartheid. It would have to create a climate of tranquillity conducive to a good quality of life and also promote nation-building. It not only had to be more than an instrument for controlling governmental power, but also reflect and respond to the baggage of apartheid as well as the consequential political, social, and economic imbalances that exist in the present South African society.

It is against the background of these concerns that an attempt was made in the Bill of Rights to go beyond merely providing for civil and political rights. While it provides for the right to life, human dignity, freedom and security, privacy, religion, freedom of association and expression, liberty, and conventional political rights, it also provides for labor rights, education, and even a right to a safe and clean environment. In the South African Interim Constitution, for example, to some extent the Bill of Rights fell short of providing for socioeconomic rights in any explicit form. Partly, this was the result of a compromise between two schools of thought, one advocating total inclusion of socioeconomic rights in a substantive form and the other seeing socioeconomic rights as essentially resource-based rights whose attainment would not be meaningfully enhanced by substantive clauses in the constitution.

Despite its limitations, the Bill of Rights represents a major achievement for protecting human rights and consolidating democracy in South Africa. It heralds a major shift from a constitutional order based on parliamentary sovereignty to a system that holds the constitution as supreme and judicial testing of parliamentary acts against the entrenched Bill of Rights as the norm. The Bill of Rights, while it does not extend to the judiciary, binds all legislative and executive organs of state at all levels of government. The role of the judiciary, particularly that of the Constitutional Court, will be crucial in providing scope and content to the provisions contained in the Bill of Rights. The courts will have to do the balancing between the interest of the state and the legitimate claims of individuals. While no right is absolute, and indeed the constitution explicitly so provides, an independent an impartial judiciary is a *sine qua non* for any system predicated on constitutional and democratic ideals. It is in this context that the constitutional guarantee of the independence of the judiciary provides a pillar for the development of democratic ethos and culture.

VII. CHALLENGES TO DEMOCRATIC REFORM AND HUMAN RIGHTS PROTECTION

While South Africa can rightly pat itself on the back for what is sometimes referred to as a "political miracle," it is a country still beset with enormous challenges. The process of democratization is still very much in its infancy and, as such, still susceptible to the vagaries of democratic experimentation and uncertainty. In a sense, South Africa, as the last African state to achieve freedom, has been in a more fortunate position than other African countries. First, it has benefited from the failures and achievements of its predecessors. In the process, it has been able not only to avoid the mistakes of other African states, but also to emulate their success stories and strategies. Second, South Africa, unlike many African states, is endowed with immense natural and human resources. It has, relatively speaking, an adequately developed modern economy and is well integrated in twentieth-century technology. South Africa's economy and technology can benefit not only its own population, but also the continent as whole. Its well-developed economic and financial infrastructure can help to stabilize fledgling economies and enhance the prospects of democratic consolidation on the continent. Thus, South Africa finds itself in a situation characterized by challenges as well as opportunities, both of which have serious implications for the process of democratization and human rights protection internally and internationally.

Institutional Infrastructure

As South Africa seeks to consolidate its democratic gains, it has to review its institutional apparatus to ensure that it is capable of supporting the democratic initiatives. The sad legacy of apartheid has been the lack of a democratic institutional base to sustain a human rights culture. The courts, civil service, police, armed forces, and, to some extent, the professions are still very much a reflection of the values of the apartheid system. While some incremental changes are slowly taking place, major institutional transformation is an obvious necessity. The culture arising from the rule-based authoritarian system of governance that characterized the apartheid system will have to give way to one embedded in the principles and ethos of participatory democracy and human dignity. In this regard, one indeed has to ask the question as to what is the role of the existing institutional arrangements and groups in civil society in the transition from the authoritarian apartheid regime to a democratic order? How can groups in civil society intervene in a manner consistent with values of democratic participation, respect for the rule of law, and more accountability?

Most of the initiatives in this regard have been taken within the context of the final constitution. The final constitution to a large extent retained the structure and principles that had formed the basis of the Interim Constitution. However, there are certain significant aspects of the final constitution that deserve special emphasis. First, the constitution has done away with the requirement for power sharing, thereby bringing to an end, at least in a legal sense, the requirement to involve minority parties in the government. The inclusion of minority parties is now left to the discretion of the majority party as is the practice in many democracies throughout the world. This has been a significant aspect of our final constitution and has in many ways demonstrated that the feelings of distrust and suspicion that characterized the pre-1994 election are gradually being overtaken by a sense of common destiny and purpose and, above all, mutual trust.

Second, the constitution entrenches the system of provincial government. In a country as diverse as South Africa, nurturing and fostering provincial autonomy has been a major component of our democratic development. Apart from the fact that such a system would facilitate easier communication and interaction with local and rural communities, it is crucial for forging national consensus and belonging. The constitution spells out areas of exclusive as well as inclusive competence for provincial governments and establishes mechanisms for resolving conflicts between national and provincial constitutions. In this connection, a new innovation of the final constitution has been the inclusion of a chapter regarding local governments whose responsibility will be to promote governance at the grassroots levels as well as promote social and economic development at municipal levels. Despite the funding difficulties that some of the municipalities are currently facing, these structures on the whole have begun to work well and do provide a good link between the central government and the grassroots communities.

Last, the other significant feature of the final constitution has been the retention of two houses of Parliament. Under the Interim Constitution we had the National Assembly and the Senate. While the National Assembly consisted of 400 members elected in accordance with the system of proportional representation of voters, the Senate was composed of ten senators for each province, nominated by parties represented in a provincial legislature. The aim was to give the provinces a direct voice in the discussions of the national Parliament. Whereas, apart from the introduction of a common voters roll, the rules governing representation in the National Assembly have not changed fundamentally, the Senate has now been replaced by the National Council of Provinces, composed of a single delegation consisting of ten delegates from each province. The nine provinces together therefore send ninety delegates to the National Council of Provinces. The important aspect of the National Council of Provinces is that its composition is now more a reflection of the representation in the provincial legislatures and has been given more extensive competences than the Senate had.

Constitutional Democracy and Transition

In recent transitions in Africa, the most vocal opponents to authoritarian rule have generally been the urban middle class and intellectuals, and the democracy they have been advocating is one that can be characterized as political democracy, liberal democracy, or polyarchy. The characteristics of such a democracy include the presence of institutionalized mechanisms by which citizens may change the personnel holding governmental power, respect for the rule of law, accountable governance, and protection of human rights.[1] The major preoccupation of liberal democracy is with party competition and elections. While these issues are legitimate concerns, the fundamental problem with the liberal approach to democracy is that usually the issue of redistribution in the economic sphere and responsiveness to the disadvantaged social classes is not part of the definition of democracy. Yet for the people of Africa in general, and of South Africa in particular, a democratic order means much more than social peace, due process in the judicial system, and political accountability. They hope for justice as well as legal order; they would like to have improved opportunities to feed and educate their children. To the popular mind, a democratic order is judged in terms of its ability to respond to these concerns.[2] Thus, while liberal democracy is an important development and, as a matter of fact, does provide for political organization previously stifled under the system of apartheid, it is not a sufficient tool to combat the socioeconomic inequities, poverty, and massive brutalization of South African society. The inherited institutional infrastructure, apart from its paucity in democratic values and orientation, suffers from the crisis of legitimacy in the eyes of the formerly oppressed and historically disempowered majority.

In order to strengthen the democratic infrastructure, the role of civil society is vital. A closer examination of the interaction between state apparatus and civil society is instructive regarding not only short-term issues relating to political liberalization, but also longer-term concerns regarding the durability of democracy and sustainability of human rights. There is little disagreement on the proposition that political accountability is a *sine qua non* for democracy, and that the degree of accountability depends upon the capacity of a robust, autonomous, civil society to curb the abuse of state power.[3] However, what seems to generate controversy is how to define "civil society," how it relates to the state, and how one should assess the role of its constituent groups in the process of democratization. It would be misleading to assume that civil society is quite distinct from the state. Apart from the danger that civil society can be manipulated by the state, as indeed was the case on numerous occasions during the apartheid system, it can also be used in the transitional phase by middle-class leaders to promote their own statuses and consolidate their privileged positions. Thus, while civil society is important in consolidating democracy in transitional society, our evaluation of its role and possible contribution must include the values and the structures that shape how people think and act politically. Such an inquiry must address the cultural repertoire of politics—that store of customs, symbols and habits of power, authority participation, and representation associated with various formal and informal groups in the civil society.[4] One of the features of democratic reform in South Africa is its fragility. The mere fact that recent political developments have brought about a regime change does not in itself mean that this will automatically lead to greater participation and representation. The reality of poverty and deprivation will continue to bring to the fore new challenges, particularly if the resource capacity is not significantly increased. It is in these grassroots areas that the civil society can make meaningful contributions and maximize its impact.

The organs of civil society in South Africa must brace themselves for heightened activity in the years ahead. There is ample scope for the nongovernmental organizations (NGOs) and community-based organizations (CBOs) to play a more active role than they have in the past. With the new democratic dispensation they possess the ability to encourage community empowerment and local initiative. Trade unions and civic and business organizations must now direct their energies to combatting the poverty inherited from apartheid. At the same time, this will require a more accommodating and receptive approach from the government. Government will have to make institutional arrangements that encourage participation of interest groups in the process of government. Similarly, the parliamentary system, whether at the national, provincial, or local level, can be adapted so as to encourage direct participation of interest groups and the public in general in the legislative process. A system of public hearings can be organized so as to facilitate such participation. In this regard, parliamentary committees could also open their debates to public hearings and public comment. We already saw examples of this, for example, during debates on the National Unity and Reconciliation Act, which established the Truth and Reconciliation Commission.

Human Rights Protection and Human Rights Culture

The weight of apartheid is nowhere more apparent than in its brutalization of South African society. Apartheid, based as it was on the negation of human rights and human dignity, has generated a society in which the worth of the human has been relegated to the lowest levels of concern. While rural communities are struggling under the weight of economic poverty and social degradation, urban centers are increasingly becoming citadels of serious crimes such as murder, rape, and robbery. Serious economic crimes are on the increase while prisons are overflowing with juvenile offenders who find themselves on the economic fringes of society. These issues will have to be given serious consideration if the process of democracy is to take root in the emerging democracy. It can be argued that the problem of rising crime is not a phenomenon peculiar to South African society. Indeed, crime is a feature of both the industrial and the developing democracies. What distinguishes the South African situation, however, is that it is rooted in historical institutionalized deprivation and threatens the very basis of democratic initiatives. Comprehensive measures have been taken by the new democratic government to address this problem. These initiatives are already yielding successes.

For South Africa, human rights protection is, therefore, a must and not an option that can, with impunity, be set aside or ignored. The challenge for the transition to democracy is how to use the Bill of Rights creatively and in a manner that will contribute to the creation of a just society. Accordingly, there is a need to review the content of the Bill of Rights. The current debate over the content of the Bill of Rights in the final constitution has rekindled the controversy over whether socioeconomic rights should be specifically provided for in the final constitution and, if so, the manner the formulation should take. It has been argued, quite rightly, that the failure of the Bill of Rights to concern itself with such rights seriously compromises its effectiveness in a society characterized by massive poverty and social dislocation.[5] There is already a perception amongst the ordinary people that the Bill of Rights is an instrument of the privileged few who can afford the often expensive litigation in the Constitutional Court and superior courts. Besides, such litigation can be highly technical and involved, making it more difficult for ordinary people to take full advantage of the redress mechanism provided for under the constitution. At any rate, one must avoid reinforcing the impression that the Bill of Rights is only concerned with civil and political rights whose direct beneficiaries are the affluent and wealthy. Regrettably, that perception is likely to be given credibility unless a mechanism is found whereby the socioeconomic rights and the fight for equality can find substantive recognition under the final constitution. Obviously, their recognition would not resolve all the controversies around their enforceability. The opponents of constitutionalizing socioeconomic rights have vehemently argued that, since these are rights whose substance is largely determined by the available national resources, it is an exercise in legal futility to provide for them in the same way as civil and political rights whose content and enforcement is less contentious. Be that as it may, the latter argument is more about effectiveness than the validity of the rights themselves. While the debate on appropriate implementation procedures is a germane one and indeed one that should be pursued, the recognition of socioeconomic rights is long overdue. It is in a way gratifying to note that the final constitution has gone some distance to address these concerns. The final constitution now provides for the right to housing and land, health, food, water, and social security, in addition to education.

It must be pointed out, however, that the mere constitutionalization of rights does not necessarily guarantee a human rights culture or even protection of human rights. First and foremost, people must know their rights. They must systematically be informed of their entitlements as well as the redress processes that are available to them. In essence, this implies that there has to be a reexamination of the entire legal system. Courts must be made more accessible, affordable, and user-friendly to make it possible for the ordinary person to approach them with ease and confidence. For those who are unable to afford the legal process, more creative thinking needs to be put into either alternative or complementary institutions that are more readily accessible, or finding ways their financial barriers can be reduced. Above all, the courts and the entire legal process must inspire confidence and faith in the efficacy and fairness of the law.

This requires that the entire criminal justice system be able to respond adequately and efficiently to the various complaints put before it. There should be certainty, for instance, on the part of the offender, that if he or she breaks the law, he or she will be arrested, prosecuted, and, if found guilty, convicted and sentenced to a punishment that he or she will carry out. Unless the criminal justice system is able to provide that kind of predictability, it will be subjected to scorn and ridicule and will prompt society to take the law into its own hands. Nothing could be more damaging to the democratic process than flagrant disregard of the rule of law and human rights. This is not by any means to suggest that one must take a pure law-and-order approach as the primary strategy to build democracy. Certainly other measures that address socioeconomic disparities and poverty must also be taken. The former processes do not in any way exclude the need to address constraints in the socioeconomic sphere. However, unless people can feel secure and confident about the state's ability to intervene effectively when their rights have been violated, it is like a house built on quicksand, its edifice constantly at the mercy of the storm. The new democratic government is conscious of the responsibilities in this regard and many initiatives that will make a positive contribution to creating safety and security are currently being implemented.

VIII. CONCLUSION

It would be wrong to assume that because a country adopts a democratic constitution, it is a democratic state. The process of democratization is not only a process of institution building, but also an arduous task that entails changing the national psyche in regard to democratic values and human rights ideals. While the latter is obviously dependent on the tenacity and resilience of the former, the degree of democratic consolidation and maturity is a function of society's willingness to accept and be governed by the democratic framework by which they have agreed to be governed. This process is usually easier and less turbulent where there is a general consensus among members of society about the values and ideals that the democratic dispensation entails. It becomes increasingly difficult in a society like South Africa, which has, over a long period, been characterized by social polarization and mutual suspicion. Both the interim and final Constitutions have attempted to address these fundamental concerns. In a sense, our democratic transition proceeded rather smoothly and, I may add, quite responsibly, as demonstrated by the peaceful atmosphere in which the last elections were held. This is supposed to be a period characterized by tolerance and political accommodation to facilitate a common consensus and platform for nation-building. Contrary to the predictions of skeptics, the government of national unity did very well and exceeded expectations. The economy is on the upswing, while South Africans are slowly but steadily finding a common purpose and destiny. Despite the weaknesses, and I am sure there are quite a few, that one can identify in the present democratic arrangement, it has nevertheless laid a basis for a common destiny. For the first time in almost 100 years, South Africa now has a constitution that is truly autochthonous—grown from the soil, reflective, and expressive of the socioeconomic and political aspirations of the broader South African society. It sets down a framework for a representative, impartial, and accountable government.

However, one must hasten to remark, that it is not necessarily the legal framework that ultimately makes a better society, but rather it is the commitment, talent, and resilience of its people that give it quality and shape its future. These will remain the main challenges to the South African people in the times that lie ahead.

NOTES

1. Newbury 1994.
2. Nyangoro 1994.
3. Robinson 1994.
4. Robinson 1994.
5. Dugard 1994.

REFERENCES

Basson, D. South Africa's Constitution (1996).

Davidson, B. AFRICA IN MODERN HISTORY (1978).

———. MODERN AFRICA: A SOCIAL AND POLITICAL HISTORY (1994).

Davis, D. *The Freedom Charter: A Challenge and Bequest, in* THE FREEDOM CHARTER AND BEYOND (Nico Steytler, ed., 1991).

Dugard, J. *Human Rights and Rule of Law in the Post Apartheid South Africa, in* SOUTH AFRICA'S CRISIS OF CONSTITUTIONAL DEMOCRACY (Robert A. Licht and Bertus de Villiers eds., 1994).

Everatt, D. *The Freedom Charter in Historical Perspective, in* THE FREEDOM CHARTER AND BEYOND (Nico Steytler, ed., 1991).

Newbury, G. *Paradoxes of Democratisation in Africa*, 37 AFRICAN STUD. REV. 1 n.1 (1994).

Nyangoro, J. *Reform Politics and the Democratization Process in Africa*, 37 AFRICAN STUD. REV. 133 n.1 (1994).

Paul, C.N.J. *Developing Constitutional Orders in Sub-Saharan Africa: An Unofficial Report*, THIRD WORLD LEGAL STUD. 1 (1988).

Robinson, Pearl T. *Democratization: Understanding the Relationship between Regime Change and the Culture of Politics,* 37 AFRICAN STUD. REV. 39–67 n.1 (1994).

Part III

Constitutions, Rights, and Reframing

10

The Right to Freedom of Religion and Secularism in the Indian Constitution

Ratna Kapur

On December 6, 1992, the mobs of the Hindu Right destroyed a sixteenth-century mosque, the Babri Masjid, demolishing history, trammeling over the rights of religious minorities, and in the process shaking the edifice of Indian democracy. Salman Rushdie, in his book, *The Moor's Last Sigh*, describes the process of obliteration:

> The mosque at Ayodhya was destroyed. Alphabet soupists, "fanatics," or, alternatively, "devout liberators of the sacred site" . . . swarmed over the seventeenth-century Babri Masjid and tore it apart with their bare hands, with their teeth, with the elemental power of what Sir V. Naipaul has approvingly called their "awakening of history." The police, as the press photographs showed, stood by and watched the forces of history do their history-obliterating working.[1]

The "alphabet soupists" of Rushdie's novel include the *Bhartiya Janata Party* (BJP), the political arm of the Right, in power at the national level in 2001; the *Rashtriya Swayam Sevak*, the main ideological component of the Right; and the *Vishwa Hindu Parishad*, the exponents of the Right's religious doctrine. Other parties include the militant and virulently anti-Muslim *Shiv Sena*. These organizations collectively promote the ideology of *Hindutva*—an ideology that seeks to establish a Hindu state in India.

In real life, the Supreme Court bemoaned the event:

> Within a short time, the entire structure was razed to the ground. Indeed, it was an act of "national shame." What was demolished was not merely an ancient structure; but the

faith of the minorities in the sense of justice and fair play of the majority. It shook their faith in the rule of law and constitutional process. A five hundred year old structure which was defenseless and whose safety was a sacred trust in the hands of the State government was demolished.[2]

These fine words suggested that the Court at least was committed to upholding the principles of secularism and holding back the tides of intolerance and Hindu majoritarianism. But the record of the Supreme Court is not what it should be, and its performance in promoting tolerance and a respect for the rights of religious minorities was less than stellar.[3]

This chapter examines the recent legal narrative of secularism in the Supreme Court and the extent to which the Hindu Right's deployment of equality and secularism, the cornerstones of a liberal democratic state, have been, to some extent, validated by the Indian Supreme Court.

In the first section, I examine the competing understandings of secularism that have emerged in India. I look at the model of secularism that is being promoted by the Hindu Right and the validation this model has received from the electorate, and more importantly, from the Supreme Court. I then discuss the importance of the Supreme Court decision in 1995 vindicating *Hindutva*.[4] In the concluding section, I briefly suggest ways in which we might contest the ideological and discursive battle being waged in the courtroom by the Religious Right in order to safeguard the Indian secular state, specifically through a reconfiguring of the principle of toleration.

SECULARISM

Secularism has long been the site of political and constitutional struggle and controversy in India. The struggle to secure its place in the Indian polity has had many enemies. Increasingly the enemies of secularism are waging their war not in opposition to secularism, but in and through it. Secularism has become the site of intensive political contestation, in which right-wing, religious, and fundamentalist forces endeavor to claim the terrain as their own. In India, the Hindu Right has increasingly staked out its own claim to secularism, arguing that it alone is committed to upholding this constitutional principle. Indeed, secularism has become the central and powerful weapon in the Hindu Right's quest for discursive and political power.[5]

In India secularism has never been based on the idea of the separation of religion from the state. Since independence, almost all debates on the subject of secularism have been based on the idea of *sarva dharma sambhava*—equal respect of all religions. This approach to secularism does not require a wall of separation between religion and politics. It is based on the idea of equal respect of all religions within both the public and private spheres. This concept was propounded by Mahatma Gandhi and has been the governing model of secularism over the past fifty years.[6] Like the liberal democratic vision of secularism, the Indian model is based on equality and freedom of religion. However, toleration displaces the third principle of the liberal vision (neutrality) in the Indian model.

The meaning to be given to secularism in India depends to a large extent on the meaning given to each of these constituting principles. To some extent, the meaning of secularism turns on the meaning of equality. If equality is understood in the formal sense—treating likes alike—then secularism will insist on treating India's various religious communities alike. By contrast, if equality is understood in a more substantive sense—of addressing disadvantage—then secularism will allow for an accommodation of difference between religious groups and the protection of the rights of religious minorities.

Indian secularism has, to a large extent, been based on a more substantive approach to the principle of equal respect and toleration of all religions, which has allowed for the protection of religious minority rights. But the Hindu Right has increasingly been trying to cast itself as the true inheritors of India's secular tradition, that is, as promoters of "genuine" secularism. Contrary to the dominant understanding of secularism in India, the Hindu Right is committed to a vision of secularism based on a formal approach to equality. In its vision, secularism requires that all religious communities be treated the same. Any protection of the rights of religious minorities is cast as "appeasement," and a violation of the "true spirit" of secularism. Within this vision of secularism, all religious groups are to be treated the same, that is, the same as the majority. Within this formal approach to equality, then, the majority becomes the norm against which all others are to be judged. Secularism is no longer about protecting the rights of religious minorities, but rather, becomes about the assimilation of these minorities.

The principle of equal respect and toleration of all religions is used to establish the supremacy of Hinduism as the only religion that truly respects difference and toleration (since, unlike Islam and Christianity, it is not proselytizing). According to the logic of the Hindu Right, since secularism is about toleration, and only Hindus are tolerant, then only Hindus are truly secular. The principle of protecting minorities virtually disappears. The various laws through which these minority rights have been protected are attacked as "special treatment" and as a violation of the constitutional mandate of equal treatment. Within this vision of the Hindu Right, then, secularism comes to be equated with a Hindu state, where religious minorities must be treated the same as the Hindu majority (i.e., where those religious minorities are effectively assimilated into the Hindu majority). It is a vision in which there is no respect, no toleration, and no protection of religious minorities, and it is the antithesis of Indian secularism.

THE SUPREME COURT'S SEAL OF APPROVAL

In 1994 and 1995 the Supreme Court of India decided two cases, both involving the Hindu Right and the meaning of secularism in India, that revealed the Court's inconsistent record and its recent failings in protecting against the erosion of India's secular foundation.

The 1994 *Bommai* decision involved a challenge to the declaration of presidential rule in four states following the destruction of the Babri Masjid.[7] The full constitutional bench of the Supreme Court upheld the declaration's validity. The Court unanimously affirmed the importance of secularism to the Indian Constitution while emphasizing the distinctively Indian concept of secularism—the equal respect of all religions. The decision contained not only statements about secularism—as religious tolerance and equal treatment of all religious groups—but also a very strong condemnation of those political forces committed to undermining this constitutional ideal.

The *Bommai* decision recognized that the Hindu Right's strategy was an attack on the religious freedom of minorities, and that its strategy undermined secularism. *Bommai* represents a high watermark in the Court's recent protection of secularism. The decision followed the destruction of the mosque, when India was experiencing its most violent manifestation of communal politics. The discourse of the Hindu Right, as powerful as it may be, was not powerful enough to mask or obscure the death and destruction brought on by its forces.

But a year later, in 1995, the Supreme Court delivered its opinion in what has come to be known as the *Hindutva* cases.[8] These cases represent a low watermark in the Court's protection of secularism. In the *Hindutva* cases, the election of *Shiv Sena*/BJP candidates in the December 1987 State Assembly elections in the western state of Maharastra was challenged on the grounds that the candidates had committed corrupt practices in violation of section 123 of the Representation of the People Act, 1951. This section prohibits candidates from appealing to religion, race, caste, community, or language to further their chance of election, and also prohibits candidates from promoting feelings of enmity between different classes of citizens on the grounds of religion, race, caste, community, or language. Charges were brought against twelve members of the Hindu Right—including Bal Thackeray, the head of the militant *Shiv Sena*, and Manohar Joshi, the then chief minister of the state of Maharastra.[9] Although the Court found several of the accused—most notably Thackeray—guilty of appealing to religion to gain votes, and promoting religious enmity and hatred, it also held that *Hindutva*—the ideological linchpin of the Hindu Right—simply represented "a way of life of people of the subcontinent."[10]

According to the Court, *Hindutva* could not to be equated with or understood as religious fundamentalism or as a depiction of an attitude hostile to persons practicing other religions. Rather, *Hindutva* was to be used to promote secularism, to emphasize the way of life of the Indian people and the Indian culture, or to criticize the policy of any political party as discriminatory or intolerant.[11] The Court held that *Hindutva* was neither an appeal to religion nor a promotion of religious hatred, and thus not a violation of the Act.

The Court's conclusion on the meaning of *Hindutva* is legally, historically, and politically unsupportable. The historical and political context within which

Hindutva has been given meaning reveals that it is (1) an appeal to religion and (2) a promotion of religious enmity and hatred. The history of *Hindutva* demonstrates that the term has long been an appeal to religion. The writings of the ideological leaders describe *Hindutva* as the mental state or attitude of the Hindu race and the Hindu nation—a race and a nation that were, at their very core, about religion.[12] *Hindutva* propagated the idea that the "holy land" for Christians and Muslims lay elsewhere and that their presence in India made them a threat to the Indian nation. This idea allowed the ideological leaders to construct Muslims and Christians as foreigners, aliens, and invaders.

Beyond its failure to recognize the highly communal nature of the contemporary deployment of *Hindutva* by the Hindu Right, the decision represents a further erosion of India's secular foundations. The Court held that the speeches in fact promoted secularism. It stated, "It cannot be doubted that a speech with a secular stance alleging discrimination against any particular religion and promising removal of the imbalance cannot be treated as an appeal on the ground of religion as its thrust is for promoting secularism."[13] In accepting, without any critical analysis, this discourse as secular, the Court fell into the complex trap set by the Hindu Right—in which a fundamentally nonsecular project (of Hindu supremacy and the assimilation of religious minorities) has been packaged, sold, and consumed as a secular one.

Not surprisingly, the decision was immediately hailed as a victory by the Right. In its 1998 election manifesto, the BJP used the decision to continue to legitimize its model of secularism, citing the Supreme Court decision as an endorsement of the "true meaning and content of *Hindutva* as being consistent with the true meaning and definition of secularism."[14]

TURNING TO THE WALL

The crisis has led some commentators to argue in favor of a return to some notion of the wall of separation of religion and state. Yet some U.S. cases indicate that the problem of majoritarianism may not be avoided by a constitutional principle of state nonintervention.[15] There are two clear tensions evident in the struggle over the meaning of secularism, or where the line should be drawn between the church and the state in the United States. The first is the tension implicit in the very idea that there can be a wall of separation. The second is that even if there is a wall, there is an increasingly strong pull within constitutional discourse as well as within the legal academy to shift toward a model of secularism that is based on the "equal treatment of all religions," a model that until now was considered to be a distinctively Indian model.

Few commentators believe that there really is a wall of separation between religion and the state in the United States. Despite the establishment clause, there are in fact a broad range of widely accepted state-sanctioned religious activities: the U.S. currency, displaying "In God We Trust"; opening prayers at state assemblies; and state funding of chaplains in the armed forces. From the point of view of the comparativist, religion is seeping into the public arena, partly through the avenue of the courts, and more openly challenging the rigid separatism that has ostensibly been established by the wall. There are a series of cases that have been chipping away at the wall, leaving the outsider questioning its impermeability. Many critics have argued that the requirement of state nonintervention and neutrality has served to reinforce the power relations of the status quo, and thus the dominant position of religious majorities. For example, in one decision the U.S. Supreme Court upheld the constitutionality of the Sunday closing laws, which had been challenged by religious minorities whose Sabbath—or weekly day of rest—fell on a day other than Sunday, as violating their right to freedom of religion and the establishment clause.[16] They argued that they should be allowed to close on their own Sabbath, while remaining open on Sundays. While conceding that the Sunday laws were originally religious in nature, the Court upheld them on the ground that their present purpose and effect was to impose a uniform and neutral day of rest for all citizens. The fact that this uniform day of rest was of particular significance to Christians was not considered to be an obstacle to this secular objective. The case reveals how, in the name of secularism, the dominant norms of the Christian majority were reinforced at the expense of the norms of the minority.[17] In his dissent, Justice William Douglas recognized this implicit majoritarianism. He wrote: "No matter what is said, the parentage of [the Sunday closing] laws is the Fourth Commandment. . . . They serve and satisfy the religious predispositions of our Christian communities."[18]

In contrast, in a later decision in *Thornton v. Caldor*, the Supreme Court struck down a Connecticut law that allowed Sabbath observers the right to not work on their Sabbath.[19] Other workers simply had the right to a day off, but not to designate that day. The fact that only Sabbath observers had the right to designate their day off was, in the Court's view, a violation of the constitutional requirement of neutrality. As a result of the Court's decision, a state can force all individuals to take off Sunday (the traditional Christian Sabbath) as long as it does not do so in the name of the Sabbath, but is not permitted to accommodate the Sabbath of non-Christian observers by allowing workers to take off on their own Sabbaths.[20]

As my coauthor, Brenda Cossman, and I have observed, a similar majoritarian religious bias is evident in *Lynch v. Donnelly*. The Supreme Court there held that the public display of a creche—the nativity scene of Jesus, displayed during Christmas—does not violate the establishment clause.[21] "The City . . . has principally taken note of a significant historical religious event long celebrated in the Western World. . . . The display is sponsored by the City to celebrate the Holiday and to depict the origins of that Holiday. These are legitimate secular purposes."[22] As we have commented, in this reasoning, the explicitly Christian religious holiday has apparently become so invisible from the unstated norm of the majority that the Court can simply claim the holiday to be secular in nature.

Again, in the name of neutrality, the dominant norms of the Christian majority were reinforced.[23]

In contrast, the Supreme Court held that student-led prayer at high school football games violates the establishment clause. The case involved an appeal from the Fifth Circuit Court's decision in *Doe v. Sante Fe Independent School District*, which struck down a school policy to permit the saying of prayer at a high school graduation ceremony and extended that to high school football games. The issue was whether the way in which the school policy was framed violated the establishment clause and the strict separation of church from the state. The Supreme Court held that the delivery of a message such as an invocation "on school property, at school-sponsored events, over the school's public address system, by a speaker representing the student body, under the supervision of school faculty, and pursuant to a school policy that explicitly and implicitly encourages public prayer" could not be characterized as "private" speech.[24] The Court held that the delivery of the invocation, broadcast over the school's public address system, to a large audience that assembled as part of a regularly scheduled, school-sponsored function conducted on school property, amounted to an endorsement of the message by the school.

In December 1999, a federal district judge in Cleveland struck down a school voucher program passed by the Ohio legislature, largely on the grounds that the program violated the establishment clause.[25] Many of the schools participating in the program had a pervasive religious orientation. The U.S. Supreme Court will likely review the issue, and the final outcome will be determined against a history of the previous four decades that have witnessed an unsteady erosion of the wall.

The tension in these cases is indicative of the broader tension between promoting or endorsing religion and failing to make room for religious exercise. Neutrality ostensibly means noninterference in any religion, that the state shall adopt a neutral position with regard to all religions. Yet, as feminist legal scholar Martha Minow has stated, neutral means might not produce neutral results, given historic practices and social arrangements that have not been neutral.[26] Accommodation of religious practices may look nonneutral, but failure to accommodate may also seem nonneutral as it burdens the religious minority whose needs were not built into the structure of mainstream institutions. In other words, if the government does nothing, the structures that have continued to operate remain unaltered and in place, and minorities remain unaccommodated.

So the problem of majoritarianism remains unaddressed in the separation model. State neutrality has served in the United States to reinforce the majority practices, and the power of the majority to define the norm. There is little reason to believe that its performance would be any better in the Indian context.

There is a second emerging tension in the American context that I will mention. Through the 1990s there has been gradual chipping away at the wall primarily by the Christian Right, which is making serious efforts to bring religion more and more into the public sphere. It is attempting, with a considerable degree of success, to introduce a new standard into the doctrine of secularism, based on the equal treatment of all religions. The public discourse has become distinctly more religious throughout the 1990s. For example, in the presidential campaign of 2000, the candidates felt obliged to reveal their faith credentials in order to establish their legitimacy. George W. Bush set the tone by declaring that his favorite political philosopher was "Christ, because he changed my heart."[27] Not to be outdone, Al Gore boasted that he decided important questions using the religious shorthand "W.W.J.D.—for a saying," he explained, "that's popular now in my faith, 'What would Jesus do?' " Gore also described himself on a nightly news program as a born-again Christian.[28]

Some recent cases also make explicit the effort to introduce a move away from the strict separation standard toward one based on the equal treatment of all religions. For instance, Christian Right groups have begun seriously to push the boundaries of earlier Supreme Court rulings, that have permitted nonproselytizing, nonsectarian prayer or benedictions to be given at graduation ceremonies. Christian groups are arguing that these rulings are still discriminatory and violate the establishment clause as they do not permit sectarian proselytizing speech but do allow ecumenical speech. One reason that the issue is so contentious is that it involves educational spaces, a zone of contest, and highly prized breeding ground for right-wing ideology. Recently, some conservative state legislatures have attempted to introduce a mandatory "moment of silence" in public schools.[29] This issue has become extremely contentious. The Concerned Women of America are supporting the right to school prayer while the American Civil Liberties Union is filing a challenge to the provision in federal district court arguing that a moment of silence breaches the establishment clause.[30] These challenges are set against a backdrop of cases in which the Supreme Court refused to permit prayer in schools and the posting of the Ten Commandments in classrooms. However, the new challenges also have to be determined against a run of cases that have succeeded in chipping away at the wall as well as the fact that the discourse of the Religious Right and the idea of equal treatment of all religions has since permeated the public arena.

What is evident in these cases and public declarations is that the religion in question is Christian majoritarian values. The issue of prayer is directly about the right of public expression by the Christian majority. Even voucher programs indirectly raise related issues when the proponents express concern that "extreme" religious groups or "cults" might operate schools that receive vouchers. Neither program invites religious minorities to perform their rights of worship or prayer in schools or to set up sectarian schools based on their religious values and principles.

The tensions emerging in the U.S. context demonstrate how state neutrality has served to reinforce the majority practices and the power of the majority to define the norm. The turn to a strict separation of religion and politics and its requirement of state neutrality does not appear to have resolved the problem of majoritarianism in the American context. At the same time, recent efforts to introduce an equal treatment of all religions standard into legal and public discourse amounts to an implicit acknowledgment that the wall is crumbling.

Thus, to repeat a point made elsewhere, we are left then with a dilemma—both the principle of toleration that underlies the equal respect of all religions and the principle of neutrality that underlies the separation of religion and politics have been shown by their critics to reinforce majoritarianism. The dilemma can only begin to be resolved by recognizing that not only does religion remain present in the various models of secularism, but the unstated norm of the dominant religion also remains present. A model of secularism that is premised on the separation thesis is least likely to acknowledge the presence of religion, since its very premise is the prohibition of religion in politics.[31] The model based on the equal respect of all religions, in contrast, though it is complicit in majoritarian politics, may be able to meet the challenge insofar as it acknowledges the presence of religion in politics. It can use its own premise, that is, the principle of equality, to critique the way in which this model of secularism has been applied to undermine the equality of religious minorities.

NEW SECULARISM

In this section, drawing upon and summarizing prior work by Cossman and me, I make some tentative suggestions for working in and through the dominant discourse of secularism in an attempt to revitalize this discourse with democratic principles. Secularism's three basic tenets—equality, freedom of religion, and toleration—need to be revisited.

The recognition of the importance of minority rights within a more substantive understanding of equality is crucial in challenging the majoritarianism of the Hindu Right's approach to secularism.[32] This discursive challenge will not be an easy one because the formal understanding of equality that informs the Right's approach to secularism has come to capture the popular imagination—it has become a part of a truth claim, a part of collective common sense.[33] Like the conservative assault on affirmative action in the United States, the Right has led the charge on "special treatment" and "appeasement." This position is summed up in the BJP slogan, "Justice for All: Appeasement for None." It sounds both logical and reasonable. But it is precisely this powerful discursive move that must be countered if secularism is to be reappropriated from the Right and revisioned in accordance with a more democratic political vision.[34]

More important, the principle of toleration must be refashioned and democratized. It must be unlinked from its majoritarian and religious foundations. But then we encounter a troubling paradox: the majoritarian and religious character of toleration is precisely the characteristic that gives Indian secularism its distinctive nature.[35] So should we then abandon this concept of secularism in favor of one that returns to the principle of neutrality? Yet it is this dominant discourse of secularism that seems to offer the most political promise. The dilemma then becomes how to escape from this paradox without abandoning the dominant discourse of secularism as the equal respect of all religions.[36]

Rather than disarticulating toleration from its religious moorings altogether, a second option might be to pluralize the cultural and religious traditions on which it is based. Rather than emphasizing the exclusivity of Hinduism as a tolerant religion, this pluralizing strategy would search for toleration's historical roots in the multiplicity of India's religious traditions.[37] This pluralizing strategy always runs the risk of majoritarianism. In the *Ayodhya* decision,[38] for example, the Supreme Court attempts to tell a story of India's rich tapestry of toleration by weaving together a pastiche of citations from famous speeches and decisions that in turn cite other famous works and speeches. But, this pastiche does not amount to a particularly rigorous historical methodology.[39] And invariably the scriptures cited are Hindu—revealing again the extent to which the unstated norm of the majority slips into judicial discourse, in subtle and not so subtle ways.[40]

The problem of majoritarianism remains. Arguably the way out is to decenter the unstated norm and to make the historical basis of the Indian tradition of toleration truly pluralized. But this move still runs certain risks. It is a move that begins to approximate the strategy advocated by Ashish Nandy, who argues that secularism as a nineteenth-century import from Europe should be abandoned in favor of a "tolerance that is religious" and that is located "outside the ideological grid of modernity."[41] In essence, he is arguing for a return to premodern forms, uncontaminated by India's encounter with colonialism and modernity.[42] It is a strategy that runs the risks of nostalgic idealism and cultural essentialism—of searching for the elusive authenticity of religious and cultural traditions, of assuming that those traditions can be discovered rather than constructed and negotiated, and of reconstructing those traditions as static, immutable, and monolithic.[43] Arguing in favor of "return" does not provide an adequate or feasible response to a critique of modernity. Such archeological expeditions are misguided at best and unworkable at worst, as they assume that there is a purity of culture that can be excavated and restored in all its pristine glory. This position ignores the fact that, as Cossman has observed, India is a country that itself was forged on the anvil of colonialism, and the traditions of the subcontinent have been reconfigured and reshaped through invasions, wars, and the colonial encounter. There is no possibility of returning to the authentic, as all religious traditions have been hybridized through the history of global expansion and imperialism.[44]

A second limitation with a religious conception of toleration is that it does not extend beyond a toleration of religious difference. This religious toleration could not speak to the importance of tolerating those who think, act, and live differently, if those differences were based on something other than religion. It would not be applicable in the context of political differences or moral differences, where toleration may be called for. For example, homosexuality and sexual difference is an issue around which there is a high degree of controversy.

In the United States and elsewhere, there are conservative political movements that not only do not tolerate homosexuals, but also strive to eliminate homosexuality altogether. Similarly, one wonders whether other sexually different groups would be tolerated in India.[45] A religious conception of toleration may not support an argument for toleration toward such sexual subgroups.[46] Nor is it likely that a religious conception of toleration would be up to the task of promoting tolerance toward racial[47] minorities, or of accommodating political differences like communism or pacifism. A principle of toleration must be one that is up to the challenge of promoting respect of difference not only along religious lines, but also along a range of other fault lines.[48]

An approach to toleration that may accommodate a fuller range of conflicts and cleavages may be found in a political conception of toleration. It is a conception of toleration that acknowledges the irreversible mark that modernity has made on our times and recognizes that a commitment to living together across our differences will have to be carved out of this modernity, not in opposition to it.[49] Within the context of legal and political discourse, toleration would no longer need to be derived from ancient sources. It would be approached as a constitutional value in its own right. It would begin from the basic premise of accepting people and their practices despite our disagreements and disapproval. It is a conception of toleration that means not only accepting differences, but also accepting differences that at some level we find unacceptable. It is a conception that goes beyond the mere acceptance of different forms of worship. It is a normative commitment to accepting a broad range of differences in beliefs, practices, and ways of being, made necessary by the pluralistic and fragmented world in which we live.[50]

Yet doesn't this approach represent a secular—that is, an antireligious—bias and displace the very recognition of religion that lies at the root of the distinctive nature of Indian secularism? Perhaps it does. However, at a pragmatic level, the intention is not to banish a reliance on religious conceptions of toleration altogether. To the extent that a reliance on this religious toleration may assist in challenging the rising tides of majoritarianism and recreating a public space that respects the rights of those who are different, it should be used in day to day struggles for recuperating a democratic vision of toleration.[51] The suggestion is not to exclude the possibility of a religious conception of toleration from the secular equation altogether. Rather, it is to point out its risks and limitations, to suggest that a religious conception of toleration is insufficient, and to argue in favor of a broader political conception.

This proposal is made specifically in relation to this legal and constitutional discourse, where it is important for the courts to disentangle toleration from its religious and majoritarian basis. Proponents of secularism may find it strategically useful to deploy a religious conception of toleration on occasion—in public discourse and popular culture, for example—but it may not have a place in law. The courts should not feel compelled to search ancient texts to legitimate the rightful place of toleration in the Indian Constitution, but rather, should confidently assert toleration as its own constitutional value.[52]

THE DILEMMAS OF TOLERANCE

Toleration is generally said to require that we accept people and their practices, even when we strongly disagree and disapprove of them.[53] But, this statement of principle leaves many difficult questions unanswered. What kind of state action does this acceptance require? Does tolerating subgroups involve nonintervention in their affairs? Or does it require a more substantive accommodation of group differences?[54] Minow argues that if toleration simply involves nonintervention in the views and practices of the subgroup, it will fail to adequately respect the subgroup.[55] In her view, the protection of cultural minorities requires more than toleration—it requires a respect for cultural diversity, which, Minow suggests, may "call for accommodation of subgroup practices and, therefore, changes in dominant institutions."[56]

Mere nonintervention may be inadequate to the task of accommodating the subgroup; indeed mere nonintervention perpetuates the very oppressive conditions that subgroups struggle against for their very survival. At the same time, nonintervention may be all that stands in the way of the goal of assimilation. From the point of view of the cultural minorities that are under attack from the Hindu Right, even weak toleration as mere nonintervention may seem to be an increasingly attractive and elusive norm.[57]

A second recurring question that plagues the principle of toleration is whether the principle is to be extended to subgroups who do not accept toleration. Partha Chatterjee has explored this dilemma of toleration and suggests that the problem of the rise of the Hindu Right and its assault on minorities should be reconfigured not as a problem of secularism, but as a problem of toleration.[58] He argues that the principle of respect for persons can serve as the moral basis for defending the principle of toleration. It simultaneously provides the basis for respecting the rights of cultural groups.

Chatterjee reframes the kind of treatment that the dominant community will have to extend to subgroups and argues that toleration will have to involve more than the mere right to be different.[59] It will require accepting "that there will be political contexts where a group could insist on its right not to give reasons for doings things differently provided it explains itself adequately in its own chosen forum."[60] Cultural minorities will need to ensure that procedures and processes exist through which they can "publicly seek and obtain from [their] members consent for [their] practices insofar as those practices have regulative power over the members."[61] It is a call for some kind of internal accountability or democracy that becomes the prerequisite for extending the principle of toleration and, in turn, for accommodating a cultural minority's right to do things differently.[62]

Chatterjee's critique and proposal are provocative. In part, he may be read as relinquishing too much autonomy to highly conservative, even orthodox, communities to manage their own affairs without adequate concern for toleration within their own ranks. His proposal appears to cede all normative universality in favor of an extreme cultural relativism. But there are some safeguards built into his proposal. There are underlying universal norms informing his vision. These include a process of democratic accountability and the respect for persons, autonomy, and self-representation. In his refashioned vision of toleration, it is the existence of some structures of accountability and democratic representation that operate as the prerequisite for the dominant community's willingness to extend toleration to the subgroup.[63] The members of the subgroup must consent. Chatterjee attempts to formulate a middle ground, "somewhere in between" universal principles and the recognition of difference.[64]

Many questions remain unanswered. It is difficult to imagine how his propositions could be translated into the legal domain. For example, would courts accept the principle of a right not to give reasons, given that this legal arena is all about giving reasonable argument? Could or should courts be called upon to adjudicate issues such as whether cultural minorities have met the minimal requirement of internal accountability? Would we not expect to encounter precisely the same problem of majoritarianism? And has Chatterjee prematurely abandoned the importance of the "mere right to be different"—a right that is little in evidence in the discourse of the Hindu Right?[65] Nevertheless, it is important to engage his proposals, as they provide the basis for some kind of principled defense of some degree of autonomy for cultural minorities, on the condition that those minorities abide by a basic degree of democratic accountability.

As Cossman and I have noted, Minow's and Chatterjee's efforts at refashioning the scope and content of toleration provide insight into the effort to ground secularism within a more democratic politics. In particular, their insistence on the importance of group rights and of the rights of cultural minorities to some degree of self-governance and self-determination is an important contribution to redemocratizing the principles that inform Indian secularism. They also share a belief that the principle of respect for persons should be the basis for toleration. It must serve as the arbiter in attempting to resolve the dilemmas that toleration continues to present. It is this principle of respect for persons that must inform efforts at resolving the questions of when to tolerate those who do not appear to hold toleration as a cherished value and how to balance a commitment to universal norms with a respect for cultural difference.[66] The principle of respect can provide the prerequisite for the extension of toleration—that only those communities that demonstrate respect towards their members will qualify for toleration.

A revisioning of toleration along the lines proposed creates space for an approach to secularism that does not preclude the recognition of group differences. In fact, it begins with an affirmation of the importance of accommodating these differences. The equal toleration of all religions does not necessarily imply equal treatment or that the practices and views of religious minorities be brought into line with those of the dominant community in order to qualify for toleration. Instead, the equal toleration of all religions, based on a substantive vision of equality, recognizes that difference can be accommodated and respected, including those differences with which the majority community may disagree or disapprove.

CONCLUSION

The Hindu Right is producing crude fantasies about Hinduism and Hindu history. They are contriving new belief systems and structures through the process of invention and fabrication rather than truth or evidence. Their ultimate fantasy has been produced in the struggle over Ayodhya, where the Hindu Right has staked a signpost on the spot where God was born.[67] Their construction of the Hindu faith and religion is the very antithesis of pluralism. Nevertheless, their fantasies are capturing the popular imagination, and it is for this reason that we need to monitor the discursive shifts and moves of the Right in order to protect the rights of religious minorities, rights that constitute the cornerstone of any democracy.

The core of the Hindu Right's approach to secularism and the rights of cultural and religious minorities lies in its policy of assimilation. It is a policy that aims at denying and, ultimately, eradicating these minorities. Although their policy is specifically directed at the Muslim minority, it also includes other religious minorities that pose any threat to, or are in any way different from, the dominant Hindu norm. Any effort to defend secularism from the attack of the Hindu Right requires a direct confrontation over the issue of minority rights.[68] And this in turn requires that the principle of secularism be revisited and revitalized in a way that enables cultural minorities to be free to pursue their own beliefs. It requires that the state be obligated to accommodate group differences. The argument in favor of a political conception of toleration—one that is not ensnared in religious and majoritarian traps—can recognize and accommodate difference within minority communities, provided these communities demonstrate democratic accountability and respect to their own members.[69]

Secularism is a concept that will not remain static and requires constant monitoring. Its meaning will shift with changing political and historical contexts. In the contemporary moment, the meaning of secularism is hostage to the ideological agenda of the Hindu Right. In order to release this ideal from the grip of the Right, secularism, within legal discourse, must be detached from its current religious bondage. This process involves a reconfiguration of secularism in ways that it becomes a unifying, rather than a fragmenting concept. The pursuit of *Hindutva*'s fantasy and its political project of the "demolition" of cultural and religious minorities[70] in and through liberal rights discourse, requires a direct confrontation if secularism is to be rescued from being overwhelmed by the false godheads of Hinduism.

NOTES

I am grateful to Brenda Cossman who has permitted me to draw on our collaborative work in writing this article, in particular, SECULARISM'S LAST SIGH? *Hindutva* AND THE (MIS) RULE OF LAW (1999). Substantial portions of this chapter appeared originally in that book and are reprinted here, without separate quotation marks, with permission of Professor Brenda Cossman and our publisher, Oxford University Press.

1. Salman Rushdie, THE MOOR'S LAST SIGH, Jonathan Cape (1995), 363.

2. *M. Ismail Faruqui v. Union of India*, A.I.R. 1994 S.C.W. 4897, paragraph 7.

3. SECULARISM'S LAST SIGH? *Hindutva* AND THE (MIS) RULE OF LAW (1999) at XV.

4. *Prabhoo v. Prabhakar Kasinath Kunte et. al.*, 1995 S.C.A.L.E. 1.

5. *Supra* note 3 at 63–72.

6 *See* Asgar Ali Engineer, *Secularism in India—Theory and Practice, in* SECULARISM AND LIBERATION: PERSPECTIVES AND STRATEGIES FOR INDIA TODAY 40 (Rudolf C. Heredia & Edward Mathias eds., 1995).

7. *Bommai v. Union of India*, 3 S.C.C. 1 (1994).

8. *Supra* note 4; with *Shri Bal Thackeray v. Shri Prabhakar Kasinath Kunte and Ors.*; *Manohar Joshi v. Nitin Bhaurao Patil*, A.I.R. 1996 S.C. 796; *Ramachandra G. Kapse v. Haribansh Ramakbal Singh*, A.I.R. 1996 S.C. 817; with *Pramod Mahajan v. Haribansh Ramakbal Singh* and *Anr., and Sadhvi Reetambrara* [*sic*] *v. Haribansh Ramakbal Singh and Anr.*; *Ramakant Mayekar v. Smt. Celine D'Silva*, A.I.R. 1996 S.C. 826; with *Chhagan Bhujbal v. Smt. Celine D'Silva* and *Anr., Balasaheh Thackeray v. Smt. Celine D'Silva*; *Shri Moreshwar Save v. Shri Dwarkadas Yashwantrao Pathrikar*, A.I.R. 1996 S.C. 3335; *Chandrakanta Goyal v. Sohan Singh Jodh Singh Kohli*, A.I.R. 1996 S.C. 861; *Suryakant Venkatrao Mahadik v. Saroj Sandesh Naik*, 1995 S.C.A.L.E. 92.

9. *Id.* The charges were brought under section 123 (3) and (3A) of the Act. The former prohibits candidates from appealing to religion, race, caste, community, or language to further their prospects for election, and the latter provision prohibits candidates from "promoting feelings of enmity or hatred between different classes of the citizens of India on grounds of religion, race, caste, community or language" for the purposes of securing votes or prejudicially affecting the votes of another candidate.

10. *Prabhoo*, 1995 S.C.A.L.E. at 24.

11. *Id.* at 24–25.

12. *See* M.S. Golwalkar, WE OR OUR NATIONHOOD DEFINED (1939) and V.D. Savarkar, WHO IS A HINDU? 3 (4th ed., S.P. Gokhale 1949)

13. *Supra* note 4 at 11–12.

14. Bharatiya Janata Party, Election Manifesto 2 (1998).

15. Although the idea of a wall of separation goes back to the words of Jefferson, it was only given judicial expression as a basic principle of constitutional law by the U.S. Supreme Court in the 1940s. In *Everson v. Board of Education of Ewing Township*, 330 US 1 (1947), Justice Black, writing for the majority, emphasized the requirement of strict government neutrality on issues of religion.

16. *McGowan v. Maryland*, 266 U.S. 420 (1961).

17. *Supra* note 3 at 98–99.

18. *Supra* note 16 at 572–73.

19. 472 U.S. 703 (1985).

20. *Supra* note 3 at 99.

21. 465 U.S. 668 (1984). See also *County of Allegheny v. ACLU, Greater Pittsburgh Chapter*, 492 U.S. 573, 635 (1989) (O'Connor, J., concurring in judgment) (concluding that city display of a menorah alongside a sign saluting liberty and a Christmas tree was not an endorsement of Judaism or religion in general).

22. *Lynch*, 465 U.S. at 680–81.

23. *Supra* note 3 at 99.

24. *Sante Fe Independent School District v. Doe*, 530 U.S. 290, 310 (2000).

25. *See* Order of Judge Solomon Oliver, Jr., dated August 24, 1999, in Case No: 1: 99 CV 1740 and Case No. 1:99 CV 1818 pending in the United States District Court, northern district of Ohio, Eastern Division, in *Doris Simmon-Haris, et al., v. Dr. Susan Tave Zelman, Superintendent of Public Instruction, State of Ohio, et al.*, and *Sue Gatton v. Dr. Susan Tave Zelman, Superintendent of Public Instruction, State of Ohio.*

The program was enacted to address an educational crisis in the public schools in Cleveland in the wake of a U.S. District Court–ordered takeover by the state of the administration of the Cleveland City School District. The project includes a scholarship program to enable students to attend "alternative schools" (the voucher program). The private schools that want to participate in the program must register with the state superintendent. Those students eligible are chosen by lot and receive a fixed amount of the tuition charged by the alternative school of their choice up to the amount of $2,500. A large majority of the schools participating in the program are sectarian, as are most of the students receiving the scholarship.

26. Martha Minow, *The Supreme Court 1986 Term: Foreword: Justice Engendered*, 101 HARV.L.REV. 10 (1987).

27. Todd J. Gilman, *Bush's 'Christ' Response in Debate Surprises Some Scholars*, DALLAS MORNING NEWS, Dec. 18, 1999, at 36A.

28. Sally Quinn, *The G-Word and the A-List; In a Social Setting, There's One Subject Washington Avoids Religiously: God*, WASH. POST, July 22, 1999, at C01.

29. Gustav Niebuhr, *Ideas and Trends; God and Man and the Presidency*, N.Y. TIMES, Dec. 19, 1999, § 4, at 5.

30. *See* Laurel MacLeod, School Prayer and Religious Liberty: A Constitutional Perspective, September, 2000. <http://www.cwfa.org/library/freedom/2000-09_pp_schoolprayer.shtml> (site visited December 7, 2000); ACLU Challenges Virginia's Moment of Silence Law, The Associated Press, June 23, 2000. <http://www.freedomforum.org/templates/document.asp?documentID=12762> (site visited June 7, 2000).

31. *Supra* note 3 at 101.

32. *Supra* note 3 at 107.

33. *Id.*

34. *Supra* note 3 at 108.

35. *Supra* note 3 at 118.

36. *Id.*

37. *Id.*

38. *M. Ismail Faruqui v. Union of India*, AIR 1995 SC 605 (upholding the constitutionality of the Acquisition of Certain Land at Ayodhya Act (1993)). Justice Verma, writing for the majority, rejected arguments that the Act was biased in favor of Hindus or discriminated against Muslims. Justice Bharucha, in dissent, found that the Act was slanted toward Hindus, and thus offended the basic principle of secularism.

39. *Supra* note 3 at 119.

40. *M. Ismail Faruqui*, 1994 S.C.W. at paragraph 144.

41. *See* Ashish Nandy, *The Politics of Secularism and the Recovery of Religious Tolerance*, 13 ALTERNATIVES (1988), *reprinted in* SECULARISM AND ITS CRITICS (Rajeev Bhargava ed., 1998).

42. *Supra* note 3 at 120.

43. *Id.* On the critique of cultural essentialism, *see* Stuart Hall, *Cultural Identity and Cinematic Representation, in* BLACK BRITISH CULTURAL STUDIES: A READER 210 (Houston A. Baker, Jr. et al. eds., 1996). *See also* Ratna Kapur, *A Love Song to Our Mongrel Selves: Hybridity, Sexuality and the Law*, 8 SOCIAL AND LEGAL STUDIES 353, 352–68 (1999).

44. *Supra* note 3 at 140.

45. *Id.* at 122.

46. *Id.*

47. *Id.*

48. *Id.* at 122.

49. *Id.* at 122–23 (noting Chatterjee's efforts to construct a political concept of tolerance).

50. *Id.* at 123. For an argument on the value of toleration, *see* T.M. Scanlon, *The Difficulty of Tolerance, in* Rajeev Bhargava ed., *supra* note 41.

51. *See supra* note 3 at 123: "The question that remains unanswered for us, however, is the extent to which such a religious conception of toleration *can* be used in challenging majoritarianism. Our anxiety around this religious conception of toleration continues to be the extent to which it appears to have been, in practice, deeply majoritarian. We do not want to close the door on a potential useful resource for promoting toleration, but we remain unconvinced of its ability to do so." *Id.* at 124.

52. *Supra* note 3 at 125.

53. *See generally* Scanlon, "*Toleration*," *supra* note 50.

54. *Supra* note 3 at 126.

55. Martha Minow, *Putting Up and Putting Down: Tolerance Reconsidered*, 28 OSGOODE HALL L. JNL. 409 (1990).

56. *Supra* note 3 at 126, quoting Minow, *supra* note 55 at 422–23.

57. *Supra* note 3 at 127.

58. Partha Chatterjee, *Secularism and Toleration*, EPW, July 9, 1994, at 1768.

59. *Supra* note 3 at 130.

60. *Id.* (quoting Chatterjee).

61. *Id.* (Chatterjee). Chatterjee elaborates: "It is not necessary that there be a single uniform pattern of seeking consent that each group will be required to follow. But it is necessary, if toleration is to be demanded, that the processes satisfy the same condition of representativeness that is invoked when a legislative body elected under universal franchise is found unsuitable to act on matters concerning the religion of minority groups. In other words, even if a religious group declares that the validity of its practices can only be discussed and judged in its own forums, those institutions must have the same degree of publicity and representativeness that is demanded of all public institutions having regulatory functions."*Id.*

62. *Supra* note 3 at 130.

63. *Id.* at 131.

64. *Id.* at 131. In some ways, Chatterjee can be seen to have simply shifted the nature of the problem—from one of toleration to one of accountability and democracy. He does not appear to be completely breaking out of the imposition of some normative framework

on cultural minorities. Yet the prerequisites of some form of representation does seem to be the appropriate one within the context of a political project expressly committed to a democratic vision. *Supra* note 3 at 131–33, n.76.

65. *Supra* note 3 at 132.
66. *Supra* note 3 at 133.
67. *Supra* note 3 at 136.
68. *Id.* at 138.
69. *Supra* note 3 at 140.
70. *M. Ismail Faruqui*, 1994 S.C.W. at paragraph 7.

11

The Shaping of a New Democracy Within the Context of Tradition: Equality and the Respect for Diversity

Dennis M. Davis

> The dominant theme of the Constitution is the achievement of equality while considerable importance is also given to cultural diversity and language rights so that the basic problem is to secure equality in a balanced way which shows the maximum regard for diversity. . . . The objective should not be to set the principle of equality against that of cultural diversity but rather to harmonise the two in the interests of both. Democracy in a pluralist society should accordingly not mean the end of cultural diversity, but rather its guarantee, accomplished on the secure bases of justice and equity.[1]

It was the fear that equality would trump diversity that led to a tenacious fight by traditional leaders at the Constitutional Assembly, who argued that customary law should not be made subject to the bill of rights. In this debate, the approach adopted in *Lovelace v. Canada*[2] proved to be of some concern to the traditional leaders. In *Lovelace*, the UN Human Rights Committee accepted that an enactment prohibiting Lovelace from residing on a reservation because she had married a person who was a "non-Indian" constituted an interference with her right under Article 27 of the International Covenant on Civil and Political Rights to enjoy an indigenous culture. The committee did acknowledge that laws could be passed justifiably to define access to the native community if they were reasonable and necessary to protect the community's resources and to preserve its identity. However, the essential finding appeared to be that the individual's right to enjoyment of cultural and community life trumped the community's interest in preserving a distinct ethnic identity through a legal mechanism.[3]

My intention in this chapter is to examine how a constitution born in Africa with a Canadian, American, and German pedigree is to be interpreted, and thus developed, by South African courts.[4] This inquiry is perhaps best illustrated by the inclusion of a constitutional protection of cultural rights. In the development of a coherent jurisprudence, the South African courts will be required to give proper meaning to cultural rights without compromising the foundational aspirations contained in the constitution, that is, a society based upon freedom, human dignity, and equality.

Unquestionably, much of the existing body of African customary law, particularly where women's rights are concerned, would appear to be in conflict with a constitution founded upon the value of equality. But an uncritical acceptance of this conclusion raises the specter of a hallmark of colonial rule whereby customary rules and practices were declared repugnant if they offended western moral standards. Thus the relationship between customary law and the constitution requires a different discourse and a treatment that is nuanced to the context of South African society in which both bodies of law are located.

This chapter attempts to explore the possibility that such a discourse holds implications not only for the reconciliation between customary and constitutional law, but also for the broader issue of constitutional interpretation.

KEY ELEMENTS OF CUSTOMARY LAW THAT ARE AT RISK OF CONSTITUTIONAL ATTACK

In terms of the Black Administration Act,[5] customary law wives who live with their husbands are in the position of minors for the purposes of contractual capacity and legal standing.[6] In short, while a woman cannot be denied her action, she requires assistance to bring her case to court, such assistance coming from her guardian or a *curator ad litem*.

A related issue concerns the important practice of *lobolo*, that is, bride wealth. In order to form a valid marriage, the man's family traditionally had to give cattle to the guardian of the prospective bride. The idea was that the transfer of the cattle represented consideration for the transfer of the woman and her reproductive capacity from the father's family to that of the husband. Compliance with the obligations regarding bride wealth resulted in the husband and his family having full parental rights to any children born of the marriage. Although the modern practice is to pay bride wealth in cash, the practice continues and shows a significant measure of resilience.[7]

Customary law obliges the head of the household to use all property under his control for the benefit of the family. Whatever the problem may be with this institution, it takes on a more serious difficulty when the marriage is dissolved. As the wife has no proprietary capacity, she stands to lose all property. In theory, the woman is absorbed back into her own family while the children remain with, and are supported by, the father.[8]

The controversial institution of polygyny is part of the customary dispensation. It has been argued that the institution helps to absorb women into domestic units and thus prevent the breakdown of marriage through adultery.[9] Only the first wife is compelled to submit to a polygynous union against her will; subsequent wives have a choice. By contrast, polyandry has never formed part of the customary social fabric of South Africa.

THE EQUALITY CHALLENGE

> I am a traditional leader because I am the first male child, even though I am the fourth born. . . . This is because of our system, which is accepted by the people. Now my fear is that my son can be successfully challenged for my throne by my daughter. . . . So now my daughter who is first born, can take my son to court and I have no doubt that my son will come second.
>
> —Chief Mwelo Nonkonyama[10]

Equality is a foundational value of the constitution. Section 1 provides that South Africa is one sovereign, democratic state that is founded upon human dignity, the achievement of equality, and the advancement of human rights and freedoms as well as nonracialism and nonsexism. Section 7—the foundational set of obligations contained in the bill of rights—proclaims that the rights of human dignity, equality, and freedom are the cornerstones of the new South African democracy. The final constitution borrowed from the Canadian Charter of Rights and Freedoms to include in section 9(1)—the general equality guarantee—the right to equal benefit of the law, a change that was intended to introduce a concept of substantive equality into South African constitutional jurisprudence.

The apartheid past looms large in the background when these provisions stand to be interpreted. As O'Regan J. said in *Bernstein and Others v. Bester and Others NNO*,[11] "An enduring legacy of the past is profound inequality. The poverty in which many of our citizens live materially compromises their enjoyment of the rights of freedom and equality. There is much to be done, by the State and citizens, to ensure that the entrenched rights have meaning in the lives of all South Africans."

In a context of a history that is saturated in racial and gender prejudice, the commitment to prevent such discrimination is of equal significance to the potentially redistributive concerns of section 9(1). In dissenting against a majority decision that upheld a presidential decision to grant amnesty to women prisoners who were single parents to minor children but not to men in a similar position, Kriegler J. said "in my view the notion relied upon by the President, namely that women are to be regarded as the primary care givers of young children, is a root cause of women's inequality in our society. It is both a result and a cause of prejudice; a societal attitude which relegates women to a subservient occupationally inferior yet unceasingly onerous role. It is a relic and a feature of the patriarchy which the Constitution so vehemently condemns."[12]

The equality challenge has become more potent as a result of the introduction of a provision that extends the scope of the bill of rights beyond its traditional vertical concerns. In terms of section 8(2) of the constitution, rights guaranteed in the bill of rights bind individuals if, and to the extent that, they are applicable, taking into account the nature of the right and the duty imposed by such right.

The inquiry thus envisages an answer to two questions: does a right bind individuals? and what is the extent of the binding nature of such right? These questions are answered by means of a process of interpretation of the reach of the right. Thus, a right to equality is of such a nature that it is applicable not only to the state, but also to the relationships fashioned by individuals. By contrast, a right to citizenship would not be so applicable.

In the event that a right is found to be so applicable, a court has either to canvass whether any legislation or common law right provides protection as guaranteed in the bill of rights or to develop the common law to so provide content for the constitutionally applicable right. There can be no doubt that the equality right will impact directly upon those arrangements that are sourced in customary law. But the problem is less about the application of the equality right to private relationships that are justified in customary law and more about the relationship between equality and the right to culture, specifically the extent to which the former has the potential to destroy the latter, or at the least to negate its essential content.

In its report on the harmonization of the common law and the indigenous law, the South African Law Commission correctly noted that the manner in which the bill of rights included the right to culture, an equality guarantee, and a provision that expands the scope of the entrenched rights to apply to private relationships, meant that the overall effect was to require greater respect for customary law with a filter through which the customary rules must be interpreted.[13] Likewise, the right to culture does not appear to be a right that protects individuals against the action of the state exclusively. Since cultural integrity is as vulnerable to private power as it is to public power, the right should protect its holders when the dispute is between two private parties.[14]

POTENTIAL CONFLICT

It is these commitments that have fueled Chief Nonkonyama's anxiety about the effect of the constitution upon customary law and practice. The chief is not alone in positing the debate in this fashion. Thus, J.W. Bennett observes that the constitution could well give rise to a confrontation "between two cultural traditions that is reminiscent of the encounter between Victorian encounters and African values in the nineteenth century."[15]

The Law Commission suggests that, although courts should respect an individual's freedom to choose a particular law, they should not do so at the expense of another party's rights. Thus, if a party sues under the common law and the defendant acquiesces, the court should not hesitate to apply the common law. But if the defendant, for example, argues on the basis of customary law, the court "would be obliged to investigate the parties' relationship more deeply to discover another basis for deciding what law to apply."[16] In both cases, the commission acknowledges that the decision must be in harmony with the "supervening value system of the country, the Bill of Rights."[17]

This concession is more easily stated than implemented. This may be illustrated thus: a woman is married under customary law. She approaches a court to challenge her minority status by relying upon the equality clause. The husband relies upon section 31. The traditional way in which the solution is posited is that either the court decides that equality trumps the right to culture or, if not, then the right to equality is given a lesser weight by the court.

The issue becomes more complex when the issue of consent is introduced. Thus, Charles Dlamini argues that as long as a customary union has been entered into freely and voluntarily by the parties, and hence without compulsion on the woman, the latter cannot complain that these institutions discriminate against her.[18] To date, these complications have not confronted the courts. In the two cases where these issues have been raised, the courts have managed to uphold diversity without employing equality as a trump. In one instance this gave rise to a result which was congruent with the spirit of the constitution; in another, the product was pure jurisprudential obfuscation.

In *Ryland v. Edros,*[19] the court was confronted with a divorce of parties married by Muslim rites. Among the questions that required decision was whether a court was bound by an agreement entered into by parties pursuant to a potentially polygamous marriage. Prior to the commencement of the constitution, the Appellate Division had held in *Ismail v. Ismail*[20] that a court could not recognize a marriage or give effect to the consequences thereof when such marriage was contrary to public policy on the grounds of polygamy. In declining to follow *Ismail*, Farlam J. held that it "was quite inimical to all the values of the new South Africa for one group to impose its values on another and that the Courts should only brand a contract as offensive to public policy if it is offensive to those values shared by the community at large, by all right thinking people in the community and not by one section of it."[21]

This conclusion raised another problem, namely, the court's ability to pronounce upon doctrinal matters. In canvassing this issue, Farlam J. said "it seemed to me that there is a distinct danger that by making rulings on the issues before the Court I might unwittingly become entangled in doctrinal matters which it is inappropriate and indeed undesirable, for the reasons given in the American decisions (see for example, *Jones v. Wolf* 443 U.S. 595 (1979)) for a judge in a secular Court to do in a country which has a constitution which entrenches every person's freedom of conscience, religion, thought, belief and opinion. . . ." (as ours does in section 14(1)).[22]

Although Farlam J. observed that the absence of an establishment clause distinguished the South African instrument from the American text, he was not required to decide the question and held that nothing in section 14 of the constitution precluded a decision of the issues in that case. Farlam J. left open the question of the role of the courts in cases in which doctrinal disputes lie at the heart of the case.[23]

Ryland may have been a case dealing with a Muslim marriage, but it has a greater relevance in that it illustrates the difficulty that a court may well face when it enters into a dispute about the content of a cultural right in which distinctly competing traditions lie at the heart of the dispute. This specific issue falls outside the scope of this chapter save, however, for the manner in which a court needs to be sensitive to competing claims upon the process of constitutional interpretation, which is examined below.

The consequence of a refusal to engage the problem was unfortunately thrown into sharp relief in *Mthembu v. Letsela*, in which a woman had been married in terms of customary law. Her husband died intestate, leaving her with a minor child. The deceased's father claimed the deceased's estate by virtue of the customary rule of succession. The woman argued, *inter alia*, that such a rule infringed the constitutional right to equality. The trial court found that, in terms of customary law, a widow may remain at the deceased's home and continue to use the estate property. Hence, Le Roux J. said "if one accepts the duty to provide sustenance, maintenance and shelter as a necessary corollary to the system of primogeniture . . . I find it difficult to equate this form of differentiation between men and women with the concept of 'unfair discrimination' as used in [section] 8 of the Constitution . . . in view of the manifest acknowledgment of customary law as a system existing parallel to the common law by the Constitution . . . and the freedom granted to persons to choose this system as governing their relationships, I cannot accept the submission that the succession rule is necessarily in conflict with [section] 8."[24]

On appeal to the Supreme Court of Appeal, the appellant urged that the court develop "the rule . . . so as to allow all descendants, whether male or female, legitimate or illegitimate, to participate in intestacy . . ."[25] Mpati AJA held that, as the minor child was excluded from inheriting because she was illegitimate, it was purely an academic question as to whether the rule being attacked conflicted with the constitutional prohibition against gender discrimination in that "she would be in the same position as, for example, illegitimate male children."[26]

This, of course, hardly represented the essential problem, and the court recognized that this finding alone would constitute an inadequate response. The further and more critical question concerned the rule that illegitimate children were disinherited because they belonged to the mother's family, which "is obliged to provide for him or her. Such child may ultimately have rights of succession in the mother's family."[27] Thus, the court held that it was not prepared to disturb the rights of the respondent that had vested in him before the introduction of the constitution, "for the present is not a case where the recognition and respecting of previously acquired rights would be grossly unjust and abhorrent, in the light of the present constitutional order that they cannot be countenanced. . . ."[28]

Thus, the court turned down the invitation to develop a rule of customary law that would have prevented a minor illegitimate child from being placed in a financially detrimental position. While the judgment may receive superficial support for its justification that vested rights should not be disturbed, a more careful reading compels a different conclusion. The refusal to recognize injustice as defined by the new grundnorm, the constitution, as well as the finding that it should not follow a previous decision that did extend a duty of support to those married only by religious rights because that case did not deal with potentially competing rights, reveals an inability to transcend the narrow preconstitutional framework in which courts functioned. Yet the entrenchment of equality as a foundational value in the constitution mandates an engagement with the problems raised by the appellant in *Mthembu* in order to move toward some form of reconciliation.

The Law Commission's recommendations as to the problem of reconciliation are encapsulated in the following passage of its report:

> the residual power to decide which law to apply lies with the court, not the parties. . . . [P]arties should be free to choose the applicable law, provided that their choice does not infringe rights acquired by others. If no express choice is made . . . then, the court should be free to infer a choice, which suggests that an implied agreement may be attributed to the parties. . . . Any sense of unease about allowing parties freedom to apply customary law to their relationship and thereby evade the Bill of Rights or principles of public policy may be laid to rest, since our courts have always had a residual power to refuse to give effect to contracts infringing public policy and the Bill of Rights.[29]

This passage reflects the essential problem. It is a relatively easy matter to establish choice of law rules between customary law and common law; the difficulty is one of establishing a principled basis by which to determine that the content of the applicable law does not infringe the bill of rights while preserving the litigants' right to culture.

THE PROSPECT OF RECONCILIATION

Some commentators consider the potential for conflict to be exaggerated. Will Kymlicka, for example, argues that culture underpins every exercise of individual rights. Hence, "minority rights can form an important part of a recognizably liberal theory of equality. . . . [M]inority rights help ensure that the members of minority cultures have access to a secure cultural structure from which to make . . . choices for themselves and thereby promote liberal equality."[30]

Kymlicka argues that a comprehensive theory of justice in a multicultural state demands equal concern and respect for all citizens. However, "equal concern and respect does not demand equal treatment of all citizens in all cases."[31] The demand is, however, that people are enabled to choose a concept of the good life and "to reconsider that decision, and adopt a new and hopefully better plan of life."[32]

The question arises as to whether such a view is sustainable when the protection of culture results in the maintenance of an unequal position among the members of the group. Is there not an obligation on this line to eradicate social practices that impose preferences upon others, such as Chief Nonkonyama's preference for a patriarchal life?[33]

South African commentators have been divided as to the answer. F. Kaganas and C. Murray suggest that claims based upon culture alone cannot displace the fundamental values enshrined in the constitution, particularly as the parties to the constitutional negotiations were committed to a vision of a nonsexist egalitarian society. That is also the view of some members of the constitutional court as is apparent from the views expressed by Sachs J. as set out in the Gauteng legislature case.[34]

By contrast, I. Currie[35] has argued that the eradication of certain customary institutions would have serious consequences for rural women. *Lobolo*, for example, became an extremely important source of cash for the family, and, without adequate social security mechanisms in place, abolition would be at the expense of the most marginalized in society. Similarly, Dlamini argued that the traditional African family offered considerable protection to members beyond what would have been possible in the nuclear family.[36]

RECONSIDERING THE TERMS OF THE DEBATE

On the basis of historical evidence, it can be argued that there is no static body of customary law to be tested against the constitution and, if necessary, to be set aside.[37] As historian Terence Ranger has noted, "customary law does not mean . . . the ending of flexible custom and the operation of a rigid code operating in the interests of patriarchy. Rather it means a setting apart of a sphere—restricted, tolerated—in which an assumed static customary code in fact deals flexibly with matters below or beyond the concern of the state. The barrier has always been porous, it just needs to be recognized."[38]

This approach lends support to the argument that the debate between culture and equality has incorrectly been framed in terms of a binary opposition. Hence, the debate usually takes place as follows: A woman married in terms of customary law comes to court to challenge the regime regulating property relations, in particular that the family estate is inherited by the general heir of the husband.[39] The argument is framed in terms of equality overriding the right to culture. Thus, if she is successful in her litigation, it will be classified as a victory for the right of equality over that of traditional cultural values. If her case is dismissed, the court will be considered to have favored cultural rights over the foundational constitutional value of equality.

This is not the only way in which to examine this litigation. If the body of customary law is seen as a vibrant code that is developed over time and is itself a product of struggles within the community, a different conclusion can be drawn. In her study of the women of Phokeng, Bellinda Bozzolli writes, "in their early lives, the young girls were socialized within the chiefly patriarchy into which they were born. . . . Their (later) enthusiastic embracing of Christianity and schooling and of the opportunity to work in the cities should not be seen as evidence merely of their colonisation or eventual impoverishment as blacks. *They were also means whereby the struggles in the precapitalist household over age hierarchies and gender relations could be tipped more in their favour*."[40]

This analysis reveals that customary relationships were not static but were lived and changed by the communities in terms of their own relationships, which in turn were shaped by a host of different material, social, political, and religious forces.[41]

The constitution cannot, and indeed should not, on the basis of this argument be seen as a western trumping of cultural rights and customary law. Rather, as Victoria Bronstein notes, "when a woman comes to court to argue about her status, she does not dislodge herself from her culture. The fight . . . is between two different interest groups battling to retain/change power relations within their very culture—a culture which is constantly evolving."[42]

Take the institution of *lobolo*, or bride wealth. On one level, payment of an often substantial sum of cash or amount of livestock in exchange for a bride equates to the sale of a woman, particularly when it is spoken in terms of a *quid pro quo* for the man acquiring rights over his wife. Further it has a deterrent quality in that if the wife wishes to obtain a divorce, her family is required to return the bride wealth.[43]

The constitution insists that women have full majority and citizenship, which alters the traditional balance of power by the provision of a foundation whereby women can fight for equality. The question thus becomes what the implications of an institution such a bride wealth are.

Bennett has argued that a prohibition of bride wealth would be inadvisable in that it has proved to be an institution to which many remain deeply attached to the extent that prohibitions would be ignored. Further, the institution does not itself affect the validity of marriage, dictate the marital obligations, or determine rights to children.[44] That may well be so, but only if the woman's role in the process is fundamentally altered. An example of what is required can be found in the effect of the Legal Age of Majority Act of Zimbabwe. As a result of all persons over the age of eighteen years enjoying majority status under this act, it is Zimbabwean women, and not their fathers, who have the choice of insisting upon implementation of *lobolo*. The woman now has the choice of saying that her parents should receive lobolo before she will agree to marry.[45]

In this way, the constitutional value of equality changes the power relations within the community, thereby allowing the members of the community to develop customary institutions rather than imposing a constitutional ban thereon. Tanzania has attempted to deal with polygyny in a similar fashion. Before a marriage takes place, the parties agree upon whether the marriage is intended to be monogamous. Wives only have the right to veto their husbands' subsequent marriages in cases where the marriage was originally intended to be monogamous.[46] This is arguably a weak nod in the direction of the value of equality, but it is an attempt to allow women to shape the institution, rather than having it the subject of an immediate declaration of constitutional invalidity.

The Law Commission has recently offered its recommendations as to the indicated solution to the possible clash between the two legal regimes. It has attempted to follow a similar line of engagement between the constitution and culture. The commission is concerned that a sufficient body of customary law is vulnerable to constitutional attack in that, were section 31(2) to be strictly applied, "the constitutional recognition given to customary law in 1996 would be an empty gesture. No one in South Africa today would wish customary law to be relegated to its former position; and if the courts and Parliament are sincere in their respect for African cultural traditions, they must construe application of the Bill of Rights in such a way that the common law does not again emerge as the dominant regime."[47]

But the Law Commission grapples with the demarcation of the boundary over which constitutional scrutiny should not intrude. It appears to move in the direction of a view that culture, in terms of section 31, should only be protected to the extent that it facilitates the autonomy of all its members. Thus, culture alone may not limit an individual's right to equal treatment under section 9.[48]

The struggle is not the subject of easy resolution. The South African Constitution has been described as a bridge to help transport a society from a racist, authoritarian past to a nonracial, nonsexist deliberative democracy.[49] The maintenance of the constitution's integrity is thus vital to the establishment of a new democracy. However, customary law retains a potency as a value system.[50] Customary law has continued to play a significant part in the lives of many South Africans, and for this reason alone it will not be easily abandoned.[51] For this reason, it is important to view culture as being vibrant with the potential to change through contact with other cultures.

The constitutional ideal of a state based upon freedom, human dignity, and equality seeks to empower all members of society. Through the process of guaranteeing women the right to be treated with equal concern and respect, they are empowered to challenge existing cultural practices and fight for the progressive transformation of institutions that shape their communities and, indeed, their identities. As Bronstein correctly observes, "Thus the fight for equality is not simply the process of progressive Westernization. African institutions, like their western counterparts can be progressively transformed in accordance with the principle of equality."[52]

CONCLUSION

The problem with our justice system is . . . its total disregard of African principles of justice which ought to underpin our legal system as an African country. In this regard why is it so important and a source of pride that our law is based on the Roman-Dutch tradition.[53]

A true culture cannot be summed up, for it resides in the very effort to cultivate it.[54]

South Africa is not alone in dealing with the problem of reconciling the right to culture with apparently contrary commitments in the constitution. The range of concern about the role of Aboriginal law in Australia that was triggered by the Mabo cases[55] is indicative of a similar problem of recognition. In his analysis of the position in Australia, Duncan Ivison suggests that the challenge is to establish how customary law and "Australian law" can best work alongside each other equally, given the complex circumstances in which Aboriginal people find themselves in liberal constitutional states.[56]

The idea that cultural autonomy is a constitutional right worth preserving finds recognition in some jurisdictions. The Canadian Supreme Court has granted a considerable level of meaningful autonomy in *R. v. Sparrow*.[57] In this case, the court interpreted section 35(1) of the Constitution Act as constituting a recognition and an affirmation of existing Aboriginal practices that are integral to Aboriginal identity. Thus, it held that "for the Musqueam, the salmon fishery has always constituted an integral part of their distinctive culture."[58] This approach appears to be grounded upon the idea that Aboriginal culture deserves protection by the courts, which, in turn, implies that cultural difference forms part of this sphere of protection. As argued above, the protection of autonomy coupled with the recognition of the rights of members of the community to shape the culture of their community may well be the most plausible way to reconcile the two constitutional rights.

South Africa faces equally profound challenges. It has given clear constitutional recognition to customary law, but within a profoundly egalitarian constitutional enterprise. The latter runs the risk of delegitimation if the principles of equality so trump vast parts of the body of customary law that the constitution is viewed as anti-African. Even if the argument that customary law is both vibrant and always in a state of development is accepted, the balance between customary law and the bill of rights remains to be struck so that cultural rights are given a sense of significance in the new South African constitutional democracy.

The challenge posed by this seeming dichotomy between competing constitutional rights and arguably differing visions of a constitutional community recalls Robert Cover's concept of legal interpretation. In particular, I have in mind the view that "legal interpretation takes place on a field of pain and death . . . legal interpretative acts signal and occasion the imposition of violence upon others: A judge articulates her understanding of a text and as a result, somebody loses his freedom, his property, his children, even his life."[59]

For Cover, law, and state law in particular, pulls in opposing directions, for while state law participates in the generation of normative meaning, it also plays in the domain of social control, employing violence to impose a particular concept of order.[60] In his writings, Cover develops the concept of the "jurisgenerative" potential of law. In short, judges may, like their antislavery predecessors, help to transform their society by destroying the very norms they inhabited in order to bring about another world.

The South African Constitution as initially introduced in 1994 promised a radical break from an apartheid past. It required that judges in particular and lawyers in general not only contest the legal meanings of apartheid, but also go further and destroy the normative base upon which the previous legal order rested. But that would not implement the promise of an open democratic society predicated upon freedom, human dignity, and equality as prefigured in the constitution—particularly were the result to set up but another set of norms that denied the contested nature of legal meaning, which was then viewed as the imposition of a model of progressive Westernization upon all institutions and communities, particularly those that are of an African nature. This would be to reproduce the other in similar fashion to that which occurred under apartheid.

By recasting the debate between culture and equality in terms of intracultural struggles within the group, fought in particular by "internal women," the debate about the future of customary law does not reduce it to a state where African cultures give way to North American and German notions about a constitutional community. Similarly, if the process of interpreting a constitution that has a pedigree drawn from these jurisdictions can follow this framework, the constitution can support pluralism and deliberation, rather than violence and imposition. In this way, the constitution can be lifted into the position of widespread legitimacy from which a new democracy can be sustained.

NOTES

1. Ex parte Gauteng Provincial Legislature, 1996 (3) SA 165 (CC) at para. 52.
2. ILR 17 (1985).
3. *See*, by contrast, the Australian decision in *Gerhardy v. Brown* 159 CLR 70 (1985), where a South Australian act had granted land to members of an Aboriginal group and allowed only members of that group access. An Aborigine from New South Wales who was consequently denied access to the reserve argued that to allow only members of a specific ethnic group to enjoy such a right was in breach of a number of antidiscrimination laws, particularly the Commonwealth Racial Discrimination Act of 1975. The court held that while the legislation was discriminatory, it was a special measure designed to secure the advancement of a distinct ethnic group. *See also* the Belgian Linguistics Case, 1968 European Court of Human Rights, Series A, Vol. 6 at 34.
4. The drafting of the South African Bill of Rights was heavily influenced by the Canadian Charter of Right and Freedoms. The American and German constitutions were also used as important sources of comparative authority in the drafting process, although it was the Canadian instrument that provided the basic framework. For a discussion of this process, *see* L.M. DUPLESSIS AND H.M. CORDER, UNDERSTANDING SOUTH AFRICA'S BILL OF RIGHTS (1994).

5. Act 38 of 1927.

6. For the purposes of this chapter, it is unnecessary to engage in a comprehensive summation of the entire body of customary law. For such an examination, *see* T.W. BENNETT, HUMAN RIGHTS AND AFRICAN CUSTOMARY LAW (1995); Charles Dlamini, INDIGENOUS LAW AND THE BILL OF RIGHTS IN BUTTERWORTHS BILL OF RIGHTS COMPENDIUM (looseleaf series). In this analysis I have drawn on these two works together with that of Victoria Bronstein, *Reconceptualising the Customary Law Debate*, 14 SAJHR 388 (1998); I. Currie, *Minority Rights*, *in* M. Chaskalson et al. (eds.), CONSTITUTIONAL LAW IN SOUTH AFRICA (looseleaf series).

7. *Supra* note 6, Bennett remarks at 119 that "any prohibition on bridewealth would, in any case, be highly inadvisable. Surveys indicate that, whatever its drawbacks, people remain deeply attached to the institution, and laws that have attempted to ban it or to restrict the amount payable have proved easy to circumvent."

8. *Supra* note 6, Dlamini at 6A-34 submits that the usual way in which the woman seeks maintenance is for her to approach the husband's relatives, failing which she can return to her own family.

9. *See supra* note 6, Bennett at 120–21.

10. THE STAR, August 21, 1993.

11. 1996 (2) SA 751(CC) at 816 C.

12. *President of the Republic of South Africa and Another v. Hugo*, 1997 (1) SA 1(CC) at 37 C-D. *See also* Cathi Albertyn and Beth Goldblatt, *Facing the Difficulties of Transformation: Difficulties in the Development of an Indigenous Jurisprudence of Equality*, 14 SAJHR 248 (1998); Karl Klare, *Legal Culture and Transformative Constitutionalism*, 14 SAJHR 146 (1998).

13. South African Law Commission Project 90, *The Harmonization of the Common Law and the Indigenous Law: Report on Conflicts of Law* (1999) at para. 1.64.

14. *Supra* note 6, Currie at 67.

15. *Supra* note 6, Bennett at 47.

16. *Supra* note 13 at para. 1.70.

17. *Supra* note 13 at para. 1.71.

18. *Supra* note 6, Dlamini at para. 6A-43.

19. 1997 (2) SA 690(A).

20. 1983 (1) SA 1006(A).

21. *Supra* note 19 at 707G. *See*, in general, F. Cachalia, *Citizenship, Muslim Family Law and a Future South African Constitution*, 56 THRHR 392 (1993); *Prior v. Battle and Others*, 8 BCLR 1013(Tk) (1998).

22. *Id.* at 703B.

23. *Id.* at 703I.

24. 1997 (2) SA 936 at 945–46.

25. *Mthembu v. Letsela* and another unreported judgment of the Supreme Court of Appeal, May 30, 2000, at para. 32.

26. *Id.* at para. 33.

27. *Id.* at para. 37.

28. *Id.* at para. 38.

29. *Supra* note 13 at para. 1.101.

30. WILL KYMLICKA, LIBERALISM, COMMUNITY, CULTURE (1989) at 190–92.

31. WILL KYMLICKA, MULTICULTURAL CITIZENSHIP: A LIBERAL THEORY OF MINORITY RIGHTS (1996) at 6.

32. *Id.* at 80.

33. *See* F. Kaganas and C. Murray, *The Contest Between Culture and Gender Equality under South Africa's Interim Constitution*, 21 J.L. Soc. 409 (1994).

34. *Supra* note 2.

35. *Supra* note 6, Currie at 35.

36. C.R.M. Dlamini, *The Role of Customary Law in Meeting Social Needs*, Acta Juridica 71 (1991).

37. In considering this possibility, I am much indebted to an instructive contribution by Victoria Bronstein. *See supra* note 6.

38. T. Ranger, Legitimacy and the State in 20th Century Africa 101 (T. Ranger and O. Vaughan eds., 1993). *See also* B. Bozzolli and M. Nkotsoe, Women of Phokeng: Consciousness, Life Strategy and Migrancy in South Africa 1900–1983 (1991).

39. For a general discussion of marital property relations, *see supra* Bennett note 5, at 122–23.

40. *Supra* note 39, Bozzolli and Nkotsoe at 236. My emphasis.

41. *Supra* note 6, Bennett at 60. He writes that "because a living form of customary law is distilled directly from current social praxis, it is subject to continual and imperceptible change, and probably exists only in an oral tradition. . . . Unlike western law . . . it tends to be both volatile and uncertain." *See also* J. Goody, The Interface Between the Written and the Oral (1987).

42. *Supra* note 6, Bronstein at 403.

43. It would appear that often the family forces her to stay in an unhappy relationship rather than having to repay the bride wealth. A.K. Armstrong et al., *Uncovering Reality: Excavating Women's Rights in African Customary Law*, 7 Int'l J.L. Family 314, 317–18 (1993).

44. *Supra* note 6, Bennett at 119.

45. Welshman Nkube, *Released from Legal Minority: The Legal Age of Majority Act in Zimbabwe*, *in* A. Armstrong (ed.), Women and Law in South Africa (1988) at 193.

46. *Supra* note 6, Bronstein at 408.

47. *Supra* note 13 at para. 1.63.

48. *Id.* at para. 1.65.

49. E. Mureinik, *A Bridge to Where? Introducing the Interim Bill of Rights*, 10 SAJHR 31 (1994).

50. *Supra* note 6, Bennett at 47.

51. Another related and powerful reason is that of the ideology of a resurgent Africanism in which the desire is to treat European borrowings with great circumspection.

52. *Supra* note 6, Bronstein at 410.

53. Mathatha Tsedu, Cape Times, September 13, 1999.

54. Emmanuel Levinas, Difficult Freedom: Essays on Judaism (1990) at 252.

55. *Mabo v. State of Queensland*, ALJR 408 (1992).

56. Duncan Ivison, *Decolonising the Rule of Law: Mabo's Case and Post Colonial Constitutionalism*, 17 Oxford J. Legal Stud. 253, 277 (1997).

57. 1 SCR 1075 (1990).

58. *Id.* at 1106.

59. Robert Cover, *Violence and the Word*, 95 Yale L.J. 1601 (1986).

60. Robert Cover, *Nomos and Narrative*, *in* Martha Minow, Michael Ryan, and Austin Sarat (eds.), Narrative, Violence and the Law (1995).

12

A European Perspective: Economic and Social Rights in the French Constitution

Jean-Pierre Théron

I would like to share some thoughts with you on the theme of human rights and particularly economic and social rights in the current French Constitution and in some prior constitutions. It seems to me that this question is a significant one in comparative constitutional law for at least two reasons.

The first is that, particularly in France, human rights—that is to say, civil and political rights and economic and social rights—have increasing importance in the constitution because of the influence of our Supreme Court (Conseil Constitutionnel) and other courts. For approximately twenty-five years, constitutional law in France has evolved because of case law regarding human rights.

The second is that a constitution's treatment of human rights reveals a country's political conception of the state. Thus, constitutional provisions can be very different according to the history and political choices of countries. In certain countries, the constitution gives priority to civil and political rights, in others, to economic and social rights. In France, it is interesting to note that in the Constitution of 1958 we find the two categories of rights. Specifically, the Preamble to the Constitution of 1958 includes the preamble to the former constitution (of 1946), and the latter incorporates the Declaration of the Rights of Man and of the Citizen of 1789. This causes problems of constitutional interpretation, as I will now explain.

I. GENERATIONS OF RIGHTS IN THE FRENCH CONSTITUTION

Most often, national sources, or, for that matter, international texts, sanction an extreme diversity of rights, generally considered as evidence of an enhancement of rights. The entire evolution is expressed by a notable extension and deepening of individual rights as, for example, in the preamble of the French Constitution. This extension, which at times discloses a radical heterogeneity, raises the question of the coherence of decisions and their constitutional support.

A. What is the Meaning of "Generations of Rights"?

Often used in France, this expression is quite ambiguous. It tends to support the idea, frequently refuted by the facts, of a linear progression of rights allowing the transition from the first to the second generation even before a third generation can be recognized. This arises from a somewhat optimistic perspective. In reality, the term implies a certain hierarchy of proclaimed rights: the first generation is superior to the second. For liberal countries like France, civil and political rights take precedence over economic and social rights. The most important thing is, in fact, protecting people's physical integrity and intellectual freedom. Other rights are complementary. Characteristic is the preamble of the current French Constitution. It states that "[t]he French people hereby solemnly declare their dedication to the rights of Man and the principle of national sovereignty as defined by the Declaration of 1789, reaffirmed and complemented by the Preamble to the 1946 Constitution." (It is in the preamble of the 1946 constitution that economic and social rights are recognized.) We can notice that, on the international level, this priority is sometimes apparent since it is felt, for example, that jurisdiction exists only in cases of civil and political rights. This perception is not at all the same in countries like Vietnam or even in North Africa. There, a minimum level of development is considered a prerequisite: economic and social rights must be guaranteed before establishing civil and political rights. But in a system like the French one, there is a double affirmation of rights: civil and political and economic and social. But the problem is, if there is an ideological hierarchy, in law the two kinds of rights are at the same level despite their very different characteristics.

B. The First Generation: Civil and Political Rights

The clearest affirmation of first generation rights results from the 1789 Declaration of the Rights of Man and of the Citizen. As I stated earlier, this declaration is included in the preamble of the current French Constitution. The Conseil Constitutionnel decided in 1974 that this declaration is supreme, as is the whole preamble, with regard to all laws. Without going back over the often referred-to analysis of this text, we will simply call to mind that legal rights are general, abstract, universal, and individual in the sense that the person is the only recipient of the proclamation of rights.

Liberty, equality, and individual security are the fundamental rights attached to the individual, who holds them by gift of nature itself, and those rights come before those of the government. These proclaimed rights are in perfect conformity with the idea of natural rights, very popular at time of the Declaration of the Rights of Man and of the Citizen. The objective was to mark boundaries that the government could not cross. The prerogatives of the government, even though incontestable, should never challenge those of the individual. If the government violates the foregoing rights, the people have a right to revolt—to resist oppression. In accordance with this perspective, we see that this concept envisions a certain relationship between the individual and the government. These rights are freedom to act, and not entitlements. The state should not involve itself in the individual's sphere of action. It does not have to call into question natural rights. All legal structure resulting from this liberal notion flows from a rigorous definition. In this matter, liberal abstention postulates that the State be enclosed within a circle of activities as restricted as possible.

By slightly distorting a complex reality, one could affirm that these rights are recognized against the State. Tied to the very nature of man, they are absolute within the limits provided by the law. This conception of the Declaration of 1789 of the Rights of Man and of the Citizen has greatly influenced the Conseil Constitutionnel. In 1974, a number of cases addressing freedom of speech, free communication of thought, and individual security, emphasized the importance of this conception of civil and political rights. Consequently, all the principles contained in this declaration are constitutional rules. The difficulty, as we will see, is that the 1789 Declaration of the Rights of Man and of the Citizen is very different from the other text included in the same preamble regarding economic and social rights, which are accorded the same legal significance.

C. The Second Generation: Economic and Social Rights

The constitutional recognition of economic and social rights results from a slow evolution and involves a dimension radically different from the very notion of civil and political rights. Hence, the Declaration of the Rights of Man and of the Citizen of 1793 brought about the organization of public aid and the right to education. The Preamble of the constitution of 1848 seems to reinforce the idea of more concrete liberties and, most of all, the necessary intervention of the State in spreading freedom, by beginning to recognize the right to employment. The Preamble of the constitution of 1946 marked the official emergence of the economic and social rights of the "second generation."

Several factors explain this constitutional evolution. Periods of war or economic crisis have led to an increase in state interventions. This does not merely concern the economic sector. The idea developed that state intervention was necessary to secure freedom. The state interventions in the field of freedom are also a way of remedying the excesses of hard-line liberalism. The formal character of civil and political rights was put into question. In order to put them into practice, human rights must be concretely defined. The state should not exercise restraint but should intervene to benefit human rights.

Legally, the Preamble of the French Constitution of 1946 did not effect a radical departure in comparison with former declarations because it gave the Declaration of 1789 of the Rights of Man and of the Citizen as a reference. It contains, however, highly original elements resulting from political, economic, and social principles particularly necessary in our days. Thus it affirms, for example, the right to employment, the right to strike, the right for workers to participate in the collective determination of their conditions of work, protection of the family and health, and equal access to legal education. Hence, civil and political rights are included in the French Constitution of 1958 because its preamble includes the preamble of the constitution of 1946.

II. THE SIGNIFICANCE OF CONSTITUTIONAL EVOLUTIONS

The presence in constitutional texts of different rights and liberties raises the question of the consistency of the sources of those rights and liberties. It has to do with the differences not only in the contents of recognized rights, but also in the implied relationship between the citizen and the government. Therefore, courts must choose between two very different conceptions of rights and thus have great power in the interpretation of constitutional texts.

A. A Very Different Conception of Liberty

The conception of liberty that results from economic and social rights is a fundamental departure from that contained in the Declaration of 1789 of the Rights of Man and of the Citizen. In the place of abstract, theoretical man, man *in situ* is substituted. In the original, liberal conception, the individual is the only thing taken into account. The grouping of that individual is unknown and even remote. However, the principles particularly necessary to our times take into account the individual in his relationship to groups. And it is interesting to note that, in the preamble of 1946, directly or indirectly, these groups became subjects of proclamations, such as those of the family or of labor unions.

More concretely, economic rights are no longer characterized by the abstract universalism of the Declaration of 1789 of the Rights of Man and of the Citizen. They vary according to one's social class, one's economic status, and one's age: women, children, and workers. Economic and social rights are no longer the prerogatives naturally held by the individual, rather they are largely characterized as liberties to be acquired, thereby establishing the preeminent role of the government.

B. The Relationship Between Freedom and Power

Without a doubt, this is one of the most essential aspects of the differences in declared rights. In fact, the question is not just one of the nature of declared rights, civil and political in one case, economic and social in the other. It is the very question of the relationship between power and freedom that differs fundamentally.

The State is no longer the potential enemy of freedom, one who should be enclosed within a circle of activities, as restricted as possible. Economic and social rights make the government the provider of freedom. For example, the preamble of the constitution of 1946, included in the constitution of 1958, states that "[t]he Nation assures the individual and the family the conditions necessary to their development." And further, it "guarantees to everyone health insurance, material security, rest and leisure activities."

This change, from enemy to provider, is fundamental with regard to the theoretical role of the State. But it is even more important in developing procedures and techniques for the protection of rights. In the classic liberal conception, the State should do nothing that would undermine individual freedoms. Yet, in terms of the evolution symbolized by the preamble of 1946, entitlements must be provided, and, accordingly, social and economics structures must be created to assure their effective provision. Such is the case of labor participating in the management of firms or even of nationalization when there is a national public service or a monopoly as a matter of fact. Thus, the preamble of the constitution of 1958, which contains the Declaration of 1789 of the Rights of Man and of the Citizen and the preamble of 1946, reflects perfectly the evolution of human rights.

III. CONCLUSION

Rights of different natures, implying a different relationship between the individual and the government, are juxtaposed in the French Constitution. This contradiction is the reflection of the ambiguities of the liberal regime. On the one hand, the rightful claims of individual freedom vie against the increasing control of the state in private relations. On the other hand, state intervention is constantly solicited in order that freedoms may be enjoyed.

13

Comparative Constitutional Law in an Age of Economic Globalization

David Schneiderman

Comparative law has aspired to comprehend differences across national boundaries.[1] Comparative constitutional lawyers now aim to dissolve difference. Recent literature emphasizes that constitutional systems are converging toward a single dominant system that "points very strongly to the existence of universal principles of law."[2] These exercises in comparativism purport to generate legal principles that transcend national borders and legal cultures,[3] consonant with a tendency within comparative law to isolate the "common core" of legal systems.[4]

This interest in comparative constitutional law arises at the very same time when differences across borders are assumed to be disappearing as a consequence of the processes associated with globalization. What David Held describes as the stretching and deepening of social relations and institutions across space and time[5] has also compressed distances between national elites. Unbounded by geography and facilitated by the easy exchange and retrieval of information, a transnational discussion around the rules and structures of constitutional law has intensified. The rise in the production of comparative constitutional law, in its academic, juridical, and political manifestations must be considered, then, as a part of this larger process of globalization.

The conditions giving rise to this resurgence in comparative constitutionalism—an increased urgency that we concern ourselves with the legal and institutional conditions of life in other nation-states—arise at the very same time that political alternatives seemingly have shrunk. The demise of the Eastern Bloc and "actually-existing socialism" appears to have prompted a desire to influence conditions elsewhere. For many citizens of the former Eastern Bloc, and in countries where active citizenship remains an elusive idea, this influence may help to improve the material and spiritual conditions of life. But in the rush to embrace universality, comparative constitutional lawyers run the risk of neglecting the ambiguities and contradictions inherent in processes associated with globalization.

The present course of globalization presents both "new opportunities as well as unparalleled risks," risks that threaten "existing democracy to the core."[6] Among the intended aims of economic globalization is to secure commitments from national governments to eliminate local regulations that constrain unduly the movement and operation of market actors, in other words, to empower the already powerful.[7] Many, like Philip Alston, concede far too much when they express the hope that the process of convergence underway in the field of global economic law can be replicated in the field of human rights under constitutional bills of rights.[8] This movement within comparative constitutionalism may help to seal the hegemony of the constitutional and legal project associated with economic globalization, that of limited government and the subordination of politics to economics—in short, the ideology of neoliberalism. Coating the disciplines of economic globalization with the rule of human rights law, oftentimes in the guise of constitutional reform, renders the discourse of constitutional rights a riskier business than is usually acknowledged.

The comparativist project traditionally has been concerned with the abstraction and classification of local legal systems.[9] This project, particularly its North American variant, aimed to explore intercultural differences and to understand and map legal traditions in a horizontal movement.[10] It has been, according to one observer, "typically a sterile taxonomy saved by a pragmatic experimentalism."[11] What is important to salvage from that tradition, according to commentators Boaventura de Sousa Santos and Annelise Riles, is the emphasis on plurality and diversity, on "passion" and "empathy" for difference but also for "similarities."[12] What should be abandoned, I argue here, is the propensity to divorce questions of international power and authority from the content of local legal rules.

David Kennedy recently has argued that there is a family resemblance between comparative law and private international law. In the private international law tradition, law is portrayed as developing outside of the realms of government in the private and autonomous spheres of the market and civil society. This is contrasted with its "ideal-type" other: the public international law tradition that aims to construct the rules and institutions for good global governance. For scholars working within this tradition, sovereignty and legal particularities are problematic. The objective of the internationalist is to shift "outside or above" differences between legal cultures.[13] The comparativist, according to this account, is more closely associated with private law and the classification of legal systems—not with questions of political and economic power.[14] Comparative constitutionalists, nonetheless, appear to be moving in the direction of the public international law tradition by worrying about sovereignty and good governance, while continuing to abstain from asking questions about political and economic power.

I argue here that recent work in comparative constitutional law, in welcoming universality, embraces aspects of the internationalist tradition, maintains a comfortable distance from questions of political and economic power, and marginalizes the possibility for pluralism in the realm of the economy. This chapter aims to construct the outlines of a universal and humanitarian public law, but demurs any association with the project of neoliberalism. By reflecting on these unspoken connections, I aim to narrow that critical distance so as to better understand constitutionalism's role in framing the rules and institutions associated with economic globalization.[15]

THE GLOBAL AND THE INTELLECTUAL

Current streams of comparative constitutional law appear to have rejected comparativism's traditional concern with empathizing and understanding differing local law. Instead, the object is to participate actively in the construction of a constitutionalism that makes liberal legal rights the common constitutional inheritance of humankind.[16] Though transcending the local, these projects are instantiated largely through local agents (such as the judiciary and the bar), the traditional locus of legal understanding for the comparativist.

Roberto MacLean argues that a previously anarchic legal world is generating a body of uniform laws, evolving ultimately toward a unified global legal community.[17] For MacLean, local national judicial systems in the South are an obstruction to the achievement of the universal ideal of an independent and impartial judiciary, an administration of justice free of corruption, and a democratic culture in which legal security for both majority and minority is fully enjoyed. His project is to identify the mechanisms—such as judicial independence and judicial training—that will help to institutionalize a global legal culture. This project moves beyond comparison to find "common denominators" and "minimum standards" required for a fully functioning national judicial system. The agency for this global movement are local bars and judiciaries schooled in the values of legal cosmopolitanism. MacLean, however, looks to international arbitration and other mechanisms for alternative dispute resolution to take a leadership role in instructing local judiciaries. They can be the "conscience" of judicial understanding and the "guardians" of justice and equity, of "freedom, exchange, development, [and] distribution of wealth."[18]

Lorraine Weinrib considers the post–World War II model of rights, such as that found in the constitutional systems of Canada, Israel, and South Africa, as sharing in a single transnational project, that of advancing the gradual convergence of national constitutional systems around the principle of rights protection and promotion.[19] In such a world, comparative constitutional analysis becomes central to this ongoing collective enterprise of liberal rights and equality protection. Weinrib acknowledges that hers is not a project that embraces new international institutions. The local is less problematic for her, as it is a stepping stone to the Kantian ideal of a gradual convergence of national constitutional systems.

For both MacLean and Weinrib, the constitutional world is converging on one model: a variant of liberal constitutionalism with an emphasis on judicial review. Both authors unhesitatingly situate comparative lawyers as critical to this project of making material a global regime of constitutional law. Theirs is no mere objective description of the world or cataloguing of indigenous legal difference, but a vital project in which comparativists and the institutions with which they are associated are the key agents in shaping judicial minds and global public opinion.

THE GLOBAL AND THE ECONOMIC

What is missing from these accounts is the element of political economy. Might it be no mere coincidence that we are undertaking new work in comparative constitutional law at the very time there is a narrowing of options available to structure constitutional regimes? In a world where the market rules, where structural adjustment programs mandate legal reform that privilege economic interests, states increasingly are under pressure to adopt constitutional regimes that replicate the model upon which economic success more likely will be secured.

From this perspective, the objective of constitutional convergence is not only to enhance civic life, but also to lock in those gains made in the post-1989 international economic environment—the general tendency toward open markets and limited government—by constraining, through the force of constitutional and constitution-like limitations, the capacity of government to intervene in the market.[20] Constitutional law, according to this view, aspires to generate one large free trade zone.

Regional and transnational legal regimes, such as the North American Free Trade Agreement and the Uruguay Round General Agreement on Tariffs and Trade (GATT) World Trade Organization, facilitate the concretization of economic globalization within national legal regimes. This is accomplished not only by policing trade and investment disputes from without, but also by internalizing the values of liberalized trade within. In this way, international trade rules and domestic constitutionalism complement each other, argues Ernst-Ulrich Petersmann. International trade law "is an expression of, and gives precision to, the liberal constitutional obligations of governments towards their own citizens."[21] Regional and international economic rules and institutions act as external constraints, or "conditioning frameworks,"[22] on the range of political possibilities available to secure domestic social change.

The reform of domestic legal regimes remains, however, a critical objective if the neoliberal gains of the post-1989 world are to remain locked in. Enhancing economic performance and liberalized trade through legal reform has been a singular goal of the World Bank's "good governance" project. According to the

Bank's 1997 report, "markets rest on a foundation of institutions" and, without rudimentary legal protections for property rights, markets cannot develop.[23] The Bank maintains that states must establish the critical supports for property rights in order for markets to develop—prohibitions against theft, protection from arbitrary government action, and a reasonable and fair judiciary. It is the second support that is most revealing of the Bank's intentions. By "arbitrary government action," the Bank means not merely outright corruption, but a range of activity including, "unpredictable" rule-making or "ad hoc regulations and taxes." "Capricious" and "arbitrary" state action, the misuse of state power, gives rise to issues of "credibility"[24] and what the Bank terms the "lawlessness syndrome."[25]

The Bank emphasizes that stability and predictability in legal rules and institutions are the hallmarks of a successful developing market.[26] Constitutionalizing rules that facilitate market transactions signals to foreign investors that a state is serious about participating fully in the processes of global capitalism. Increasing the number of checking points on domestic political processes—slowing down politics and restraining "constant legislative changes"[27]—is the stated objective of the Bank's good governance strategy. By subordinating political to economic processes, the Bank makes clear that democratic politics are less important than securing the conditions for the entry of foreign direct investment.

Here lies one point of contradiction in the contemporary discourse of globalization. The speeding up of time and the narrowing of distances—together with the evolution of legal processes seemingly outside of the state system—has not resulted in the removal of the state. The state is necessary to secure the conditions in which private property will be safeguarded and returns on investment assured. In emphasizing movement, the discourse of globalization obscures this element of fixity.[28] It is at this point that constitutional regimes institutionalize some of the processes associated with economic globalization. It is also here that comparative constitutional law, by its silence, elides its complicity.

THE GLOBAL AND THE LOCAL

Numerous examples from the contemporary global scene point to a strategy of convergence—of the kind celebrated in recent comparative constitutional law work—in instantiating neoliberal legal reform. According to the chief justice of the Supreme Court of Israel, Aharon Barak, Israel has witnessed a "constitutional revolution"[29] by virtue of the enactment in 1992 of two Basic Laws concerning "Freedom of Occupation" and "Human Dignity and Freedom." Justice Barak and his colleagues on the Supreme Court of Israel have elevated these legislative enactments to the status of constitutional law. The scope of these rights has a decidedly conservative cast. Ran Hirschl has argued that enactment of the Basic Laws were initiated by a multiparty "Thatcherite" coalition representing a neoliberal agenda.[30] Both Basic Laws, Hirschl suggests, constitutionalize neoliberal values that emphasize "the importance of an autonomous economic sphere and free economic initiative, calling for the state's withdrawal from the labor relations and collective social and welfare spheres."[31] Examining both the text of the Basic Laws and recent jurisprudence, Aeyal Gross writes that Israel's constitutional revolution risks freezing "the economic status quo in a way that is tilted against redistribution and against regulatory or protective labor legislation."[32]

The 1995 *Gal Law* decision[33] is representative of the problem. At issue was a law protecting the Israeli agricultural sector from its creditors. The United Mizrahi Bank challenged the validity of the law on the basis that it offended the protection of property in Article 3 of the Basic Laws: Human Dignity and Liberty. The Supreme Court upheld the law and, in the course of this landmark decision, Chief Justice Barak in a lengthy opinion articulated reasons why the Israeli courts had the authority to invalidate laws of the Knesset inconsistent with the Basic Laws (a *Marbury v. Madison* moment).[34] Though the Gal Law did violate the property rights of banks, it survived constitutional challenge as it was a permissible limit on those rights authorized by the limitations clause (an interpretive approach resembling the limitations model found in the Canadian Charter of Rights and Freedoms[35]).

It is the finding that property rights were infringed that should cause comparativists to pause. Justice Barak interpreted the right to property broadly, to include every interest that has a "financial value."[36] Every dimunition in a property interest will give rise to an infringement of the Basic Laws, unless the restriction is too insignificant to matter. "Theoretically," wrote the president of the court, "the right to property is infringed when the property value of an interest is less than its value before the legislation."[37] This would implicate most every state regulation of market activity. As Richard Epstein and others have argued, virtually any regulation of the market can be seen to impair the value of a property interest.[38] This raises the specter of wholesale judicial review of all economic regulation and the rolling back of the redistributive state. Acknowledging the threat to state law posed by this all-embracing definition, Justice Barak preferred to postpone discussing the scope of the right any further, leaving unaddressed the real concerns raised by his judgment.[39]

Other examples of this use of constitutional change to freeze or roll back regulation of the market are the series of constitutional and quasi-constitutional reforms adopted by countries in Latin America throughout the 1990s.[40] These reforms have put an end to the older constitutional model mandating the nationalization or the management of key economic sectors. The "state capitalist" model of economic development, in which the regulatory and redistributive role of the national state is mandated constitutionally, largely has been dismantled.[41] The Calvo clause, intended to protect Latin American states from foreign intervention at the behest of foreign investors, or property clauses declaring that property serves a social function and authorizing the expropriation of property on the payment of less than full market value are being erased from Latin American constitutional texts.

Those texts with a residue of the old style are under pressure to conform to the new model of constitutionalism. The Colombian Constitutional Court was presented with just this kind of conflict in 1996 when it was asked to certify a bilateral investment agreement between Colombia and the United Kingdom. The agreement contained provisions for the protection and promotion of foreign investment standards in most investment agreements signed in the 1990s. These include broad prohibitions on expropriations, stringent standards of compensation in the event of an expropriation, and standing to foreign investors to enforce these obligations before international trade tribunals. The court held (by a majority of 6:3) that the treaty was contrary to the constitution in two respects.[42] First, it had the effect of de-activating provisions of the Colombian Constitution—the constitution permits, in the interests of equity, expropriation without the payment of any compensation. The government could not waive the exercise of a power delegated to it by the constitution by conceding the payment of prompt, adequate, and effective compensation. Second, the investment treaty offended the equality provisions of the constitution by granting to citizens of British nationality preferential treatment in respect of expropriations—preferred treatment not available even to Colombian nationals.[43] In other words, the agreement offended Calvo's edict that foreign nationals not be entitled to preferential treatment over domestic nationals. The court reached a similar conclusion in regard to a Cuba-Colombia bilateral investment treaty (BIT).[44]

The Colombian government—anxious to reassure foreign investors that Colombia was open to foreign investment—pledged to remove this remnant of a bygone era, though no government in modern Colombian history has expropriated foreign property, and investors have not expressed any concern that the risk of expropriation is high in Colombia.[45] Moreover, there is some doubt that any benefits will accrue to Colombia as a consequence.[46] A recent UN study confirms that investment protection agreements are relatively insignificant in determining amounts of foreign direct investment (FDI).[47] Other factors such as market size and growth, exchange rates, and country risks are more important determinants of FDI. Nonetheless, the Colombian government was intent on removing the offending language from the constitution, deploying investment policy and constitutional reform to "symbolize a commitment to economic liberalism."[48] The two relevant paragraphs of constitutional text were repealed in August 1999.[49]

CONCLUSION

Globalization often is portrayed as something going on "out there," rather than happening "in here." The aim of this chapter has been to situate work in comparative constitutional law in the structuration of economic globalization.[50] This preliminary investigation into the linkages between comparative constitutional law and the rules and structures associated with economic globalization reveals disquieting affiliations between the two legal projects.[51] By narrowing the distance between projects for human rights and those for neoliberalism, the problematics of this alliance begin to reveal themselves.[52] It has not been my object to outline the tensions and inconsistencies between these two projects here, but to render the comparative constitutional law project more attentive to these tensions in its research endeavors. The comparativist project might begin anew by reflecting on the contemporaneous proliferation of constitutionally binding human rights mechanisms and the seeming decline in the power of the national state to exercise its power in regard to economic matters. There are interesting but unexplored connections between diminishing sovereignty over the economy and the affirmation of national sovereignty via constitutional bills of rights. A fruitful line of inquiry is suggested by Wolfgang Streeck. He observes an alliance between nationalism and neoliberalism, whereby states are no longer held responsible for economic outcomes but retain sufficient domestic sovereignty and political legitimacy so as to foreclose "investing supranational bodies with sovereignty of their own."[53] Has the project of comparative constitutionalism helped to foreclose the possibility for supranational governance?

Constitutional comparativists also might reflect on the fact that, in the world of constitutional convergence, there seem to be few spaces of difference in the steady march of neoliberal constitutionalism. They could begin by noting that, if the tradition was overly preoccupied with understanding legal difference through historical retrieval, the current project seems overly preoccupied in seeking the outlines of the universal without reference to past. Neither provides a fully satisfactory approach.[54] The universalist fails to acknowledge that much of what we claim as universal merely is a particularism gone global.[55] Conversely, the global impacts the local in ways that the particularist often will miss in the quest for seeking out difference. A relational understanding should assist constitutional comparativists as they seek to find spaces where difference and similarity reside, and endeavor to understand how these legal spaces are undergoing change even as they concretize the values of the neoliberal order.

I have urged the proposition that we cannot comprehend other constitutional regimes without taking into account the international economic dimension as a conditioning framework or structuring agent. Once we insert political economy into the enterprise of comparative constitutional law, we should understand that enterprise as amounting to more than a renewed enthusiasm for comparison. Rather, the comparativist's task should be reconceived as one of describing and understanding the concrete ways in which globalization is being made manifest in constitutional regimes throughout the world. In this way, the comparativist is less an agent of economic globalization and more a champion of contingency, opening up spaces for critique and democratic self-government.[56]

NOTES

This chapter originated as comments on papers by Roberto MacLean and Lorraine Weinrib delivered to the Comparative Constitutional Law conference at Georgetown University Law Center, September 17, 1999. Although this chapter has been revised substantially, their two papers continue to provide insightful and helpful points of departure for my discussion. I am grateful to Vicki Jackson and Mark Tushnet for the invitation to present, to Ran Hirschl for comments, and to Dennis Davis for a helpful hint.

1. To be sure, one object of the comparativist enterprise has been to classify differences so as to remove those "that are obstacles to free and cordial intercourse between nations or may impose unnecessary hardships on individuals." This movement toward the unification of law traditionally was provoked, H.C. Gutteridge explains, to ease the flow of commercial relations. See H.C. Gutteridge, *Comparative Law: An Introduction to the Comparative Method of Legal Study & Research* (Cambridge: Cambridge University Press, 1946) at 157, 155; Rudolf B. Schlesinger, *Comparative Law: Cases and Materials* (Brooklyn: The Foundation Press, 1950) at 381–82.

2. David Beatty, "Law and Politics" (1996) 44 *American Journal of Comparative Law* 131 at 141.

3. See L. Amede Biora, "Toward an Auspicious Reconciliation of International and Comparative Analyses" (1998) 46 *American Journal of Comparative Law* 669; David Beatty, *Constitutional Law in Theory and Practice* (Toronto: University of Toronto Press, 1995) at 105. This is not so for all of the new literature: see Sujit Choudhry, "Globalization of Justification: Toward a Theory of Comparative Constitutional Interpretation" (1999) 74 *Indiana Law Journal* 819; Mark V. Tushnet, "The Possibilities of Comparative Constitutional Law" (1999) 108 *Yale Law Journal* 1225.

4. An objective common to modern comparative scholarship has been to identify and explain the "common core" in differing legal systems (Rudolph B. Schlesinger, "The Past and Future of Comparative Law" (1995) 43 *American Journal of Comparative Law* 477–81 at 479). See, for example, Alan Watson, *Legal Transplants: An Approach to Comparative Law* (Charlottesville: University Press of Virginia, 1974). More ambitiously, the comparative law and economics movement attempts to account for legal imitation in the name of efficiency. See Ugo Mattei, *Comparative Law and Economics* (Ann Arbor: The University of Michigan Press, 1997). Mattei argues that the "general convergence of modern legal systems" in the area of takings law, for instance, "despite the variety of institutional backgrounds, could be explained as a movement toward efficiency" (at 129).

5. David Held, *Democrat and the Global Order: From the Modern State to Cosmopolitan Government* (Cambridge: Polity Press, 1995) at 20.

6. James Bohman and Matthias Lutz-Bachmann, "Introduction," in James Bohman and Matthias Lutz-Bachmann, eds., *Perpetual Peace: Essays on Kant's Cosmopolitan Ideal* (Cambridge: The MIT Press, 1997).

7. See Colin Hay and Matthew Watson, "Globalisation: 'Sceptical' Notes on the 1999 Reith Lectures," *The Political Quarterly* (1999) 418–25 at 420.

8. Philip Alston, "A Framework for the Comparative Analysis of Bills of Rights," in Philip Alston, ed., *Promoting Human Rights Through Bills of Rights: Comparative Perspectives* (Oxford: Oxford University Press, 1999) 1 at 14.

9. See Boaventura de Sousa Santos, *Toward a New Common Sense: Law, Science and Politics in the Paradigmatic Transition* (New York: Routledge, 1995) at 272–73.

10. David Kennedy, "New Approaches to Comparative Law: Comparativism and International Governance" 1997 *Utah Law Review* 545.

11. Martin Shapiro, "The Success of Judicial Review," in Sally J. Kenney, William M. Resinger and John C. Reitz, eds., *Constitutional Dialogues in Comparative Perspec-*

tive (New York: Macmillan, 1999) at 193. Also see Mattei, *supra* note 4 at 97; William Twining, *Globalisation & Legal Theory* (London: Butterworths, 2000), c.7.

12. Annelise Riles, "Wigmore's Treasure Box: Comparative Law in the Era of Information" (1999) 40 Harvard Journal of International Law 221 at 229. See also *supra* n. 9 at 273; see also Vivian Grosswald Curran, "Dealing in Difference: Comparative Law's Potential for Broadening Legal Perspectives" (1998) 46 *American Journal of Comparative Law* 657.

13. *Supra* note 10 at 554.

14. *Id.*, at 583. To be sure, Kennedy admits, there is a branch of comparative law having to do with public law and questions of governance, like their colleagues in public international law, most marked in comparative federalism studies (at 587).

15. This is not an argument that constitutionalism is determined by, or reducible to, powerful economic forces. Rather, it is to say that there is an unspoken relationship between the two that needs unearthing. On the relationship between law and society in contemporary comparativism, see William Ewald, "Comparative Jurisprudence (II): The Logic of Legal Transplants" (1995) 43 *American Journal of Comparative Law* 489 at 509. On the tendency to appeal to globalization "as a causal factor of process working, apparently independently, of the actions, intentions and motivations of real subjects" see Colin Hay and David Marsh, "Introduction: Demystifying Globalization," in Colin Hay and David Marsh, eds., *Demystifying Globalization* (Houndmills: Macmillan, 2000) 1–17 at 6. For a parallel, but more acerbic, account of the postcolonial critic's complicity in the structuration of global capitalism, see Arif Dirlik, "The Postcolonial Aura: Third World Criticism in the Age of Global Capitalism," (1994) *Critical Inquiry* 20 (1994) at 328–56 ("To put it bluntly, postcoloniality is designed to *avoid* making sense of the current crisis and, in the process, to cover up the origins of postcolonial intellectuals in a global capitalism of which they are not so much victims as beneficiaries" at 353).

16. Gutteridge explained in 1946 that the "universalist" theory of law (a variant of natural law) "may still be invoked in aid of the project for the unification of private law, [but] it is no longer regarded as explaining the necessity for the employment of the comparative method" (Gutteridge, *Comparative Law* at 6–7).

17. See Roberto G. MacLean, "Abstract of the Paper 'Judicial Systems: Challenges for the Twenty-first Century' " (August 1999); see chapter 8 this volume.

18. *Id.* at 3.

19. Lorraine E. Weinrib, "Constitutional Conceptions and Constitutional Comparativism"; see chapter 1, this volume.

20. See generally, David Schneiderman, "Investment Rules and the New Constitutionalism," (2000) *Law and Social Inquiry* 25 at 757–787.

21. Ernst-Ulrich Petersmann, *Constitutional Functions and Constitutional Problems of International Economic Law* (Fribourg: Switzerland University Press, 1991) at 220–21.

22. See Ricardo Grinspun and Robert Kreklewich, "Consolidating Neoliberal Reforms: 'Free Trade' as Conditioning Framework," (1994) *Studies in Political Economy* 33 at 33; Eyel Benvensiti, "Exit and Voice in the Age of Globalization" (1999) 98 *Michigan Law Review* 167.

23. The World Bank, *World Development Report 1997: The State in a Changing World* (New York: Oxford University Press, 1997) at 41.

24. *Supra* note 23 at 99.

25. *Id.* at 41.

26. See Douglass C. North, *Institutions, Institutional Change and Economic Performance* (Cambridge: Cambridge University Press, 1990); James M. Buchanan and Gordon Tullock, *The Calculus of Consent: Logical Foundations of Economic Democracy* (Ann Arbor: The University of Michigan Press, 1962).

27. *Supra* note 23 at 100.

28. See David Schneiderman, "Investment Rules and the Rule of Law" (2001) 8 *Constellations* 503–37.

29. Justice Aharon Barak, "A Constitutional Revolution: Israel's Basic Laws" (1993) 4 *Constitutional Forum* 83.

30. Ran Hirschl, "The Political Origins of Judicial Empowerment through Constitutionalization: Lessons from Four Constitutional Revolutions" (2000) 25 *Law and Social Inquiry* 91 at 113.

31. Ran Hirschl, "The 'Constitutional Revolution' and the Emergence of a New Economic Order in Israel" (1997) 2 *Israel Studies* 136 at 147.

32. Aeyal Gross, "The Politics of Rights in Israeli Constitutional Law" (1997) 3 *Israel Studies* 80 at 98.

33. *United Mizrahi Bank plc v. Migdal Cooperative Village* (1995) 49(iv) P.D. 221. The extract translated into English on which I rely can be found in Omi, "Leading Decisions of the Supreme Court of Israel and Extracts of the Judgement" (1997) 31 *Israel Law Review* 764 [hereinafter *Mizrahi Bank*].

34. Justice Barak, like Marshall C.J. in *Marbury*, finds the constituent authority for constitutional review in "the people" (*Mizrahi Bank, supra* note 33 at 781).

35. *Mizrahi Bank, supra* note 33 at 787, 792. On the parallels to the Canadian Charter, see Lorraine Weinrib, chapter 1 this volume and in "The Canadian Charter as a Model for Israel's Basic Laws" (1993) 4 *Constitutional Forum* 85.

36. *Mizrahi Bank, supra* note 33 at 785, per Barak J.

37. *Id.* at 786, per Barak J.

38. Richard Epstein, *Takings: Private Property and the Power of Eminent Domain* (Cambridge: Harvard University Press, 1985); Ellen Frankel Paul, *Property Rights and Eminent Domain* (New Brunswick, N.J.: Transaction Books, 1987).

39. *Mizrahi Bank, supra* note 33 at 786, per Barak J.

40. The following two paragraphs are drawn from my paper "Constitutional Approaches to Privatization: An Inquiry into the Magnitude of Neo-Liberal Constitutionalism," (2000) 63 *Law and Contemporary Problems* 83.

41. See Robert Cox, "The Global Political Economy and Social Choice," in Robert W. Cox and Timothy W. Sinclair, eds., *Approaches to World Order* (Cambridge: Cambridge University Press, 1996) at 201.

42. Colombian Constitutional Court Decision C-385/96.

43. Carlos M. Calvo, *Le Droit International Théorique et Practique*, 2nd ed. (Paris: Amyot, 1870).

44. Colombian Constitutional Court Decision C-379/96.

45. National Trade Data Bank, *Colombia: Investment Climate* (August 13, 1996), International Market Insight available in Lexis/Nexis.

46. M. Sornorajah, *The International Law on Foreign Investment* (Cambridge: Cambridge University Press, 1994) at 235–36.

47. United Nations Conference on Trade and Development, *World Investment Report 1999: Foreign Direct Investment and the Challenges of Development* (New York: UNCTAD, 1999) at 117; United Nations Conference on Trade and Development, *World In-*

vestment Report 1997: Transnational Corporations, Market Structure and Competition Policy (New York: UNCTAD, 1997) at 37.

48. Kenneth J. Vandevelde, "The Political Economy of a Bilateral Investment Treaty" (1998) 92 *American Journal of International Law* 621 at 628.

49. The amendment, by Acto Legislativo 1/99 of August 4,1999, excised the provisions concerning equitable expropriation: "Con todo, el legislador, por razones de equidad, podrá determinar los casos en que no haya lugar al pago de indemnización, mediante el voto favorable de la mayoria absoluta de los miembros de una y otra Cámara. Las razones de equidad, así como los motivos de utilidad pública o de interés social, invocados por el legislador, no serán controvertibles judicialmente" [trans: Still, the legislative, for reasons of equity, may determine those cases in which there is no ground for indemnification through an affirmative vote of the absolute majority vote of the members of both chambers. Reasons of equity, as well as motives of public necessity or social interest invoked by the legislative, will not be judicially reviewable].

50. On "structuration," referring to "the dynamic processes whereby structures come into being," see Anthony Giddens, *New Rules of Sociological Method*, 2d ed. (Stanford: Stanford University Press, 1993) at 125–35; on structuration in a global context, see Roland Robertson, *Globalization: Social Theory and Global Culture* (London: Sage Publications, 1992) at 53.

51. Once again, this is not an argument that human rights are reducible to economic imperatives. See discussion *supra* note 15.

52. On this tension, see Upendra Baxi, "Voices of Suffering and the Future of Human Rights," *Transnational Law and Contemporary Problems* 8 (1998): 125–169.

53. Wolfgang Streeck, "Public Power Beyond the Nation State: The Case of the European Community," in Robert Boyer and Daniel Drache, eds., *States Against Markets: The Limits of Globalization* (London: Routledge, 1996) 299–315 at 307.

54. See David Harvey, *Spaces of Hope* (Berkeley: University of California Press, 2000) at 16.

55. De Sousa Santos refers to this phenomenon as "globalized localism," *supra* note 9 at 263.

56. The kind of critique suggested here has affinities to neo-Foucaldian work. See Nikolas Rose, *Powers of Freedom: Reframing Political Thought* (Cambridge: Cambridge University Press, 1999) at 19–20; Mitchell Dean, *Governmentality: Power and Rule in Modern Society* (London: Sage Publications, 1999) at 36–38.

For Further Reading

Andrews, Penelope, and Stephen Ellman. *The Post-Apartheid Constitutions: Perspectives on South Africa's Basic Law*. Columbus: Ohio State University Press, 2001.

Asmal, Kader. "Constitutional Courts: A Comparative Survey." *Comparative and International Law Journal of Southern Africa*, vol. 24, no. 3 (1995): 315.

Beatty, David M., ed. *Human Rights and Judicial Review: A Comparative Perspective*. Boston: Martinus Nijhoff, 1994.

Beer, Lawrence W. "Constitutionalism and Rights in Japan and Korea." In *Constitutionalism and Rights: The Influence of the U.S. Constitution Abroad*. Edited by Louis Henkin and Albert J. Rosenthal. New York Columbia University Press, 1990.

Brewer-Carías, Allan-Randolph. *Judicial Review in Comparative Law*. New York: Cambridge University Press, 1989.

Brown, Nathan J. *The Rule of Law in the Arab World: Courts in Egypt and the Gulf*. New York: Cambridge University Press, 1997.

Cappelletti, Mauro. *The Judicial Process in Comparative Perspective*. Oxford University Press 1989.

Desfosses, Helen, and Abdo I. Baaklini, eds. *Designs for Democratic Stability: Studies in Viable Constitutionalism*. Armonk, NY: M.E. Sharpe, 1997.

Epp, Charles R. *The Rights Revolution*, Chicago: University of Chicago Press, 1998.

Finer, S.E., Vernon Bogdanor, and Bernard Rudden. *Comparing Constitutions*. New York: Oxford University Press, 1995.

Galanter, Marc. *Law and Society in Modern India*. London: Oxford University Press, 1989.

Greenberg, Douglas, Stanley N. Katz, Melanie Beth Oliviero, and Steven C. Wheatley, eds. *Constitutionalism and Democracy: Transitions in the Contemporary World*. New York: Oxford University Press, 1998.

Holland, Kenneth M., ed. *Judicial Activism in Comparative Perspective*. New York: St. Martin's Press, 1991.

Jackson, Donald W., and C. Neal Tate. *Comparative Judicial Review and Public Policy*. Westport, CT: Greenwood Press, 1992.

Jacob, Herbert, Erhard Blankenburg, Herbert Kritzer, Doris Marie Provine, and Joseph Sanders. *Courts, Law, and Politics in Comparative Perspective*. New Haven: Yale University Press, 1996.

Klug, Heinz. *Constituting Democracy: Law, Globalism and South Africa's Political Reconstruction*. Cambridge: Cambridge University Press, 2000.

McWhinney, Edward. *Supreme Courts and Judicial Law-Making: Constitutional Tribunals and Constitutional Review*. Boston: Martinus Nijhoff, 1986.

Nino, Carlos Santiago. *The Constitution of Deliberative Democracy*. New Haven: Yale University Press, 1996.

Pasquino, Pasquale. "Constitutional Adjudication and Democracy: Comparative Perspectives—USA, France, Italy." *Ratio Juris*, vol. 11, no. 1 (1998): 38.

Schwartz, Herman. *The Struggle for Justice in Post-Communist Europe*. Chicago: University of Chicago Press, 2000.

Shapiro, Martin. *Courts: A Comparative and Political Analysis*. Chicago: University of Chicago Press, 1981.

Stotzky, Irwin, ed. *Transition to Democracy in Latin America: The Role of the Judiciary*. Boulder, CO: Westview, 1993.

Symposium: The Constitution of Japan—The Fifth Decade. Edited by Percy R. Luney (Special Editor). *Law & Contemporary Problems*, vol. 53, nos. 1 & 2 (1990).

Tate, C. Neal, and Torbjorn Vallinder, eds. *The Global Expansion of Judicial Power*. New York: New York University Press, 1995.

Volcansek, Mary L., ed. *Judicial Politics and Policy-Making in Western Europe*. London: Frank Cass, 1992.

Widner, Jennifer. *Building the Rule of Law*. New York: W.W. Norton, 2001.

Index

About the Editors and Contributors

EDITORS

VICKI C. JACKSON is Professor of Law, Georgetown University Law Center. She has written numerous articles on federalism and is the coauthor of *Comparative Constitutional Law* (1999).

MARK TUSHNET is Carmack Waterhouse Professor of Constitutional Law, Georgetown University Law Center. He has written extensively on U.S. constitutional law and is the coauthor of several casebooks, including *Comparative Constitutional Law* (1999), and is the author of *Taking the Constitution Away from the Courts* (1999), among other books.

CONTRIBUTORS

WINFRIED BRUGGER is Professor of Law, Heidelberg University. He has served as dean of the faculty of law and has written on U.S. and German constitutional law. His books include *Liberlismus, Pluralismus, Kommunitarismus: Studien zur Legitimation des Grundgesetzes* (1999) and *Einfuehrung in das oeffentliche Recht der USA* (2nd ed., 2001).

DENNIS M. DAVIS is a judge in the Cape Provincial Division of the High Court of South Africa and a Professor of Law at the University of Capetown. He was the director of the Center for Applied Legal Studies at the University of Witwatersrand and is the Honorary National Director of the Society for the

Abolition of the Death Penalty. His books include *Democracy and Deliberation* (1999) and the coauthored *Rights and Constitutionalism: The New South African Legal Order* (1996).

THOMAS FLEINER is Professor of Constitutional and Administrative Law and the General Theory of the State at the University of Fribourg, Switzerland, where he also directs the Institute of Federalism. He is the honorary president of the International Association of Constitutional Law and has held positions as visiting professor at universities in Israel, France, Yugoslavia, Germany, Belgium, and the United States. He has written numerous articles and books on comparative administrative and constitutional law and political theory and philosophy, including *What are Human Rights?* (1999) (in German, English, French, Spanish, Chinese, Portuguese, Russian, and Serbo-Croatian).

RATNA KAPUR is a director of the Centre for Feminist Legal Research in New Delhi, India. She had been a visiting Professor of Law at Cleveland-Marshall College of Law, Dalhousie Law School, New York University School of Law, and Georgetown University Law Center. She has lectured and published extensively on issues of secularism, freedom of expression, equality, and women's rights. Among other printed works, she edited *Feminist Terrains in Legal Domains: Interdisciplinary Essays on Women and Law* (1996) and coauthored *Subversive Sites: Feminist Engagements with Law* (1996) and *Secularism's Last Sigh?: Hinduvata and the (Mis)Rule of Law* (1999).

DONALD P. KOMMERS is Joseph and Elizabeth Robbie Professor of Political Science and Concurrent Professor of Law, Notre Dame University. He has written widely on U.S. and comparative constitutional law, and he is the author of *The Constitutional Jurisprudence of the Federal Republic of Germany* (2d ed., 1997), among other books.

ROBERTO G. MACLEAN is a commissioner at the United Nations Compensation Commission and served as Distinguished Visiting Professor of Law at Southern Methodist University from 1998 to 2001. He has also been an associate justice of the Supreme Court of Peru, Peruvian ambassador to the United States, a judicial specialist for the World Bank, a member of the Permanent Court of Arbitration at the Hague, and adjunct Professor of Comparative Law at Georgetown University Law Center. He has written on comparative judicial systems.

GEOFFREY MARSHALL is former provost of Queen's College, Oxford University. He is a leading scholar of British constitutional law and has written many books and articles, including *Constitutional Theory* (1971) and *Constitutional Conventions: The Rules and Forms of Political Accountability* (1984).

WILLIAM H. REHNQUIST is Chief Justice of the United States.

DAVID SCHNEIDERMAN is Associate Professor of Law, University of Toronto Law School. Previously he served as research director for the Canadian Civil Liberties Union and as executive director of the Centre for Constitutional Studies, University of Alberta. He has written on Canadian constitutional law and constitutional law and globalization.

JUSTICE ADEL OMAR SHERIF is the Chief Commissioner of the Supreme Constitutional Court of Egypt. He has written and edited numerous books and articles on constitutional law in Egypt and other Islamic countries, including *Democracy, The Rule of Law and Islam* (1999), *The Role of the Judiciary in the Protection of Human Rights* (1997), and *Human Rights and Democracy: The Role of the Supreme Constitutional Court of Egypt* (1996).

DULLAH OMAR is the Minister of Transport in the government of the Republic of South Africa from 1999 to date. He served as Minister of Justice from 1994 to 1999 and was the author of the legislation to set up the Truth and Reconciliation Commission and was responsible for overseeing its work during his period as Justice Minister. He is a member of the National Executive Committee of the African National Congress. He was a member of its Constitutional Committee and negotiating team, which drafted the constitution for the new democratic order. As an attorney and advocate (solicitor and barrister) in practice, he represented deprived communities in matters arising from South Africa's apartheid laws, and represented numerous political prisoners and labor unions. He also was defense lawyer in numerous political trials for a period of over thirty years.

KAZUYUKI TAKAHASHI is Professor of Law, University of Tokyo. He is the coauthor of *Perspectives in Japanese Constitutional Law* (1992) and coeditor of *Japanese Constitutional Law* (1993). He has been a visiting Professor of Law at the University of Michigan Law School.

JEAN-PIERRE THÉRON is Professor of Public Law at the University of Toulouse. He specializes in theory of the state, legal theory, human rights, and administrative law. He has published various works, most notably in the area of human rights.

LORRAINE E. WEINRIB is Professor of Law and Political Science at the University of Toronto. Before joining the faculty of law, she served as Deputy Director of Constitutional Law and Policy at the Ministry of the Attorney General (Ontario). She has written extensively on Canadian constitutional law, including on its influence upon the Israeli and South African rights-protecting systems. Her current research focuses on the converging judicial role in protecting fundamental rights and the core principles of liberal democracy in the aftermath of the Second World War within widely contrasting constitutional structures and traditions.